Jesus was making it clear that the first birth is a flesh birth, but the second birth is a spiritual birth. God is a Spirit (John 4:24), and being born again means that the second birth is to be born of God in a spiritual birth.

To be born again (or to be saved, as the book of Romans describes salvation) is to believe that Jesus Christ paid the penalty for your sins and literally rose from the dead. You must trust completely. The Bible tells us that the penalty, or punishment of sin is death. God told Adam if he disobeyed and ate of the forbidden tree, the penalty for that sin would be death. The Bible tells us that all have sinned and come short of the glory of God. (Romans 3:23).

Jesus Christ never sinned. As God in the flesh, He lived a perfect and sinless life. Jesus Christ could have stood before God the Father and rightfully claimed that He had never sinned and therefore did not deserve to die. Why then did Christ die on the cross?

When Jesus Christ died on the cross, He was paying the penalty for the sin of all mankind. Our sin and the judgment of our sin were laid on Him, and by dying on the cross, He paid the penalty that really was ours to pay. He did not deserve to die but He died for us. *But God commendeth his love toward us, in that while we were yet sinners, Christ died for us.* (Romans 5:8) *For the wages of sin is death, but the gift of God is eternal life through Jesus Christ our Lord.* (Romans 6:23)

To be saved, you must put your faith (belief) in Jesus Christ as being the One who paid the penalty for your sin, you must trust completely in what He has done for you to provide salvation. *But as many as received Him, to them gave He power to become the sons of God, even to them that believe His name.* (John 1:12). *For whosoever shall call upon the name of the Lord shall be saved.* (Romans 10:13). If you understand and believe these things, turn to Jesus Christ to be your Savior; accept His gift of salvation that He offers to you.

In Luke 18:13, the sinner prayed, *"God be merciful to me a sinner."* If you believe these things, you can turn to Jesus Christ and accept His gift of salvation. No amount of good works or other prayers at church will save you. It is God that saves you. Just take God at His word and receive His salvation by faith. You may want to pray something like this:

> **God, I know that I am a sinner. I believe Jesus Christ paid the penalty for my sin by His death on the cross. I believe He rose from the dead and at this very moment wants to be my Savior. I turn to Him now and receive the gift of salvation and everlasting life. Save me.**

If you have made this decision to believe in Jesus Christ to be your Savior, we'd like to know about it and help you further in your new life in Christ.

For help, contact us on our website: http://www.searchforthetruth.net

SIX STEPS TO CHRISTIAN GROWTH

1. Go to a Bible-believing church.
Hebrews 10:25 – *Not forsaking the assembling of ourselves together, as the manner of some is; but exhorting one another, and so much the more as ye see the day approaching.*

2. Read your Bible daily:
1 Peter 2:2 – *As newborn babes, desire the sincere milk of the word, that ye may grow thereby.*

Acts 17:11 – *These were more noble than those in Thessalonica, in that they received the word with all readiness of mind, and searched the scriptures daily, whether those things were so.*
Start in the New Testament with the book of John.

3. Obey Christ and be baptized:
Matthew 28:19 – *Go ye therefore, and teach all nations, baptizing them in the name of the Father, and of the Son, and of the Holy Ghost.*

Acts 2:41 – *Then they that gladly received his word were baptized: and the same day they were added unto them about three thousand souls.*

Acts 8:36, 37 – *And as they went on their way, they came unto a certain water: and the eunuch said, See, here is water; what doth hinder me to be baptized? And Philip said, If thou believest with all thine heart, thou mayest. And he answered and said, I believe that Jesus Christ is the Son of God.*

Baptism does not make a person a Christian but it is an outward showing of an inward decision.

4. Witness to others of Christ:
Acts 1:8 – *But ye shall receive power, after that the Holy Ghost is come upon you: and ye shall be witnesses unto me both in Jerusalem, and in all Judaea, and in Samaria, and unto the uttermost part of the earth.*

5. Thank God daily in prayer:
Philippians 4:6 – *Be careful for nothing: but in everything by prayer and supplication with thanksgiving let your requests be made known unto God.*

Matthew 7:7 – *Ask, and if shall be given you; seek and ye shall find, knock, and it shall be opened unto you.*

6. Honor God with the tithe:
Malachi 3:10 – *Bring ye all the tithes into the storehouse, that there may be meat in mine house, and prove me now herewith, saith the Lord of hosts, if I will not open you the windows of heaven, and pour you out a blessing, that there shall not be room enough to receive it.*

1 Corinthians 66:2 – *Upon the first day of the week let every one of you lay by him in store, as God hath prospered him, that there be no gatherings when I come.*

Fijian Prayer:

Noqu Turaga, Jisu, Au vakabauta ni'u sa tamata i valavalaca, kau' sa kerea kina oqo nomuni veivosoti, au vakabauta ni ko ni a sa colata na qua i totogi ni valavalaca e na nomuni a mate ka tucake tale mai na i bulubulu. Vinaka vakalevu na nomuni sa vakabulai au ka vosoti au e na tiki ni gauna sara ga oqo, e na yaca i Jisu. Emeni.

"A rau sa kaya, vakabauta na Turaga ko Jisu Karisito ko na bula kina." - Cakacaka 16:13.

"Come now, and let us reason together," saith the Lord, "Though your sins be as scarlet, they shall be as white as snow;..."
– Isaiah 1:18

"Instead of complaining that God had hidden himself, give Him thanks for having revealed so much of himself."
- Pascal, Blaise, philosopher and mathematician

January 1
Christian Truth

We forget our past at peril to our future.

Almost every university in America was started as a Bible college in order to train future leaders in various areas of biblical knowledge. The very word 'university" is a combination of the Latin word *uni* – meaning "one" and *veritus* - meaning "truth." Thus the central purpose of our centers of knowledge and training (universities) was to link knowledge to biblical truth. Yet today in many universities, morality has become relative, sin is no longer even acknowledged as real, there is no unifying source of truth, and the Bible is ignored or ridiculed. **But God's Word remains the foundation of all truth whether acknowledged or not.** For instance:

- Almost all **LAWS** are based on some view of limiting "bad" behavior and enforcing "good" behavior. Yet with no basis *outside* of humanity to determine right from wrong (such as the Bible), the persuasive, powerful, or majority simply define right and wrong to suit themselves while laws become numerous, arbitrary, and twisted. Society deteriorates. That is exactly what is happening in America today.
- There are only two possible explanations for our existence – either distinctly different types of animals were created or simple organisms (such as bacteria) turned into more complicated things (such as people). Once the biblical account of life's origins is rejected, much of **BIOLOGY** is simply misinterpreted.
- **ECONOMICS** is a biblical concept based on the stewardship of creation in order to develop the resources of the earth in a way that respects people as having been made in God's image and pleases God. With the rejection of a Creator, economics has no ultimate purpose.
- Rejection of the reality of a Biblical world-covering flood means that most of **GEOLOGY** and the time frame of history get distorted and misinterpreted.
- Even the study of **THEOLOGY** becomes distorted. Theism acknowledges God as being ultimately in control (*The Creator is God*). Atheism assumes God does not exist, so the human intellect is supreme (*I am God*). Pantheism believes that creation itself is all that there is and therefore worships creation (*Everything is God*). Since a biblical God is left out of a students' thinking throughout our public school system, the behavior of many students reflects some blend of atheism and pantheism.

We ignore the foundational purpose of our universities (one truth) at peril to our future.

Professing themselves to be wise, they became fools.
~ Romans 1:22

January 2

Biology

Imagine an ant hill made out of pine needles seven feet high! That's what you can find in Northern Europe and cold Siberia. These wood ants don't build ant hills out of sand but collect massive amounts of pine needles and pile them on tree stumps. The rotting vegetation causes heat, providing warmth during the winter, and during the summer, the pine needle pile is full of holes and tunnels for ventilation and air conditioning. It is steep-sided to shed water. To prevent fungal or bacterial infections, the ants apply pine resin to their bodies as a disinfectant. **These wood ants know what to do; they do it because of instinct**. Instinct is what God has built into these wood ants, so they know how to build their pine needle nest, how to ventilate it and how not to get infections. All this is provided by a God who takes care of every detail. If He cares this much for a wood ant, how much more does He care for you?

(For after all these things do the Gentiles seek:) for your heavenly Father knoweth that ye have need of all these things.
~ Matthew 6:32

Geology

January 3

Imagine that you drive into a deserted town and happen to stop at a closed restaurant. You go around to the back of the building and peer in the window, and there on the kitchen counter is a stack of food-encrusted plates. By looking at the plates, you really cannot know how long they have been there nor can you know how much time passed between the placing of the first plate at the bottom of the stack and the plate located at the top of the stack. It could have been mere seconds from the placing of the first plate until the placing of the last plate. Or perhaps the stack was made on a weekend or the dishwasher had a day off and days passed between the placement of the plate at the bottom of the stack and the placement of the final plate at the top of the stack. **The stack itself reveals nothing about the time frame – only that the bottom plate was deposited first and the top plate was deposited last.**

In a similar way, the geologic layers of the earth, in no way, prove an enormous age for the earth. The sedimentary layers are very much like this stack of plates. They simply reveal which plates (layers) were laid down first during the worldwide flood of Noah and which plates (layers) were laid down during the final stages. The geological column is the record of what was laid down during the year-long Flood of Noah's time, not how old the layers are.

**The fear of the Lord is the beginning of knowledge, but fools despise wisdom and instruction.
~ Proverbs 1:7**

January 4

History

When we hear the word "cavemen," we often think of primitive people wearing bear skin clothing and carrying wooden clubs. In fact, people have lived in caves throughout history; some even live in caves today.

In the Yellow River region of China, some **20 million people are still living in caves**. These caves are carved out of silty soil and are packed so hard that they do not need support. The caves usually measure 10 feet by 13 feet and extend 20 to 25 feet into the hillside. They are warm in the winter and cool during the hot summer. **They have many modern comforts such as plumbing, electricity, and even cable television**. Caves are a great place to live, to which 20 million Chinese can attest. Are these people primitive? Hardly!

Based purely on evolutionary ideas, people assume that humans who lived in caves were primitive brutes. In chapter 10 of Genesis, we find the account of the tower of Babel. As people migrated across the earth, some sought shelter in caves as they built more permanent homes. Today we often find their archeological remains in caves. Neanderthal man is one such example. The fact that they lived in caves did not make them primitive; it is just another housing choice.

Then he came there to a cave and lodged there...
~1 Kings 19:9

Biology

January 5

What ant-sized crustacean resembles a bright iridescent blue jewel but disappears in the blink of an eye? It is the sea sapphire, which lives in tropical and subtropical oceans around the world.

This amazing creature can appear and disappear before our very eyes because of the cell structure on its back. A sea sapphire has microscopic layers of honeycomb-shaped crystal plates embedded in its skin cells. The crystal plates are all the same thickness, but the spacing between the stack of plates determines the wavelength of light (color) that is reflected back. The space between these plates is four ten-thousandths of a millimeter, about the same distance as a wavelength of blue light, so blue light is reflected back. If the angle of viewing changes to 45 degrees, the reflected light shifts from the visible light range to the invisible ultra-violet range, **making it disappear before our very eyes**. How intricate and precise! Our Creator loves to delight us with the smallest details - even beautiful, disappearing crustaceans aptly named sea sapphires.

And above the firmament that was over their heads was the likeness of a throne, as the appearance of a sapphire stone
~ Ezekiel 1:26

January 6
Cosmology

Under the inspiration of the Holy Spirit, Jeremiah compared the future descendants of Israel, "*… as countless as the stars of the sky and as measureless as the sand on the seashore*" (Jeremiah 33:22). Jeremiah was explaining that Jews would become so widely dispersed around the earth that no census could count them, just as all the stars in the universe or grains of sand upon the earth could never be counted. Yet in his day, all the visible stars could be counted. At that time, 600 B.C., early astronomers counted about 3,000 stars in the night sky. It was not until the 20th century that astronomy affirmed that the stars were indeed countless by humans.

The Hubble telescope captured a long time-lapsed image in a seemingly dark part of the universe near the Big Dipper. **The area they photographed would be equivalent to our standing on earth and holding a grain of sand at arm's length**. When this image was compiled, this completely dark region was found to contain more than 10,000 galaxies, with each galaxy containing an estimated 100 billion stars (Hubble Ultra-Deep Field). Now imagine grains of sand covering the night sky and behind each grain being more than 10,000 galaxies, each containing 100 billion stars! What an immense number of stars. Truly the numbers of stars are as countless as the sands on the seashore! Our minds can hardly grasp the multitude of stars! Today it is estimated that there are roughly 10^{24} (10 followed by 24 zeros) stars. And the Jewish descendants are indeed scattered around the globe in numbers so large that no census can count them all. When God speaks on science, what he has to say is absolutely accurate. Should that be any surprise? After all, He's the one who made science!

The heavens declare the Glory of God.
~ Psalm 19:1a

Biology

January 7

Have you heard of "buzz pollination"? About 8% of flowering plants have their pollen so tightly locked away that most pollinating insects cannot reach it. With these flowers, only a loud sound of a certain frequency will release a shower of pollen.

The Virginia Meadow Beauty is one of these flowers; it will not release its pollen unless "buzzed" by a bumblebee. A honeybee can crawl around the flower all day and never get any pollen. Only the correct buzzing sound releases the pollen! In America, bumblebees are required for proper tomato flower pollination. These bumblebees make a buzzing sound at exactly middle C (261.63 Hz). No other frequency causes the pollen to be released from the tomato flower! Honeybees work in silence; therefore, no pollen is released for them. Dr. Sarah Smith Greenleaf demonstrated this process using a tuning fork. When she struck a middle C and placed the tuning fork near the tomato flower, a cloud of yellow pollen appeared. Only bumblebees buzz at the correct frequency to unlock the pollen.

How did buzz pollination come about? What advantage would this be for the flower - to lock pollen from a pollinator? Why would the bumblebee develop the right frequency to unlock the pollen when he could get pollen from other plants that do not require buzz unlocking? We are observing design in this process, and God is that Designer.

**All things were made by him; and without him was not anything made that was made.
~ John 1:3**

January 8

Microbiology

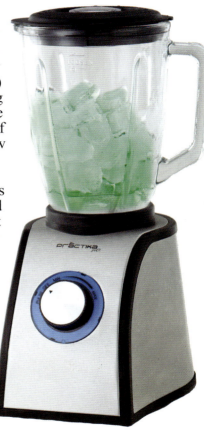

Imagine finding a very large bullfrog hopping through your backyard. Biochemists tell us that this frog contains hundreds of thousands of complex chemicals. Thus all the parts needed for life are contained within its body. **So what will happen if we drop the bullfrog into a kitchen blender and add lots of energy by blending it?** Will a new form of life develop since all the parts are present? We may create a frog smoothie, but we will never create a new form of life. Even if you take the frog smoothie and add other forms of energy (by microwaving, baking, or electrocuting) you are only going to end up with a frog smoothie – not some new form of life. We could continue adding various forms of energy for millions of years – still no new form of life will ever develop.

It is not enough to have the correct parts for life; these parts must also be arranged in a perfect sequence – all in the correct place. Yet life is more than just having the correct sequence. What makes life? Science textbooks can describe the mechanisms of **how** life operates but not how life came about. If our bullfrog was dead, how would it become alive again? All the parts are present, but life is missing! Life is not within our grasp to understand. We cannot restore life to the dead bullfrog, let alone create life in a blender. The Bible tells us that God created life; He is the source of all life!

Thou sendest forth thy spirit, they are created...
~Psalm 104:30a

January 9

Design

Imagine you are. an engineer working for Tupperware[tm] and given the following assignment - design a new container and its food with the following characteristics[1]:

- The container is one color when the contents are not aged sufficiently for peak taste, then changes to a different color when the food is perfect to eat, and changes to a third color when the food inside has gone bad.
- The container is hard to open when the food is not ready to eat and easy to open when the food is ripe.
- The food inside changes texture as it ages. During transport the food is hard and durable. At peak taste the contents will soften to a perfect texture, and once past prime, it will become soft and gooey.
- The food inside naturally contains a wide variety of vitamins and minerals.[2]
- It is so easy to produce that billions can be sold at a few pennies per unit.
- The shape allows for single-handed handling, opening and eating while talking on the phone or conversing with a friend.
- The serving size is perfect for one average adult without waste.
- One last specification is that the food and container are capable of reproducing themselves.

A team of thousands of engineers, working for their entire career, might as well quit and find other jobs because they have been assigned a humanly impossible task. Yet, we already have it - the banana! God shows His power through what He has made; He truly is the Master Engineer!

O taste and see that the Lord is good; blessed is the man that trusteth in him.
~ Psalm 34:8

January 10 — Botany

The bunchberry dogwood plant has a built-in trebuchet. A what you ask? A trebuchet is a medieval projectile-launcher. Envision it as a complex catapult. During the Middle Ages, trebuchets were designed using the principles of leverage to propel large objects faster and farther than a simple catapult. Bunchberries carpet the spruce-fir forests of North America in late April to May. The flower centers (where the pollen is produced) are only 0.1" tall so the pollen needs to be propelled upward to reach other flowers. High speed video cameras were needed to see how this plant sends its pollen flying. Scientists first tried with a camera that was able to take 1,000 pictures a second, but this proved to be too slow to capture the trebuchet's speed. So they brought in cameras capable of capturing 10,000 pictures a second. What they saw amazed them.

As bunchberry flower petals open, each petal is separated and flipped backwards (out of the way). Almost instantaneously, the stamen unfurls, catapulting pollen into the air and sending it off to pollinate other bunchberries. What is so amazing is the speed at which this process takes place. The unfurling of the petals to the launching of the pollen takes only four-tenths of a thousandth of a second. This causes the pollen to be subjected to 2,400 times the force of gravity. This is quite a projectile launcher!

Building a trebuchet took planning and design in the same way the bunchberry's miniature trebuchet took planning and design. When you see a design, you know there must be a designer. It is difficult to imagine how a plant evolved to have each of its individual petals rapidly flip down and out of the way at just the right time. If the stamen's miniature trebuchet was not ready to fire, nothing would happen. In the same way, a rapid fire pollen launcher would not be needed unless the petals burst open at the right time. Everything has to be coordinated perfectly from the beginning to do exactly what is needed.

Great is the Lord, and most worthy of praise.
~ Psalm 48:1

Biology

January 11

A wonder of the ocean is the porcupine fish. This creature has three lines of defense. If a predator comes too near the porcupine fish, it quickly gulps a large amount of water, almost **doubling its size**. Hopefully, the fish is now too large to be swallowed.

If the predator persists, the second line of defense kicks in, and **2 inch long spines** stand out in every direction, making the fish look like an underwater porcupine.

The third line of defense is **poison within its body**. If a predator eats the fish, it will get sick and won't likely eat one again. The porcupine fish does not have many predators!

How do evolutionists explain the way these three lines of defense came about over millions of years? Even Darwin in his book *The Voyage of the Beagle* did not try to explain how the porcupine fish got its three lines of defense. We know! The Creator designed this fish to survive in this manner.

Great is the Lord, and greatly to be praised;
And His greatness is unsearchable.
~ Psalm 145:3

January 12

Biology

One of the weirdest creatures in the ocean is the sea cucumber, which looks like a cucumber with small spines. Some sea cucumbers eat sand with other small pieces of food, while others filter food out of the water with their tentacles. But the weirdest behavior of a sea cucumber occurs when under attack - it spills its guts, literally!

The sea cucumber throws up long, sticky threads - which are its own internal organs. These sticky threads can glue a predator's throat shut, which will eventually kill the predator. Does the sea cucumber die? Of course not. His body parts are soon regenerated, and he continues on without harm. **How did the first sea cucumber survive the first time he spilled his guts?** From the very beginning, he had to have the ability to vomit out his sticky organs and then have the ability to regrow them. Evolution would have us believe that this defense method came about by slow stepwise processes. If this were true, there would be no sea cucumbers today.

Lord, You are God, who made heaven and earth and the sea, and all that is in them.
~Acts 4:24

January 13

Biblical Accuracy

Have you ever tried to count the clouds? At any given moment, about one half of the earth's surface is covered with clouds. These clouds are either made of water droplets or ice crystals. Of the three types, the cumulus or "cotton ball" clouds last from 5-40 minutes. **The number of clouds in the sky is constantly changing - yet at every moment of time, God knows the number of clouds!**

God asks Job a rhetorical question in Job 38:37, "Who has the wisdom to count the clouds?" **By implication, God is telling us that He is capable of exactly that!** Just as God knows the number of hairs on our head; He knows the number of clouds in the sky at a given moment. God is all-knowing concerning his creation. He also knows every desire of your heart, every thought in your mind, every temptation you face, and every challenge you have to overcome. So take a moment, look up into the sky, marvel, and trust your Maker.

Who has the wisdom to count the clouds?
~ Job 38:37

January 14 — Paleontology

News flash: Fossilized squid ink used in modern ink pen! Recently in Wiltshire, UK, a fossilized ink sac was removed from a squid fossil. The dried ink was ground up, mixed with an ammonia solution, and used to draw a picture of the extinct squid with its Latin name written underneath. How could a soft and sloppy ink sac fossilize? How could it still be black? Evolutionary dating puts it at 150 million years old. No protein structure could survive that long!

Obviously, this squid was not slowly covered with sediment over millions of years; it had to be covered recently, rapidly, and deeply in order to preserve such a find. The worldwide Flood of Noah's time (about 4400 years ago) is a far better explanation for the preservation of this fossil squid ink.

> And God said unto Noah, The end of all flesh is come before me; for the earth is filled with violence through them; and, behold, I will destroy them with the earth.
> ~ Genesis 6:13

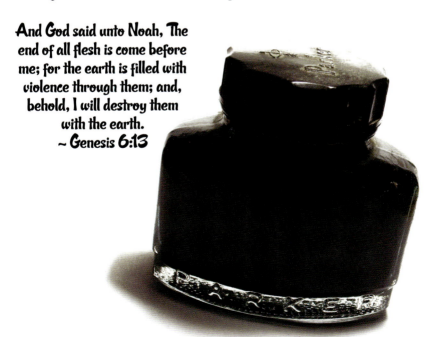

Biology

January 15

Did platypuses evolve in Australia? There are two monotremes (mammals that lay eggs) in Australia - the platypus and the echidna. These animals have all the normal characteristics of mammals (backbone, hair, milk glands), yet they lay eggs instead of giving birth to live young. We only find platypuses and echidnas in Australia. So how did they get there?

Noah took two of each kind on the Ark, which landed in the Middle East (Mt. Ararat). Echidnas and platypuses spread out to various parts of the world, yet it seems they only survived in Australia. During the Ice Age, the interior of Australia would have been well-watered and very lush, allowing the platypus and echidna to spread out and fill Australia. Only after the Ice Age ended did the enormously dry Australian desert areas develop. When the sea levels rose at the end of the Ice Age, Australia was cut off from Asia, isolating its unique animal life on this very big island.

Did platypuses evolve? **Fossil platypuses are essentially identical to modern platypuses; no transitional forms have been found**. The Bible says God created fully formed land animals on Day 6 of Creation week. When we look with our "biblical" glasses, we can understand why platypuses are found in Australia.

Bring forth with thee every living thing that is with thee, of all flesh, both of fowl, and of cattle, and of every creeping thing that creepeth upon the earth; that they may breed abundantly in the earth, and be fruitful, and multiply upon the earth. ~ Genesis 8:17

January 16

History

Since the discovery of their bones in the 1800's, Neanderthals have been presented as ignorant, evolving, humanoid ancestors to modern man. Yet over the last few decades, anthropologists have discovered that Neanderthals demonstrated sophisticated human behavior. For example, they traded jewelry, made cosmetics, developed sophisticated glues, cooked with utensils and spices, and had grave rituals. Creationists have long taught that Neanderthals were just post-Babel, fully-human descendants of Adam and Eve. They were nomadic hunters with sophisticated javelins living in shelters of hides on wooden frames and occasionally in caves.

The Max Planck Institute for Evolutionary Anthropology has recently found and analyzed a specialized bone tool used in leather working at two French Neanderthal sites. Microscopic analysis of the tools revealed wear and tear consistent with today's tools used to make supple, lustrous hides. **In other words, Neanderthals were also great leatherworkers!** Once again, science is confirming the biblical viewpoint. Neanderthals were not some primitive, subhuman creature, but fully human nomads in Europe that lived a rugged life during the Ice Age.

Before the mountains were brought forth, or ever thou hadst formed the earth and the world, even from everlasting to everlasting, thou art God.
~ Psalm 90:2

Biology

January 17

How do fish swim in murky water or schools without running into each other? It's the fish's lateral line. On either side of the fish, running from the gills to the tail, is a line of small pores that are filled with hairs (neuromasts). **These sensory hairs pick up very tiny vibrations and pressure changes traveling through the water** and convert them to electrical impulses that are sent to the brain. With a line of many hair clusters (neuromasts) picking up information at different points on the lateral line, the fish has the ability to figure out what is happening around it.

Scientists have successfully copied the fish's lateral line and hope to install them on submersibles and other underwater vehicles. **These scientists used great engineering skills to develop this new technology.** It would be an insult to their intelligence to say their artificial lateral line happened by accident and chance. Then why would we say the fish's lateral line happened by accident and chance? It was created by the Great Engineer Himself, God. So the next time you pick up a fish, look for the lateral line (on some fish it is hard to see) and praise the Great Engineer for His great design.

Or speak to the earth, and it shall teach thee: and the fishes of the sea shall declare unto thee. Who knoweth not in all these that the hand of the Lord hath wrought this?
~ Job 12:8-9

January 18

Christian Truth

God commanded us to "*have dominion over [creation]*." The original word translated as "dominion" means to study, understand, and control. This is the essence of science. So do you want to be a science detective? First, let's define science. There are two broad categories of science: operational and historical.

Operational (or observational) science is the type of science that one might do in a laboratory. It is about experiments that are repeatable. For example, at sea level, water will always boil at the same temperature: 212 degrees F. Operational science builds stuff like rockets, smart phones and other inventions.

Historical science deals with what happened in the past. No scientist has a time machine. No scientist can go back into the past to perform experiments. The past cannot be directly observed or tested, so interpretations are involved. For example, suppose a dinosaur fossil is dug up. How long ago did it live? We don't know for sure. But Christians have an eye-witness report through which to interpret the present. God is the eye-witness, and He recorded it in the Bible. There was a great Flood, and this flood would have recently buried the dinosaurs that would have rapidly become fossils. But this is still historical science.

So, when you go on vacation to places like Yellowstone National Park, you will see signs such as, "*Over the course of 16.5 million years, approximately 15-20 massive eruptions have left immense calderas (craters) to dot the landscape…*", have fun separating **interprtation/ historical science** (*millions of years*) from **observation/operational science** (*immense calderas*). Remember, it is only the observable that can be tested. All else is opinion, based on starting beliefs. Spend your next vacation being a science detective!

...have dominion over the fish of the sea, and over the fowl of the air, and over every living thing that moveth upon the earth.
~ Genesis 1:28b

Anatomy

January 19

Have you ever thought about how a scab is made? Do you realize that it takes a 12-step process to form that scab? In order for blood to clot, there must be 12 specific individual chemicals reacting in a domino effect for a clot to form. Think about a row of dominos. **If you remove one domino from a perfectly spaced line of dominoes, the dominoes following the gap will not fall**. It is exactly the same principle with blood clotting. If one of these chemicals is missing, then a person may bleed to death. If less than the required amount of a specific chemical is present, the person has pain. Too much of the chemical causes a clot in the blood stream, however, and may bring on a heart attack or stroke.

If evolution were true, how did this process happen by accident and chance? How did these chemicals first get placed in the right order, in the right amount, and at the right time? All this had to be correct from the very beginning; otherwise, we would have bled to death. When we see a perfectly spaced row of dominoes, we know there was a designer. God designed the clotting of blood, so we would know of His existence.

Let thy work appear unto thy servants,
and thy glory unto their children.
~ Psalm 90:16

January 20

Botany

The Venus flytrap is a carnivorous plant that grows only in bogs located in a tiny part of the world covering about 700 miles along the coast of North and South Carolina. These humid, sunny bogs lack nutrients that the plant needs, so this plant traps and eats insects! **These insects are like vitamin pills for the plant.**

How does this plant trap and digest insects?

- First, it has to get the insects to come to it, so it produces a sweet smelling aroma.
- Second, it has to know the insect is there. As the insect moves around on the "open mouth", it triggers two hairs inside of the plant's leaves.
- Third, the plant has to trap the insect. When these two hairs are triggered, the trap snaps shut faster than the blink of an eye. These leaves snap by changing from convex (outward –curving) to concave (inward –curving) - similar to the way a tennis ball cut in half can be quickly flipped inside out.
- Fourth, the plant must "eat" the insect. Trapped inside the imprisoned leaves, the insect is digested in three to ten days – leaving nothing but its exoskeleton. Then the trap reopens – allowing the exoskeleton to be blown away in the breeze.

If you believe in evolution, this trap had to develop over eons of time and thousands of generations. How did the plant, which had no brains, know what aroma to make to lure the insect? How did the plant know to use two hairs to trigger it shut and not just one? How many times did the trap close needlessly until it realized it needed to evolve two hairs to trigger its trap? Once the insect captured, how did the plant know how to develop the correct digestive juices in correct quantity? **If it made too much, it could digest itself.** The Venus flytrap was made by the Creator from the beginning. He put together a way for this plant to get extra vitamins that the soil lacked. He made the Venus flytrap with the right aroma, the right trapping mechanism, the right amount of digestive juices and much more so that it could survive and thrive in a small niche in this world. A Venus flytrap testifies that there is a Venus flytrap maker, and that maker is God.

O give thanks unto the Lord...who giveth food to all flesh:
for his mercy endureth for ever.
~ Psalm 136:1,25

Biology

January 21

Orcas, commonly called "killer whales", are neither whales nor killers of humans. Orcas are the largest mammal of the dolphin family and have a unique herding method more in common with sheepdogs than ocean creatures.

When a pod of orcas find a school of herring, they start a coordinated, circular swimming pattern in order to corral the fish into a tight ball and force them to the surface. The orcas work as a well-orchestrated team to herd the fish upward, using bubbles, clicking calls, flashing their white underside to frighten the fish, and swinging their tails to keep any fish from escaping. The herring become so tightly packed that the surface of the ocean containing the herring ball looks like it is literally boiling. According to cetacean biologist Tiu Simila, *"It's like a ballet, so they have to move in a very coordinated way; and communicate, and make decisions about what to do next."*

While some of the orcas continue to keep the school of fish corralled, others in the pod take turns slapping the underwater ball of herring with their tails, resulting in a few stunned fish dropping out of the school. The herring normally move far too fast for orcas to catch, but by working as a team, the Orcas can take turns eating the stunned fish, one by one.

How can we explain such sophisticated behavior? Believers in naturalism credit it to "evolution" - as if the mere mention of the word explains such complex behavior. Yet, the use of a word actually explains nothing. **Such complex, instinctual behaviors have never been explained by evolution.** Such coordinated hunting methods are only useful once they exist. So how could pre-orca dolphins, not possessing such behavior, have learned to act in such a coordinated method? If they couldn't do it from the beginning, they would go hungry!

God created all creatures with the ability to survive and thrive. It is this complex instinctual behavior that shouts "DESIGN."

(He) doeth great things past finding out; yea, and wonders without number.
~ Job 9:10

January 22

Geology

The White Cliffs of Dover are an impressive sight. These stark white cliffs, over 1300 feet thick, are made of 98% pure, fine-grained calcium carbonate (commonly known as chalk). This sedimentary layer formed from the cells of microorganisms called foraminifera and common calcareous algae known as coccoliths and rhabdoliths. **At today's accumulation rate, millions of years would be needed to form a sedimentary layer this thick, and this is used as a prime example of why the rock layers of the earth must be millions of years old**. But there are several problems with this assumption.

First of all, there is nowhere on earth today where chalk of this purity is forming. As plankton and algae die and slowly settle to the bottom of oceans, their shells become mixed with sediment and the remains of many other creatures. In order to form a pure layer of chalk, a massive amount of organisms would need to die, settle, and be buried extremely rapidly.

Second, the commonly quoted average accumulation rate (½ inch per thousand years) is characteristic of current conditions. Explosive growth of ocean microorganisms would have been common at various times during the Flood of Noah's time. What typically limits the growth of algae in water are temperature, mixing, carbon dioxide concentration, and nitrogen nutrition sources. At unique locations during the Flood, enormous volumes of warm ocean waters would have been filled with nutrients from decaying vegetation and with massive amounts of CO_2 from volcanic activity. All of this would have led to ideal conditions for explosive chalk-forming microorganism blooms. Today we only observe small localized bloom areas; during the Flood, there would have been large regional blooms resulting in the geological features we see today such as the White Cliffs of Dover. These blooms (with the organisms dying, settling to the bottom and being rapidly buried) would have happened in a matter of weeks, not millions of years! The White Cliffs of Dover proclaim that Noah's Flood did happen, just as Scripture tells us.

Then I beheld all the work of God, that a man cannot find out the work that is done under the sun: because though a man labour to seek it out, yet he shall not find it; yea farther; though a wise man think to know it, yet shall he not be able to find it. ~ Ecclesiastes 8:17

Design

January 23

Our frontline troops need night vision goggles, but often times, these goggles had a limited field of vision - seeing only 30-40 degrees. What was needed was a greater field of vision AND to be smaller and lighter. The engineers at BAE Systems looked to a tiny parasitic fly's eyes (Xenos peckii). This parasitic fly's compound eyes are different from other insect eyes; instead of thousands of tiny lenses, this fly has 50 lenses in each eye. Researchers were able to achieve the same imaging effect using only nine lenses.

Each lens is about the size of a cell phone camera lens and is arranged on a curved surface. They call it the "Bug Eye." These new "Bug Eye" night vision goggles gives the wearer a 60 degree field of vision, almost double that of normal goggles. Also, the new "Bug Eyes" are lightweight and compact. **Thousands of man hours went into developing this new technology**. It would be an insult to tell these engineers that these new "Bug Eye" goggles happened by chance and accident. These engineers were only copying what had already been made by the great Designer, God Himself!

Blessed be the Lord God, the God of Israel,
who only doeth wondrous things.
~ Psalm 72:18

January 24

Biology

Have you considered how a one-humped dromedary camel survives a harsh, hot, dry climate? The camel's hump is like a fatty backpack - not a hollow water storage reservoir. This fat is actually food stored for later use. When food is not available, nourishment is provided by the stored fat in the hump. When nourishment is taken out of the hump and not replenished over a long period of time, the hump actually shrinks and flops over. When food becomes more plentiful, the hump swells to become a fatty backpack again.

Most mammals distribute fat all over their bodies (including humans – much to our displeasure)! However, fat is a great insulator, and if camels stored fat all over their bodies, the heat would be held in - not a desirable design in extremely hot desert climates. **A camel's design allows it to store energy for future use without becoming overheated**. In addition, the design of the camel's hump protects the vital organs below from the heat of the sun beating down on the topside of the camel. Dromedaries thrive in extremely hot, dry climates because of this ingenious fat storage design. How would a camel know it needed to store the fat in one place and not over all its body? How would it get all its fat cells together in one place in its hump? Dromedaries are wonderfully designed to live in hot, dry deserts, and their hump is just one of many parts which testify to the genius of their Creator.

Cast thy burden upon the Lord, and he shall sustain thee: he shall never suffer the righteous to be moved.
- Psalm 55:22

January 25

Biblical Accuracy

Is the Bible true? Again and again, archeology confirms that the Scriptures are true.

Here a few discoveries archeologists have made.

- The Bible tells of Israelites being attacked by Moabites. Guess what they dug up in 1869? *The Moabite stone which records the Moabites attacking Israel.*
- The Bible tells of Jerusalem being attacked by King Nebuchadnezzar in 586 BC (2 Kings 24:10). Guess what was found? *In southern Israel, in the 1930s, the Lachish letters showing that Nebuchadnezzar did attack Jerusalem.*
- The Bible speaks about Abraham and Isaac, and Sodom and Gomorrah. Guess what they dug up in northern Syria in the 1970's? *The Ebla Tablets mentioned these two people groups and these two cities.*
- The Bible mentions the city of Jericho and how the Israelites marched around the city's mighty walls once a day for six days. On the seventh day, they marched around the city seven times with the priests blowing their trumpets and the people shouting, and then the walls fell down (Joshua 6). So what have archeologists find in 1997? *Evidence that "the wall fell beneath itself."*
- The Bible mentions slings and stones being used as deadly weapons. David used them when he killed Goliath (1 Samuel 17), and 700 Benjamites used slings and stones and never missed (Judges 20:16). So what have we discovered? *Archeologists now recognize that the ancient armies' most important weapon was the sling!*

Archeology continues to show that God's word is true!

Among all this people there were seven hundred chosen men lefthanded; every one could sling stones at an hair breadth, and not miss. ~ Judges 20:16

January 26

Cosmology

The best preserved meteorite impact crater on earth can be found near Flagstaff, Arizona. This impressive hole in the ground is almost a mile across and 570 feet deep. Yet, it took over 150 years to acknowledge that it was indeed caused by the impact of a meteor on the earth. From its discovery in the early 1800's, until 1960, it was thought to be the result of volcanic activity.

Grove Gilbert first studied the crater for the US geological survey in 1891, but he found no evidence of an iron meteorite or any magnetic anomaly in the area that would testify to the presence of an underground meteorite. Therefore, he concluded the crater was the result of a volcanic steam explosion. Undeterred, a mining engineer named Daniel Barringer did not believe the report and spent 27 years, from 1903 -1930, looking for "an estimated 200 billion pounds of iron" that he believed must have been buried by the iron meteorite. He found nothing. It wasn't until the rock compressions from similar craters and craters formed from nuclear testing were compared with the Barringer crater that scientists finally realized that the Barringer crater formed almost instantly by a rapid catastrophic impact.

The meteorite that caused the crater is estimated to have weighed 600 million pounds (not 200 billion), and it instantly vaporized upon impact leaving only traces of iron deep underneath the crater. This event would have happened after Noah's Flood of about 4400 years ago, for the crater goes through several of the top sedimentary layers laid down by the Flood. **Our entire solar system was apparently pummeled with meteors**. Just look at all the meteorite impacts on the moon's surface! The moon's craters could have happened either during its formation or during the Flood of Noah. If the meteors pummeled our solar system during the Flood, perhaps the thousands of feet of water covering the earth's surface during this time explain why there aren't more meteorite craters apparent around the globe. The meteor to hit Arizona's Barringer Crater was one of the last stragglers to hit the earth - long after the Flood ended.

The pillars of heaven tremble and
are astonished at his reproof.
~ Job 26:11

Design

January 27

Have you considered the poisonous snake's venom and delivery system? This amazing delivery system is intricately designed, requiring eight parts:

1. **Venom** - either a neurotoxin or hemotoxin.
2. **Venom gland** to store venom.
3. **Canal to transfer the venom** to the fangs.
4. **Hollow fangs**, like a hypodermic needle, to inject the poison.
5. **Muscles** to contract the venom reservoir.
6. **A nervous system to signal** the muscles to contract.
7. **Spring loaded fangs** to drop down when ready to bite.
8. **Instincts** to know when and how to use all this against prey or predator.

All these parts needed to be present from the beginning for venomous snakes (such as the rattlesnake or cobra) to be able to deliver their venom, kill its prey, and have their lunch. If everything was present except for the hollow fangs, it would not work. If there was no venom, it would be just a bite. If the fangs were not able to drop down, the snake would poison itself. What good is "part of a snake"? All the parts needed to be there from the beginning. When we see such intricate designs, we know there must be a Designer, and that would be God.

Spring-loaded Hollow Fangs

Venom Canal

Venom Glands

He shall suck the poison of asps: the viper's tongue shall slay him.
~ Job 20:16

January 28

Geology

If the Genesis Flood took place, what kind of rock layers would have been produced? One such strong evidence supporting the biblical Flood is the world-wide occurrence of folded rock layers. Geologists find entire strata sequences that are folded without fracturing. This is only possible if the sedimentary layers were still soft and pliable (like modeling clay) when bent. In the same manner, if the molding clay dries out, it becomes hard and brittle, unable to bend without breaking or shattering. Many of these folded rock sequences show no sign of breaking or shattering.

So how do evolutionary (huge time period) geologists explain this? **They ASSUME that deep in the earth, under enormous pressure and high temperatures, rocks can bend without shattering**. Yet if this were true, the characteristics of the rocks would be changed by the heat. They would show metamorphism. When geologists examine many of these folded rocks, they find no evidence of metamorphism; **therefore, these rocks were bent without enormous pressure and high temperatures**. These folded sedimentary rocks are still sedimentary rocks! This can only mean that these folded rocks were still soft and pliable when folded. During the Genesis Flood, there would have been rapid movements of the plates on the earth's crust. No sooner would the floodwaters have laid down great quantities of sand and mud than rapidly moving plates would have pushed the sediment while still soft and pliable - resulting in folded rocks. The Genesis Flood would have been a powerfully destructive event leaving this type of evidence around the world.

And I will establish my covenant with you, neither shall all flesh be cut off any more by the waters of a flood; neither shall there any more be a flood to destroy the earth.
~ Genesis 9:11

January 29
Paleontology

Wisconsin is home to a very important fossil find – the jellyfish. So what's the big deal about a fossil jellyfish?

In Central Wisconsin, near the town of Mosinee, there is a rock quarry. But this is no ordinary quarry; it contains many thousands of fossilized jellyfish. Why are they there? In the oceans, jellyfish are squishy blobs of clear gel. How could squishy jellyfish fossilize? Generally, hard substances become fossils – not soft substances. Also, if you have ever been to the beach, you have probably noticed seagulls eating things washed up on shore, maybe even a jellyfish. When animals wash up on shore, there are predators around to eat them – they simply do not lie on the shore waiting to be fossilized. Furthermore, when a jellyfish washes up on shore, it pumps its bell, trying to get back to the water. This will leave behind little rings in the sand. In this rock quarry, no evidence exists of fossilized rings around these jellyfish. A jellyfish is 96% water and would dry out and shrink if exposed to air. There is no fossil evidence that these jellyfish have shrunk.

Moreover, these jellyfish were not found in just one layer but were found buried in seven layers of the quarry over a thickness of 12 feet. So, what does all this evidence tell us? These jellyfish had to have been covered and fossilized quickly – and not just once – but repeatedly – to form the many layers. What event in history would have fast, quick coverage with mineral-filled sediment and no oxygen (the recipe for making fossils), so the creatures could be fossilized? The Flood of Noah!

And, behold, I, even I, do bring a flood of waters upon the earth, to destroy all flesh, wherein is the breath of life, from under heaven; and everything that is in the earth shall die.
~ Genesis 6:17

January 30

Geology

Every day, cliffs are weathering away. Water seeps into tiny crevices and separates the rock by freezing (expanding) and then thawing (contracting). Tree roots make gaps in the rocks, and rainwater can cause chemical changes to weaken rock. **Every year at Mt. Rushmore, workers rappel down the cliff face to inject glue into newly formed cracks on the presidents' faces**.

Normal cliffs erode rapidly. Weakened cliffs result in rocks tumbling to the canyon floor. These rocks on the canyon floor are called talus. If you believe in evolution and the earth having been here for billions of years, these talus piles should be enormous - reaching to the top of the cliff. Yet, what we see in places like Monument Valley or the Grand Canyon talus piles are small. To an evolutionist, this is a mystery. Where is all the missing talus that must have formed over millions of years? Why are the world's talus piles/slopes so skimpy?

If we view these talus slopes from a biblical viewpoint, however, it confirms the Bible. The piles of talus are so skimpy because they are only thousands of years old, having begun at the end of the Flood of Noah's time (about 4400 years ago). The mystery of the missing talus is not a mystery at all when viewed from a biblical perspective.

The waters wear the stones: thou washest away the things which grow out of the dust of the earth.
~ Job 14:19

History

January 31

When did the concept of millions of years of earth history first creep into academic thought? For thousands of years of human history, in almost every culture around the world, it was universally acknowledged that humanity was a relatively recent creation of God. Modern textbooks imply that it was during the "rise of science" in the 1700s that geologists "discovered" that the rock layers of the earth were millions of years. In reality, this **revisionist history has turned the truth completely upside down**. The rejection of God's Word came first, resulting in the misinterpretation of the earth's rock layers.

In 1492 Columbus first crossed the Atlantic and "discovered" America. In actuality, he landed on what is now the Dominican Republic, and after exploring the area, he returned to Spain in 1493, taking with him some native North Americans. **To understand the impact of this event, you need to understand the culture of that day**. The church strongly influenced both governmental and social structures in all European countries and was arguably the most powerful social institution of the day. It controlled educational thought and, in the 1400s, still accepted the early parts of the Bible as true historical events. Thus, it was widely taught that the worldwide Flood of Genesis 6-9 was a real event and all people on earth were descendants of Noah's sons – Shem, Ham, and Japheth. Furthermore, it was widely accepted that the Europeans were primarily descendants of Japheth, Africans were primarily descendants of Ham, and Asians were primarily descendants of Shem. They believed this explained the very different skin coloring and facial characteristics of different races of people. **What they did not understand is that the genetic composition of all people was already created within the DNA and both Adam and later Noah.** The children of Shem, Ham and Japheth would have displayed a wide variety of appearances, not just the narrow variation which came after the tower of Babel.

When Columbus arrived back in Europe, he disembarked with people who did not look like Europeans, Africans, or Asians. Since it was widely taught that all people descended from Noah's sons, and these "creatures" did not look like any of the sons of Noah (Europeans, Africans, or Asians), the church had a huge mystery on its hands. Some church leaders argued that these Naive Americans could not even be human! Eventually the church came to a faulty conclusion – since these people did not look like the sons of Noah, they could not be descendants of Noah.

They solved the mystery by rejecting what the Word of God teaches. They arbitrarily concluded that there had never been a world-covering flood upon the earth in spite of the fact that the Bible is crystal-clear on this issue.

It took about 100 years for this general consensus to be widely accepted, but by the 1700's, when earth scientists were studying the rock layers of the earth, many of them no longer accepted that these sedimentary rocks (and the fossils they contained) were a testimony to the worldwide Flood from the days of Noah. Therefore, the only other logical explanation for the existence of extensive layers of sedimentary rock (in some places thousands of feet deep) was enormous periods of time and slow accumulation. Thus millions, and later billions, of years of earth history became accepted as a "fact of science." **Long forgotten is that this is just a faulty interpretation** of the rock layers based on the rejection of the truth (a world-covering flood created these layers).

Slow changes over enormous time became the only accepted viewpoint in the 1700's to explain the geology of our planet (geological evolution); leading directly to the belief in slow changes over enormous periods of time to explain all of biology (biological evolution) in the 1800's; leading directly to slow changes over enormous periods of time to explain all the matter and energy in the universe (cosmic evolution) in the 1900's.

Today, evolutionism is the only explanation taught to students. It is so widely repeated throughout our educational, museum, and media systems that few people question its assumptions or understand how this philosophical framework for interpreting the world around us arose. **It was the rejection over 500 years ago of what the Bible teaches about geology (the worldwide Flood) that ultimately led to the current situation where most of Western civilization has rejected all of God's Word as accurate and relevant.** An ever-increasing proportion of people are now rejecting the very existence of God Himself. Ideas have consequences! Ideas not based on God's truth have dire consequences!

You have made the earth tremble; You have broken it;
Heal its breaches, for it is shaking.
~ Psalm 60:2

"Greater love hath no man than this, that a man lay down his life for his friends."
– John 15:13

"I have found that there are three stages in every great work of God: first, it is impossible, then it is difficult, then it is done."
- Hudson Taylor, Pioneering Missionary to China in 1800's

February 1
Christian Truth

While on the cross, Jesus experienced a taste of hell in at least six very real ways:

1. Jesus was **conscious during His time** of suffering on the cross. He felt the scourging, nailing, and torturing pain of crucifixion. Hell is a place of "weeping and gnashing of teeth" (Luke 13:28, Matthew 13:50). **In hell, one will be conscious of suffering.**
2. **Darkness** was experienced by Jesus "from the sixth hour (12 noon) until the ninth hour (3 pm)" (Matthew 27:45). Hell will be the blackest of darkness.
3. Jesus was **surrounded by demonic powers**. Colossians 2:15 states, "And having spoiled principalities and powers, he made a shew of them openly, triumphing over them in it [the cross]". We do not fully see this spiritual conflict taking place on Calvary, but this dark force of demons would have poured out their evil jeers and hatred on Christ.
4. Jesus bore our sins in His body on the tree (1 Peter 2:24) because God made Him who knew no sin to be sin for us (2 Corinthians 5:21). God laid the iniquity of us all on Him (Isaiah 53:6). **Christ was our sin-bearer.** In Hell, we will bear our sins.
5. Jesus experienced hell on the cross by taking **the punishment for sin**. During those hours of darkness, He bore our sins and endured our punishment. God poured out His wrath on sin. That is what Hell is, receiving the punishment for the sins we deserve.
6. Christ was **separated from the love of God**. To be separated from God's love is to be removed from all that is wonderful and lovely.

Hell is being conscious of suffering, in total blackest darkness, surrounded by demonic powers, bearing the guilt of sin, coming under the judgment of God, and being eternally separated from love. The hell of hells is knowing that you could have followed God and that you passed up this opportunity--forever!

Hell is for real. But, God has provided a way out. It is through His son Jesus Christ. He was the one that paid the price for your sins. All you need to do is *admit*: I am a sinner; *repent*: I am sorry for my sins; *believe*: Jesus paid the price by dying on the cross; and *accept*: Jesus is my Lord and Savior. The invitation is given; the time is now.

> For we have not a high priest which cannot be touched with the feeling of our infirmities; but was in all points tempted like we are yet without sin.
> ~ Hebrews 4:15

February 2

Geology

Scientists have discovered that gold veins can be produced in an instant (a few tenths of a second) and do not require huge time periods. Veins of gold are produced when hot fluids flowing through cracks deep in the earth's crust depressurize rapidly - causing the minerals and metals to fall out of the hot fluid solution. The "flash deposition" of gold is a result of earthquakes opening up cracks. Gold can often be found in these sideways, zigzagging fault jogs - cracks that are connected to main fault lines in rocks. Earthquakes can make gold veins in an instant as cracks open and the pressure drops, causing the precious metals to be flash deposited. **Gold does not take millions of years to form within the rock layers of the earth**. During the Flood of Noah's day, there would have been intense earthquake activity that could have produced gold in a flash as it precipitated out of solution.

It is sad how much death, human misery, slavery, and corruption has been caused by the search for gold and riches. Heaven is described as a place where gold is so common the streets are paved with it. Things humans typically value (such as gold) turn out to be rather commonplace in the end. The world desires gold, yet gold pales in comparison to God's Word and the wisdom and meaning it can bring to our lives.

More to be desired (is God's Word) than gold, yea, than much fine gold:....
- Psalm 19:10

Biology

February 3

The giant silk moth can have a wing area of over 60 square inches with a tail over 8 inches long. Cleaning this insect off your windshield just might empty your washer fluid! Yet every portion of the wings and tail is covered with intricately-designed scales, which produce beautiful iridescent patterns. But why are they so beautiful? The Christian perspective is that their beauty reflects the character of their Maker. The evolutionary perspective is that they are simply a product of chance. Which perspective is correct?

Those working to explain all of life without God make up stories to explain why butterflies are so beautiful. They say the gorgeous colors exist to draw mates or camouflage the insects from predators. Yet the brilliant coloration does the opposite of hiding the insects. **The 1500 known species of the giant silk moth fly only at night when the brilliant coloration cannot be seen**. Why would a moth with "eyespots" need these spots when it only comes out at night?

Butterflies and moths confound those who wish to believe God does not exist. Not only do both kinds of flying insects transform themselves from a leaf-chewing, land-bound caterpillar into a nectar-sucking, flying wonder, but each can be breathtaking in its beauty. Neither the origin of this flying insect, nor the explanation for its beauty, can be explained by evolution; it is only by looking at God that we find the answer. He is the master Creator of beauty – all-knowing and all-powerful!

He hath made everything beautiful in his time....
~ Ecclesiastes 3:11

February 4

Biology

Have you ever noticed how the colors on a butterfly or moth wing seem to change and almost glow as it flies through the air? Pilots flying above the rainforests in South America have reported seeing the bright blues of the morpho butterfly up to half a mile away! What makes the butterfly wing so vibrant and colorful? Butterfly wings are covered with two or three layers of microscopic scales separated by air. Light passing through these layers is scattered, and depending on the angle of view, the light waves recombine in different combinations of different wavelengths. This is called diffraction, which produces iridescence. The multiple layers of scales on a butterfly wing create these intensely shifting color hues.

The scales of butterfly wings are made of very thin layers of a hardened protein called chitin. Your hair and nails are made of this same protein. These scales protect and insulate the insects and aid in the flow of air along their wings. The scales also help the butterfly absorb heat. Since butterflies are cold-blooded, they rely on external sources of heat.

But where did the butterfly's beauty and complexity come from? Neither the beauty nor the structure of the butterfly wing has ever been explained by evolution. **Those who reject creation throw the word "evolution" at such complex creatures and assume that just using the word explains how they developed**. To produce these iridescent colors requires complex optical physics and mathematics. Could this phenomenon of iridescence happen by accident and chance? Caterpillars are not made of chitin scales, but butterflies are, so how would the caterpillar develop this characteristic slowly and randomly over time in order to become a butterfly? If evolution were true, we should first find a butterfly without chitin scales and then a butterfly with chitin scales. We find nothing like this in the fossil record. The oldest butterfly and moth fossils are fully formed and developed, looking essentially identical to current moths and butterflies.

Butterflies, with their beauty and complexity, proclaim there is a God!

Let them praise the name of the Lord: for his name alone is excellent; his glory is above the earth and heaven.
~ Psalm 148:13

February 5
History

Have you considered that the Garden of Eden was meant to be understood as real history? Does this mean that there was a walking, talking snake? If any of this were true, we would expect people to remember some of the details and carry that memory with them when they left the Tower of Babel. **We find such details in a 12 foot tall, bronze, fruit tree that was excavated in 1986 near Guanghan, China** (dated about 4000 years old, secular dating).

Attached to this 12-foot bronze fruit tree were a **human hand** and a **snake with feet**. Genesis 3:6 records that Eve took **forbidden fruit** from the tree and ate. Genesis 3 continues with the snake being cursed by God such that it was changed to move about on its belly. This implies that previously the snake had legs and walked. The temptation of Eve was a real event in history and the Chinese recorded it in one of their artifacts.

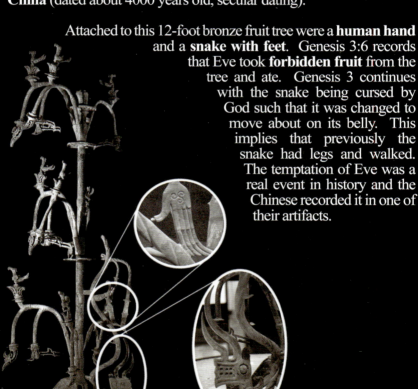

*Upon thy belly shalt thou go,
and dust shalt thou eat all the days of thy life.
~ Genesis 3:14b*

February 6

Biology

Marine loggerhead turtles are found in all of the world's oceans with the exception of the Arctic. They have the longest known migration route of any marine animal. For example, a little hatchling on the coast of Japan swims to its feeding area along the coast of California and back to the exact beach where it was hatched each year. **Over its lifetime, it will migrate millions of miles!**

It has been known for decades that loggerheads have a built-in "compass" in their heads that allow them to know their latitude; the equator is 0 degrees while the north or south pole is 90 degrees. When traveling north to south, the magnetic field will vary in intensity. Recently scientists were amazed to find that loggerheads can also detect longitude, traveling east or west. Longitude is very difficult to discern because earth's magnetic field does not vary much east to west; only the *angle* of the magnetic pull changes and only to a very minute degree. **Loggerheads were found to have not just a "compass" but a built-in "GPS" system detecting both the intensity and *angle* of the magnetic field**. It took humans hundreds of years and a great deal of money to build instruments measuring longitude. Does ANYONE believe mankind's GPS systems happened by accident and chance? Loggerheads have astounding migration abilities by using their GPS. And who is their GPS Maker? God Himself.

All thy works shall praise thee, O Lord....
~ Psalm 145:10

February 7

Christian Truth

Did you know that the planet Mercury is a testimony to creation? Back in 1974-75, the space probe *Mariner 10* discovered that Mercury has a magnetic field. Thirty-six years later, in 2011, space probe Messenger documented that Mercury's magnetic field strength had fallen 8%. So what, you say! This means that the magnetic field on Mercury has a half-life of only 320 years. In other words, every 300 years or so, Mercury loses half the strength of its magnetic field. If Mercury is billions of years old, or even hundreds of thousands of years old, it could not possibly have any magnetic field left. This recent discovery is enormously strong evidence from the field of cosmology that our solar system had to have been recently created. But it gets even better!

The validity of any scientific theory is based on its ability to predict as yet unmeasured or unseen events. Dr. Russell Humphreys, a Bible-believing, creation scientist, correctly predicted rapid decay of Mercury's magnetic field decades **before** *Messenger* measured the planet's field strength. His correct prediction was based on his theory that all the planets were initially formed about 6000 years ago. He also correctly predicted the strength of Uranus' and Neptune's magnetic fields - before spacecraft measured these magnetic fields. **In EVERY case of predicting magnetic fields, the predictions of old-age evolutionary astronomers were wrong!** But of course, Dr. Humphreys would be correct; he started with the Bible to develop his mathematical models. The universe is young, just as the Bible says. Mercury's magnetic field is a testimony to creation!

**The heavens declare the glory of God;
and the firmament sheweth his handywork
~ Psalm 19:1**

February 8

Biology

Does a bumblebee have two or four wings? It has four wings. The wings are in pairs coupled together by a row of hooks on the back wing that grip in a groove on the rear edge of the front wing. As the bee gets ready to fly, its wings unfold causing the hooks to fall into the groove and lock in place. Now the wings are a single, large flight surface. A bumblebee can fly up, down, sideways, backwards and forwards, with a speed over 6 mph. **The bee flaps its wings about 200 times a second**, causing the buzzing noise we hear.

Why is a bumblebee made with short wings? Watch it move around inside a flower to see the bee fold its wings and lay them along its back. Long wings would stick out and the bee would not be able to turn in tight spaces. **The wings are specially designed**. The way the bee's wings couple together with hooks in a groove could not have come about by accident and chance; it was specifically designed for the work the bumblebee does.

If I take the wings of the morning,...
~ Psalm 139:9

Microbiology

February 9

Bacteria are both the most diverse and the most numerous life forms upon earth. **You actually have more bacteria on and within your body than human cells**. The diversity of these bacteria continues to amaze scientists. Dr. Kenneth Nealson leads a team of scientists that has discovered a new type of bacteria--electric bacteria--which can survive on pure electricity. These bacteria have the ability to both deposit and remove electrons directly from surfaces as their "food". His team has identified over 1000 varieties of bacteria which make use of electricity for survival. Six of these bacterial strains have the ability to survive on electricity alone. Electric bacteria should not "shock" us; God designs beyond our imaginations! Science now has an entire new area to "think God's thoughts" and see how He has put it together.

Even though these bacteria have a unique method of survival, they are made from biologically useful chemicals which have only been shown to exist and be produced by living cells. These complex bio-chemicals have never been shown to exist outside of a cell. So what implication does this discovery have on the origin of life?

- Electricity did not bring them alive; it is used for survival.
- These bacteria are made of complex bio-chemicals that only exist inside a living cell.
- The coded DNA information in these bacteria is so complex that it would be impossible for it to have written itself.
- There is no link between non-living chemicals and these bacteria. These distinct forms of life show no indication of turning into anything other than copies of themselves.

Yet the researchers who discovered these bacteria attribute their existence to "evolution". In other words, they assume that they simply created themselves. They further speculate that similar forms of life have made themselves all over the universe. Billions of dollars are being spent to search our universe for any other signs of life. Yet not a shred of evidence has been found.

In actuality, **the diversity of life does nothing but demonstrate the power and creativity of the Creator of life.** The more we learn about its complexity and diversity, the less excuse we have for ignoring God's existence.

> O give thanks unto the LORD; call upon his name:
> make known his deeds among the people.
> ~ Psalm 105:1

February 10

Design

Have you considered that the earth is perfectly designed for life?

1. **The right rate of spin**. 24 hours is just right. If the earth spun slower, nights would become colder, and days would be hotter.
2. **The right length of year**. Winters are just short enough for creatures to survive while summers are just long enough for plants to produce food for us to eat.
3. **The right axis of rotation tilt**. This tilt produces the seasons. Winter and summer seasons trigger the timing of when plants bloom and creatures court.
4. **The right distance from the sun**. If earth were 10 % closer to the sun, earth would feel like a furnace. If it were 20% farther away, we would be an icy desert.
5. **The right orbit**. Earth's orbit is nearly circular. This allows the sun to evenly heat us.
6. **The right surface smoothness**. The earth surface is surprisingly smooth. If the mountains were only 10% higher, the local weather conditions would be extreme.
7. **The right materials**. Apart from the organic materials such as wood, earth has an abundance of the right kind of metals: aluminum, iron, lead, tin, copper, zinc, titanium, gold, silver, etc. The most abundant also tend to be the most useful!

The earth is perfectly designed for life!

For thus saith the Lord that created the heavens; God himself that formed the earth and made it; he hath established it, he created it not in vain, he formed it to be inhabited: I am the Lord; and there is none else. ~ Isaiah 45:18

February 11

Biology

There is a small bird known as the "little dipper", or water ouzel, that loves to dip into the water beside a fast-flowing river. This little bird flies, swims, and strolls along the bottom of the stream turning over rocks with his beak looking for food. He does not have webbed feet, so he uses his **wings as oars** to move through the water. He uses his **air sacs to rise** to the surface and compresses the air out of these sacs to submerge. The dipper's eyes have a **special lens curvature** for underwater vision and **nasal flaps** in his nostrils that close when diving. After all, who wants water up one's nose?

Evolutionists will say this bird evolved. Why would he "evolve" all this underwater equipment when he could just as easily have gotten his food off the ground? Our heavenly Father just loves to show His creativity!

Hear, O ye kings; give ear, O ye princes; I, even I, will sing unto the Lord; I will sing praise to the Lord God of Israel.
~ Judges 5:3

February 12
Christian Truth

Your skin is literally crawling with millions of harmful viruses and bacteria, yet infections and diseases ONLY start when contamination finds its way inside. In a similar way, the Christian church faces its greatest danger, not from persecution and skeptical attacks, but from those within the faith who twist and distort the Word of God to justify non-biblical beliefs. Combining God's Word with evolution (and its required millions of years) is Christianity's greatest internal threat.

You need only observe the reaction to creation conferences hosted on public universities to see this reality in action. Venomous and insulting attacks preceding such conferences by unbelieving faculty and students are not at all surprising – the very idea of a Creator to whom we are accountable strikes at the very core of their belief system. But all too often "Christian" groups show up at such conferences to pass out evolution-promoting literature. And every year **thousands of churches set aside the Sunday closest to Charles Darwin's birthday to celebrate "Darwin Day"!** Most Christian Bible colleges and seminaries teach that it is perfectly acceptable to believe that God used billions of years to slowly change pond slime into human beings (i.e. molecules-to-man evolution). Well-funded organizations are spending millions to convince Christians that evolution and the Bible blend seamlessly. Yet, the exact opposite is true.

I recently helped my son tear out almost every wall in his "fixer-upper" home in preparation for a major remodeling. While we were rebuilding, three critical tools were needed: a level, square, and chalk line. The Bible gives us an unchanging standard for understanding not just morality, but history and science also. **God's Word is the only suitable level, square, and chalk line standard with which to interpret these subjects.** Almost universally, Christians have compromised God's Word by making science, majority opinion, or their own experience the absolute with which to judge and re-interpret God's Word. This is exactly equivalent to bending the square, misaligning the level, or smearing the chalk line to fit a crooked wall. It may work for a while, but ultimately, the structure will become distorted as mistake, builds upon mistake and it will become hopelessly unstable and destroyed from within.

God repeatedly warns us to make His Word - not the teaching of church leaders, scientific consensus, or popular opinion - our primary guide of truth.

Beware of false prophets, which come to you in sheep's clothing, but inwardly they are ravening wolves. ~ Matthew 7:15

Paleontology

February 13

Most Christians are not aware that there is much evidence supporting the belief that dinosaurs lived only thousands of years ago - alongside of mankind. Here is a brief list:

1. The archaeological evidence: For example, the engravings in brass around Bishop Bell's tomb at Carlisle Cathedral in the north of England dated 1491 show two intertwined long-necked dinosaurs. Worldwide, **there are many dinosaurs depicted in ancient sculptures, paintings, and carvings**. The variety and frequency of such evidence supports the reality that mankind has lived with these creatures.
2. **Soft tissue has been found inside of multiple dinosaur bones**, which means they must have been buried recently, not millions of years ago.
3. **DNA has been found in dinosaur bone cells**, which means they must be relatively young.
4. **Carbon-14 has been found in dinosaur bone**. C-14 is used to date organic matter (not rocks), and it has a short 5,730 year half-life. After about 100,000 years, there should be no detectable C-14 left. Yet, C-14 levels hundreds of times above the equipment detection limit has been found.
5. Before the word "dinosaur" was invented, **creatures fitting the description of dinosaurs were mentioned in the Bible** - the Behemoth of Job 40:15-41 and the Leviathan of Job 41.

Dinosaurs have been the "poster child" used to promote the belief in evolution for decades. With these findings, dinosaurs can now be missionaries of biblical truth. **Everyone loves dinosaurs**. Let's show people how they fit a recent biblical creation viewpoint far better than a millions-of-years evolutionary perspective.

Canst thou draw out leviathan with an hook.... Out of his mouth go burning lamps, and sparks of fire leap out. Out of his nostrils goeth smoke, as out of a seething pot or caldron. His breath kindleth coals, and a flame goeth out of his mouth. ~ Job 41:1, 19-21

February 14

Biology

A pig farmer in the UK heard an evolutionist academic talk about how the breeding of farm animals shows evolution. At the end of the lecture the pig farmer said, "Professor, I don't understand what you are talking about. When I breed pigs, I get pigs—if it were not so I would be out of business!"

Evolutionists understand that the addition of new, increasingly complex information is required if a bacterium is to evolve into a man. For a reptile to change into a bird would require new genes to transform scales into feathers. The odds of random natural processes (like mutations) creating a new gene coding to make feathers (instead of reptilian scales) is essentially zero. Mutations always degrade the information found on the DNA molecule. Mutations never result in increasingly complex information. As ardent evolutionist Carl Sagan admitted: "... *mutations occur at random and are almost uniformly harmful—it is rare that a precision machine is improved by a random change in the instructions for making it.*" **Rare indeed – and in most cases, NEVER!**

There are many breeds of dogs, chickens, cats, and pigs, but they are all dogs, chickens, cats and pigs. The reshuffling of different genes produces the great variety **within a kind,** but the variety is limited to the genes that are present. If there are no genes for feathers, then feathers will not be present. Variation within a kind is not evolution! Galapagos finches are still finches, peppered moths are still peppered moths; they just show variety within a kind, not evolution. Things reproduce after their kind just as the Bible states. As the pig farmer said to the evolutionist, "I would be out of business if pigs did not produce pigs!"

And God said, Let the earth bring forth the living creature after his kind, cattle, and creeping thing, and beast of the earth after his kind: and it was so.
~ Genesis 1:24

February 15

History

Is there really a lost city of Atlantis, or is this just a myth?

Let's consider what happened after the Flood. Within a few hundred years, the rapidly expanding human population was spreading across the earth after being dispersed from the Tower of Babel. The end of the Flood also marked the beginning of the Ice Age. The Flood warmed the oceans of the world causing increased evaporation. This resulted in a wetter, colder climate worldwide with massive snowfall in high north and south latitudes. Fine ash particles from the massive volcanic activity during and after the Flood also worked to keep the earth cool and snow from melting.

This resulted in enormous amounts of water being removed from the oceans. **Most experts believe the oceans were 300 feet lower during the height of the ice age**. It is estimated that this one and only Ice Age lasted about 700 years. It seems likely that many people spreading out at this time of earth history would have settled along coastlines. At the end of the Ice Age, the icepacks began to melt - returning the water to the oceans and causing the sea level to rise about 300 feet. This caused flooding of coastal cities all over the world.

Today we are discovering more and more underwater archeological sites: Yonaguni near Japan, old Dwarka near India, Yarmuta near Lebanon and underwater cities off the coasts of Greece and Cuba. The submerged megaliths off southern India are a boon for the local fishermen. The temples and walls provide a place for the fish to congregate. The local fishermen are constantly snagging their nets on the buildings and must dive to loosen them. These local fishermen have the privilege of seeing the submerged kingdom of Kumari Kandam with its columns, pyramids, stone walls and lion statues. In other words, the ancients were building megalithic cities during the Ice Age that were submerged as the Ice Age ended.

Was the city of Atlantis a myth? Let's just say these are exciting times for this new field of study, underwater archeology.

For he saith to the snow, Be thou on the earth; likewise to the small rain, and to the great rain of his strength.
~ Job 37:6

February 16

Biology

Each fin on a fish is needed to move the fish. If the tail fin (caudal) was not there, the fish could not propel itself forward. If the pectoral fins and the pelvic fins were not present, the fish would not be able to steer. If the dorsal or anal fin was missing, the fish would not be able to stay upright and would tip sideways. All the fins are needed AND at the same time. Darwinian evolutionists believe that living organism developed and diversified from simple to complex during earth's history. Yet, a fish with only two or three fins would not survive. All the fins, with their functions, were needed from the beginning in order for the fish to successfully swim.

Evolutionists believe that hundreds of millions of years ago fish evolved from some worm or sponge or other invertebrate. Not one single fossil has revealed this intermediate form of half-fish and half-invertebrate. And as J.R. Norman, an evolutionist from the Department of Zoology, British Museum of Natural History, London, states, "The geological record has so far provided no evidence as to the origin of the fishes…" **Fossils of invertebrates have been found, and fossils of fishes have been found, but nothing in-between!** There are no transitional fossils showing the evolution of a fish. Scripture states that God created the swimming creatures, including fish, on Day 5 of the creation week. He created them as fully formed fish.

O Lord, our Lord, how excellent is thy name in all the earth!....
~ Psalm 8:1

Biblical Accuracy

February 17

Are unicorns real? An AP report coming out of an Italian nature preserve announced, *"Single-Horned 'Unicorn' Deer is Found in Italy."* Sounds like fantasy, doesn't it? But unicorn merely means "one horn", and that is what was discovered in Italy.

Interestingly, its twin has two horns, so in this case, the one horn is probably a genetic flaw or birth defect. **What is interesting is that the horn is positioned in the center of its head.** Unicorns are mentioned in the King James Bible multiple times (Deuteronomy 33:17; Numbers 23:22, 24:8; Psalm 22:21, 29:6, 92:10; Isaiah 34:7). Ancient artwork also has images of unicorns. Remember that a unicorn is just a one-horned animal but depictions do not look like rhinos. They could be a one-horned deer, goat, or some other animal. Unicorns were some kind of four-legged mammal with either a genetic mutation for a single horn (like the one found in Italy) or an extinct variation of a species still alive today.

God brought them out of Egypt; he hath as it were the strength of an unicorn.
~ Numbers 23:22

February 18

Anatomy

Two United Kingdom twins turn heads because **one twin sister is white and the other twin sister is black!** Lucy is "white" with blue eyes, and Maria is "black" with brown eyes, yet they are twins. Their father is "white" and their mother is part-Jamaican. These two girls help answer a troubling question about the Bible. If there were only one man and one woman in the beginning, then where did all the "races" come from? Why do people of such diverse facial appearance and skin color exist?

Lucy and Marie show that it is simply a matter of genetics. Skin color is based on a pigment called melanin. If you have a lot of melanin you will be dark; if you have just a little melanin, you will have light skin. If Adam and Eve were medium brown, subsequent generations would have had melanin skin colors from very dark to very light. Following the Genesis Flood, the people built the tower of Babel, God caused confusion in their languages, and people spread out across the world (Genesis 11). This resulted in the genetic pools being isolated and the different people groups developing. We are all literally sons and daughters of Adam and Eve. Twin sisters Lucy and Maria Aylmer from the UK show us that we are all related. **Skin color is only skin deep and nothing more**. We are all one race, the human race.

And hath made of one blood all nations of men for to dwell on all the face of the earth...
~Acts 17: 26

February 19 — Botany

People are fascinated by insect eating plants such as the Venus flytrap. Venus fly traps are designed to snap their leaves shut, trapping the insect inside. This provides the nutrients for the plant that the soil does not provide. Another mechanism of trapping insects is seen in the pitcher plants. Their leaf-like structures form a cavity that fills with liquid in which insects are attracted and then drown. The dissolved insects provide nutrients which the plants need.

The Borneo giant pitcher plant, *Nepenthes rajah*, is so large **it can hold almost a gallon of liquid**. With a reservoir so large, any nutrients from insects would be too diluted to do the plant much good. So biologists were curious how the Borneo's giant pitcher plant got its nutrients. They discovered an amazing process whereby the plant lures rats and tree shrews with sweet nectar, not to eat them, but to feed them. During the day, the tree shrews come to lick the nectar from the rim and defecate into the plant. During the night, rats come to lick the sweet nectar and also **use the pitcher plant as a toilet**.

The tree shrew/rat gets a valuable food source, nectar, while the pitcher plant gets to catch and absorb the "poop" from the shrew/rat, which supplies it with much-needed nitrogen. The plant needs the rat, and the rat needs the plant. Did this mutualism happen by accident and chance? When we see such a mutually benificial design we know it points to a Designer.

And he answering said unto him, Lord, let it alone this year also, till I shall dig about it, and dung it. ~ Luke 13:8

February 20

Biology

The dragon fish lives 1,500 to 4,500 feet below the surface of the ocean – it is what is known as a "deep-sea" animal. At that depth, light is minimal, and most deep-sea creatures can only see blue light because other wavelengths do not penetrate the ocean to such great depths.

In spite of this, the dragon fish can see red light because he has chlorophyll in his eyes. Yes, that's right, chlorophyll - stuff that makes plants green. This chlorophyll allows the dragonfish to see in the red spectrum, giving the dragonfish a secret weapon. It pulses far red light which allows it to see its prey without itself being seen. You could say that **a dragon fish's eyes act like a night vision scope on a sniper's rifle**. How can evolution explain a dragon fish evolving chlorophyll, the stuff of green plants, within its eyes? And how did it know that this chlorophyll would help it to see in the red spectrum? And why would it evolve the ability to see in the red part of the light spectrum when it could not have known that red light even existed? Does anyone believe that a night vision sniper scope happened by accident and chance? The dragon fish's sniper scope eyes bear witness to a powerful and unique designer, God Himself.

And the light shineth in darkness...
~ John 1:5a

February 21

Design

Automakers are busily developing self-driving automobiles which are capable of sensing danger and instantly reacting to it. Imagine that you are in such a car and it senses that a large tree has fallen across the road, blocking your path forward. The response from such a vehicle would be to slam on the brakes and come to an immediate stop.

Now think about that response. Why did the car stop? **Did the fallen tree in some way communicate with the car and cause it to stop?** Not at all. The car had internal sensors to identify the barrier and internal programming to adapt to the changing circumstances. To believe that the tree caused the car to stop would be both naive and misguided. **Yet, this is exactly how biologists are trained to think about life**. Their literature is filled with examples that imply that the environment in which an organism lives causes it to adapt and change. The idea that the presence of drugs causes a bacteria to evolve or a sooty environment caused the peppered moths population to shift from light to dark coloration is the common perception among biologists. This is as misguided as believing that the fallen tree caused the car to stop.

Life adapts to changing environments because it has been designed with programming that allows it the flexibility to adapt. It is the organism, guided by prior programming, that adapts to changes, not the environment that causes the changes to happen. The primary reason biologists do not think in this manner is because it implies that a source of this programming is required, and they are trained to believe the environment made the organism. Thus, they miss the One who did the programming. God, the great programmer!

Yea, if thou criest after knowledge, and liftest up thy voice for understanding; If thou seekest her as silver, and searchest for her as for hid treasures; Then shalt thou understand the fear of the Lord, and find the knowledge of God. ~ Proverbs 2:3-5

February 22

Design

Most animals flee from forest fires, but not the black fire beetles (*Melanophila acuminate*). **They flock toward the fire!** These unique beetles mate, and then the female lays her eggs in the bark of the still smoldering wood. The eggs hatch and burrow into the tree, free to munch away on trees without interference from the tree's protective defenses.

During its lifetime, any given black fire beetle is statistically unlikely to ever experience a forest fire where it lives, so how does it find a burning forest for reproduction? On the underside of these beetles are tiny pits equipped with infrared radiation detection sensors. This infrared radiation detection system **can detect the invisible heat rays given off by a forest fire up to 50 miles away!** Do infrared radiation detection systems happen by accident and chance? Hardly! In fact, scientists are trying to copy this system in order to install them around forests to alert foresters when there is a fire. Scientists are only copying a good design. When we see an infrared radiation detection system, we know there must be an infrared radiation detection system Maker! And that Maker is God!

O Lord, there is none like thee, neither is there any God beside thee, according to all that we have heard with our ears.
~1 Chronicles 17:20

Cosmology

February 23

Have you considered how well archaeological evidence provides support for the recent creation of mankind? All anthropologists know that key human technological advancements – agriculture, the wheel, pottery, and horse domestication – were developed less than 10,000 years ago. The oldest plow is about 4,000 years old. It was discovered in Lavagnone, Italy in a peat bog. What about agriculture in general? Archaeological excavations have shown that agriculture has existed less than 10,000 years. What about the wheel? Even secular history books admit the wheel was invented 5,000 - 6,000 years ago and not in just one area but in Germany, Switzerland, Slovenia, and Mesopotamia. What about pottery? The earliest pottery found was in Iran, Japan, and China and has been dated less than 7,000 years old. Some of the pottery was found to be just as sophisticated in design as recent pottery. What about horse domestication? Again, the most ancient date advanced is that horses were domesticated less than 6,000 years ago. Archaeological evidence shows that the three most ancient civilizations, the Egyptian, Mesopotamian, and Indus civilizations, arose 6,000 (or less) years ago.

Even the oldest written languages date back about 5,000 years, and these languages show no evidence of evolving in complexity. In fact, the most ancient languages were just as complex and sophisticated (often more so) than modern languages – having complex grammar and structure. When we examine the evidence of human activity through archaeology, we find overwhelming support for a recent creation of man. If man had been evolving over millions of years, we should find evidence to support this, but we do not. What we find is man leaving his evidence dating back far less than 10,000 years. This is exactly what we would expect by reading the Bible as accurate, literal history.

Please inquire of past generations, And consider the things searched out by their fathers.
- Job 8:8 (NASV)

February 24

Botany

Michael Faraday (1791-1867) is second only to Isaac Newton as the greatest physicist who ever walked the Earth. Faraday was credited with the invention of electromagnetic induction, the electric motor, the electric transformer, the electric generator and made major contributions to our understanding of magnetism, polarized light, the liquefaction of gases, the development of rubber, optical glass, alloys of steel, electroplating, and artificial rubies. In addition, his greatest contribution to science was the development of field theory in physics. He is ranked by science historians as the greatest of all experimental physicists – adding a whole new vocabulary to modern science – anode, cathode, ion, electricity, electrode, anion, cation, magnetic field, lines of force, and electrolysis.

Faraday's work so changed modern science that two basic units of physics were named in his honor – the faraday (a unit of electrical quantity) and the farad (a unit of capacitance). Yet, as much as Faraday contributed to scientific advancement – he drew more from his deeply held Christian faith. His actions were strongly guided by Biblical truths, and his Bible contained nearly 3000 meticulously written notations in the margins. His good friend John Tyndall wrote of Faraday, *"I think that a good deal of Faraday's week-long strength and persistency might be due to his Sunday exercises. He drinks from a fount on Sunday that refreshes his soul for the week."*

Just like Newton before him, Faraday drew strength and meaning from the reality that the universe displays order and meaning as a direct result of being created by God. It is not a meaningless assembly of atoms which created itself, but an orderly arrangement – designed by an incredible intelligence outside of the physical universe. This acknowledgement did not hinder the incredible discoveries of these great scientists, but provided the foundation which motivated them.

> **And whatsoever ye do, do it heartily,
> as to the Lord, and not unto men
> – Colossians 3:23**

Biology

February 25

Wouldn't it be fun to walk right up the side of a wall or dash across the ceiling without tumbling to the floor? Only in comic books can fantasy heroes accomplish such feats. Inspiring such fiction are spiders, flies, and many other insects that have no trouble scurrying upside down across the ceiling. But no creature defies gravity like the gecko. **Scientists have spent decades trying to discover how this heavy lizard, weighing hundreds of times more than an insect, can run upside down across surfaces as smooth as glass.**

Originally, it was believed that tiny features on the gecko's feet functioned like suction cups to suspend the lizard. Later, the real secret was discovered – hundreds of millions of microscopic hair-like filaments on the gecko's feet exploit weak electrostatic attraction (van der Waal forces) that act as tiny magnets to hold the lizard to the ceiling[1]. But the mystery of how the gecko could turn these forces on and off to prevent its foot from remaining stuck to the ceiling remained.

More recent work has shown that the gecko hairs are curved like little bent hairs that can be snapped back and forth as the lizard moves across a surface allowing a rapid attachment/detachment mechanism to take place. Even researchers who believe in evolution describe the gecko with words like, "*...amazing, finely balanced, and finely tuned this whole system is...*" Mankind can invent imaginary wall-clinging heroes like Spiderman, but only God can create real creatures capable of displaying such amazing abilities.

The spider taketh hold with her hands, and is in kings' palaces.
~ Proverbs 30:28

February 26
Biblical Accuracy

The Bible is full of prophecy – which simply is advance knowledge of the future. Since time is part of the physical universe, and God is the one who created the universe, God is "outside of time." The fact that the Bible is filled with specific prophecies, that have come true, is one of the ways we can know the Bible is inspired by the One who is outside of time – God, the Eternal One.

One such prophecy concerns Edom. Edom was an ancient nation located near the Dead Sea. In Ezekiel 35:3-4, 9, God pronounced a curse on Edom, stating that this large nation would become desolate, all its cities would disappear, it would never be inhabited by humans, and it would be overrun by animals and beasts.

Today, we find nothing but traces of uninhabited towns in this area. Even the capital of Edom, Petra, considered one of the wonders of the ancient world with its buildings hewn out of beautiful rose-red solid rock, now stands in ruins. The only inhabitants are birds, reptiles, and assorted other animals. **Imagine if a prophet of today came to New Jersey, which is about the size of Edom, and prophesied that New Jersey would become desolate, never to be reinhabited by humans and would be home only to wild animals and beasts**. We would say that is ridiculous. Yet that is what has happened to Edom. The Edomites only existed for 1,700 years; their cities and even their language have utterly disappeared. The desolation of this land is a testimony to fulfilled prophecy.

I am against thee, and I will stretch out mine hand against thee, and I will make thee most desolate. I will lay thy cities waste, and thou shalt be desolate, and thou shalt know that I am the LORD....I will make thee perpetual desolations, and thy cities shall not return: and ye shall know that I am the LORD. ~ Ezekiel 35:3-4, 9

Cosmology

February 27

Every time NASA sends a probe to a new location within our solar system, it sends back images that astonish scientists. Why the surprise? **Because probe after probe sends back images that would not be expected if our solar system were billions of years old.** Evidence for the recent creation of our solar system abounds - from the moon of Jupiter (Io) which is inexplicably volcanically active (it should be a cold moon, if millions of years old) to the raging storms and heat radiating from Neptune (it should be a cold planet if millions of years old); from the magnetic field of Mercury (which should not exist if this solid planet was billions of years old) to stable rings of dust orbiting the sun within the asteroid belt between Mars and Jupiter (which should have long ago been pulled apart by the gravitational attraction of the sun). The latest discovery supporting the recent creation of our solar system is the __smooth__ surface of Pluto.

In July of 2015, NASA released photographs taken during the *New Horizons* space probe's fly-by of Pluto. Again evolutionary scientists were stunned by the evidence. Pluto's surface showed very few craters. If Pluto had been in existence for billions of years, there should have been millions of craters on the surface from impacts of objects hitting it, and any gas in the atmosphere around the planetoid should be long gone. Yet, Pluto was inexplicably found to have very few craters and a nitrogen atmosphere. Both are best understood as perfectly logical because our solar system is a recent creation by God only about 6000 years ago – rather than a chance formation billions of years ago. Pluto's smooth surface, along with the existence of an atmosphere, cries out, "Pluto is young!"

God looked down from heaven upon the children of men, to see if there were any that did understand, that did seek God. ~ Psalm 53:2

February 28

Paleontology

All over the world, we find dinosaur prints captured in mud or shale, which subsequently turned to rock. These footprints are commonly found on top of coal seams, as seen in the College of Eastern Utah's Prehistoric Museum at Price, Utah. In fact such dinosaur footprint fossils are so common that **people in this area use them as door stops!** But how did all of these footprints survive the worldwide Flood? Here is one possible scenario.

The worldwide Flood literally pulverized the world that existed before the Flood. The coal seams of the world (which formed during Noah's Flood) required almost ten times more vegetation on the planet before the Flood than we find alive today. This pre-Flood vegetation must have floated around for months, as wave after wave sorted and dropped sediment in underwater valleys thousands of feet deep below.

During the Flood, many land animals would have sought to survive by clinging onto these huge floating islands of vegetation. Much of this vegetation would have been beached at some point during the year-long Flood as water levels fluctuated from place to place. Between the beaching of these mats and subsequent covering with more layers of water and sediment, dinosaurs could have made their footprints, followed by a subsequent drowning and burial of their bones. The "age of the dinosaurs" is taught to have extended from 250 million years ago to 65 million years ago, but in reality we are just seeing bones buried at different levels during an extremely complex worldwide Flood about 4400 years ago.

Dinosaurs buried early in the Flood are misinterpreted as having existed over 200 million years ago whereas those destroyed and buried later in the Flood (after leaving their footprints on the newly laid and exposed sediment layers) are misinterpreted as having lived less than 100 million years ago. Because evolutionists leave the world-restructuring Flood out of their thinking, **they draw incorrect conclusions about the rocks, fossils, and the age of the dinosaurs**. The existence of dinosaur footprints on the top of coal seams points to a catastrophic event such as the Flood.

Whereby the world that then was, being overflowed with water, perished. - 2 Peter 3:6

February 29

Anatomy

Incredible complexity shows up in every area of the human body. The study of any one of our organs (our heart, liver, stomach, lungs, eyes, ears, and dozens of others) is enough to totally discredit the belief in slow evolutionary development. Doctors spend a lifetime specializing in understanding the operation of just one specific human organ and understand that even tiny variations in one of a thousand different specifically designed parts of the organ wreaks havoc with the human body. To believe that even one of the complex systems listed below developed itself is to believe in pure fantasy.[1]

In his chapter "Purposeful Design," Geoffrey Simmons, M.D. lists 81 facts that he believes point to design rather than chance as postulated in Darwin's theory of evolution.[2] Simmons points out that Darwin had little knowledge of genetics, physiology, and conception. So how could his theory still be accepted as valid?

- Every significant change in a human male reproductive system as he evolved from a less-than-human ancestor had to have been matched at exactly the same time with a reciprocal change in the female reproductive system (or vice versa).
- The egg has to know when it's time to ovulate, how to pop out of the ovary, how to travel through the fallopian tube, how to receive a single sperm and immediately shut out other sperm, and how to eventually implant itself into the uterus.
- A cell resembles a miniature industrial complex more complicated than a General Motors or Boeing manufacturing plant.
- The brain can store between 100 trillion and 280 quintillion bits (1 followed by 20 zeros) of information in a mere three pounds of matter. By comparison, the largest computer array

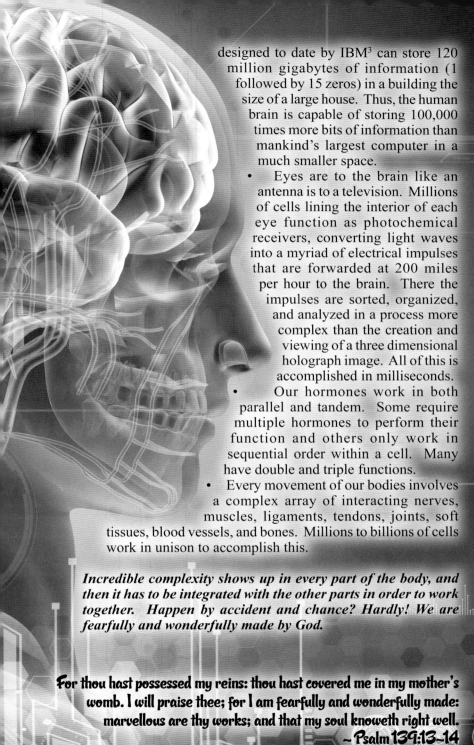

designed to date by IBM[3] can store 120 million gigabytes of information (1 followed by 15 zeros) in a building the size of a large house. Thus, the human brain is capable of storing 100,000 times more bits of information than mankind's largest computer in a much smaller space.

- Eyes are to the brain like an antenna is to a television. Millions of cells lining the interior of each eye function as photochemical receivers, converting light waves into a myriad of electrical impulses that are forwarded at 200 miles per hour to the brain. There the impulses are sorted, organized, and analyzed in a process more complex than the creation and viewing of a three dimensional holograph image. All of this is accomplished in milliseconds.
- Our hormones work in both parallel and tandem. Some require multiple hormones to perform their function and others only work in sequential order within a cell. Many have double and triple functions.
- Every movement of our bodies involves a complex array of interacting nerves, muscles, ligaments, tendons, joints, soft tissues, blood vessels, and bones. Millions to billions of cells work in unison to accomplish this.

Incredible complexity shows up in every part of the body, and then it has to be integrated with the other parts in order to work together. Happen by accident and chance? Hardly! We are fearfully and wonderfully made by God.

For thou hast possessed my reins: thou hast covered me in my mother's womb. I will praise thee; for I am fearfully and wonderfully made: marvellous are thy works; and that my soul knoweth right well.
~ Psalm 139:13-14

"If Christ be not raised, your faith is vain...Christ (is) risen from the dead...the last enemy that shall be destroyed is death. For he has put all things under his feet." - 1 Corinthians 15:17, 20, 26,27a

"I have found nature to be a conserver. Nothing is wasted or permanently lost in nature. Things change their form but never cease to exist. After I leave this world I do not believe I am through. God would be a bigger fool than even a man if He did not conserve the most important thing He has yet done in the universe."
- George Washington Carver, scientist and inventor

March

Christian Truth

March 1

Why spend time talking about the evidence for creation, aren't we, "justified by faith?" (Romans 5:1)

Romans 1:19-20 states that all people are without excuse for lack of belief in God because all people can clearly see what He has made by observing the creation. The world is filled with people who can see the intricacies and design of life and the vast scale of the universe – but are still blinded to the reality of God's existence. Therefore, more than physical evidence is needed to convince people that God exists, that He has died for our sins, and that we must accept His sacrifice for our sins to come back into fellowship with Him. Mature Christians understand that this awakening to the truth is the working of the Holy Spirit within people's lives, but hearing the evidence from creation opens people's spiritual eyes. **Immature Christians absolve themselves of any responsibility to do anything to reach others with this truth by assuming that it is the Holy Spirit's job to reach people** and that people have been given the freedom to reject the obvious (if they choose to).

God has always used people to reach other people. Yes, all the credit for a person's spiritual eyes being opened goes to God, but He commands us to be the ones who place the truth in front of others. He has always used people to reach other people with the truth. The greatest teacher, Jesus Christ, was both fully man and fully God. Thus God Himself became a man to reach other men with the truth. We MUST explain to others that God is the Creator and evolution is just a story. Christians need to get out of the bleachers and into the game and speak of God the Designer/Creator/Redeemer.

How beautiful are the feet of them that preach the gospel of peace, and bring glad tidings of good things! ~ Romans 10:15b

March 2

Biology

For thousands of years, the bee's honeycomb has fascinated man. Pappus of Alexandria, a third-century A.D. astronomer and mathematician, was intrigued by the honeycomb shape found inside of hives. He asked himself, "Why is the honeycomb cell six-sided? Why isn't the honeycomb cell a circle, triangle, or square?"

Pappus found that the six-sided shape, the hexagon, holds more honey and **takes less wax to produce than any other shape**. It was not until modern calculus was invented over a thousand years later that the shape of the cap at the end of the honeycomb cell was analyzed. Each cell cap is a pyramid made of three rhombuses. **This cap shape was found to require the smallest possible amount of wax for construction**. Each bee knows how to build this type of cell and cap. Some say they are great engineers; however, it is the One who designed the programming that controls the honeybee who is really the great engineer. That would be Jesus!

My son, eat thou honey, because it is good; and the honeycomb, which is sweet to thy taste: ~ **Proverbs 24:13**

March 3

Biology

Have you ever thought about how a honeybee communicates to the rest of the colony where the new source of nectar is? **She does a dance!** If the food source is near, she just dances in a circle. If the food source is over 100 yards away, she does the "waggle" dance, which is like a figure eight. The center of the "waggle" reveals the direction and distance to the flower. The bee uses the sun as a reference point to signal the direction to the flower from the hive. If the flower is toward the sun, the bee "waggles" up the vertical comb. If it is away from the sun, it "waggles" down the comb. If it is 60 degrees to the east of the sun, it will "waggle" at a 60 degree angle and so forth. The type of "waggle" is either fast or slow that communicates the distance and quality of the nectar. The dance is a complex but efficient form of communication.

Evolutionists believe that this dance came about slowly over a long period of time. Really? If only one bee came up with the idea and the others did not understand, the result would be no nectar gained. If this dance slowly evolved, how would all the bee ancestors have survived? **If they survived without this complicated dance, why would they need to invent the dance?** God programmed within the honeybee this unique form of communication. The honeybee's communication style is so precise and complex that it shouts design! And God is that Designer!

O clap your hands, all ye people; shout unto God with the voice of triumph. For the Lord most high is terrible; he is a great King over all the earth.
~ Psalm 47:1-2

March 4

Geology

During the Flood of Noah's day not only was the earth covered with water but also with a large number of volcanoes. In fact, you can travel to the very throat of one of these super volcanoes, Yellowstone National Park. That's right; almost the entire park is a collapsed volcanic cone or caldera. It is 44 miles long and 34 miles wide and covers 1500 square miles in area. Imagine this super volcano spewing out ash and lava!

Evolutionary geology believes in enormous time periods, so it places eruptions that formed the Yellowstone area at 2.1, 1.2, and 0.64 million years ago. Yet these dates are based on dating methods that have been proven to be both inaccurate and subjective. The fact that the collapsed caldera of Yellowstone remains geologically active – creating the geysers, mud pots, hot springs, and fumaroles found throughout the area - actually testifies to its recent creation during the Flood of Noah about 4400 years ago. **It remains hot and active because the eruption which created this area DID NOT occur millions of years ago.** The underground magma remains hot and close to the surface because the entire area was recently created.

In the six hundredth year of Noah's life, in the second month, the seventeenth day of the month, the same day were ALL THE FOUNTAINS OF THE GREAT DEEP BROKEN UP, and the windows of heaven were opened. ~ Genesis 7:11

History

March 5

One of the stories from ancient Norway speaks of the existence of a magical glowing stone called the "sunstone." It was believed that these fabled sunstones aided mariners when the days were so cloudy that the sun was obscured. Vikings write of using these prized sunstones to navigate the perilous Arctic seas. It turns out that sunstone stories are true, there is a transparent spar crystal found in Iceland that creates a double refraction or image. (You can see this for yourself by placing an Iceland spar crystal on a newspaper and seeing a double image appear).

Vikings would mount this crystal of Iceland spar into a wooden block and rotate the block until the two fuzzy images of the sun equalized; from that position, the Vikings could determine the sun's exact position without a visible sun. Knowing the sun's location allows sailors to calculate their exact latitude upon the globe. The ancient Vikings were one of the dispersing clans from the Tower of Babel as the Viking civilization is amongst the earliest of European settlers. As one of the earliest human cultures, were they unsophisticated, primitive humans? No, the very opposite is true. They developed advanced technologies needed to survive in the harsh post-Flood world and sailed the globe in search of new resources.

And God said, "Let us make man in our image, after our likeness...."
~ Genesis 1:26

March 6

Botany

Botanists have long been fascinated by the design of the giant Amazon water lily (*Victoria amazonica*) with its raised rim that surrounds floating leaves reaching eight feet in diameter. In fact, **the lily's floating leaves can easily support a full-grown adult lying on the thin leaf structure!** The secret to the strength of these leaves is the well-engineered supporting veins on the underside of these floating marvels.

Before the very first World's Fair, being held in London, England in 1851, the organizing committee announced a contest for the best and most original design for the Great Exhibition Hall. Architects and engineers from around the world sent in their designs. Yet, it was not a trained architect, but a botanist named Joseph Paxton, who won the contest. His "Crystal Palace" was to be constructed with 200,000 panes of glass, weighing an estimated one million pounds, supported by a thin iron framework. The entire building was to stand 108 feet tall and cover 18 acres. **Experts declared that the foolish structure would collapse before being finished**.

Paxton based the design of his building on the same design used to support the heavy leaves of the giant water lily. Not only were the experts wrong, but **the beautiful glass building stood as a testimony to the genius of God's design ability for the next 80 years** before being destroyed by fire. Paxton realized that the giant water lily was well engineered; he just copied the greatest Engineer, God Himself.

Through wisdom is a house built.
~ Proverbs 24:3a

Cosmology

March 7

The universe exhibits the same precise movements as a finely crafted clock.

Beginning with our own solar system, we find that the planets orbit in the same direction, counter clockwise as viewed from above the earth's North Pole. Each planet's orbit is stable and precise. A planet's orbital momentum tends to send the planet in a straight line, but the sun's gravity pulls the planet's path into a circle (or nearly a circle, an ellipse). If the planets did not have orbital motion, the sun would pull them in and burn them up. Nearly circular orbits prevent planets from straying into another planet's orbit. All the planets orbit the sun in about the same plane (called the ecliptic). This allows them to be easily located from earth AND for the large gas giants to protect earth from comet-sized bodies.

The Milky Way Galaxy also shows clockwork design. The stars in our galaxy orbit the central hub in such a manner that gravity keeps the stars in a stable orbit. These billions of stars all travel in the same direction, thereby preventing collisions.

Such clockwork motion implies that there must be a clock-maker. We do not say a clock made itself. Clockwork motion means there is One who is a clockmaker, and that One is God. The heavens do declare the glory of God!

The heavens declare the glory of God....
~ Psalm 19:1

Biology

March 8

Have you considered the bird called the whip-poor-will? I remember sleeping at Grandma's and hearing the night music of the whip-poor-will putting me to sleep. This jay-sized bird makes its home where jack pine forests or oak savannas meet meadows and pastures. This nocturnal bird hunts mosquitoes, moths and beetles. **On a moon-lit night, you might see it doing aerial stunts like banking, dipping, diving and hovering to catch its prey**. It doesn't build a nest but lays two eggs on the forest floor in fallen leaves. Both parents care for the young, making frequent hunting trips bringing back regurgitated bug porridge. They also exhibit one other fascinating characteristic - whip-poor-wills time their eggs to hatch exactly 10 days before the full moon. But why?

The bird chicks are at their hungriest about 10 days after hatching. Ten days after they come out of their eggs, the moon is at its brightest. Insects are the easiest to see and catch during a full moon. How did the first whip-poor-will come up with this idea? Did it have a calendar of when the full moon would appear, and then counted back 10 days for the hatching? A bird does not think about this; it comes about by instinct. **The precise timing had to be preinstalled on the bird's software, i.e. its brain.** When we see such preinstalled software, we know there must be a software engineer. So, when you hear the night music of the whip-poor-will, think of the greatest software engineer, God.

The flowers appear on the earth; the time of the singing of birds is come, and the voice of the turtle is heard in our land;
~ Song of Solomon 2:12

Microbiology

March 9

One of the most famous chemistry experiments ever performed was the Miller experiment - first reported in 1952. Over 60 years later this experiment is still presented in biology textbooks worldwide as proof that life formed by itself early in the earth's history. In this experiment, a researcher named Stanley Miller circulated ammonia, methane, hydrogen, and water vapor through a tube and added sparks in order to cause amino acids to form (coined the "building blocks of life"). Yet, students are seldom told the rest of the story.

In order for these amino acids to form proteins, they must link up in a polymerization reaction that requires both ends of the molecule to remain reactive until the entire protein molecule has formed. Visualize a stack of Lego^{tm} blocks – you can keep adding blocks to the top or bottom of the stack until a block with a flat, undented surface is added to either side. Then no more blocks can be added to that side of the stack. It is now no longer "reactive". In the Miller experiment, a "flat topped Lego block" is always formed - it is called formic acid. Formic acid is the most common molecule formed during the Miller experiment. The instant formic acid reacts with an amino acid the molecules **stop linking up**. As a result, no useful protein molecules are ever produced in this experiment.

What this experiment actually demonstrates is that life could not possibly have formed in this way! When problems like this are not shown to students, it is deception, not education. So why is this experiment, which does not work to explain life, still cited in biology books over sixty years later? Textbook writers simply cannot accept the logical conclusion that life can only come from a Creator outside of the time, space, and matter universe. The correct explanation for the existence of life (creation by God) has been eliminated from the thinking of generation after generation of students reading such textbooks. Where does life come from? It's still a mystery to evolutionists but not to Bible-believing Christians - life comes from God.

And the Lord God formed man of the dust of the ground, and breathed into his nostrils the breath of life; and man became a living soul.
~ Genesis 2:7

March 10 — Microbiology

In the last decade, it has become apparent that bacteria are far more varied and versatile than any other kind of creature on Earth. Scientists estimate there is somewhere between 10 million and 1 billion different species of bacteria and have discovered that they are essential for all forms of life – including us! Bacteria help digest the food we eat, provide nutrients, prevent diseases, and produce oxygen. **It has also been discovered that bacteria can readily exchange DNA fragments with other bacteria.** Because they reproduce so rapidly, this allows the bacteria to test different defenses and environments, capabilities, and strategies for survival. Those that don't succeed die out while characteristics with an advantage prosper.

So why do bacteria vary so widely? Evolutionists teach that changes in the environment drive bacteria to change; however, that is not true. It is the internal programming of the bacteria that allows them to vary in order to thrive in a wide variety of environments. Evolutionists use the fact that bacteria can transfer DNA coding from one type of bacteria to another as proof of evolutionary advancement, but don't be fooled by the sleight of hand. **What they call evolution is just bacteria doing what they were programmed to do**. No one has ever identified a microbe in either the laboratory or the fossil record which is evolving into another kind of creature. They are always clearly identifiable as bacteria.

The vast majority of bacteria are either helpful or harmless, but a small percentage have degenerated into harmful organisms. Even this testifies to the reality of Scripture – death entered into creation because of our rebellion against our Creator, and even the smallest of creatures have become part of the penalty of death, which we brought upon ourselves.

But whoso hearkeneth unto me shall dwell safely, and shall be quiet from fear of evil. ~ Proverbs 1:33

Design

March 11

If we open our eyes, we will see the handiwork of God everywhere. One of these areas is in the design of flowers. Flowers are critical for the complex mechanism by which God reproduces flowering plants. This multiple-step process involves the pollination of flowers to produce seeds, which then produces the next generation of plants. Flowers draw the pollinator to the flower, yet we find some flower designs that just perplex us. Flowers exhibit a dizzying variety of complexity, design, and beauty. **What purpose is there for a flower to look like a monkey, a bird flying or a person?** What evolutionary function is served by this beauty? Absolutely none! They exist purely for our enjoyment and to reveal God's incredible genius and creativity.

Check out just a few examples of God's creativity in the design of flowers:

Why would an orchid decide to make itself look like a monkey?

How could a flower decide to make itself look like a flying bird?

This flower looks like a person!

He hath made everything beautiful in his time....
~ Ecclesiastes 3:11

March 12

Geology

How old are diamonds? Scientists have found carbon-14 in diamonds. Carbon-14 (^{14}C) has a half-life of 5730 years, and so anything older than 100,000 years should contain no detectable levels of ^{14}C. Finding ^{14}C in diamonds means they are less than 100,000 years old. Yet all diamonds contain measurable amounts of ^{14}C even though they are the hardest known naturally occurring substance, which is impervious to outside contamination. ^{14}C in diamonds means they are young. There are also other clues revealing the actual age of diamonds.

Kimberlite is a volcanic rock which often contains diamonds. These carrot-shaped rocky tubes begin at the earth's mantle and rapidly carried diamonds from deep within the earth to the surface. A wooden log that was fresh and unpetrified has been discovered deep within a Canadian kimberlite pipe. There have been other such reports of finding unpetrified wood in kimberlite pipes. How did this wood get deep within the earth, and why is it not petrified or rotted if it has been there for millions of years? Scientists think the logs got there by local catastrophic forces. Fresh unpetrified wood in the same rock as diamonds means diamonds are young. Also, consider that artificial diamonds are rapidly made by the exact same processes of high pressure and temperature as natural diamonds. **An artificial diamond can be made in the same amount of time that it takes to wash a car!** If we can make artificial diamonds so rapidly, why would we assume it takes billions of years to make natural diamonds?

The evidence of ^{14}C in diamonds, fresh wood found in kimberlite, and the ability to rapidly make artificial diamonds all cry out, "The earth is young."

(Mankind) putteth forth his hand upon the rock; he overturneth the mountains by the roots...where shall wisdom be found? and where is the place of understanding?
~ Job 28:9, 12

Geology

March 13

For more than 100 years, oil or "black gold" has fueled our cars, trucks and economy. But how did these vast fields of oil form? The chemistry of oil offers some important clues. One of the chemicals in crude oils is porphyrin. Most petroleum geologists believe crude oils form mostly from plants, such as diatoms (single-celled marine and freshwater photosynthetic creatures), and beds of coal (huge fossilized masses of plant debris). The moderate heating of brown coals in the lab can produce crude oil and natural gas containing porphyrin. Keep in mind that animal blood also contains porphyrins. Oil can be made from animal slaughterhouse waste within two hours.

For porphyrins to be present in today's crude oils means they have been kept from the presence of oxygen because porphyrins break down rapidly in the presence of oxygen. We do not see oil containing porphyrins forming today because oxygen destroys them during the oil formation. Yet worldwide, we find vast petroleum deposits that do contain this chemical. This supports the conclusion that much of the world's oil reserves are the direct result of a worldwide catastrophic flood covering trillions of pounds of vegetation and animals. They were buried so rapidly that oxygen was not present to destroy the porphyrins. Deep rapid burial by additional sediments would have created sufficient heat to generate crude oils and natural gases. Subsequently, these migrated, became trapped in reservoir rocks, and accumulated to form gas and oil deposits. So, from what is oil made? Primarily squished vegetation and animals that were rapidly buried in the Flood of Noah's day.

And, behold, I, even I, do bring a flood of waters upon the earth....
~ Genesis 6:17

March 14 — Biology

Electric eels are not eels but fish that live in the murky waters of South America. They can reach 6 feet long and weigh 45 pounds. All living things generate electrical charges in their cells. The electric eel has thousands of modified cells in its tail that are lined up like batteries in a flashlight. Each cell can generate only about 0.15 volts, but stacked together, the 6,000 cells make one giant battery that can generate as much as 600 volts. In comparison, a car battery generates 12 volts yet has enough power to start a large car engine.

Pure water is a very poor conductor of electricity, but the waters where electric eels live have enough salt and other minerals to make the water a good conductor. To shock their prey, electric eels bring their positive end, located in their head, close to the negative end, located in their tail. The electric shock is sent out from the positive end to the negative end of the "battery." **How did the eel know to trap its prey between its head and tail such that the electrical discharge would stun or kill its prey?** Basic physics teaches that bringing two opposite electrical poles together concentrates the electric field. Evolutionists call eels "primitive creatures", but creationists studying eels are not "shocked" by their level of sophistication. God created these creatures to glorify Him.

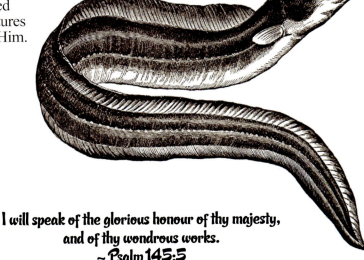

I will speak of the glorious honour of thy majesty, and of thy wondrous works.
~ Psalm 145:5

Cosmology

March 15

One of the greatest mysteries of science is the exact structure of creation. What keeps electrons moving? What is light? What is space? What is a charged particle? Why is there so much energy contained within empty space at absolute zero (zero point energy)? Why are galaxies commonly found in a spiral shape? Why are red shifts in distinct bands (quantitized) rather than a continuous smear of shifted values? Why does the speed of light, the mass of atomic particles, and Plank's constant all seem to have a changing value with time? *Who stretchest out the heavens like a curtain.* - Psalm 104:2

These are profound mysteries, and even the observation of changing values for atomic constants are frequently denied or ignored because of the implication upon traditionally accepted physics. The primary reason modern physics is helpless to adequately explain these type of inquiries is because it starts from the wrong assumption.

Modern physics accepts an enormous age for the universe and attempts to explain everything based on this starting assumption. Thus, it needs a very weak force (gravity) and lots of time to explain all of reality. Yet, this explanation cannot even explain the formation of a single star and relies on unseen faith in things like "dark matter" and "multiple universes" in an attempt to explain the impossible. A brilliant physicist from Australia, Barry Setterfield, has developed a plasma model of physics that seems to unify the anomalies that are not explained by the Big Bang model. Setterfields' theory accepts the scriptural teaching that God stretched out the heavens and realized that this must have been accompanied by enormously accelerated radioactive decay, red shifting of light in quantized bands, and energy added to the fabric of space (analogous to how a stretched rubber band is filled with energy). According to Setterfield, this process "wound up" the universe, providing the energy necessary for star and galaxy formation – all within a very brief period of time.

Who stretchest out the heavens like a curtain.
~ Psalm 104:2

March 16
Paleontology

In Peru, there is a 370 acre deposit containing at least 346 wonderfully preserved fossil whales. A whale graveyard! These bones are buried in a sedimentary rock called diatomite. Diatomite is made from the remains of diatoms - or single-celled algae. Today when diatoms die, their microscopic glass-like skeletons accumulate on the ocean bottom. It takes about 400 million skeletons to make one gram of diatomite. An inch of diatom skeletons on the ocean bottom would currently take about 1,000 years to accumulate. **These whales are buried in 260 feet of fossilized diatoms**.

That means--if the evolutionary timeframe of the earth is correct--it would have taken millions of years for these whales to be covered. **If it took millions of years to cover these bones, there is no possibility that they would exist!** Scavengers and bacteria would have decayed these whale bones long before they could have been covered, yet we find them well-preserved and intact - with no evidence of decay. Along with these 346 whale fossils, fossils of porpoises, turtles, seals, ground sloths, and penguins are also found. For these dead creatures to avoid decay, they had to have been buried rapidly, deeply, and catastrophically. The biblical model of a recent catastrophic Flood of Noah's day would fit such evidence far better than the millions of years of slow sediment accumulation. This whale graveyard shouts that the Flood of Noah's day was a real event!

And God said unto Noah, The end of all flesh is come before me; for the earth is filled with violence through them; and, behold, I will destroy them with the earth. ~ Genesis 6:13

Biology

March 17

You have probably have heard of the monarch butterfly migrating some 4,000 miles round trip, but have you heard of the painted lady butterfly migration? This butterfly migrates between Europe and Africa, flying an incredible 9,000 miles round trip. Why has this not been discovered until recently? People have not spotted these butterflies migrating because they fly at altitudes up to 3,000 feet and at speeds of 30 mph. Radar recently discovered millions of these butterflies migrating high up in the atmosphere. More than 60,000 sightings of painted lady butterflies have also been made as far north as the Arctic Circle.

The 9,000 mile migration takes six generations to complete. A butterfly might fly from Norway to Britain where it will breed and die, and then the next five generations will carry on the migration, breeding, flying, dying in an effort to fly all the way to Africa and returning to Norway. This is amazing! The tiny creature, weighing less than a gram, with a pin-sized head, having no opportunity to learn the migration route from older butterflies, undertakes and succeeds at this epic migration. How do they know where to go? Evolution says this all happened by chance. How could it? **How would the painted lady evolve the ability to fly to a place it has never been before?** God set this up from the beginning to show His great power. God has woven this information into the genetic code of each butterfly so that each generation "knows" what stage of the migration cycle the butterfly is in. This information is passed on to each generation. Such a delicate mechanism shouts intelligent design!

Yea, the stork in the heaven knoweth her appointed times; and the turtle and the crane and the swallow observe the time of their coming...
~ Jeremiah 8:7

March 18

History

Evolution always has been, and always will be, inherently racist. The foundational concept of evolution is that mankind evolved from some sort of ape-like creature, and since some groups of humans are still genetically more closely related to their ancestors than others, more evolved humans are superior and therefore of more value. Modern evolutionists like to downplay this inherent nature of their belief, but it was widely acknowledged early on. For instance, the full title of Darwin's classic book is *The Origin of Species by Means of Natural Selection—or **The Preservation of Favoured Races** in the Struggle for Life* (emp. added). Imagine the response to any scientist today who wrote the following (excerpted from Darwin's book):

*"At some future period, not very distant as measured by centuries, **the civilised races of man will almost certainly exterminate, and replace, the savage races throughout the world**. At the same time the anthropomorphous apes, as Professor Schaaffhausen has remarked, will no doubt be exterminated. The break between man and his nearest allies will then be wider, for it will intervene between man in a more civilised state, as we may hope, even than the Caucasian, and some ape as low as a baboon, instead of as now between the negro or Australian and the gorilla (p. 521)." (Emphasis added)*

Clearly, Darwin was convinced that the more "civilized races" (e.g., Caucasian) would one day exterminate the more savage races (e.g., African Negroes and Australian Aborigines), which he considered to be less evolved (and thus more ape-like) than Caucasians. The chief promoter of evolutionism in the 1800's was Thomas Huxley who wrote:

*"It may be quite true that some Negroes are better than some white men; **but no rational man, cognisant of the facts, believes that the average Negro is the equal, still less the superior, of the white man**. And, if this be true, it is simply incredible that, when all his disabilities are removed, and our prognathous relative has a fair field and no favour, as well as no oppressor, he will be able to compete successfully with his bigger-brained and smaller jawed rival, in a contest which is to be carried on by thoughts and not by bites." (Emphasis added)*

The fact is that a historical understanding of evolution implies that some groups of humans are closer to our alleged ape-like ancestors in their mental faculties than others. Thus, some groups of humans supposedly are superior to others. The Bible teaches exactly the opposite. There are not different species or races of men; there is just one race, the human race. All people were created by God "in His image" from the very beginning of creation.

And hath made of one blood all nations of men for to dwell on all the face of the earth... ~ Acts 17:26

Biology

March 19

Why are elephant's tusks shrinking? African elephants and Asian elephants (living in India) have smaller tusks today than those measured in the 1850s; in fact, they average half the length. Ivory trade statistics and hunting records have revealed this fact. Why is this happening?

Hunters target elephants with large tusks and have been doing so for decades. **This has culled out the elephants with large tusks, leaving only the elephants with smaller tusks or no tusks to propagate**. Tuskless elephants are ignored by hunters and so survive to pass on their genes to the next generation. This is not evolution but selective pressure by hunters; you could say artificially-imposed selection. The consequences of trophy hunting are also impacting the antlers of moose and the wild bighorn sheep, as they are also experiencing smaller antler sizes. When trophy animals are culled out of the population, their genes are not passed down to future generations; there is a loss of information. Once the genes for larger size are lost, they are gone forever! New useful, functioning information is never added to the DNA. What nature reveals is a deterioration and reduction of information and features. The world is indeed in "bondage to decay" (Romans 8:21 NIV).

For the creature was made subject to vanity, not willingly, but by reason of him who hath subjected the same in hope, because the creature itself also shall be delivered from the bondage of corruption.... ~Romans 8:20-21

March 20

History

Drawings or descriptions of two-headed dragons seem to strain credibility. But we have seen many examples of snakes and turtles with multiple heads. About 400 cases of two-headed snakes have been recorded in modern times. A two-headed reptile was even discovered fossilized in China. Perhaps two-headed reptiles gave rise to the idea of multi-headed dragons - like the Hydra that Hercules conquered.

The Bible even mentions a multi-headed dragon in Revelation 12:3. **Having two heads is a detrimental developmental abnormality**. The accident does not occur due to permanent mistakes in the DNA code (mutations) but in the process of forming the embryo. In this case, the embryo partially splits into two individuals, creating the two-headed reptile. If the embryo did split completely, it would result in identical twins. No new genetic information has been added to create a two-headed creature.

The two-headed creatures remind us that there are two ways of interpreting evidence - evolution or the Bible. Evolution believes that two-headedness is a natural part of biological variation; evolution in action. The Bible on the other hand, teaches that suffering, sickness, death and two-headedness are a result of man's rebellion in the Garden of Eden against their Creator.

For we know that the whole creation groaneth and travaileth in pain together until now.
~ Romans 8:22

History

March 21

Evolutionary ideas can actually kill people. In 1893, based on the belief in evolution, there were 83 human features considered to be useless leftovers from our ancestral past. One of these was the thymus gland. The thymus gland is located behind the breast bone in the upper chest. In babies and children, it is quite large and active, but this gland shrinks with age.

One of the functions of the thymus gland is to produce white blood cells called T lymphocytes, which attack foreign invaders such as bacteria and viruses. The white blood cells leave the thymus gland and settle in the spleen and lymph nodes where a new batch of white blood cells is produced. The thymus serves throughout life but is most active during childhood. Throughout the 1930's, the thymus was considered a useless evolutionary leftover that was harmful to infants because of its large size. In misguided preventive measures, **infants were exposed to x-rays in order to reduce the size of this "unncecessary evolutionary leftover" from the past.** Follow-up studies found that infants who received the radiation treatment had abnormal growth and higher rates of infections that persisted longer than normal. In addition, the unintended consequence of the x-rays was cancer in the nearby thyroid gland - resulting in the death of many of these children from thyroid cancer some 10-15 years later. **The misguided belief in microbe-to-man evolution is not only wrong, it is dangerous!**

All of this unfathomable pain caused to these children and their parents could have been avoided if it had been acknowledged that we have a Creator who had a purpose in creating the various parts of our bodies. There are no junk leftover vestigial organs in our bodies; all parts have been created to serve a purpose. Your child's ability to fight disease is in large part due to God's creative design of the thymus gland.

*There is a way which seemeth right unto a man,
but the end thereof are the ways of death.
~ Proverbs 14:12*

March 22

Botany

Mangrove trees live alongside the ocean where their roots are flooded by salty ocean water. You would not expect ants, which build their home underground, to build nests in such a wet location. Believe it or not, some ants (*Polyrhachis sokolova*) thrive within Australia's mangrove swamps. They build their cities deep into the mud some 18 inches below a mangrove tree. **Twice a day, at high tide, their city is flooded!**

The ants have designed their mound with two entrances that collapse at high tide - plugging the entrances and ensuring the safety of the ants inside. When seawater does leak into the underground tunnels, the ants scurry around moving their eggs and brood to different galleries. The bell-shaped galleries ensure that air is trapped, saving the ants from drowning. When the water recedes at low tide, the ants repair their city and others hunt small crustaceans on the mud flats. Two times a day…seven days a week…365 days a year, the ants repair their entrances and go hunting! **Why would ants choose to live in such a way?** It would be much easier to build their city in a place not covered with seawater twice a day. They did not choose it. God designed them to survive and thrive in this location.

Go to the ant, thou sluggard; consider her ways, and be wise: which having no guide, overseer, or ruler, provideth her meat in the summer, and gathereth her food in the harvest. ~ Proverbs 6:6-8

Biology

March 23

Dolphins navigate and find their prey by using echolocation. A dolphin emits clicking calls and listens for their returning echoes. The greater time for the return of the echo, the further away an object. Echolocation is similar to sonar. So how is echolocation produced in a dolphin? The dolphin sends out ultrasonic clicks through its nasal canals. These vocalizations travel through a fatty protrusion on its forehead. This melon-like structure is actually a "sound-lens" designed to focus the sound waves into a beam that can be directed. This sound lens uses different fatty compounds to bend the ultrasonic sound waves in different ways. **These specifically placed and designed fatty compounds have to be arranged in the right shape and sequence in order to focus the sound waves properly.** These fatty compounds are different from normal blubber fats and are made by a complicated chemical process that requires a number of different enzymes.

Once the dolphin focuses and directs his ultrasound signal, the noise hits an object and bounces back to the dolphin. Sinuses filled with special oil located within the dolphin's lower jaw recieve the returning echo. The sonic information then passes to the inner ear which changes the sound waves to nerve impulses. These signals are then sent to the brain. This sonar system is so precise that it can detect a fish the size of a golf ball 230 feet away. **The dolphin's sonar system is the envy of the U.S. Navy**. For such an organ to evolve by random mutations is hard to believe because it took years for inventors to develop the sonar used on ships. Consider just the sound-lens in the dolphin's sonar system. It needed to have the right enzymes to make the **right fatty compounds,** and the lens had to be the **right size** and the **right shape** and be in the **right location**. A partially functioning system is no system at all. Ships and submarines have man-made sonar; dolphins have God-made sonar.

They that go down to the sea in ships, that do business in great waters; These see the works of the Lord, and his wonders in the deep.
~ Psalm 107: 23,24

March 24

Geology

In a remote part of Utah lies Kodachrome Basin State Park. The National Geographic Society named this park because of its beauty. Some 60 towering stone spires jut up from the valley floor and are displayed against the backdrop of multi-colored sandstone layers. Evolutionists are at a loss to explain how these spires formed. When we put on our biblical glasses, we can view their formation from the Flood perspective.

During the Flood, many sedimentary layers were laid down. One of the layers would have been a squishy sand layer. Earthquakes could have caused this squishy sand mixture to be injected upward through the other sedimentary layers, like toothpaste being squished upward in its tube. This "plume" of sand then cemented together. **At the end of the Flood, waters eroded the less cemented layers away, leaving the cemented plumes or sand pipes**. Clusters of sand pipes can be found in other remote parts of the Colorado plateau. This same formation can be seen with mounds, like Ayers Rock in Australia. The sand plumes can be traced down to the source layer of sand. Secular geologists believe that the source bed was millions of years old prior to its injection. Would the source bed remain uncemented for millions of years? Hardly. These sedimentary sand pipes give evidence that there was little time between the layers being laid down, injected and eroded. The fact that sand pipes exist at all is evidence that little time passed from deposition to squeezing.

*And spared not the old world,
but saved Noah the eighth person,
a preacher of righteousness,
bringing in the flood upon the world of the ungodly;
~ 2 Peter 2:5*

March 25

Design

Today, there is great concern over football players receiving concussions. Have you thought about the woodpecker banging its head against a tree trunk? Why doesn't a woodpecker get a concussion or brain damage? On average, he bangs his head 12,000 times a day, each time reaching speeds of 13-15 mph. As he pecks, his beak stops abruptly when it hits the wood. The deceleration force has been measured to be 1,200 times the acceleration of gravity (1200 g). **Decelerating one's heads at just 300 g would leave a person with serious brain injury or a concussion**. Through slow motion footage, x-ray images, tomography, and CT scans, scientists discovered four features that enable the woodpecker to sustain this type of head-banging existence:

1. The beak is made of an elastic material.
2. The woodpecker's hyoid bone is different than a human's. It loops around the entire skull, acting like a seat belt. In a human, this bone sits just above the "Adam's apple".
3. The spongy bone behind the beak and at different places in the skull act as shock absorbers.
4. A special skull bone contains spinal fluid.

Researchers emphatically claim that all four of these features have to be present at the same time in order for the woodpecker not to destroy his brain. Evolution says that these four features would have come about by accident and chance over millions of years. **If this is true, would we have woodpeckers?** All four special design features needed to be present from the beginning in order for the impact force to be spread throughout the skull.

One last amazing fact - every time the woodpecker hits a tree, his eyes close simultaneously – otherwise his eyeballs would pop out of his skull! Of course, learning to close his eyes simultaneously with hitting his head against the tree also needed to work the first time, or we would have lots of blind woodpeckers. God is an amazing designer of woodpeckers!

For thou art great, and doest wondrous things: thou art God alone.
~ Psalm 86:10

March 26

Biology

Lest you think everything to be discovered has already been discovered, a recent examination of whales has revealed a previously unknown organ – completely different from any other structure found throughout the animal kingdom. Researchers studying blue whale carcasses in Iceland used MRI scans to identify this unique fluid-filled sac (the size of a small cushion) within their chins. This new organ helps the blue whale coordinate its mouth movements during lunge feeding.

Blue whales are the largest creatures on the earth and feed by lunging through the water. At just the right moment, they open their mouths so wide that they screech to a halt like a drag-racer deploying a parachute. Before they come to a stop, they gulp enormous amounts of water filled with krill (shrimp-like creatures). Whales swallow the equivalent of their enormous body mass (400,000 pounds) of water with each gulp. For many years, scientists have wondered how they co-ordinate their jaw movement in order to capture and filter the krill so efficiently.

The newly discovered organ within their mouths has provided the answer. This organ contains millions of microscopic, finger-like nerve structures and blood vessels that change shape as the jaw moves. This enables the mouth to open extra wide at just the right moment. But here is the most amazing example of modern man's intellectual blindness. Because the nerves from this newly discovered organ go through the jaw cavity to the whale's brain, these researchers attribute the existence of this organ to "*a tooth socket earlier in whale evolution*"! In other words, **they would rather believe that a toothache turned into a complex organ** (with absolutely no evidence to support such wild speculation) than to acknowledge that the existence of the blue whale, with all of its intricate design, involved a Creator.

We all need to stand back and marvel at God's detailed handiwork.

O Lord God, thou hast begun to shew thy servant thy greatness, and thy mighty hand: for what God is there in heaven or in earth, that can do according to thy works, and according to thy might?
~ Deuteronomy 3:24

History

March 27

The dodo bird was a strange bird. These large, flightless birds lived on an island in the Indian Ocean. Sailors found this bird so easy to catch and eat that by 1662, it was extinct. No one seemed to notice. Decades later, scientists did not believe that the dodo ever existed. It was widely believed that legends of such a bird were pure myth. Just think about the evidence:
1. A strange creature
2. No one can find one in existence
3. Nothing but old accounts, fanciful drawings and vague descriptions

The dodo might still be considered a prehistoric animal or myth had it not been for a few dodo specimens found in the basements of museum collections. By the 19th century, scientists realized the dodo was a real bird that became extinct. There is a stuffed dodo bird on display in the Prague Museum of Natural History today.

In the same way, consider dragons:
1. A strange animal
2. No one can find one in existence
3. Nothing but old accounts, fanciful drawings and vague descriptions

But there is a significant difference between the dragon and dodo evidence. There are massive numbers of dragon accounts, drawings and descriptions from around the world. Many of these dragon descriptions fit a creature that we know by a different name – dinosaur. Dragons (dinosaurs) were considered real creatures for over 4000 years of human history. **It was not until the 20th century that we began to teach that any firsthand human knowledge of dragons/dinosaurs was a myth**. Dragons living after the Flood could have become extinct through environmental changes, man killing them off, or many other reasons.

Most dragon legends speak of dragons as viciously attacking and then being killed. In Scriptures (Revelation 12:3), Satan is portrayed as a vicious dragon. If dragons were a myth, then the description of Satan being a dragon would also be mythological. Satan wants people to deny his existence. This idea, that dragons are only a myth and not real, could be just another attack on God and His Word. **Dragons were real creatures that went extinct** - just like the dodo.

And there appeared another wonder in heaven; and behold a great red dragon, having seven heads and ten horns, and seven crowns upon his heads. ~ Revelation 12:3

March 28

Design

In November 1974, as a jumbo jet took off from the Nairobi airport, the plane shuddered violently, stalled, crashed to the ground and broke into pieces. The pilots had forgotten to deploy the slats on the leading edge of the wings that allow a plane to fly at much lower speeds without stalling. The development of this leading edge slat to help with landing and take offs has been a key factor in modern aviation. And guess what? **Birds deploy such a wing slat on the front edge of their wings just as jumbo jets do!** Large birds, like the steppe eagle, use this front slat (alula or bastard wing) to prevent them from stalling during landing. Such design did not happen by accident and chance, either in the jumbo jet or these large birds. Clearly, there is a Designer behind this "leading edge" technology.

They shall mount up with wings as eagles....
~ Isaiah 40:31

Geology

March 29

The Roberts family bought the famous Belle Tout lighthouse at Beachy Head, UK, in 1996 as a bed and breakfast. At that time, it was 300 feet from the high chalk cliffs. Four years later, the couple fled in the middle of the night as the cliff started to fall away leaving the lighthouse precariously perched just 10 feet from the edge. On average, **six inches of the cliff erode away every year**, keeping the white cliffs white by preventing shrubs, grasses, and trees from growing. Most people don't realize that significant erosion is happening along coastlines. In recent history entire, English coastline villages have been lost into the ocean.

On the Outer Banks of North Carolina, USA, Cape Hatteras Lighthouse was built in 1872 and sat about 1,800 feet from the shore. In just 130 years, the coastline had eroded 1,680 feet such that the light house sat only 120 feet from the sea. **The lighthouse has since been moved**. The amount of coastal erosion we observe does not match the evolutionary timeline, but it is consistent with the Bible's timeline. About 4400 years ago, there was a global flood, and the continents' coastlines have been eroding ever since. Coastal erosion is a world-wide problem, causing beaches to vanish and houses to toppling. Fast coastal erosion points to the world being young.

And the earth shall wax old like a garment,....
~ Isaiah 51:6b

March 30

Geology

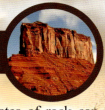

Earthquakes are movements of the earth; huge plates of rock can move sideways or slide vertically. Modern earthquake movements have seen land masses move the land as much as 30 feet, resulting in enormous damage. Compare this with the earthquakes during the Flood; many moved large chunks of the land 2 miles or more at a time! What havoc this would have caused!

When an earthquake happens underwater, a tsunami is formed. In an open ocean, a boat on the surface would experience a gentle movement upward. But once this tsunami reaches a shallow shoreline, the water builds up creating a wall of water. The tsunami that hit Japan, in March 2011, displaced the water below the ocean bottom about 30 feet - creating a 124 foot wave, which crashed onto the shore and killed some 15,000 people. Now imagine the tsunamis during the Flood with earth movements of 10,000 feet! **The resulting tsunamis would pulverize EVERYTHING in its path and cover entire continents**. Imagine a wall of water dwarfing the tallest building on earth! Earthquakes during the Flood would have been unstoppably destructive. The safest place to be during the Flood would have been on the Ark in the middle of the ocean. The Flood of the ancient world was truly a horrific event!

And spared not the old world, but saved Noah the eighth person, a preacher of righteousness, bringing in the flood upon the world of the ungodly;... The Lord knoweth how to deliver the godly out of temptations.... ~ 2 Peter 2:5, 9

Paleontology

March 31

Soft tissue found in dinosaur bones has been found in over a dozen documented examples. Laboratory studies indicate that soft tissue decays within about **1 YEAR**, and it is known that even the most stable biological proteins would break down within **30,000 YEARS**. So how do evolutionists explain soft tissue within fossilized bones - yet still hang on to their belief that these bones are over 65 million years old?

According to research results from evolutionist, Dr. Mary Schweitzer (the discoverer of the original soft tissue found in a T-rex fossil reported in a 2005 paper), iron from our blood can bond to tissue immediately after death and decrease the decay rate of biological tissue by orders of magnitude. Dr. Schweitzer used TOTALLY unrealistic conditions in her experiments.

Dr. Mark Armitage is a creationist who was fired from the University of California in 2013 after publishing the implications of his discovery of soft tissue in a Triceratops horn (found in the Hell Creek formation in Montana). He makes the following observations about Dr. Schweitzer's latest paper, *"There is no way the iron could have preserved the tissues (blood vessels) which Schweitzer is talking about because blood clots within 20 minutes [locking up any available iron]...iron could not have preserved the soft BONE sheets I found because they are in impermeable bone and they never come in contact with the blood. PLUS Schweitzer used an ANTICOAGULANT in her experiment and separated all the other blood products in order to isolate and highly concentrate the iron. She also kept it sterile (i.e., no fungi, microbes, plants, water, ice) which is way different from [any natural conditions]..."*

In other words, **evolutionists start with the assumption that the huge time periods are true and then manipulate experiments to get the results they desire** - even though such

Behold now behemoth, which I made with thee;....
~ Job 40:15

conditions or experiments in no way reflects reality. They then present the findings as proof that the huge time periods are true. This type of research is poor science. We need to do good science and go wherever the facts lead us. Soft tissue in dinosaurs is puzzling for evolutionists but not for Christians. Finding many examples of soft dinosaur tissue means they died in the recent past.

Christian Truth

April 1

Imagine a student coming into his teacher's office and declaring that he did not believe that oxygen existed. Before the teacher could even respond, the student bursts forth with a long series of justifications for his conclusion starting with the fact that "no-one had ever seen an oxygen molecule" and the question, "where would this molecule come from?"

A good teacher would not get defensive and go into an insulting tirade against such a student. The teacher would be confident in the truth and would lead the deceived student to the truth with patience and logic.

In the same way, evolutionists are like the student, insisting that everything can be explained without the existence of God. God has repeatedly stated that it is the evidence from creation that testifies to His existence (Roman 1:18-31). The very fact that rational thoughts are possible proves the existence of a Creator. Our minds have been purposefully created. We are not random arrangements of chemicals. Otherwise, our thoughts are just chemicals and electricity zipping around our brain randomly. If I were to have you think of a pink elephant and then cut your skull open, would I find a pink elephant there? No, a pink elephant is a thought while your brain is a physical structure. You are body and soul. Where did this soul come from? God. There is a God who reveals Himself through what He has made. To those who have been taken captive by the philosophy of this world, we need to be patient and explain the truth.

Who hath put wisdom in the inward parts?
Or who hath given understanding to the heart?
~ Job 38:36

April 2

Biology

Have you ever tried to hold onto a slimy, slippery fish? It is very difficult. Now imagine birds that primarily eat fish, such as penguins or loons, trying to hold onto a fish! These birds are designed with unique backward pointing spines on their tongue and the roof of their mouth. **These spines hold onto the slippery fish, and as the fish wiggles, the spines force the fish further down the throat**. The spines act like a conveyor belt, moving the fish into the bird's throat and down to the stomach.

As the loon hunts for fish, it swims along with its eyes just below the surface. Upon spotting a school of fish, it dives and chases the fish. **Loons can dive as deep as 200 feet and hold their breath for as long as 10 minutes!** When the loon gets close to the fish, it thrusts its head forward and grabs the fish. The loon has no problem holding onto the fish and swallowing it because of the backward pointing projections in its mouth. Interestingly, the fish can only be swallowed head first because the fish's scales only allow them to slide forward in that direction. When we see special designs, like spines on a bird's tongue and the roof of its mouth, we know there must be a Designer! God thought of all the details, even holding onto a slimy fish.

I will meditate also of all thy work, and talk of thy doings.
~ Psalm 77:12

Geology

April 3

Rock layers (strata) show much more evidence for rapid formation than evidence for formation over eons of time. Here are some evidences for rapid formation of rock strata:

- **Polystrate fossils,** like fossilized tree trunks running through multiple rock layers (supposedly millions of years old) had to have formed rapidly. If it did not happen quickly the trunks would have rotted away as they waited for the next layer to be laid down.
- **Ripple marks and footprints in rocks** are delicate surface features preserved on underlying rock units. If there were millions of years between layers, these delicate features should be gone. Think of an animal footprint in mud being undisturbed for years - even that is impossible.
- **Lack of soil layers** in rock strata.
- **Lack of erosion features** in rock layers. If there were millions of years between the layers, there should be gullies and other erosion features everywhere we look.

The rock layers (strata) that we see today were laid down during the year-long Flood of Noah's time. The rock layers testify that God's word is true about the world-wide Flood.

And the rain was upon the earth forty days and forty nights....And the waters prevailed upon the earth an hundred and fifty days....And the waters decreased continually until the tenth month....
~ Genesis 7:12, 24; 8:5

April 4

Biology

Termites are famous for eating wood, especially in houses. Yet, termites cannot digest wood. It is the microbes in the gut of the termite that break down the wood that allows it to be digested. **The termites cannot exist without the gut microbes, and the gut microbes cannot exist without the termites; both need each other in order to survive**.

Science calls this symbiosis or mutualism. Some scientists say this relationship evolved by accident and chance. Why would termites begin to eat wood if they could not digest it? Why would gut microbes make their home in termite guts if they were not getting the food they needed? Both termites and gut microbes had to be together from the beginning, mutually depending on each other. Who would have thought that termites and their gut microbes give glory to God!

I will sing unto the Lord as long as I live:
I will sing praise to my God while I have my being.
~ Psalm 104:33

Biology

April 5

Have you considered that birds like gannets and blue-footed boobies dive into the water at high speeds and do not break their necks! How do birds survive a dive like that? These birds come equipped with their own built-in "air bags"!

Gannets and blue-footed boobies like to go fishing. They flock together high in the sky, usually hovering over schools of herring, menhaden, or other fish. Then one of the gannets will single out a certain fish, tuck his wings close to his side and dive from heights of 100 feet. **The gannet will slam into the water headfirst at 60 mph like a missile**. What keeps his neck from breaking upon impact? Beneath the skin near the neck are air sacs that the bird fills by taking a gulp of air just before impact. This provides cushioning for the bird, just like the airbags in a car. Do we say that airbags started appearing in cars by chance? When we see an airbag, we know there must be an airbag designer. And who is the airbag designer in these birds? God our Creator. He designed the first airbags for the safety of birds like gannets.

For who in the heaven can be compared unto the Lord?...
~ Psalm 89:6

April 6

Biology

Have you heard of a cave weta? This New Zealand insect lives in mountain top caves that can experience -10 °F during the winter. This insect actually freezes solid for three months - showing no brain activity or respiration. **Then in the spring, it thaws out and proceeds with life as normal – doing whatever big bugs enjoy doing in the spring.** They can go through six such freeze-thaw cycles in their lifetime, often living up to six years.

When humans freeze, crystals form in our blood, bursting our cells and causing our death. Wetas, however, have high levels of glucose, a sugar which keeps these crystals from forming. Evolutionists assume this all happened by accident and chance. What would have happened to the first weta that had not yet evolved a high enough sugar level in its blood? **We'd have a dead weta!** Evolutionary advancement would have ended, along with the first wetas! God had to design the cave weta to survive freezing from the beginning. Creation is shouting God's glory!

O Lord my God, thou art very great;....
~ Psalm 104:1

April 7

Design

Have you considered that the Sun provides the right amount of brightness on earth, and even on a cloudy day, there is still enough light? Why? Earth's atmosphere makes this happen. When the Sun's rays hit our atmosphere, they bounce off the air molecules, causing the light to scatter in all directions and lighting the sky. **If we did not have our atmosphere, our sky would be pitch black - like the Moon's.** When the astronauts were on the Moon during the daylight, the sky was all black except when they looked right at the Sun. God has provided the right type of atmosphere so that when the Sun's rays hit it, it provides the perfect amount of brightness…and a beautiful blue color.

*Truly the light is sweet, and a pleasant thing
it is for the eyes to behold the sun:
~ Ecclesiastes 11:7*

April 8

Biology

Have you heard of the coywolf? Genetically it is ¼ wolf, 1/10 dog and the rest coyote. The coywolf is a hybrid twice the size of a coyote, able to hunt in both the woods (traditionally the place for wolves) and on the prairies (traditionally the place for coyotes). With the help of the dog genetics, it is able to hunt in urban areas by eating rodents and pets or scavenging. If you spot one in suburbia, you will even notice that **it may look both ways before crossing the street!**

How did the coywolf come about? When the wolves of southern Canada experienced environmental problems of deforestation and drastic hunting, they began to interbreed with both coyotes and large breeds of domesticated dogs. The coywolf is not the result of evolution but the in-built diversity of genetic code that God has placed within the dog kind. It has also been demonstrated that wolves, coyotes, and domestic dogs are the same kind since they can successfully interbreed.

And at evening let them return; and let them make a noise like a dog, and go round about the city. Let them wander up and down for meat, and grudge if they be not satisfied. ~ Psalm 59:14-15

Microbiology

April 9

Do you realize that the evolutionary view of molecules-to-man can have a detrimental effect on scientific advancements? The latest example was the belief in "junk DNA." For over twenty years, it was widely accepted that less than 2% of the coded information on the human DNA molecule was used to produce proteins (little molecular machines within the cell).[1] Thus 98% of the human DNA sequence was assumed to be useless, leftover junk from our evolutionary past. This was accepted evolutionary dogma for many years, so scientists had no incentive to look for a purpose for this supposed "junk coding." Thus, evolutionary preconceptions slowed scientific advancement in this area of genetics for decades.

Dr. Francis Collins (head of the Human Genome Project) stated in his book, *The Language of God*, that roughly 45% of the human genome is made of repetitive flotsam and jetsam and that this junk provides "compelling" evidence for the evolutionary origin of humanity. Yet, we can now conclusively show that **essentially all the DNA's coded sequence (including repetitive sections) serves multiple purposes and functions**.[3]

God doesn't make junk, not even junk DNA!

Surely your turning of things upside down shall be esteemed as the potter's clay: for shall the work say of him that made it, He made me not? or shall the thing framed say of him that framed it, He had no understanding? ~ Isaiah 29:16

April 10  Design

How many ways are there to fasten shoes? Old-fashioned shoes often had buttons; tennis shoes frequently use laces. Other shoes even use elastic or zippers. Some shoes, like children's shoes and women's sandals, often use Velcro™. Where did mankind get the idea of creating Velcro?

One day in 1941, after going for a walk in the woods, Swiss electrical engineer George de Mestral noticed cockleburs stuck to both his pants and his dog. Instead of just cleaning them off, he decided to figure out what gave them their incredible sticking nature. He discovered they were designed with thousands of ingenious, flexible, barbed "fingers", which allowed them to easily attach for a free ride on the fabric of clothing and hairs of an animal. So after eight years of research, Velcro™, with its "hook and loop," was invented. de Mestral used two strips of fabric, one with thousands of tiny hooks and another with thousands of tiny loops; de Mestral coined the term Velcro from the combination of the words "velvet" and "crochet." **The inventor observed the design that God had built into the cockleburs and came up with one of the most versatile and useful attachment systems ever developed!** He was not the original designer; he just copied what THE Designer had already made!

O the depth of the riches both of the wisdom and knowledge of God!
~ Romans 11:33a

Biology

April 11

When an adult California ground squirrel discovers a rattlesnake lurking nearby, it often harasses it. In this area, baby ground squirrels make up 69% of the rattlesnakes' diet. Therefore, the adult ground squirrel harasses the rattlesnake by dashing around it, nipping at its tail, kicking sand on it and waving his tail at it. The rattlesnake is not as fast or agile as the ground squirrel. If bitten, the ground squirrel doesn't die because adult squirrels have proteins in their blood to neutralize the rattlesnake venom. Baby California ground squirrels, however, have not yet developed enough proteins to neutralize the poison.

The ground squirrel will even taunt the rattlesnake by shunting extra blood to its tail, so it will heat up. Rattlesnakes can see heat (infra-red) and, therefore, lunges for the extra hot tail. Eventually the rattlesnake becomes frustrated and retreats. Interestingly, ground squirrels also harass gopher snakes – 50% of the gopher snakes' diet also is baby ground squirrels. Gopher snakes, however, do not see heat, so the ground squirrel does not shunt extra blood to its tail when fighting with this kind of snake. **How does a ground squirrel know that a rattlesnake can see heat and a gopher snake cannot?** God knew the California ground squirrel would need this for its offspring's defense, so He designed it to discern the difference.

O Lord, how manifold are thy works! in wisdom hast thou made them all: the earth is full of thy riches.
~ Psalm 104: 24

April 12
Biblical Accuracy

What if….you took 40 different people….from all different walks of life, social status, and vocations…living on three different continents… separated by thousands of years….writing in different moods (from sorrow to joy)… writing in three different languages….and writing about diverse topics. Would you expect to have a unified, harmonious story? Or would the result be a disjointed jumble of different ideas?

The Bible was written
- **By 40 different authors**: shepherds, kings, soldiers, religious leaders, common men, statesmen, doctors, government officials
- **In different places**: palaces, towns, large cities, deserts
- **At different times**: times of war and peace, of prosperity and need
- **In different moods**: joy and sorrow, fear and security
- **On three different continents**: in Africa (Egypt), Europe (Italy), and Asia (Turkey)
- **In three different languages**: Hebrew, Greek, Aramaic
- **About many topics**: the nature of God, moral issues, religious ceremonies, history, science, documentation of facts
- **In multiple styles**: poetry, songs, historical accounts, sermons, advice, personal letters, prophetic utterances, lineages, royal edicts, allegory
- **Over a 1500 year period**

Yet, these 66 books share a common storyline - creation, fall, redemption - God's love for us and His means of salvation to all who repent of their sins and follow Him with all their heart, soul and mind. This golden thread weaves its way throughout the Bible. It is the unified, harmonious story of God's Word. In all 66 books, there are no historical errors or internal contradictions. The Bible is no ordinary book; it is the inspired Word of God!

All Scripture is given by inspiration of God...
~ 2 Timothy 3:16a

Biology

April 13

What is the secret to an owl's ability to rotate its head 270 degrees? Why are there not thousands of dead owls on the forest floor after having experienced a stroke from rapidly twisting their heads? Sudden head movements in humans--like whiplash--can cause the fragile blood vessel lining to stretch and tear, producing clots that break off, causing a deadly stroke.

Biologists have discovered many features allowing owls to turn their heads almost completely around. First of all, owls have 14 vertebrae in their necks whereas humans only have seven. In addition:

1. The blood vessels at the base of the neck get larger as they get closer to the brain. This acts as **a reservoir that continues feeding the brain** when the twisting neck slows the blood supply.
2. The owl's neck bones have holes 10 times the diameter of the artery traveling through it. This extra space allows for **greater flexibility and movement of the artery**. In humans, the holes are the size of the artery.
3. The vertebral artery enters the neck higher up than in other birds, creating slack, so **the artery is not twisted shut** as the neck turns.
4. Owls have small vessels connecting both the carotid and neck bone arteries; humans do not. During neck rotation, if one of the vessels becomes blocked, the **others can still let the blood flow** uninterrupted.

All these unique features had to be there from the beginning; otherwise, the forest floor would be littered with dead owls. God uniquely created owls from the very beginning.

Who is so great a God as our God? Thou art the God that doest wonders: ~ Psalm 77:13b–14a

April 14

Paleontology

When living creatures look exactly like their fossil counterparts, they have been called "living fossils." There are actually thousands of examples of fossils (many believed by evolutionists to be hundreds of millions of years old) that are identical to modern counterparts. For example:

- Bacteria fossils are found identical to bacteria today. This means that some bacteria stayed the same while other bacteria mutated and turned into human beings?
- Sponge fossils have been found identical to sponges today. So, some sponges stayed sponges while others turned into other complex sea life such as whales?
- Starfish fossils are identical to starfish today. So, some starfish stayed starfish while other starfish turned into sharks, tuna, and octopuses?

The list goes on and on. The only reason these fossils exist is because they were buried during Noah's Flood. **The similar creatures alive today are not "living fossils"; they are just the same kind of creatures that survived the Flood.**

Thou openest thine hand, and satisfiest the desire of every living thing.
~ Psalm 145:16

April 15

Biology

Ancient sailors spin yarns of mermaids, sea monsters, giant octopuses, sunken cities, and flying squid. The mermaid stories are based on fanciful storytelling; however, the **stories of flying squid, sunken cities, and giant octopuses have turned out to be absolutely true!** As a matter of fact, squid have now been documented to soar as high as 20 feet above the ocean surface on flights of over 180 feet. So how do animals with no wings and bodies designed to swim manage to soar above the water's surface? And more to the point, why would a squid bother to fly?

Each flight has three distinct phases:

1. A sudden contraction of the squid's body shoots water out of its funnel shaped rear end in a jet stream and propels them it the air.
2. During flight, the squid spreads out his front fins like wings and arranges his rear tentacles in a fanlike pattern (not unlike the tail fins of a plane). This aerodynamic position allows him to glide long distances after the jet propulsion stops.
3. He folds his fins and tentacles back against his body to end his glide with a controlled dive in order to minimize the impact and maximize the forward movement as he reenters the water.

Researchers have discovered that a squid's jet propulsion moves it three times farther in air than the same exertion in the water. Thus by "flying," a squid can travel much longer distances using far less energy. Evolutionists believe that squids evolved this ability to "fly" over millions of years, yet in the fossil record we see squids are squids (even though evolutionists have taught us the fossil ancestors are over 200 million years old).

The creativity and design of the squid's jet propulsion testifies to the creativity and intelligence of its designer, not evolutionary development.

For God is king of all the earth: sing ye praises with understanding.
~ Psalm 47:7

April 16

History

By studying the effects of recent volcanic eruptions, we can better understand what happened during the Flood of Noah. On April 5, and again on April 10 of 1815, Mount Tambora, the highest peak on a South Pacific Island, literally blew its top - sending a stream of ash upward over 25 miles into the earth's atmosphere. An ash cloud the size of Australia blackened the sky, dropping ash over 6 feet deep on surrounding islands and creating floating fields of pumice that traveled over 2000 miles. Iceberg-sized chunks of pumice created hazards for ships for years afterwards. Explosive percussions of the mountain's collapse could be heard on other South Pacific islands located over 1000 miles away as the top two thousand feet of the mountain disappeared in a fiery detonation. This powerful eruption killed over twelve thousand natives who died instantly from the explosion and subsequent tsunamis. Ultimately though, far more people around the world died, as this one volcano affected the history of our entire planet.

Fine volcanic ash from Tambora was ejected far into the earth's upper atmosphere where it affected weather patterns around the earth for the next year or more. Fiery red and purple sunsets were visible around the globe for several years. In Europe and North America, there were severe storms, excessive rain, and snow that fell far into the summer months of 1816, causing crop failures, food shortages, famine, riots, and political unrest. Mass migrations in search for food occurred as people traveled from Europe to America, and out of New England to the Midwest. Religious revivals broke out across America as stable communities were transformed into groups of wandering beggars and the worst typhus epidemic in history broke out. 1816 became known as "the year without summer," and this one volcano changed the history of both individual families and our entire planet in profound ways that are still being studied.

Now imagine the impact of thousands of volcanic eruptions during the Flood of Noah's time, which were hundreds of times more powerful than this one volcano, accompanied by a world-covering flood that lasted for over a year. Volcanic reverberations would have continued for decades during and after the Flood of Noah. Weather patterns would have been affected for centuries as the world was plunged into an extended Ice Age. The Flood of Noah's day had a profound effect on our planet. That is why every human culture has a remembrance of this Flood in their ancient traditions.

**He looketh on the earth, and it trembleth:
he toucheth the hills, and they smoke.   ~ Psalm 104:32**

Biology

April 17

Did you know that there is a direct connection between bats and the Ebola virus? News reports of the Ebola virus never seem to address the source of the virus. People in the tropical regions where fruit bats live often sell these bats at market for consumption. These bats have been found to serve as natural reservoirs of the Ebola virus. In the Western culture, the eating of bats has never been considered appropriate, but why? Perhaps because both the USA and Western European cultures were established on Judeo-Christian principles. **Bats are listed among food to be avoided and considered as detestable as rats in our culture**. Thus, we are spared from many diseases rampant elsewhere.

When reading the Scriptures, we find many of our practices (like washing our hands under running water and not touching a dead body), originated from the Bible long before germs were understood. Our forefathers believed God and incorporated many practices from the Bible into their everyday lives, and these practices have been passed down to us. Did our forefathers know the consequences of eating bats? No. But our heavenly Father knew and wanted to protect us.

And these are they which ye shall have in abomination among the fowls; they shall not be eaten, they are an abomination: the eagle, and the ossifrage, and the ospray, ...and the bat.
~ Leviticus 11:13-19

April 18

Christian Truth

Mankind has often pondered the question, "What comes after this life?" Do we just simply cease to exist and return to the dust of the earth? Or is there more to our existence than our physical bodies?

The Bible is clear that we will be held accountable for our lives after death, "*it is appointed unto men once to die, but after this the judgment*" (Hebrews 9:27). It also states, "*ALL have sinned and come short of the glory of God,*" (Romans 3:23 emp. added) and "*There is none righteous, no, not one*." (Romans 3:10) We will face a holy and just God after death, and this is indeed a scary reality for those who have not accepted the forgiveness offered through the sacrificial death of Jesus. Yet, how do we know there will be a life after death? One answer comes in the most unlikely of places – the book of Job.

Before his trials, Job was blessed with wealth, health, and happiness. He had 7 sons, 3 daughters, 7000 sheep, 3000 camels, 500 pairs of oxen, and 500 donkeys (Job 1:2-3). Stricken by disaster, which few men have endured before or since, Job lost everything. He was urged by his wife and closest friends to blame either God or his own sins for his problems - yet Job steadfastly refused to do either. Blaming God would defame the character of God, and Job knew he had not sinned in a way that should have brought such misery upon his life. Yet, it never entered Job's mind to deny the very existence of God. Job begged to know why such agony had fallen upon him and in the end, God rebuked his antagonists while rewarding Job's steadfast faithfulness by doubling his losses with 14,000 sheep, 6000 camels, 1000 pairs of oxen, 1000 donkeys, 7 more sons and 3 more daughters (Job 42:12-13).

Compare the original list with the final list. Notice that the Lord doubled all of Job's possessions …except for his children. Why? Because **death does not end our existence**. Job's original 7 children did not cease to exist; they had simply stepped through the door we call death and would see Job again (if they were judged righteous). So in reality, by giving Job another 10 children, the Lord also doubled his children. Had he been given 20 more children, it would have been as if the original 10 had ceased to exist, and this is not the case!

He had also seven sons and three daughters.
~ Job 42:13

Anatomy

April 19

The world's first artificial stomach was recently developed in Britain at a cost of $1.8 million dollars. It even vomits! The shiny, high-tech box is made of plastics and metal and is built to withstand the corrosive acids and enzymes found inside a real stomach. The two-part model is just a little larger than a desktop computer. Food, stomach acids, and digestive enzymes are poured into the stomach, which mixes them in the first chamber. The artificial stomach attempts to copy real muscle contractions to mix everything up. Software regulates how long food remains in the chamber. **Yet, scientists really don't know how well this lab bench simulator stomach replicates the real thing.** A scientist involved with this project admits, *"Our knowledge of what actually happens in the gut is still very rudimentary."*

Nevertheless, food companies are interested; one company wants to test its biscuits to see when a particular nutrient is released, and another is interested in how quickly glucose is absorbed into the bloodstream. Even though this stomach took millions of dollars and hundreds of hours to design and build, it still cannot accomplish what our own stomach can do. **If it took intelligence to make this artificial stomach, imagine the immense intelligence it took to make our own stomach!** Evolutionists would have us believe that our stomach happened by accident and chance. Did this artificial stomach, which is not even as good as our own stomach, happen by accident and chance? I just can't stomach that idea! When we see a stomach, we know there must be a stomach-maker and that stomach-maker is God!

And Jesus said, "Are ye also yet without understanding? Do not ye yet understand, that whatsoever entereth in at the mouth goeth into the belly..." ~ Matthew 15:16-17

April 20

Botany

Have you considered the sawfly larva's ingenious defense system? This North American and European pest lives in conifers. Conifers aren't bothered by too many insect pests. That's because the oils that give pine trees that nice pine scent are poisonous to insects - including the sawfly. Yet, the sawfly larva eats these poisonous pine needles without dying. How does it survive?

As a sawfly larva munches on the poisonous pine needles, he does not digest them immediately. The sawfly larva separates the poisonous oils in the pine needles from the nutritious pulp. These poisonous oils are then stored in two special sacs in his mouth which are lined with a "poison-proof" material. **These poisonous oils can then be used as the larva's defense mechanism**. When a bird or spider attacks, the foul-smelling oils are discharged - frightening the enemy away.

How could this complicated defense/storage system have developed gradually over time? How did the sawfly know to build two sacs and line them with a poison-proof coating so that he would not be killed by the poisons? How did the sawfly know this foul-smelling poisonous oil would repel birds and spiders? The sawfly did not know; God knew. God protects even the smallest of His creatures.

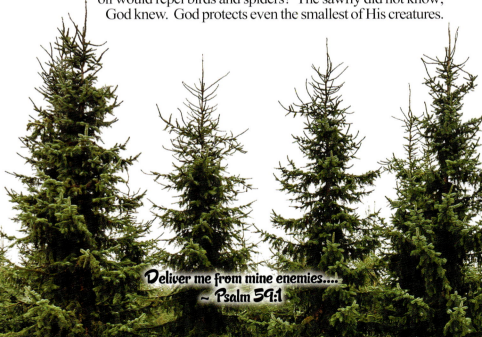

Deliver me from mine enemies....
~ Psalm 59:1

Geology

April 21

How long does it take to form large mineral formations? In 1903, in the town of Thermopolis, Wyoming, USA, someone drove an iron pipe into the ground, allowing the underground mineral-rich waters to escape. As the warm mineral waters flowed out the top of the pipe, the water evaporated leaving behind a mineral called travertine. The travertine rock mound is now 24 feet tall.

Why does this rock formation, called Teepee Fountain, surprise visitors? Because it did not take millions of years to form. When tourists view cave stalagmites and stalactites, tour guides tell them these rock formations took hundreds of thousands or even millions of years to form. The Teepee Fountain shows us this is not true - it just took the right chemical environment to make this monstrous mound. Rocks can form very rapidly.

Consider the following: At the beginning of the Genesis Flood, the Bible says all the fountains of the great deep were broken up, suggesting huge hot-water geysers erupting mineral-rich waters just like at Thermopolis. These mineral-rich waters would have been mixed with sand, mud, and other sediments during this violent Flood. As the sediments settled out and the waters dried up, the remaining minerals helped bind the sediments together to form the sedimentary rock layers that we see today. It does not take millions of years to form solid rock, just the right conditions.

Towards the end of the Flood ~ " The fountains also of the deep and the windows of heaven were stopped, and the rain from heaven was restrained"
~ Genesis 8:2

April 22

Biology

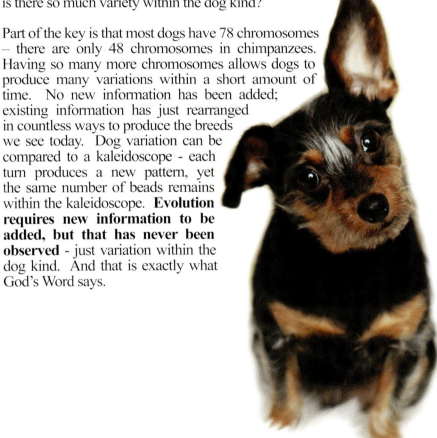

It has been widely repeated, "Dogs are man's best friend." This has proven to be true for thousands of years as dogs have benefited mankind with hunting, herding, transportation, protection, and companionship. There are over 300 dog breeds in the world - from Chihuahuas to Great Danes. Most have been bred over the last century! Why is there so much variety within the dog kind?

Part of the key is that most dogs have 78 chromosomes – there are only 48 chromosomes in chimpanzees. Having so many more chromosomes allows dogs to produce many variations within a short amount of time. No new information has been added; existing information has just rearranged in countless ways to produce the breeds we see today. Dog variation can be compared to a kaleidoscope - each turn produces a new pattern, yet the same number of beads remains within the kaleidoscope. **Evolution requires new information to be added, but that has never been observed** - just variation within the dog kind. And that is exactly what God's Word says.

And God said, Let the earth bring forth the living creature after his kind, ... and it was so.
~ Genesis 1:24

Biology

April 23

All warm-blooded animals generate heat when running. When we run fast, we get rid of heat by sweating over our entire body. **But a dog does not sweat the way humans do**. Instead, a dog "pants." Panting is a process where a dog hangs his tongue out of his open mouth and breaths over his wet tongue. This causes the wet saliva to evaporate – removing heat from the tongue in the process. This cools the tongue's blood vessels, which carry the cooled blood throughout the body.

A dog's primary method for regulating its body temperature is by evaporation through panting and sweat glands on its paws. This is a marvelous design. Imagine a dog sweating all over its body on a cold winter day; its coat would be covered with icicles. **God had to solve many engineering problems** when he created the wide variety of creatures to survive the diverse environments throughout the earth.

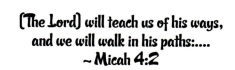

(The Lord) will teach us of his ways,
and we will walk in his paths:....
~ Micah 4:2

April 24

Design

Have you considered that the winds have weight? Winds move the air, and air has mass. If the air had no mass, then the winds would have no force. This is just what is stated in Job 28:25, "To make the weight for the wind."

It was once believed that air had no weight. Evangelista Torricelli designed an experiment to test this belief in 1641. He filled a 3 foot glass tube with mercury. He quickly turned it upside down and placed it in a bowl of mercury. The mercury in the tube dropped to 30 inches. Torricelli noticed that when the mercury rose in the tube, there were clear skies. The mercury level decreased as stormy weather approached. **Torricelli had invented the barometer**, which measured the weight of the air. God told Job of this idea, the "weight for the winds," some 3500 years earlier. Too many people are trained to think of the Bible as unscientific. The very opposite is true. Whenever God's Word speaks of science, it is true. In reality, we are just catching up with God.

To make the weight for the winds;
~ Job 28:25

Design

April 25

It is often stated that belief in God is a "leap of faith." Yet, the Bible, from the Old Testament (Psalm 19:1-4) to the New Testament (Romans 1:18-23), clearly states that the reality of God's existence is absolutely apparent to everyone, everywhere -- simply by observing creation. In other words, creation could only exist if a Creator made it.

The September 2013 journal *Science* describes a set of perfectly formed gears at the base of a lowly 2 mm-long leafhopper nymph.[1] This creature has the ability to jump several inches using a mighty thrust from its hind legs that propels the creature with an acceleration of nearly 400 G (fighter pilots risk blackout if accelerating much past 10 G). **This feat would be equivalent to a man accelerating from 0 to 200 mph in less than a second and jumping 400 feet in a single bound!**

What makes the leafhopper's feat even more amazing is that the nerve impulses cannot travel fast enough to allow both legs to push off in a coordinated fashion – meaning that with every hop, the insect should spin out of control. So how did the Creator solve this problem? **He added a set of interlocking gears to the base of the leafhopper's legs so that they are forced to move in exact coordination.**[2] This design is currently being studied as a prototype for new kinds of high-speed, directional gears. The marvels of the microscopic world and the wonders of God's creativity never cease. The belief that such a gear could "make itself" via random changes over time is

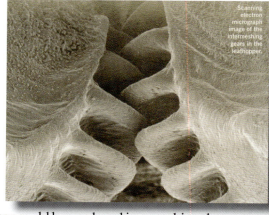

Scanning electron micrograph image of the intermeshing gears in the leafhopper.

equivalent to believing that a gear could be produced in a machine shop via random hammering of a piece of metal. When we see microscopic gears solving a leafhopper's leap, we stand in awe of our Creator!

The heavens declare the glory of God; and the firmament sheweth his handywork. Day unto day uttereth speech, and night unto night sheweth knowledge. There is no speech nor language, where their voice is not heard. ~ Psalm 19:1-3

April 26
Biblical Accuracy

One criterion for determining the reliability of any ancient manuscript is the time which elapsed from the original manuscript to its later copies; the more time that has passed between the original and the copy, the more chance for errors to develop.

So what have manuscript studies found when comparing ancient documents? Caesar's *War Commentaries* were written about 50 B.C.; we do not have the original. The only copies date from the 9th century - a 900 year gap! Aristotle's works have a 1450 year gap. Plato's works have a 1,250 year gap. Tacitus's writings have a 1,000 year gap from the original manuscript, and Virgil's works have a 300 year gap.

Now, let's compare these ancient manuscripts (whose authenticity is not questioned) with the New Testament. Major copies of every book in the New Testament are within 100 years of the original. What a short time span! The closer to the original, the more accurate it will be. **If the New Testament were a collection of secular writings, their authenticity would be beyond ANY REASONABLE DOUBT**. The New Testament stands in a league of its own, far more trustworthy than any other ancient writing!

The grass withereth, the flower fadeth: but the word of our God shall stand for ever.
~ Isaiah 40:8

Cosmology

April 27

Why isn't the earth and all life on it, fried from deadly solar radiation? The earth is protected by a magnetic force field that surrounds it. Scientists are finding, however, that this protective force field is slowly wearing down (or decaying). At the current rate of decay, the magnetic force field can be no more than 20,000 years old. This means the Earth could not be older than 20,000 years.

Measuring the strength of the earth's magnetic field began in 1845. Since that time, there have been many studies. One study showed the decay rate of 5% per century. Another study done by archeologists estimated that the earth's magnetic field must have been 40% stronger in 1000 A.D. A more recent study from 1970 - 2000 by the International Geomagnetic Reference Field measured a loss of 1.4% in the magnetic field in just 30 years! **This has far more profound implications than global climate change, yet it is largely ignored.**

For the earth to be billions of years old, as evolutionists say, the earth's magnetic field would long ago have disappeared, and we would have been bombarded by deadly solar radiation. But earth still has a force field surrounding it. When we do the math, it all points to a young earth and magnetic field. According to Scripture, the earth and the entire universe is only about 6,000 years old. Earth's magnetic field shouts a young earth!

To him that by wisdom made the heavens: for his mercy endureth forever. To him that stretched out the earth above the waters....
~ Psalm 136:5,6

April 28
Microbiology

For centuries, barnacles--crustaceans that live inside their exoskeletons--have frustrated ship owners because they like to glue themselves to ship hulls. It is difficult to remove them because their glue is so tenacious. But **how does a barnacle's glue stick to a wet surface?**

There are two steps needed for a barnacle to adhere itself to an underwater surface: first it needs to clear the water away, and then it cements itself to the surface. The barnacle larva, which is the active swimming stage of a barnacle, releases an oily droplet to clear the water from the surface to which it wants to stick itself. Then, the larva releases a phosphoprotein adhesive. **In essence, a super-glue!**

Scientists are studying this two-step process in hope of being able to manufacture the glue for surgical use. We make great claims on how scientifically smart we are, but we can always improve our science by having a better understanding of how God made the identical thing in nature. Who knows, the next time you have surgery, "barnacle superglue" may be used!

The Lord is my strength and my shield; my heart trusted in him, and I am helped....
~ Psalm 28:7

Geology

April 29

Water and wind gaps are common geological features found worldwide, yet their formation is a mystery to many scientists. These gaps form a shallow notch in the upper part of a mountain ridge. The notch is an erosional notch and is not caused from faulting (rock layer movements). Water gaps channels still have rivers running between the mountain peaks while wind gaps only have wind.

In central Wyoming, the Sweetwater River flows through such a granite ridge. How did the river cut this 330 feet deep channel? And what about **the Arun River in the Himalayan Mountains flows through a water gap that is 4 miles deep and 13 miles wide**. Why wouldn't the water have flowed around rather than through these mountains? How does a river cut right through the top of a mountain ridge? It can't! But if you put on your biblical glasses and view these gaps with the Genesis Flood in mind, the explanation becomes obvious. At the end of the Flood, as the continents and mountains of the world were rising up out of the water, enormous sheets of water would have been channelized, initially cutting a notch through the layers. As it continued to pour through the rising land surfaces, huge gaps were formed. Later, a river might run through the gap; scientists call that a water gap. If no river flows through but only wind, scientists call it a wind gap. We find these water and wind gaps all over the world… but of course we would. The Flood was a powerful, globe-covering event.

Water Gap

And the waters receded continually from the earth. At the end of the hundred and fifty days the waters decreased. ~ Genesis 8:3

April 30 — Botany

In the jungles of Borneo, a bat looks for a daytime place to roost. He sends out his sonar throughout the crowded jungle and finds the perfect place echoing back, a pitcher plant. Amazingly, sonic reflectors grow right above the pitcher plants opening, bouncing back the bat's own sonar. These sonic reflectors have tiny ridges, correctly spaced for just the right reflection. So the bat quickly finds a cool, parasite-free place in the hot rainforest to roost. But what benefit is there for the pitcher plant? It gets the bat's droppings.

Bat droppings are extremely high in nitrogen, which the plant needs. As a matter of fact, dried bat guano (droppings) is collected from caves around the world for use as fertilizer. Many pitcher plants eat insects, but not this one; it dines on the nutrients in bat waste. This mutualistic, beneficial behavior is in the category of "wacky but wonderful." Evolutionists believe that this pitcher plant (*Nepenthes hemsleyana*) was not good at attracting insects, so, it evolved a sonic reflector over millions of years in order to attract a different source of nitrogen (bat droppings). Does this make any sense at all? If a pitcher plant does not get enough nitrogen in the beginning, which is why it eats insects, wouldn't it just die? How could it change its DNA to make the exact reflector it needed? How did a plant know that a bat sent out sonar? How did a plant know that bat droppings had the nitrogen it needed? **This unusual partnership was set up by God; it did not happen by accident and chance.**

the excellency of knowledge is, that wisdom giveth life to them that have it. Consider the work of God...
~ Ecclesiastes 7:12b, 13

"Consider the lilies of the field, how they grow, they toil not, neither do they spin: and yet I say unto you, that even Solomon in all his glory was not arrayed like one of these... seek ye first the kingdom of God, and his righteousness; and all these things shall be added unto you."
- Matthew 6:28-29, 33

"We can complain because rose bushes have thorns, or rejoice because thorn bushes have roses."
– Abraham Lincoln (1809 – 1865), 16th President of the United States

May

Christian Truth

May 1

The Ten Best Evidences for a Young Earth as Confirmed in Science

1. **Very little sediment on the sea floor:** Every year, sediment washes into the sea. At current rates, oceans contain about 12 million years-worth of sediment, not billions. Even this sediment exists because of erosion at the end of the Flood – not from 12 million years of slow accumulation. So, where are the billions of years of dirt, if earth is billions of years old?
2. **Bent rock layers:** Throughout the world, we see sedimentary layers bent and folded without fracturing. This means they had to be bent when freshly laid.
3. **Soft tissue in dinosaur bones:** It would be long gone in millions of years.
4. **Faint sun paradox:** The sun gets its energy from the fusion of hydrogen into helium, deep within the sun's core. As the hydrogen fuses, the sun's core increases in temperature. This means billions of years ago, the sun was fainter or cooler. Only 3.5 billion years ago the entire earth would have been well below freezing - at a time when life supposedly evolved.
5. **Rapidly decaying magnetic field:** The earth's magnetic field is decaying so rapidly it could not be older than 20,000 years old.
6. **Helium in radioactive rocks:** Helium is released during the radioactive decay of uranium and thorium contained in rocks. All the helium should have leaked out of the rocks in less than 100,000 years. So why are these rocks still filled with significant concentrations of helium?
7. **Carbon-14 found in fossils, diamonds and coal:** C14 or radiocarbon decays quickly, so after a few hundred thousand years, no carbon-14 should be left, yet we find it in "ancient" fossils, diamonds, and coal.
8. **Short-lived comets**: Every time a comet passes by the sun, it loses some of its mass. Given the observed loss rates, it is easy to compute the age of comets; the maximum age is well below billions of years.
9. **Very little salt in the sea:** Every year salt gets transported into the sea from the continents. If the world's oceans have been around for three billion years (as evolutionists believe), we should see almost 100 times more salt within ocean waters than we do today.
10. **DNA in "ancient" bacteria:** Bacteria, believed by evolutionists to be 250 million years old, still had DNA. This is impossible unless they were quite recently buried. Also, they were shocked to find the bacteria's DNA was very similar to modern bacterial DNA. Where's the evolution?

Whatsoever the Lord pleased, that did he in heaven,
and in earth, in the seas, and all deep places.
~ Psalm 135:6

May 2

Biology

What is faster than a speeding bullet, can break aquarium glass with a single punch, and draw blood from a human finger? A five-inch peacock mantis shrimp.

In the wild, peacock mantis shrimp eat foods such as clams, snails, and crabs - all of which have tough shells. With one swift knock-out punch, **reaching the speed of a 22-caliber bullet, the shrimp shatters these shells** and has a tasty lunch. How did the peacock mantis shrimp's "club" become so powerful that it can even shatter aquarium glass? It's all in the design.

The "club" has three layers. The outer layer is rich with minerals; the middle layer is composed of chitin with minerals dispersed within it; the inner layer has chitin fibers oriented in the opposite direction. The "club" is lightweight, stiff, tough, shock-resistant, and impact-tolerant. Today, researchers are studying the peacock mantis shrimp's "club" in an effort to develop better body armor for soldiers. These scientists recognize a good "knock-out punch" when they see it! Let's hope they also recognize the designer, Jesus Christ.

For the earth shall be filled with
the knowledge of the glory of the Lord,...
~ Habakkuk 2:14

Geology

May 3

One of the most famous places to view petrified wood is at Specimen Ridge's "Petrified Forest" in Yellowstone National Park. There, 63 rock layers contain vertical, petrified trees. It has been historically taught that a forest grew at each layer and were petrified in growth position--with each forest growing up and being buried by a volcanic eruption; then a new forest grew and was buried, and so on. For almost 100 years these layers were interpreted as having been laid down over hundreds of thousands of years. Yet, the facts point to a different explanation:

1. Petrified tree rings from different layers were examined and found to match each other, indicating the petrified trees lived at the same time.

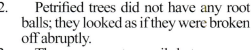

2. Petrified trees did not have any root balls; they looked as if they were broken off abruptly.
3. There were no true soils between any of the 63 layers, only debris that was undecayed. True soils would show gradations of decay.
4. Mixed throughout the layers were tropical vegetation (brought in by the Flood waters.)
5. Mineral content from the volcanic eruptions were the same. If each layer was buried under a different volcanic episode, the mineral content would be different. Yet throughout the layers, the mineral content was the same, indicating one super volcanic episode within a short period of time.

A better explanation would be a world-wide Flood. Trees were ripped by their roots and transported to this area. During the Flood they became waterlogged and sank vertically to the bottom of the water; eventually becoming covered with sediment. Yellowstone's Petrified Forest testifies to the Flood during Noah's time, not to huge peroods of time upon the earth.

the same day were all the fountains of the great deep broken up, and the windows of heaven were opened. And the rain was upon the earth forty days and forty nights. ~ Genesis 7:11-12

May 4 — History

Have you considered that **the primary motivation leading to the development of the scientific method was the sinfulness of man!** Sixteenth century Reformers acknowledged man's depravity and therefore understood that even his ability to reason could not be trusted to determine truth. Because of man's sinfulness, he has an inclination toward twisting things for his own purposes. So, science needed repeatable experimentation if its conclusions were to be accurate.

The Reformers also took seriously the command that man was to have dominion over creation, which meant he needed to study and understand it. These two ideas, man's sinfulness and dominion, birthed the scientific revolution, which produced the founders of the various branches of science. These Bible-believing scientists included:

- Sir Isaac Newton - physics, optics, invention of calculus
- Joseph Lister - antiseptic surgery
- Johannes Kepler - celestial mechanics
- Louis Pasteur - bacteriology
- Michael Faraday - electromagnetism
- James Maxwell - electromagnetic equations
- Lord Kelvin - thermodynamics
- and MANY others

These men were "Thinking God's thoughts after Him" to produce much of the technology we have today.

Sadly, much of "modern science" has returned to biased opinion over observation. As D.J. Kennedy has said in his book, ***What If Jesus Had Never Been Born***, *"It is interesting to note that science could not originate in the philosophical view prevalent in the world today. The prevailing philosophy of the Western world today is existentialism, which is irrational."*

We move away from true science, founded on the understanding that creation exists because we have a Creator, to our detriment!

And God blessed them, and God said unto them, Be fruitful, and multiply, and replenish the earth, and subdue it: and have dominion... over every living thing that moveth upon the earth. ~ Genesis 1:28

Biology

May 5

The wombat is one of Australia's many unique creatures that is found nowhere else on earth. This animal is a marsupial - meaning it has a pouch in which prematurely born young finish their development. Having a pouch is great if you are a kangaroo - but a wombat is a burrowing animal. If the pouch opened toward the mom's head, the pouch would quickly fill with dirt. So the wombat's pouch faces backwards; it opens towards the mother's hind legs. Now, where did this unique animal come from? There are only two possibilities – creation or evolution. Either the wombat was created, fully formed and fully functional, or it evolved. Our schools teach, as a fact that something that wasn't a wombat turned into the wombat. But how could this happen?

Evolutionists believe that the pouches of marsupials all started like the kangaroos, and through millions of years the wombat's pouch "evolved" to face backward. Let's try to imagine this process. First, you have a forward facing pouch in a creature that decides to burrow into the earth. Its pouch kept filling with dirt. **Its babies kept dying**. Then, one is born with a sideways facing pouch. Now, the baby can't reach the milk glands. **Its babies kept dying**. Then finally, the pouch faces backwards! But millions of years would have passed, so how could this poor creature survive the slow process of evolving; many baby wombats would have died in the process. It is clear, God created the wombat's pouch to be "backwards" from the very beginning.

Sing to the Lord, for He hath done excellent things; this is known in all the earth.
~ Isaiah 12:5

May 6

Cosmology

We do not have an ordinary sun. It is brighter than 85% of all stars and has more mass than 90% of all stars. Of all stars, 75% are red dwarfs, having less than 5% of the light output of the sun. If our sun were a red dwarf, earth would have to be closer to receive its warmth. If it were that close, it would become locked in position - causing one side of the planet to always be dark - resulting in no life. Red dwarfs also frequently have violent flares, so much so that red dwarfs are nicknamed "flare stars." The remaining stars that aren't red dwarfs are unstable and would expel too much radiation to support life on any planet orbiting close enough to support life. Our sun is a class G star. More than half of these are binary or multiple systems which would again not provide a stable climate for earth. Essentially, all of the stars we know the most about in the universe are smaller, cooler, dimmer, unstable, or part of a binary system.

Our sun is amazingly stable. For example, EV Larcertae is a red dwarf that has 1% of the sun's light output, but it had a mega-flare 1,000 times brighter than the sun. If earth were near this red dwarf, our atmosphere would have been stripped off and everything fried because of these flares. Scientists are beginning to observe that super-flares on typical stars happen once every century. These scientists question why our sun hasn't experienced super-flares in all of recorded history. Our sun is quiet, calm, and stable. One 30 year study found the sun's energy varied only .06%. Our sun is no ordinary star but; it is perfectly designed to sustain life on earth. This is no accident.

From the rising of the sun unto the going down of the same the Lord's name is to be praised.
~ Psalm 113:3

May 7

Biology

Did you know that one species of ants herds aphids? These dairy ants protect aphids in order to "milk" them for food. A common type of dairy ant is the cornfield ant. Before winter arrives, these ants collect corn-root aphid eggs and store them in their tunnels. In the spring, these aphid eggs hatch, and the ants herd the young aphids to the roots of young wild plants while they wait for the field's corn seeds to germinate. Once the corn germinates, the ants herd the aphids to the corn roots, so the aphids can feed on them. If the weather is bad, the ants carry the aphids underground for protection. When an ant wants a drink, she will stroke the aphid with her antennae causing a sweet liquid called honeydew to be secreted from the aphid. The ant is "milking" the aphid. **The aphids benefit by being protected by the ants, and the ants benefit by receiving honeydew from the aphids.** Both ant and aphid benefit from this relationship; this is called symbiosis. How did this relationship come about? They needed each other to survive. God's fingerprints are even over the tiniest creatures of His creation.

Great is the LORD, and greatly to be praised....
~ Psalm 48:1

May 8

Microbiology

We would not have chocolate if macroevolution was true.

Chocolate comes from the seeds of the cacao plant, but in order to make these seeds, the cacao flower must be pollinated by the tiny chocolate midge. This pinhead-sized "fly" is the only known insect that can work its way into the intricate cacao flower. According to evolutionary theory, flowers developed long before pollinator insects existed. Yet, **without insects to carry pollen from plant to plant, there would be no fruits, seeds, or chocolate**. Of course, insects do not know they are pollinating; the pollen just happens to stick to them as they move from flower to flower. Often it is the flower's beauty or the flower's smell that attracts the insects.

Evolutionists theorize that flowers started out drab and had no fragrances. Apparently, these early, boring plants studied the surrounding insects and then engineered their flowers to attract the insect in order for pollination to take place. Does this make sense? How did they get pollinated before the insects appeared? This "theory" simply cannot be true!

Flowers would need to be pollinated from the very beginning - if not, they would most likely go extinct. **Flowers were designed with beauty and fragrance from the beginning** to attract pollinators. Just as God's Word says, He made flowers, which are plants, on day 3 of creation week and pollinators (flying creatures such as insects) on day 4.

Chocolate testifies to a Creator - not to evolution.

And God said, Behold, I have given you every herb bearing seed, which is upon the face of all the earth, and every tree, in the which is the fruit of a tree yielding seed; to you it shall be for meat. ~ Genesis 1:29

Design

May 9

Imagine a box. How did it come about? Evolution? Let's examine this possibility.

Billions of years ago, there was a tree that fell down into water. The tree became very mushy. Many animals walked through this water stirring up the shredded tree and water. Later, the water dried up leaving a mat of shredded "paper." The wind soon picked up this paper and folded it into corrugated cardboard - each dip and ridge was nicely lined up. Then the wind folded the corrugated paper into a four-sided box with a top and bottom. Of course, glue was needed, so it came flying through the air at the right moment and hit the right parts of the box to glue it together. As time passed, black paint fell from the sky and formed the word "Amazon" on the side of the box. Is this true? Of course not! We know when we see a box, there must be a box maker.

In the same way, the ear has many parts. Sound enters through the eardrum - a tough, tightly-stretched membrane. The airwaves move the surface of the eardrum like a beating drum. The sound is transferred to three tiny bones; the anvil, hammer, and stirrup. These tiny bones amplify the sound 22 times, and they pass the amplified sound into the inner ear via an oval window. In the inner ear is the cochlea, whose twisting exterior looks like a snail shell. In this twisting, fluid-filled cavern are thousands of microscopic hair-like nerve cells, each tuned to a particular vibration. If a middle C has been sounded, then the cochlear middle C hair cells vibrate. These vibrations then make a wisp of electricity that feeds into an auditory nerve that leads to the brain where the electric signal is interpreted as a sound. **The ear is FAR more complex than a box!**

Each part of the ear had to be in its proper place and fully functioning - right from the beginning in order for us to hear. A hearing ear could not happen by chance, just like a box could not happen by accident. When we see an ear, we know there must be an ear-Maker, and that ear-Maker is God.

The hearing ear, and the seeing eye,
the Lord hath made even both of them.
- Proverbs 20:12

May 10 — Biology

Sponges are peculiar animals. They have no heart, lungs, stomach, or nerves. They are like a hollow sac with a large opening opposite its base. They are filter feeders. Most sponges eat tiny, floating particles and plankton, which they filter through their pores. Cleaner water is released out of the top of the sponge. Sponges act as super-filters cleaning the ocean of its bacteria, algae, filth, and debris. A full-grown sponge can filter the equivalent of a bathtub full of water in only one hour!

Evolutionary biologists like to refer to the 4,000 species of sponges as "simple animals." But is this really a simple animal? An experiment was done in which the sponge tissue was pressed through a fine mesh; this broke the sponge into individual cells. Amazingly, **the sponge cells rejoined, forming a whole sponge!** Don't try this with the cells of your body – you won't come back together like this "simple" creature!

You can even make a "mixed sponge smoothie", blending together the cells of different species of sponges. Each cell, from each species, will find similar cells and reconnect! Simple? Hardly! Creative ingenuity by the Creator, yes!

Remember his marvellous works that he hath done;...
~ Psalm 105:5

May 11
Biblical Accuracy

Did you know that pterosaurs are mentioned in the Bible? Not by the modern scientific name but as *"fiery flying serpents"* (Isaiah 14:29, 30:6). Also in Numbers 21, as the Israelites wandered in the wilderness, they encountered "fiery serpents" (21:6, 8). **Some modern commentators suggest these were venomous snakes**. The Hebrew words used to describe them, however, include the verb, *uph*, which means to fly or flutter, that is "flying serpent". These creatures most likely were pterosaurs with venomous bites and brilliant scales that appeared "fiery".

Notice in Numbers 21:9 and John 3:14, this creature was put on a pole. At this time, because of their disobedience, the people of Israel were plagued with poisonous flying serpents. God told Moses to have the people raise a symbol of this serpent up on a pole in the midst of the camp in order to protect them. But neither the Old nor New Testaments, in their original language, use the word "snake" to describe what is being put on the pole. The poisonous reptiles that attacked and killed the Israelites flew. Today's translations assume these creatures were venomous snakes, but why could the people not have escaped from slithering snakes? Also, a snake, from Genesis to Revelation, has been used as a symbol of Satan. Why would people look to a symbol of Satan to be saved? A much better explanation would be the now extinct pterosaur being hoisted up a pole with its wings spread out. **This would have formed the shape of a cross!** This was a foreshadowing of the final salvation coming to mankind - Jesus Christ dying on a cross.

And as Moses lifted up the serpent in the wilderness, even so must the Son of man be lifted up.
~ John 3:14

May 12
Paleontology

Carbon -14 (^{14}C) dating **can only be done on the tissue of something that used to be alive**. All plants and animals contain carbon, including some ^{14}C. As they continue to live, carbon is added to their tissues. After they die, no more carbon is added; the unstable ^{14}C begins to decay to nitrogen-14. To determine the age of a sample, scientists measure the amount of carbon-14 left. Scientists have found that ^{14}C has a half-life of about 6,000 years (5,720). So after 6,000 years only ½ of the original carbon-14 would be left. After another 6,000 years ¼ would be left and so on.

Since the ^{14}C keeps decaying, after about 18 divisions (representing a supposed 100,000 years), there is not enough left for a mass spectrometer machine to measure. After about 40 divisions (representing about 220,000 years), there should not be a single atom of ^{14}C left. For years, Bible-believing scientists have been radiocarbon dating (^{14}C) materials found at various levels in the geological rock layers. Evolution-believing scientists never bother to radiocarbon date artifacts found in rock layers because they have been conditioned to believe in evolution, and evolution requires these rocks to be millions of years old. Therefore, in their minds, it is impossible to find any ^{14}C within any creature found in these "millions-of-year-old" rock layers.

Yet, **fossils found within the rock layers still have LOTS of ^{14}C**. And the amount of ^{14}C left in the samples always seems to fall within the same range - 5% to 12% of modern levels. This same 5-12% level is found regardless of where the sample came from in the rock layers. Thus the very earliest forms of life in the rock layers (assumed to be 500 million years old) have essentially the same amount of radiocarbon as fossils found in upper rock layers (assumed to be 5 million years old). **This means ALL the rock layers were laid down during one event because all the life found in these rock layers is essentially the same age!**

So what do evolutionists do with such evidence? Basically, they assume the ^{14}C is just "background contamination." What the evidence of measurable levels of ^{14}C in fossils actually reveals is that these layers were laid down a short time ago and all at once. When we put on our Biblical glasses, these fossils were laid down about 4400 years ago in the Flood of Noah's time. The C^{14} level is so low because before the flood less C^{14} was produced and spread through more biomatter.

And, Thou, Lord, in the beginning hast laid the foundation of the earth; and the heavens are the works of thine hands: They shall perish; but thou remainest; and they all shall wax old as doth a garment;   ~ Hebrews 1:10-11

Biology

May 13

What animal only comes out to feed at night, lives in caves, uses sonar to navigate, has eyes like a deep-sea fish, hovers in place, and has a phenomenal sense of smell? If you guessed a bat you are wrong. It is actually a unique bird that lives in South America commonly known as the "oilbird." Oilbirds got their name from the native Indians who knocked them from their nests on the cave ledges with long poles so that they could melt down the fat in the bird to make oil for torches. While most other birds roost at night and are active during the day, the oilbird is the opposite. During the day, oilbirds roost on cave ledges, digesting the previous night's fruits and nuts.

Oilbirds navigate in total darkness by emitting clicking calls in rapid succession and listening for their return echoes. Unlike bats, which emit ultrasonic clicks that we cannot hear, oilbirds' clicks are audible. They leave the cave at night and use their echolocation system, their keen sense of smell, and incredible eyesight to find fruits and nuts. During these foraging trips, they do not perch, but hover in place to feed. The oilbird's retinal rods are stacked in three tiers, an arrangement seen only in deep-sea fish that live in total darkness. The density of this bird's rods is 1 million rods per square millimeter. This, in combination with its oversized pupils, gives the oilbird the greatest light-gathering capacity of any land animal!

What a bizarre bird: **it uses sonar like a bat, has eyes like a deep-sea fish, hovers in place like a hummingbird, and tracks smells like a bloodhound**. As with the duck-billed platypus, the oilbird has a hodgepodge of features from all over the animal kingdom with no clear evolutionary ancestry. This makes perfect sense if the entire animal kingdom has a common Designer--God--but defies any naturalistic evolutionary explanation.

*The works of the Lord are great,
sought out of all them that have pleasure therein.
~ Psalm 111:2*

May 14

History

Why do you think evolution caught on so quickly? That was the question the interviewer on public TV asked Sir Julian Huxley, the grandson of Thomas Huxley who popularized evolution during Darwin's day. Sir Julian Huxley was the president and founder of UNESCO (United Nations Educational, Scientific and Cultural Organization). During his lifetime, he was the world's "**ambassador for evolution.**"

What was the reason so many scientists in the 1800s accepted the unprovable assumptions of evolution - lock, stock, and barrel? Was it that Charles Darwin had superb evidences that proved the fact of evolution? Was evolution of bacteria to people proven beyond any doubt by reproducible experimentation? Did the fossil record prove evolution? Had animals been seen changing from one type into a completely different body structure? **No, none of this had ever happened.**

So, why was evolution accepted so rapidly? According to Sir Julian Huxley, "*[I suppose the reason] we all jumped at **Origins** was because the idea of God interfered with our sexual mores.*" **It wasn't scientific evidence that caused people to accept evolution but their desire to justify sexual immorality!** When evolution replaces God, then everything is permissible.

For the word of God is living and powerful, and sharper than any two-edged sword, piercing even to the division of soul and spirit, and of joints and marrow, and is a discerner of the thoughts and intents of the heart. ~ Hebrews 4:12

Biology

May 15

Earthworms help plants by plowing, aerating, and fertilizing the soil. Earthworms dig burrows that help channel water and air throughout the soil. They drag plant matter (such as old leaves and grass) down into their burrows, which they eat along with huge amounts of soil. It has been estimated that 90% of the fallen leaves in an orchard are ultimately dragged underground by earthworms! The food is then digested, and the remains "cast" onto the surface of the ground in small balls. These worm castings are high in nitrogen that is vital for plant growth. **An acre of land can contain as many as three million earthworms aerating and fertilizing the soil!** Our home sits on a 3 acre lot. That means there are more worms on our little plot of land than the population of New York City (estimated at 8.4 million people).

It has been estimated that every 300 - 400 years, every particle of soil on the top 16 inches of the earth's surface has passed through an earthworm's gut! How does evolution explain these tireless tillers? Did some earthworm just decide to start eating dirt one day in order to recycle plant material with tons of dirt and thereby provide nitrogen needed for plants? Hardly. God, the Grand Designer, knew that for us to exist on earth, we needed plants. So, God created these little creatures to plow, aerate, and fertilize the soil.

*O give thanks unto the Lord; for he is good:
because his mercy endureth forever.
~ Psalm 118:1*

May 16

Christian Truth

Few people in history have suffered as dramatically as Job. In a brief period of time, he lost his enormous wealth, his stature/fame/prestige, and every one of his ten children, and he was covered with excruciatingly painful boils - causing him continuous, unstoppable agony. His only momentary relief was to scrape his skin with a piece of broken pottery so hard that his entire body became a raw, oozing sore. His closest friends could not even recognize him, and his wife's only advice was to, "*Curse God and die!*" (Job 2:9). Yet in the face of such monumental suffering, Job correctly acknowledges this reality: "*Shall we accept good from God, and not trouble?*"(Job 2:10 NIV).

How a loving God can allow human suffering has been a central question throughout the ages – especially when we are the ones in anguish. Every human being stands sinful before God, and we deserve death for our rebellion. Yet, God **took the penalty of death upon Himself in an act of unconditional, sacrificial love**. While God sees the big picture and what the future holds, we constantly turn from Him in self-centered desires. **Physical death exists as the only possible door for believers to come back into fellowship with God**. But how could we die if disease and sickness did not exist? How could we help and empathize with others if nothing "bad" ever happened to us? How could we truly appreciate the blessings of God if we never experience the removal of these blessings? God understands suffering and knows what is best for us. It is through the tough times that we draw closest to him.

Job repeatedly acknowledged that God was both aware of his pain and was allowing him to experience it. In a classic and prophetic statement, Job declared, "*I know that my redeemer lives*." (Job 19:25 NKJ). Yet, Job cried out for an explanation of why he was going through such anguish. In the end, God did answer this question. Throughout four chapters of Scripture, in the longest recorded monolog from God to mankind, God explains His majesty, power, understanding and control over all things to Job and each one of us. Jesus Himself stated as fact, "*In this world you will have trouble*." (John 16:33 NIV) When you are suffering, concentrate on the height of God's majesty - not the depth of your sorrows.

These things I have spoken unto you, that in me ye might have peace. In the world ye shall have tribulation: but be of good cheer; I have overcome the world. ~ John 16:33

Botany

May 17

Did you know vanilla comes from an orchid, the *vanilla planifolia* plant? This orchid grows up trees as a vine. Unlike most orchids, this one blooms only one morning each year and only for a few hours and then it wilts. While it is blooming, it needs to be pollinated, otherwise no vanilla bean will develop. God has created this plant to be pollinated by a small flea-sized bee called the Mexican Melipona bee. It is the only insect capable of pollinating this orchid.

After landing on the flower, the bee lifts up the hood, collects the pollen and flies to another vanilla orchid. Once pollinated, a vanilla bean will be produced. Hernan Cortes, the Spanish conquistador who caused the fall of the Aztecs in Mexico, loved vanilla and brought back the vanilla orchid to Europe. For 300 years, Europeans grew the plant from cuttings, but no vanilla beans were produced! Then in 1836, a Frenchman went to Mexico and sat and watched the vanilla orchid. He heard the buzzing sound of the Mexican Melipona bee as it pollinated the orchid. **The secret to vanilla beans was discovered!** This bee knew how to lift the hood and go in; no other insect can do this! This bee is made for this orchid, and this orchid is made for this bee. They were made for each other. How do evolutionists explain this? If it did not work the first time, the first generation of the vanilla plants would have become extinct. So as you enjoy that delicious vanilla ice cream, thank God for a little bee and a vanilla orchid.

Sing unto the Lord; for he hath done excellent things: this is known in all the earth.
~ Isaiah 12:5

May 18 — Biology

The oceans are full of amazing creatures, but none are masters of disguise like the cuttlefish. This creature has been coined "The King of Camouflage." It can distort its body into 40 different body shapes mimicking everything from a starfish to a squid; change its skin texture to mimic its background like corals, kelps or rocks; display a dizzying array of motions from swaying seaweed to swimming fish; change colors across the spectrum from red to blue to yellow; and flash zebra-like patterns across its body. And all of these colors, textures, shapes, and patterns can be changed within seconds!

One scientist studying the cuttlefish was amazed as he watched each cuttlefish transform into a "tailor-made camouflage pattern" for a particular microhabitat. Two identical cuttlefish settled to the ocean bottom. One instantly took on the coloration and texture of sand and disappeared into the background. The other was only ten feet away where algae covered the ocean bottom, and it took on the coloration and texture of algae. Each of these two cuttlefish "tailor-made" its camouflage pattern.

How are cuttlefish able to do this when they cannot even see their skin? In fact, scientists believe cuttlefish are even colorblind, only seeing the color green! The scientist was right in calling these cuttlefish "tailor-made"; they were tailor-made by the great Tailor, God Himself!

The Lord reigneth; let the earth rejoice; let the multitude of isles be glad thereof.
~ Psalm 97:1

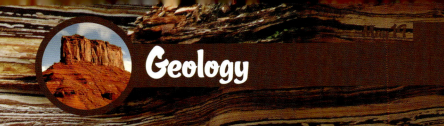

Geology

Sedimentary rock covers almost 75% of the earth's surface. Have you ever wondered how sedimentary rock layers were made? Let's find out. Fill a pint jar with ¼ cup pebbles, ¼ cup of white sand (easier to see with white sand but any sand will do) and ¼ cup of ground-up kitty litter with no additives (kitty litter is bentonite clay). Add water until almost full. Place lid on the jar and shake vigorously to mix. Let the jar stand until all the materials are settled and the water becomes somewhat clear. You should see some results of layering in 15 minutes. It will take several hours for the water to become clear (clay particles settle slowly). **Moving water has the ability to separate sediments into layers.**

During the Flood of Noah's day, rocks were ground up in the cataclysmic flood, then transported and laid down. Evolutionists believe that sedimentary layers took millions of years to form, but with your "flood jar," we observe layers being formed quickly. **Sedimentary rock layers are not a monument to time; the rock layers are a monument to the Genesis Flood.**

And he answered and said unto them, I tell you that, if these should hold their peace, the stones would immediately cry out.
~ Luke 19:40

May 20

Design

God has put many design features into our world. For example, the earth has a built-in thermostat to help keep the earth's temperature moderated. When an ocean warms, it causes the amount of water vapor entering the air to increase. If the heating continues, the water vapor will be forced higher into the atmosphere and form icy cirrus clouds. These clouds then reflect the incoming sunlight that decreases the temperature on earth. **God uses the clouds as a built-in thermostat.** Do we say a thermostat happened by accident and chance? Evolution is based on random changes over time (accident and chance). Why would anyone believe that God's "cloud thermostat" happened by accident and chance?

Also by watering he wearieth the thick cloud: he scattereth his bright cloud: And it is turned round about by his counsels: that they may do whatsoever he commandeth them upon the face of the world in the earth.
~ Job 37:11-12

Biology

May 21

The size and variety of cats are simply astounding. Yet few people looking at the amazing variety of the cat family--from lions to leopards and panthers to Persians--realize that they are extremely closely related. If it were not for the size differential, all cats could interbreed. Biologists classify different cats (such as lions/tigers, jaguars/cheetahs, margays/ocelots, bobcats/lynxes, and domestic cats) as distinctly different species. Sometimes they are even placed into different biological families because they do not naturally interbreed, live in different environments, and are of vastly different sizes. Yet a 6-pound domestic cat can breed a 15-pound margay; a 15-pound margay can produce offspring with a 30-pound ocelot; a 30-pound ocelot can be crossed with a 80-pound puma, which has been shown to be fertile with a 120-pound leopard, which has been bred with a 250-pound lion, which can produce a striped "liger" when bred with a massive 400-pound tiger.[1] Thus, the entire cat family, from one end to the other, is so inner-fertile that the various breeds and families can interbreed. Contrast that with humans and our supposedly "closely-related ancestors." **Scientists have spent years trying to cross-breed humans with apes, chimpanzees, and gorillas,** but the gulf is so vast that nothing has ever resulted - because mankind is not related to such animals.

So, how did such vastly different-looking cats originate? God placed all of the information needed to create the enormous variety of cats within an original "cat-type creature." He then created a process we call "speciation," which allows variations of offspring to mate in order to fill different environments in which they live. **Biologists have shown that it takes as few as 10 generations for a completely new species to develop!**[2]

God used Noah to preserve all the variety of animal life we find on the earth today. Noah did not need to bring dozens of different kinds of cats upon the ark but only two that had the broad variety of information upon their DNA code to speciate into the variety of cats we see in the world today. And only God would have known which cat had the correct coding. Thus it was God, not Noah, who selected the animals to be taken on the ark!

> Of clean beasts, and of beasts that are not clean, and of fowls, and of every thing that creepeth upon the earth, there went in two and two unto Noah into the ark, the male and the female, as God had commanded Noah. ~ Genesis 7:8-9

May 22

Biblical Accuracy

What is the smallest seed? The vanilla orchid seed is microscopic in size and to date is acknowledged as the smallest seed. **So was Jesus wrong** when he stated that the mustard seed was the smallest of all seeds?

Let's look at the context. Matthew 13:31-32 (NKJ) says, "Another parable He put forth to them, saying: '*The kingdom of heaven is like a mustard seed*, **which a man took and sowed** *in his field, which indeed is the least of all the seeds.*'" The mustard seed was cultivated during this time. So the mustard seed was spoken of in comparison to other seeds that were sown by the farmers. "*It is like a mustard seed which,* **when it is sown on the ground**, *is smaller than all the seeds on earth*" (Mark 4:31 NKJ). Of the common seeds that are planted by farmers, the mustard seed is indeed the smallest. The Bible is not full of contradictions and falsehoods. Upon closer inspection all questions about its accuracy have clear answers. God inspired the Bible. Biblical truth always remains!

If ye have faith as a grain of mustard seed....
~ Matthew 17:20

May 23

Biology

The Bristle-thighed curlew is an amazing bird! When the Alaskan-born chicks are just five weeks old, the parents abandon them and migrate to the South Pacific. For the next few weeks, the chicks go on a feeding frenzy, fattening themselves for the same 5000 mile journey. The young birds are on their own to find the tiny islands of Fiji in the vast Pacific Ocean. They travel non-stop without a guide and arrive with pinpoint accuracy to the same mudflats and sandy beaches where their parents have flown. Unlike seabirds that can stop, rest, and feed along the way, curlews will drown if they land on the ocean. The 5000 mile trip is all or nothing.

How do you explain a curlew's ability to navigate, untaught, to the opposite hemisphere some 5000 miles across the Pacific, flying non-stop, and landing with pin point accuracy at their winter home? **Evolution implies that all this happened by accident and chance.** What are the odds? Navigation over vast distances does not happen by accident and chance! The Creator coded within the curlew the route to take. When there is a code, there must be a code-maker, and that code-maker is the Creator God.

The Lord is good to all: and his tender mercies are over all his works.
~ Psalm 145:9

May 24

Microbiology

Certain bacteria love to live in the mud, but they do not like oxygen. So, they need to know which way is down, that is, away from oxygen found in higher concentrations nearer to the surface of the mud. Large creatures use gravity to know which way is down, but bacteria are microscopic and do not have any apparatus to sense direction of gravity's pull.

A graduate student studying these mud-loving bacteria noticed that they would congregate on the north side of the microscope's slide. So, he placed a bar magnet on the opposite side of the slide, overriding earth's magnetic field. Sure enough, the bacteria swam to the other side, thinking it was north. In the northern hemisphere, the further north one goes, the more a compass needle dips toward the center of the earth; at the North Pole, the needle dips straight down. If a bacteria had an internal magnetic compass, it would not only guide itself north, but it would have the ability to sense which direction was down and away from oxygen within a mud layer.

Upon further investigation, each bacterium was found to have molecular sized particles of magnetized iron (magnetite or lodestone), arranged in a line along the axis of the cell. Each piece of magnetite was roughly cubic and only about 50 nanometers (or one millionth of a millimeter) on each side. Mankind has never been able to make magnetite particles this small! Since that first discovery of bacteria having a built-in compass, dozens of varieties have been found displaying this same magnetic response. Bacteria with compasses; Jesus loves to surprise us with His creativity!

The north and the south thou hast created them....
~ Psalm 89:12

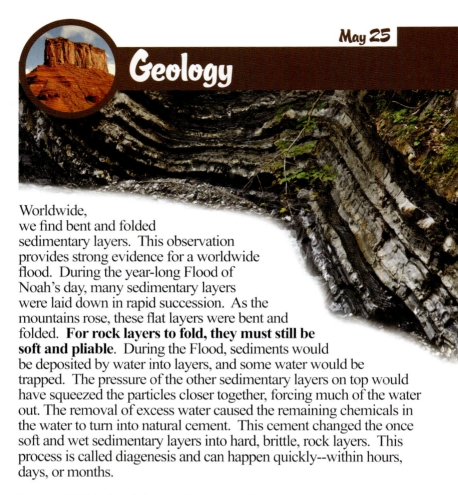

Geology

May 25

Worldwide, we find bent and folded sedimentary layers. This observation provides strong evidence for a worldwide flood. During the year-long Flood of Noah's day, many sedimentary layers were laid down in rapid succession. As the mountains rose, these flat layers were bent and folded. **For rock layers to fold, they must still be soft and pliable**. During the Flood, sediments would be deposited by water into layers, and some water would be trapped. The pressure of the other sedimentary layers on top would have squeezed the particles closer together, forcing much of the water out. The removal of excess water caused the remaining chemicals in the water to turn into natural cement. This cement changed the once soft and wet sedimentary layers into hard, brittle, rock layers. This process is called diagenesis and can happen quickly--within hours, days, or months.

Bent and folded rock layers show that all the bending and folding had to happen when the layers were still soft and pliable, in order to be folded without fracturing. Conventional thinking assumes heat and pressure could have caused these bent and folded layers; however, we do not find metamorphic rocks that would have resulted had high pressure and heat been involved. Bent and folded sedimentary layers are very common in mountainous regions and show us that these layers were laid down in rapid succession during the Flood of Noah's day, not over millions of years.

They go up by the mountains; they go down by the valleys unto the place which thou hast founded for them.
~ Psalm 104:8

May 26

Paleontology

Textbooks, TV programs, and museums place distinct 12 geological rock strata in a vertical order and name this sequence, "the geological column." In this geologic column, the rock layers or strata form a sequence from top to bottom. Yet, the complete geological column is not found at any location on earth, it is only found in diagrams!

Before the 1800s, the sequence of different rock layers (and fossils found within these rocks) were known, but **the general order was acknowledged to exist as a result of these rock layers being formed during the year-long Flood of Noah's time**. First buried were the sea creatures and later, as the flood waters increased, land creatures were buried. The geologic column was the order of what was caught in the Flood. During the late 1800s, evolution became popular, so the meaning of the geological column changed. It now was a tool for promoting the evolution of life - from bacteria to people, over millions of years. But what do we find in the fossil record of this geological column?

Near the very bottom of the geological column is the Cambrian layer. In the Cambrian layer, we find fossil remains of complex creatures from most of the major animal groups. In fact, we find representatives of every major animal phylum both alive today and those that are now extinct. This *explosion of complex life* is called the "Cambrian Explosion." The Cambrian Explosion is actually explosive evidence against slow and gradual evolution! When we study the facts, we find God's word is true. The Bible states in clear straightforward terms that God created all plants and animals on earth in six literal days. Over a thousand years later, the Flood of Noah took place, leaving behind the fossil evidence. The "Cambrian Explosion" testifies to the accuracy of Scripture.

For in six days the Lord made heaven and earth, the sea, and all that in them is, and rested the seventh day: wherefore the Lord blessed the sabbath day, and hallowed it. ~ Exodus 20:11

Biology

May 27

The beaver is uniquely designed for a semi-aquatic life. It has special valves in its nose and ears that close automatically when underwater. To see well underwater, **it has transparent eyelids that act like swimming goggles**. When a branch-carrying beaver is swimming, how does it not choke on water going down its mouth? Behind its front teeth are two flaps of skin that close tightly to prevent water from entering the beaver's throat. **Its tail is used as a rudder** when swimming or a balance support when standing upright. Its tail also radiates heat when its body is too warm. The rear feet are webbed like a duck's - for good swimming-while the front feet are unwebbed, so it can dig canals and carry branches. To keep itself from hypothermia the fur is richly oiled by two oil glands which the beaver spreads on its fur; **water rarely touches its skin**. Fat below the skin further protects it from the cold. And, of course, beavers are known for their teeth and the ability to gnaw trees down and eat them. For this, **they have continually growing incisors**. Beavers just have to gnaw!

All of these beaver features had to be present and fully functioning from the beginning in order to survive. What if their teeth never grew after gnawing on trees? They would be ground down, and the beaver could not survive. What if the mouth flaps were not present? Water would flood their throat, choking them. Imagine digging canals with webbed front feet or swimming with no webbed back feet. The beaver is a showcase of God's creativity.

Remember now thy Creator in the days of thy youth...
~ Ecclesiastes 12:1

May 28

Biology

Did you ever wonder how perching birds can sleep on branches without falling off? God has given them a special toe-locking device! In each leg is a tendon that is attached to the underside of the toes, stretching up the leg to the back of the "ankle," and attaching to the leg muscle. When the bird relaxes, it bends its "ankle" which pulls on the tendon and causes the toes to curl more tightly. The more the bird relaxes the more it bends, and the more it curls its toes. The tendon even has hundreds of ratchet-like projections that mesh with the grooves in the tendon sheath. **It is virtually impossible for a bird to fall off a perch while sleeping**. As the bird stands up, the tendon is relaxed, and the feet are released.

Evolutionists would have us believe that this special toe-locking device happened by accidental changes over millions of years. If the tendon was present without the ratchet-like projections, how would the tendon stay taunt? And what about the ratchet-like projections, they require a complimentary groove for them to function properly? These parts had to be present from the beginning. Our Creator cares even for the way a bird perches.

The kingdom of heaven is like to a grain of mustard seed, which a man took, and sowed in his field: Which indeed is the least of all seeds: but when it is grown, it is the greatest among herbs, and becometh a tree, so that the birds of the air come and lodge in the branches thereof.
~ Matthew 13:31-32

Biology

May 29

In the shallow waters of Africa lives the Black Heron, which has an incredibly creative way of catching its food. Sunlight can cause a harsh glare on the surface of water, making it nearly impossible for the Black Heron to see into the water and find fish. In addition, fish tend to avoid the bright sunshine at the water's surface. So, what does a Black Heron (also known as the "umbrella bird") do?

As he slowly wades through the shallow waters, **he spreads his wings, forming a dome-shaped black umbrella over the water**. Then, he crouches down until the wings almost touch the water's surface. The fish think this darkened area is a good place to hide, just like under a lily pad. But in the case of the Black Heron, it is actually a trap for these little fish. As soon as an unsuspecting fish swims over into the shade, the umbrella bird pokes his head into the water and comes out with a squirming fish. Ask any fisherman which part of the lake he gets the best catches and he will say, "The shady part." How did the umbrella bird learn to hunt in this way? Evolutionists call this "canopy feeding," but just because they name it doesn't mean they understand it. As Bible-believers, we do; God created the umbrella bird to fish in such a manner.

And blessed be his glorious name for ever: and let the whole earth be filled with his glory; Amen, and Amen.
~ Psalm 72:19

May 30

Paleontology

In modern-day Cambodia stands the ancient temples of Angkor, which were built in the 12th century. These temple buildings are decorated with thousands of animal images carved into the stone. Hundreds of these decorations are circular reliefs with a central animal. Many of these carved animal images are familiar - such as deer, water buffalo, monkeys, parrots, swans, and lizards. In every image, the representation is of a real creature that the artist has seen. In one of those decorative stone circles is the carving of a stegosaurus.

A stegosaurus is a dinosaur that looks like a heavily armored tank with spikes on its tail and large plates along its spine. Evolutionists say that dinosaurs became extinct over 65 million years ago. If this really were the truth, no human being could ever have seen a stegosaurus. Yet, here we see one carved on a temple dating about 900 years ago. If school children were shown a picture of this carving, they would instantly recognize it as a stegosaurus. On page 213 of his book *Angkor, Cities and Temples*, Claude Jacques describes this carving as *"an animal which bears a striking resemblance to a stegosaurus."* What does this mean? The relief carver had to have seen a stegosaurus. This should not surprise us for we were both made on the same day of creation week, Day 6. **Dinosaurs and man did live together, and ancient man recorded it in his artwork**. Dinosaurs today seem to have finally gone extinct, just like the dodo bird and the passenger pigeon, but only 900 years ago, there is evidence to support the reality that at least a few were still around.

Behold now behemoth, which I made with thee....
~ Job 40:15

May 31

Cosmology

The universe is filled with indications of great age, yet God's Word tells us, *"In six days the Lord made THE HEAVENS and the earth...."* (Exodus 20:11 emphasis added). Star deterioration, supernovas, and colossal distances all seem to testify to an extremely old universe. So how could God have made the entire universe quite recently in only "six days"?

When the Bible states:*"In six days..."*, we have to know **at what location** these "six days" of time occurred. Since the earth's rotation is the measure of a "day"--and the earth is the central focus of the biblical account of history--it seems rather straightforward that six literal earth days, measured at the earth's location within space, is the measure of time in which the universe was created. Yet, time moves at different rates depending on the location where the passage of time is occurring. **It has been found that a clock at sea-level runs a tiny fraction of a percent slower than a clock on top of a mountain.** A brilliant Bible-believing physicist, Dr. Russell Humphreys, has proven that millions of years could have passed further out in space while only six days were passing on the earth![1]

As the very fabric of space was being stretched out, time in some areas would have literally stopped. Meanwhile, millions and even billions of years could have been passing only slightly further out. Near the center of the universe, time essentially stood still in comparison to areas outside of an event boundary. Thus on "day four", when the stars were made, there would have been a massive increase in the mass of the universe, and literally billions of years could have passed outside of our solar system (as the stars of the universe were being created and aging), while only a literal day was passing here on earth.[2,3] **This is called time dilation.** This is not deceptive on the part of God - just the mathematical consequence of making and stretching out the universe.

We have to remember God's Word is true; He created in six days about 6,000 years ago (according to the genealogical biblical records). How He did it is difficult to understand. God delights in showing us His power through the things He has made.

It is he... that stretcheth out the heavens as a curtain,
and spreadeth them out as a tent to dwell in.

~ Isaiah 40:22

"If the world hate you, ye know that
it hated me before it hated you,"
– John 15:18

"You have enemies? Good! That means you've
stood up for something, sometime in your life."
– Winston Churchill (1874-1965), Prime Minister
of Great Britain during World War II

Anatomy

June 1

What do the Eiffel Tower and the thigh bone have in common? The 1889 World's Fair was coming up, and Mr. Eiffel wanted to win the architect's contest by designing the most daring structure. The winning design would commemorate this great event.

Gustave Eiffel went to an unusual source for his design idea: the human thigh bone. The thigh bone connects to the hip and extends sideways, causing the body's weight to be moved off-center. When the thigh bone's head was examined internally, it was found to have beautifully curving lines from the head, while other bone fibers crossed over it. This bony crisscross pattern is like a diagram showing the lines of stress within the loaded structure. In other words, the thigh bone was strengthened in exactly the manner and direction in which the strength was required.

Mr. Eiffel simply copied the thigh bone structure using wrought-iron in place of bone and designed the now famous, flared tower. Even though Mr. Eiffel won the contest, the competing architects scoffed and predicted the tower would collapse under its own weight. It still stands today, a century later. But of course it would; Mr. Eiffel just copied what has been allowing us to stand all these years, our thigh bone. Maybe we should rename this famous structure the "Thigh Tower" ... or better yet – "God's Tower". After all, the Eiffel Tower is really His design.

Thine hands have made me and fashioned me together round about
~ Job 10:8

June 2 — Biology

Prairie dogs are not dogs, but they are rodents classified with the squirrel family. They live in underground tunnels and chambers that create entire "towns" housing hundreds of prairie dogs on the plains of North America. Their underground tunnels contain multiple rooms - including bedrooms, nurseries, and bathrooms. These burrows even include a "listening room" close to the entrance, where the prairie dog listens for danger before going outside. One would think that the air would become stale in these underground burrows, however, the entire complex is nicely ventilated.

Each home has at least two openings. Prairie dogs surround these two holes with piles of dirt but always make one mound taller than the other mound. When a breeze blows across the top of these mounds, a pressure differential occurs, causing air to be aspirated up, creating a partial vacuum in the tunnels, and thereby drawing air into the lower opening. **These prairie dogs have engineered a passive ventilation system that uses the Bernoulli principle!** God created these animals with the instinct to build one mound higher than the other. This creates a draft or chimney effect that draws fresh air into the tunnel and allows it to circulate throughout. In essence, during the summer, the prairie dog town is "air conditioned." When the above ground temperature exceeds 100°F, the burrow temperature one foot below is a comfortable 55°F. During the winter, the snow covers the "chimney", not allowing the cold air to enter the tunnels. How does evolution explain this engineering ability? God gave the engineering instinct to these creatures, so they can survive extreme weather conditions found on the northern Great Plains.

To him who alone doeth great wonders....
~ Psalm 136:4

Geology

June 3

Scientists believe they have discovered three times more water deep within the Earth's mantle than in all the oceans of the world. But before you grab your bathing suit and surfboard and book a trip to where the Sun doesn't shine, consider that this vast reservoir of water is located 420 miles below the earth's surface (50 times lower than the deepest oil well). It is also locked up as hydrated molecules within the Earth's magma and rock crystal structure.[1]

What makes this discovery so significant is the fact that scientists cannot even explain where all the water that fills our current oceans came from, let alone more water locked deep within the Earth. This water is a total mystery to scientists studying the Earth from an evolutionary, old-age perspective. All naturalistic models for the Earth's formation require enormous amounts of heat as materials slowly coalesced to form our planet - billions of years ago. **These processes would have driven water out of the Earth's core and left little on the surface**. So, speculation has proposed that our oceans came from vast numbers of comets hitting the Earth and depositing their water. This also does not work because water contained in comets has been shown to have a very different composition of isotopes than water found on Earth.[2]

The Bible states that the Earth was recently created "out of water" (2 Peter 3:5 NKJV) and made for mankind's benefit (Psalm 115:16). Finding oceans filled with water (and even more water deep below the surface) is neither surprising nor a mystery.

Towards the end of the Flood of Noah's day, the mountains rose up, and the waters rushed off the continents into the oceans. This is where the waters that flooded the Earth now reside. Much of this water may have originally come from sources deep within the Earth when "*all the fountains of the great deep were broken up*" (Genesis 7:11 NKJV) approximately 4,350 years ago.

For this they willingly are ignorant of, that by the word of God the heavens were of old, and the earth standing out of the water and in the water: Whereby the world that then was, being overflowed with water, perished: ~ 2 Peter 3:5-6

June 4

History

Oceans cover about 70% of our planet's surface and contain enough water that, if the Earth's surface were completely flat, the water would cover the whole planet to a depth of over 8000 feet (1.7 miles). Based on actual observation, the Earth is the only planet in the entire universe to have liquid water on its surface.

Streams, rivers, and other sources of land runoff are continually flowing into the oceans and dumping various salts and dissolved minerals into that water. Using today's rate of salt input and output, scientists estimate that the oceans could be **AT MOST 62 million years old**. This is not the actual age but a maximum age. Even if the oceans started as pure distilled water (which seems highly unlikely), the salt concentration would have reached today's level in about 62 million years. **Yet, evolutionists tell us the oceans are 3 BILLION years old**. If that were true, the oceans should be <u>FAR</u> saltier! The reason the oceans currently have "62 million years-worth of salt" could be that God created the oceans with some salt, at the beginning. Then the Genesis Flood would have very rapidly added salt. The amount of salt in the world's ocean water is strong evidence that the Earth is far younger than the billions of years required for evolution. The amount of salt is actually quite consistent with a biblical age of about 6,000 years.

Biology

June 5

When looking at a pond, have you ever noticed bugs walking on the water? These bugs move across the surface of the pond so quickly that they are almost impossible to see. What you probably saw was a water strider. **This small insect uses the surface tension of the water AND the design of its legs to walk on water**.

The water strider is designed with feet that are covered with thousands of fuzzy, wax-coated hairs. Each of these tiny hairs is also covered with even smaller grooves. The leg hair of a water strider is vastly narrower than a human hair. When wet, the microscopic grooves trap air - which allows the water strider to essentially "float" on a cushion of air across the water's surface. But a property of water called "surface tension" also comes into effect. Water molecules are attracted to each other and like to stay together. This creates surface tension that acts as a delicate membrane. **Water striders move quickly across this water membrane reaching speeds equivalent to a person moving at 400 miles per hour**.

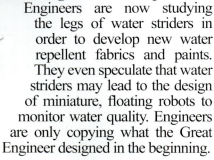

Engineers are now studying the legs of water striders in order to develop new water repellent fabrics and paints. They even speculate that water striders may lead to the design of miniature, floating robots to monitor water quality. Engineers are only copying what the Great Engineer designed in the beginning.

He hath made his wonderful works to be remembered:...
~ Psalm 111:4

June 6 — Cosmology

From the beginning of time, the night sky has caused us to look up and wonder how many stars are there. How far away are they? Early astronomers thought they were just beyond our reach up in the sky and counted about 2000 stars.

Stars are so far away that we do not measure their distance from Earth in miles but in light years. The closest star to Earth is Proxima Centauri. If you could travel at the speed of light, 186,000 miles per second, it would take 4.3 years to get there. One light year is about 6 trillion miles. Proxima Centauri is 4.3 light years or 25,278,089,104,689 miles away. It is much easier to say 4.3 light years. Our Milky Way is about 70,000 light years across or about 411,503,776,122,852,541 miles. Many stars in the universe seem to be billions of light years away. Psalm 103:11 (NKJV) tells us, *"For as the heavens are high above the earth, so great is His mercy toward those who fear Him."* The great distances to the stars help us understand God's great mercy towards us. In our natural state, we are in rebellion against God and do not deserve forgiveness. Yet in God's great mercy, He forgives the repentant sinner. How great is God's mercy? Great enough that He was willing to die to bring us back into fellowship with Him. Just as the distance to the stars seems beyond comprehension, so there is no limit to His love for us. Step outside on a starry night and gaze at the vast distances of these stars; that is the magnitude of God's mercy!

For as the heaven is high above the earth, so great is his mercy toward them that fear him.
~ Psalm 103:11

Biology

June 7

Marine iguanas are excellent swimmers and search for their food underwater. Sharks, however, love to eat marine iguanas and have sensitive hearing. They can hear the heartbeat of an iguana 12 feet away. So what's an iguana to do? **Stop its heart from beating**?

Incredibly, an iguana can stop its heart for up to 45 minutes! How do evolutionists explain this ability? A creature's ability to stop its heart requires some major internal modifications. For an iguana to stop its heart for 45 minutes without death is astonishing! Only a wise Creator would endow a marine iguana with this unbelievable ability - thereby giving glory to Himself.

Declare his glory among the heathen; his marvellous works among all nations.
~ 1 Chronicles 16:24

June 8 — Microbiology

Every microsecond, every cell in your body is converting food to usable energy in order to run the chemical processes of your body. The primary source of the cell's energy is a chemical called adenosine triphosphate (ATP). **Your body literally makes and consumes an amount of ATP equivalent to the entire weight of your body each day.** This ATP is then converted into the various chemicals and components needed to keep your body operating. So, where does all this ATP come from? Inside the mitochondria within each of our over ten trillion cells are little spinning molecular motors that operate at close to 99.99% efficiency (gasoline motors operate at about 35% efficiency.)[1] These ATP generating motors are so small that 100,000 of them would have to be lined up end to end to reach across 1 millimeter. Also, they spin at 1000 RPM while spewing out ATP molecules.

But where do these motors come from?
1. These motors are made using information coming from the DNA molecule.
2. In order to open the DNA molecule, energy from ATP is needed.
3. In order to make the ATP, the motor is needed.

The information needed to make the motors is in DNA. It takes the motor's ATP to open the DNA, but we can't make the ATP unless the information on how to make the motor is provided. Complicated isn't it! All the parts, processes, and instructions needed to be present and fully functioning from the beginning.

The more we learn about the operation of our bodies, the more we see that an incredibly intelligent Designer made every cell within our bodies.

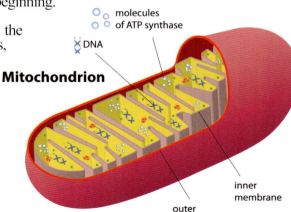

My mouth will speak in praise of the Lord, and let all flesh bless his holy name for ever and ever.
~ Psalm 145:21

Design

June 9

From peacocks to porcupines; bacteria to blue whales; raindrops to oceans - everyone in the world sees the design in nature. This is called *general revelation*. God has communicated about Himself to all persons, in all places, throughout history. He has done that through nature. When someone studies a leaf, the Moon, or the smallest cell, he sees evidence of order, design, and purpose. Who is the One who created this or that? Who is the designer? That should drive the person to find the designer.

Who is this Designer? That search leads to what is called *special revelation*, that is, the Bible. It is there, in Scripture, that a person discovers the Designer, Creator, and Redeemer of the universe. Then, the God of the Bible will tell him about how sin entered the world, how a Redeemer was sent, and how he can spend eternity with the God of the universe. Special revelation is "special" because it is the key that opens the door between Heaven and Earth. Nature (*general revelation*) is meant to be the drawing card that leads us to the God of the Bible (*special revelation*).

For the invisible things of him from the creation of the world are clearly seen, being understood by the things that are made, even his eternal power and Godhead; so that they are without excuse:
~ Romans 1:20

June 10
Biology

Have you ever thought about a spider web saving a bird? Every year, many birds are killed when they fly into window glass. Either they can't see the window glass, or they see the reflections of nearby trees, sky, and other objects - either way, they slam into the window glass and are killed. It has been found, however, that spiders that spin orb webs (spiral wheel shaped webs) use silk that reflects ultraviolet light. We can't see the UV light, as it is outside the range of human vision, but many birds and insects can see it. Biologists have discovered that the use of this UV-reflecting web material serves two important purposes:

1. It attracts insects like a neon sign; some webs even display a flower-like pattern.
2. It warns birds not to fly into the web as if to say, "I don't want to rebuild this web, so please avoid."

The Arnold Glass Corporation has copied this UV reflecting property by coating their glass with criss-crossing UV reflecting strips. This coating is invisible to humans but not to birds. Birds make every effort to avoid this UV-treated glass. **Nature is filled with design ideas, but of course, God put them there when He created the world!** His power is displayed through what He has made. Who would have thought that spider webs would lead to protecting birds!

> By the word of the LORD were the heavens made; and all the host of them by the breath of his mouth. He gathereth the waters of the sea together as an heap: he layeth up the depth in storehouses. Let all the earth fear the LORD: let all the inhabitants of the world stand in awe of him. For he spake, and it was done; he commanded, and it stood fast.
> ~ Psalm 33:6-9

June 11

Biology

Spider webs are known for their strength, but that is not the only thing needed to capture a flying insect. The web needs to be sticky, and spider webs are definitely sticky. You may have noticed this when cleaning up cobwebs – they are very difficult to remove from your hands. Spiders place tiny glue droplets, about 20 drops every 1/16 inch, along certain strands of their spider web. Their insect prey is caught by this glue. But this is no ordinary glue that just sticks things together. This glue is "smart glue."

Imagine a flying insect hitting the super-sticky web and getting glued on. The spider needs to remove the insect without getting himself stuck, but how does he do it? He waits patiently. This glue is the stickiest when the flying insect hits the web at high speed. When the insect struggles in the web at a lower speed, this glue acts like a rubber band. When the struggling insect tires and stops moving, the glue gets even less sticky - allowing the spider to pull its prey loose and retrieve its meal. **Researchers are now trying to copy this "smart glue" that has variable stickiness** according to each situation. Scientists recognize a good design when they see it. If there is a design, there must be a Designer, and that is God.

O give thanks unto the Lord; call upon his name: make known his deeds among the people.
~ Psalm 105:1

June 12
Biblical Accuracy

The continued existence of the Jewish people is one of the most amazing, fulfilled prophecies of the Bible. About 4,000 years ago, God called a man named Abram out of his country to a promised land. God promised that **a great nation of innumerable people would come from him** and changed his name to Abraham - even though he was almost 100 years old and childless. Two hundred and fifteen years later, Abraham's descendants settled in Egypt. While in Egypt, Abraham's descendants increased greatly - numbering in the millions within 500 years of Abraham's death. As they were returning to the Promised Land, Moses gave them many warnings about the consequences of being disobedient to God (see Deuteronomy chapters 28-33).

Because of their rebellion, they were again banished from their homeland in 70 A.D. The Romans destroyed the city of Jerusalem and scattered the Jewish people. For almost 1900 years, the Jews wandered the Earth. This culminated in the Holocaust of World War II. In 1948, the state of Israel was reborn, and many Jews returned to their homeland. Throughout this entire time, the Jewish people never lost their national identity. **History has shown that people who leave their homeland will lose their national identity within five generations - being absorbed into the new culture**. Have you ever heard a person say, *"I'm a Moabite, or I'm a Philistine? Ammonite? Edomite?"* These were the nations that lived around Israel. Obviously, they have not survived. Yet for the past 4000 years, people have continued to say, *"I'm Jewish"* or *"I'm an Israelite."* God is faithful to fulfill what He says!

And I will make of thee a great nation;
~ Genesis 12:2a

Paleontology

June 13

How long does it take a fossil to form? People are conditioned to think about millions of years and evolution whenever they hear the word "fossil." But is this really a valid conclusion or just storytelling?

Near York, England is the Dripping Well of Yorkshire. This place is famous for turning soft cuddly teddy bears into stone. Since the 1600's, this has been a tourist attraction where people have hung clothes, hats, shoes, and, yes, even teddy bears under a waterfall that has turned each into stone.

The waterfall's water originates underground and has an extremely high mineral content. As the water splashes onto the hanging objects, the mineral calcite (calcium carbonate) is deposited along with small amounts of other minerals. Over the months, these deposits build up and coat the object with a crust of rock. Petrifaction time depends on the size and porosity of the object. Small teddy bears turn to stone in three to five months. Larger teddy bears take six to twelve months.

This is not the only place in the world where petrifaction has been observed. Australia has its own petrified waterwheel that has become totally encased in stone in only decades, while New Zealand has a petrified bowler hat on display. It does not take millions of years for petrifaction; it just takes the right conditions.

Thou coverest it with the deep as with a garment: the waters stood above the mountains. At thy rebuke they fled; at the voice of thy thunder they hasted away.
~ Psalm 104:6,7

June 14 — Biology

How does an octopus change the color of its skin to match his surroundings in the blink of an eye? Below the top layer of protective skin, an octopus has three more layers (chromatophore layers) with thousands of tiny, balloon-like sacs filled with different pigment colors. The top layer of chromatophores has black and brown colored sacs, the middle layer has red and orange colored sacs, and the third layer has yellow colored sacs. Nerves and muscles cause the balloon-like sacs to expand and contract. When the sac expands, the color in that layer becomes more visible, and when contracted, the color becomes less visible. But the octopus camouflage system is even more complex. The fifth layer down is filled with iridophores, which are reflecting plates that give the octopus iridescent golds, silvers, blues and greens. The sixth or bottom layer contains leucophores, which mirror back colors from any surrounding environments.

Octopus skin has inspired researchers to develop a high-tech camouflage fabric. So far, the fabric can automatically shift between white and black as well as making shades of gray. One of the engineers noted that, "*…looking at moves of squid, octopuses, and cuttlefish, you just (realize) that you're not going to get close to that level of sophistication.*" This engineer knows the difficulty of making such a fabric. When man tries to copy what has already been made but cannot even come close, we must stand in awe of the original design Engineer, God, Himself!

> Let the heavens be glad, and let the earth rejoice: and let men say among the nations, The Lord reigneth. Let the sea roar, and the fulness thereof: let the fields rejoice, and all that is therein.
> ~1 Chronicles 16: 31-32

History

June 15

Have you considered that there are ancient depictions of dinosaurs in artwork from around the world? Ancient civilizations called these creatures "dragons" because the word dinosaur was not invented until 1841. In his book *Dire Dragons*, Vance Nelson documents many examples of this artwork throughout the world. These are but a few:

- On Bishop Bell's tomb (1496) in Carlisle England, there is a brass plate on the floor of the Carlisle Cathedral showing two sauropods with their necks intertwined.
- On the back of a clergy chair at St. David's Cathedral in Wales, there is a dragon which looks startlingly like a sauruopod found in Argentina known as *Brachytrachelopan mesai*.
- The Chateau Royal de Blois in France has 16th century carvings of a *Plateosaurus* dinosaur.
- Above the fireplace of the Azay-le-Rideau castle in France is a 16th century carving of a dragon that looks remarkably like modern depictions of dinosaurs. Also, a beautiful table has one of its drawers carved with a dragon/dinosaur.
- St. George's Chapel in Barcelona, Spain, "*Palau de La Generalitat*," has an altar cloth from the 1600s showing St. George slaying a dragon/dinosaur.

Artwork from Medieval Europe supports the fact that man and dinosaurs did live together.

Praise the Lord from the earth, ye dragons, and all deeps:
~ Psalm 148:7

June 16

Biology

The Texas horned toad is found all over the western United States. It has a stubby nose, horns on its head, spikes all over its body and tail. It may look dangerous to us, but it is friendly. If you are a predator, the horned toad displays a full arsenal of defensive weapons. When frightened, the horned toad first flattens itself to the ground and freezes, not moving a muscle. If a predator continues to approach, it runs with short bursts and then stops quickly - repeating as necessary. If the predator is still pursuing, it will blow itself up to be twice its size. And then there is the final trick; **the toad can shoot a stream of blood out of its eyeball up to five feet away!** He can even aim this blood stream! He can do this 2-3 times. The blood tastes nasty, so any coyote, snake, or roadrunner that wants to mess with a Texas horned toad has to be ready!

Imagine if we were to burst an artery in our eye, it would take a long time for it to heal, and it would likely leave scar tissue. Not so with the horned toad. It can shoot blood again and again without permanent harm. What if it took millions of years to develop this ability? The horned toad would have probably been eaten. No other animal can squirt blood out of its eyes. We have an imaginative Creator who is concerned for even a small, cold-blooded lizard's protection. We have a Creator that makes amazing creatures!

For the Lord is great, and greatly to be praised:....
~ Psalm 96:4

June 17

Christian Truth

Over twenty years ago, scientists first cloned a large mammal (a sheep named Dolly in 1996). **Cloning is a process where the donor's DNA is removed from the nucleus of a cell. The recipient's fertilized egg DNA is removed and replaced with the donor's DNA.** The egg is then placed within the recipient's womb. This will make an exact biological replica of the donor creature rather than the offspring being a blend of the characteristics of both the mother and father. Scientists have greatly improved their ability to clone creatures over the last twenty years, but it is still illegal in most countries to attempt to make exact replicas (i.e. clones) of ourselves. Why is this illegal, and if we could make an exact copy of ourselves, would such a person have a soul and be fully human? To answer such questions, one must consult an absolute source of truth outside of human opinion.

Let's answer the last question. There is already a model for whether exact biological duplicates of human beings will have separate souls. Identical twins come from the DNA code of one egg that divides in such a way that two biologically identical human beings result. Yet, no-one would deny that, even though their DNA is identical, they are two separate people, having two different personalities, lives, and souls. In a similar way, a human clone, should we ever be foolish enough to monkey with God's created biological machinery in order to produce one, would also have a soul and be accountable to God for his existence. Also, the process of cloning involves the killing of dozens, and sometimes thousands, of fertilized embryos in the effort to successfully produce one viable clone. This is why human cloning is and should be illegal. The entire process is a flagrant disregard for life and is the ultimate in dishonoring and ignoring our Creator - to whom all life owes its existence.

> And God said, "*Let us make man in our image, after our likeness: and let them have dominion over the fish of the sea and over the fowl of the air, and over the cattle, and over all the earth, and over every creeping thing that creepeth upon the earth.*" *So God created man in his own image, in the image of God created he him;* male and female created he them.   - Genesis **1:26, 27** emphasis added

June 18

Anatomy

In the late 1800s, after Darwin proposed his theory of life's slow evolutionary development, nearly 200 organs were considered "useless" – that is, unnecessary leftovers from our evolutionary past. The gallbladder was considered one of these "useless" leftovers. Does the gallbladder have a necessary function?

Recently, my husband had a terrible pain in his side. An ultra-sound test identified the cause of the pain to be gallstones blocking the exit duct from his gallbladder. The gallbladder is a small, pear-shaped organ on the right side just beneath the liver. This human organ stores bile, which is made in the liver. One job of the gallbladder is to release this bile, into the small intestine as needed. This bile is used for the breakdown and absorption of fatty foods. **If the gallbladder is removed, the bile oozes continually into the intestines**. If an overly fatty meal is eaten, not enough bile will be released, causing incomplete digestion - resulting in gas, bloating, and diarrhea.

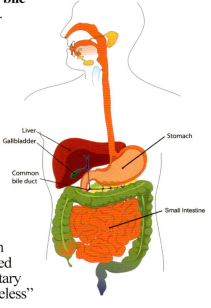

It is possible to adjust our diet such that we can function without the gallbladder, but it is far better to keep it. A person without a gallbladder needs to be a little more careful in the consumption of fatty food. But that hardly implies the organ is a worthless evolutionary leftover. Isn't it interesting how our wise Creator God knew we would have problems with our deteriorating bodies and designed them to cope with a wide variety of dietary circumstances? God doesn't make "useless" parts; the gallbladder is needed.

Know ye that the Lord he is God: it is he that hath made us,.....
~ Psalm 100:3

Botany

June 19

Why are trees round and not square? If we had a square tree, think of all the time and effort we would save when sawing them into lumber! Let's pause and think, why our Creator made trees round and not square?

1. Wood layers **grow outward** from the center in all directions.
2. Cylinders provide **maximum strength** against stresses in all directions.
3. Round trees can **bend more easily** than square-sided trees when a wind is blowing.
4. Round trees can **bend in all directions**; square trees would be more vulnerable to breaking at the corners.

The best design for trees is round; if that were not true, telephone poles and light posts would be square and not round. Sometimes, we overlook what is so common in nature, like why a tree is round. But when we stop and consider it, we see a wonderful design that gives glory to our Creator.

**All the earth shall be filled with the glory of the Lord
~ Numbers 14:21**

June 20

Biology

Have you heard of the boxer crab? **It carries around pom poms like a high school cheerleader - but its pom poms are deadly sea anemones.** The crab uses these anemones to sting small animals in order to eat them. The sea anemones then share in the meal. This is a mutually beneficial (symbiotic) relationship. The tiny boxer crab, measuring only one inch across, would be an easy lunch without the protection of the stinging sea anemones. The threat of a one-two punch from the sea anemone's "pom poms" is enough to scare most predators away. If the predator is not scared away, the stinging cells on the sea anemone's tentacles have enough poison to kill small animals - now the predator is lunch! God in His wisdom knew that boxer crabs and sea anemones would need each other and so designed this symbiotic relationship to benefit each animal.

He is wise in heart, and mighty in strength: who hath hardened himself against him, and hath prospered?
~ Job 9:4

Paleontology

June 21

The following commentary on the **fossil record** appeared in World Magazine[1]:

Darwin, while not having the benefit of cellular technology that is available to scientists today, did recognize that the fossil record posed a problem. He wrote, *"Why then is not every geological formation and every stratum full of such intermediate links? Geology assuredly does not reveal any such finely graduated organic chain, and this, perhaps, is the most obvious and gravest objection which can be raised against my theory."* [2] Unfortunately for Darwinists, the fossil record still does not support evolution, but it does fit [a biblical viewpoint].

Jonathan Wells, a biologist who holds Ph.D. degrees from both Yale University and the University of California, Berkeley, has written a book, *Icons of Evolution*, which demonstrates that **much of what is taught about evolution is wrong or even fraudulent**. Wells notes, *"Although the abrupt appearance of animal fossils in the Cambrian [period] was known to Darwin, the full extent of the phenomenon wasn't appreciated until the 1980s."* [3] He further notes, *"The fossil evidence is so strong, and the event so dramatic, that it has become known as the 'Cambrian explosion,' or 'biology's big bang.'"* [4] Thus, the fossil record does not support the theory that living things developed gradually over long periods of time, but instead appeared rather abruptly in their present form. Henry Gee, chief science writer for *Nature*, is quoted by Wells as saying, *"To take a line of fossils and claim that they represent a lineage is not a scientific hypothesis that can be tested, but an assertion that carries the same validity as a bedtime story—amusing, perhaps even instructive, but not scientific."* [5]

Beware lest any man spoil you through philosophy and vain deceit, after the tradition of men, after the rudiments of the world, and not after Christ. ~ Colossians 2:8

June 22 — Design

Golf balls made during the 1800s were made with a smooth surface. It seemed logical that the smoother the ball, the farther it flies. At some point, golfers noticed that older balls covered with nicks and grooves seemed to fly farther. By the 1930s, the standard golf ball was covered with dimples. Just as golf balls are designed with "dimples," so is shark skin.

Shark's skin is made of tough, enameled, tooth-like scales called denticles that point in the direction of the tail. When running your hand over a shark's skin, toward the tail, the skin will feel smooth. When running your hand in the opposite direction, the shark's skin feels like rough sandpaper. In the past, shark skin was even used as sandpaper.

To swim faster, a shark bristles with its denticles, causing tiny whirlpools to form within the cavities between the denticles. These tiny vortices reduce the drag. This same design can be observed with dimples on a golf ball. As the dimpled golf ball flies through the air, tiny whirlpools are created, reducing drag. **Golf balls are made with dimples to create less drag in the same way the shark skin with its "dimples" was designed**.

Would we say a golf ball happened by chance? Hardly! Neither can we assume the shark's skin made itself. God created and designed the shark's skin to maximize its speed.

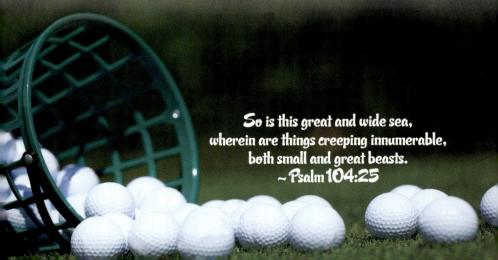

So is this great and wide sea, wherein are things creeping innumerable, both small and great beasts.
~ Psalm 104:25

Biology

June 23

One of the wonders of the Pacific Ocean is the Japanese puffer fish. During mating season this fish creates an underwater sculpture which would astound any artist and make a beautiful wall decoration in any home. Using only it fins, the tiny fish produces a perfectly circular, six-foot sculpture on the ocean bottom with uniquely placed ridges and channels. The fish cannot even see from one side of the sculpture to the other, yet it is a perfect circle and the channels it creates between the sand ridges are produced with mathematically perfection.

The fish literally has a map of the finished sculpture in its brain and works non-stop, 24 hours a day, for over a week to complete the plan. Where did this plan come from? How did it learn to move sand, shells and rocks around to create such beauty? Could such plans and ability have slowly "evolved" over time a small step at a time? Not a chance! God created such wonders to show us his creativity in the animals he has made.

For all those things hath mine hand made... ~ Isaiah 66:2a

June 24 — Botany

How can a major oil spill on the ocean be cleaned up? We use floating booms to contain the spill and absorbants/pumps to remove the oil from the surface, but what about the submerged oil droplets?

Believe it or not, technology that copies cactus spines will clean this submerged mess. The tapered spines of the cactus *Opuntia microdasys* efficiently collect water droplets from fog in the harsh ecosystems of central and northern Mexico. When micron-sized, spherically-shaped fog droplets land on the cactus spines, the spine's shape distorts the water droplet into a clam-like shape. The water droplet wants to stay spherical, so a battle between these two forces pushes the droplet to the base of the spine. The base of the spine is larger than the water droplet, and so the water droplet is immediately absorbed. Copying the cactus spine, researchers made a copper-silicon array with a cactus spine shape and submerged it into a mixture of oil and water. They blasted the mixture with ultrasonic sound waves to create micron-sized oil droplets. The underwater oil droplets collected on the man-made cactus spines in the same way fog droplets collected on real cactus spines. **God has designed everything in nature for our wonder and benefit**. It is our privilege to search out the Creator's secrets and apply them to our daily lives. In Scripture, God calls us to "have dominion" over creation; searching out the Creator's secrets and applying them to our daily life.

O God, thou hast taught me from my youth: and hitherto have I declared thy wondrous works.
~ Psalm 71:17

Cosmology

June 25

Those familiar with astronomy and cosmology have likely heard of "dark matter." Many astronomy books state as fact that 85% of all matter in the universe is dark matter – something which cannot be directly measured or observed. If it cannot be directly observed, why believe it exists?

The belief in dark matter stems from the fact that the laws of science directly contradict the belief in cosmic evolution and the Big Bang. The universal gas law ($PV=nRT$) shows that gas ALWAYS moves from high pressure to low pressure if left to itself. This means stars, galaxies, and galaxy clusters could never form themselves in the vacuum of outer space. Yet, they exist, so how do scientists explain the discrepancy? Dark matter to the rescue! By inventing a massive, invisible substance to condense and compress the "regular matter" of the universe, believers in naturalism can mathematically rescue the Big Bang explanation of how the universe could have created itself.

Dark matter is also invoked to **supposedly**:
1. Explain irregularities in Cosmic Microwave Background (CMB) radiation.
2. Explain how outer stars in galaxies can orbit faster than inner ones.
3. Explain how some of the most common elements in the universe - helium and deuterium (a hydrogen isotope) could have come into existence.
4. Support the Big Bang theory. Without dark matter, the Big Bang model for our universe collapses - thus there is enormous pressure to find proof of the existence of this unobservable, undetectable stuff.

Recent papers claim to have proven the existence of dark matter because light from certain galaxies has been bent in a "gravitational lens" effect in the way that dark matter would supposedly bend light. Yet, this is speculation, not direct observation, and the same effect can be explained in multiple other ways. Russell Humphreys, John Hartnett, and Moshe Carmeli have all shown novel physics solutions that explain the formation of the universe without the need to invent an unobservable, mythical dark matter. **All three brilliant physicists acknowledge that the only viable explanation for the origin of the matter and energy in the universe, including stars and galaxies, is a supernatural creation by God**. It is the laws of science that lead to this conclusion.

Thus, modern man is faced with two choices as he struggles to explain the origin of the material universe. Either an enormous explosion (from nothing) created the universe of mostly unobservable matter and energy, or the universe exists because an infinitely intelligent and powerful Creator made it. Modern man, in his quest to escape accountability from that Creator, all too often chooses darkness as his god and creator.

If therefore the light that is in thee be darkness, how great is that darkness! ~ Matthew 6:23

June 26 — Paleontology

Scientists recently uncovered five remarkably well-preserved octopus fossils. Octopuses are soft-bodied animals with no internal skeleton, yet each of the octopus' eight arms was fossilized with traces of muscles and rows of suckers intact. Several even had their internal gills and ink fossilized! **Today, when an octopus dies, its body rapidly decomposes into a slimy blob**. Within days, scavengers and bacteria reduce a dead octopus to nothing. To fossilize an octopus would require extremely unique conditions - fast coverage in sediment so thick that no oxygen could exist to support the growth of microorganisms. These special conditions would have been met in the Flood of Noah's day.

Furthermore, these five octopuses were enclosed in limestone. Limestone is always assumed by evolutionists to take long periods of time to form. But the Flood of Noah's time would have provided the perfect conditions for rapid limestone formation. The very nature of many fossils testifies to the Flood of Noah's day.

And the Lord said, I will destroy man whom I have created from the face of the earth; both man, and beast, and the creeping thing, and the fowls of the air;
~ Genesis 6:7a

Paleontology

June 27

Recently (2012) in Lianonig, China, the fossil of a dinosaur (*Sinocalliopteryx gigas*) was uncovered that was so well-preserved that even its stomach contents were identifiable. Its last meal must have been a Thanksgiving feast because researchers found not one, but three partially digested birds in its stomach. The birds were intact enough to identify them as pigeon-sized birds (*Confuciusornis sanctus*) with fully-formed characteristics of modern birds. The fact that this dinosaur had not one, but three partially digested birds in its stomach, indicates it was an active hunter. The report noted that the birds found in the dinosaur's stomach were "capable of powered flight" with fully-formed feathers and beaks rather than teeth. **But wait, haven't we all been told that dinosaurs slowly turned into birds?** The evolutionary story that dinosaurs evolved into birds has never been observed in the fossil record. We find either fully functional birds--complete with wings and feathers--or fully functional dinosaurs without wings or feathers. Dinosaurs evolving into birds? Not in this fossil find; the dinosaur was eating the birds! From a biblical perspective, this dinosaur was simply caught in a worldwide Flood, rapidly buried, fossilized, and dug up some 4400 years later to reveal its last meal - birds.

And God created... every winged fowl *after his kind*, and God saw that it was good.
~ Genesis 1:21 (emphasis added)

June 28

Biology

One of the most remarkable builders in the animal kingdom is the beaver. The sound of trickling water stimulates the beaver to plug the flow by building a dam. If it is a sluggish stream, the dam will be built straight across. If it is a fast-flowing stream, the beaver will construct a dam with a convex curve in the upstream direction. First, they push strong sticks down into the stream bed. Next, they fill the gaps with branches. Finally, they place heavier rocks or pieces of wood on top. **Beavers know how to compensate for the stresses and strains of water** pushing against the dam. On the upstream side of the dam, the wall is vertical and on the downstream side, the wall slopes at a 45 degree angle. Beavers also build outlet sluices for removal of overflow water.

Dams can be built short or long, high or low. **One beaver dam was 1800 feet long, 9 feet high and 18 feet wide**, strong enough for a horse and rider to use as a natural bridge! When we build dams, great engineering is needed to stop the flow and resist water pressure. Do we say that the engineering of our dams happen by accident and chance? It takes years of schooling to be a good dam builder, but beavers know instinctively how to build a dam. Even if a beaver is born in a zoo and let go in the wild, it still knows how to build a dam. Beavers do not need to learn how to build a dam, they just know; it's called instinct. If there is instinct, there must be an instinct maker and that instinct maker is God.

Give thanks unto the Lord, call upon his name,
make known his deeds among the people.
~1 Chronicles 16:8

Paleontology

June 29

Much publicity has been given to feather-like structures found in amber (assumed to be 70 million years old).[1] Why is this significant? If someone does not want to believe that birds were created fully-formed and fully-functional, the only other possibility is that some other animal must have evolved into a bird. Thus, it is widely taught that dinosaurs changed into birds. Since this feather-containing-amber is from the "age of dinosaurs"… it is assumed that these feathers came from feather-covered dinosaurs. But let's look at what was actually found – some fuzzy structures and some modern-looking feathers.

According to the researchers, *"We've got feathers that look to be little filamentous hair-like feathers, we've got the same filaments bound together in clumps, and then we've got a series that are for all intents and purposes identical to modern feathers," McKellar said. "We're finding some that look to be dinosaur feathers and another set that are pretty much dead ringers for modern birds."*

No bones, no skin, no pictures. **In other words, bird feathers and frayed fragments of who-knows-what were preserved in amber. Ignored are fully-formed birds found in lower rock layers**. Ignored are all the other creatures found in amber: well preserved insects, flowers, moss, lizards, and mammal hair. Of course, that is exactly what we would find if there was a world-wide flood as trees were ripped up and knocked against each other, releasing resin. During the raging Flood of Noah's day, huge floating log mats would have had trees oozing resin in which feathers, insects, fuzz and other critters would have been captured. Then sediments would cover them and amber would be formed.

Dinosaurs and birds were created together during that first week of creation. Both were wiped out in vast numbers and buried during the Flood of Noah - which is when the world's amber deposits formed. The feathers found in this amber are simply from a bird, not a dinosaur.

*And God created… every winged fowl after his kind:
and God saw that it was good.
~ Genesis 1:21*

June 30

Cosmology

A planet that orbits around a star that is not our Sun is called an "exoplanet." Since the 1990s, NASA has reported the existence of more than 1000 exoplanets. These planets come in a variety of sizes and distances from their suns. None have been found to be the perfect size and distance from its sun to allow life. Should Bible-believing Christians be afraid that finding other planets revolving around stars will prove life could pop up anywhere and God is irrelevant? One should not become confused with finding an earth-*sized* planet with an earth-*like* planet. Earth is unique in that it is the perfect distance from the Sun; and has the perfect gravitational pull, the perfect atmospheric gases, and copious amounts of liquid water resulting in the perfect "habitable zone" for life. **Just because other planets exist outside our solar system does not mean life is there**. Examine our own solar system with its Earth-*like* planets Venus and Mars. They are the right size and approximately the right distance from the Sun, yet they contain absolutely no life. Our Earth is special! It was designed to be a stable, safe place for people to inhabit. Isaiah 45:18 acknowledges this, "He formed it to be inhabited." Exoplanets just show God's power and creativity!

For thus saith the LORD that created the heavens; God himself that formed the earth and made it; he hath established it, he created it not in vain, he formed it to be inhabited: I *am* the LORD; and *there is* none else.
~ Isaiah 45:18

"All scripture is given by inspiration of God, and is profitable for doctrine, for reproof, for correction, for instruction in righteousness; that the man of God may be perfect, thoroughly furnished unto all good works."
– 2 Timothy 3:16, 17

"The Bible is worth all the other books which have ever been printed."
– Patrick Henry (1739-1799), Virginia Governor, Declaration of Independence signer, American Founding Father

Christian Truth

July 1

Peter's sermon on the day after Pentecost resulted in three thousand souls being saved (Acts 2). The people who heard his message were familiar with the Old Testament; they believed in the Creator God and understood sin and its penalty of death. As Peter preached to the Jews, he was able to build on their existing foundation of truth and reality.

Compare this with Paul speaking to the Greeks in Acts 17:22-34. The Greeks did not believe in a separate Creator God who held them personally accountable for their lives and actions. To them the "gods" were really just part of the universe and world around them. They did not have the same background as the Jews. So what was Paul's approach? **He began by explaining that God was not part of the universe, but the <u>Creator</u> of Heaven and Earth**. He began with creation.

Today, our culture does not know the Bible, and people increasingly think of evolution, i.e. creation itself, as their creator. We need to begin reaching the lost in our culture by explaining that there is a God, who is the literal supernatural Creator of everything. Unlike the Acts 2 crowd, our culture does not know the Bible. Americans have become like an Acts 17 culture. **Just like Paul, we need to start with the evidence for creation in order to explain the God of the Bible to them.**

Then Paul stood in the midst of Mars' hill, and said, Ye men of Athens, I perceive that in all things ye are too superstitious. For as I passed by, and beheld your devotions, I found an altar with this inscription, To The Unknown God. Whom therefore ye ignorantly worship, him declare I unto you. God that made the world and all things therein, seeing that he is Lord of heaven and earth,....."
~Acts 17: 22-24

July 2 — Biology

The caterpillar of the tropical butterfly *Heliconius sara* eats <u>nothing</u> but the leaves of the passion vines. Problem - these leaves contain cyanide packets along with enzyme packets so that when chewed and mixed together, **deadly cyanide gas is released!** The result for unwary, hungry insects – death!

However, H. sara caterpillars do not die. Why? Biologists found that when these caterpillars munched on the leaves, the caterpillars released a neutralizing enzyme that changed the cyanide into a harmless chemical. Evolutionists would have us believe that these caterpillars evolved the ability to neutralize the cyanide by accident and chance. Any insect that munched on the passion vine leaf without the neutralizing enzyme would face instant death. H. sara caterpillars had to have this special enzyme from the beginning! God, the greatest Chemist, designed this neutralizing ability from the start in order for the beautiful tropical butterfly *Heliconius sara* to exist.

For he spake, and it was done;....
~ Psalm 33:9

Geology

July 3

Coal deposits are found on every continent - even Antarctica. The deposits range from several inches thick to hundreds of feet thick. They can cover small areas or stretch for thousands of square miles. Evolutionists believe that coal formed in swamps over millions of years. As plants and trees died, they fell and accumulated at the bottom of the swamp. Over millions of years, the pressure and heat from slowly accumulating, overlying sediment transformed the swamp peat into coal. But students are seldom exposed to the problems with this story.

Today, we do **NOT** find swamps turning into coal deposits. Also, scientists have been able to identify many of the plants that were transformed into coal; most grow on the sides of mountains, not in swamps. In addition, small **marine animals, not land creatures,** are often found in the coal. All of this evidence leads to the conclusion that the material making up coal was transported from other locations. A modern example of this happened during the 1980's Mt. St. Helens volcanic eruption. At the base of the volcano was Spirit Lake. The eruption caused an 800-foot wave to wash up the slope and drag a million logs back into the lake. These trees ended up floating in the lake. As wind blew the logs back and forth across the lake, the bark was rubbed off making a foot thick layer of bark at the bottom of the lake; this is the beginning of a peat deposit.

The Genesis Flood with its violent floodwaters and earthquakes would have ripped up all the plants and trees on the entire planet - resulting in huge floating log mats. As the log mats moved back and forth, the bark and waterlogged vegetation would have rubbed off and settled to the bottom. The violence of this Flood caused plant debris to be buried quickly and deeply - forming coal within a short time. The enormous coal beds that we find all over the world are a reminder of the Flood of Noah's day.

They did eat, they drank, they married wives, they were given in marriage, until the day that Noe entered into the ark, and the flood came, and destroyed them all. ~ Luke 17:27

July 4

History

Throughout America's Midwest are hundreds of raised mounds and earthworks. Radiocarbon dating places the age of artifacts found in these mounds around 3,000 years old. Archeologists believe an extinct race of settlers known as the Adena culture built them. In Lower Michigan, from 1850 to 1910, some of these mounds were excavated. A number of engraved plates made of slate, copper, and clay were recovered. A book published in 1910 photographically documented 40 engravings that reveal amazing knowledge of this ancient people.[1]

One of the engravings shows a scene of people drowning during a heavy rainfall. The third panel on this engraving shows a boat and a bird flying away with a branch in its beak. The fourth panel shows the boat on shore with the animals coming off in pairs while a man and three sons raise their hands in praise. **Sounds very similar to the biblical account of the Flood**, doesn't it? How did the Adena culture in America know of this event some 3,000 years ago? They or their ancestors left the tower of Babel with this knowledge. As they spread across the world, they took this knowledge of true history with them. These people knew of God and the Bible, then over time, this knowledge was not passed down to their children.

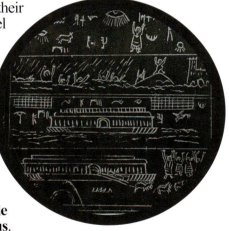

We need to make sure those following in our footsteps do not forget the God of the Bible and all that He has done for us.

And also all that generation were gathered unto their fathers: and there arose another generation after them, which knew not the Lord, nor yet the works which he had done for Israel. ~ Judges 2:10

Biology

July 5

What are the *"evolutionist's tree of life"* and the *"creationist's orchard"*?

Darwin originally proposed that all life had a common-origin ancestor and the various forms of life could be lined up into a "tree of life" showing what turned into what. "Common descent" is still the foundational principle ruling modern biology. Evolutionists believe that all of today's species are descended from one common ancestor and that every organism we see today evolved from one simple cell.

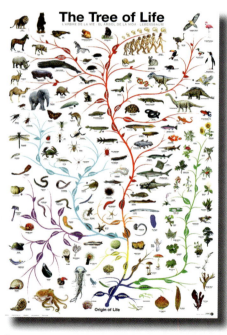

In contrast, the creationist's orchard has diversity occurring with time, but always within the basic body types or the Genesis "kinds." In the beginning, God created the creatures "according to their kinds" (Gen. 1: 11-12, 21, 24-25). **Each of these kinds was created with a vast amount of information but always within limits**. Written into the DNA coding of each "tree" within the biological orchard of life, is enough variety that descendants can adapt to a wide variety of environments. Creatures only breed with other creatures of their own kind. For example, dogs, wolves, and coyotes belong to the canine kind while cats, lions and tigers belong to the feline kind. There is no connection between the canine tree and the feline tree. There is no shared ancestry. We do not find "cogs" and "dats" but cats and dogs. The biblical orchard best fits what we observe in nature.

And God made the beast of the earth after his kind, and cattle after their kind, and every thing that creepeth upon the earth after his kind: and God saw that it was good.
~ Genesis 1:25

July 6

Cosmology

Have you considered our solar system? It has a nice, neat organized structure. Our planets all have stable and relatively round orbits. This structure, prevents planets from colliding with each other. In fact, this design protects Earth from being hit by another large planet. As scientists examine outer space, they are now discovering other planets orbiting other suns. They are finding that many of these exoplanet orbits are so erratic that collisions with other planets are a real possibility. How did our solar system become so organized? Evolution is about chaos and random changes - not design, organization, or systems. Our solar system shows order.

Even the name we give it, the solar "system," shows we know it is organized. **We do not call it the "solar accident," "solar non-system" or "solar disorder"…but the solar system**. Even those who believe in evolutionary processes as the explanation for everything cannot help but use words that signify design and order. Order does not happen by accident and chance. Order means there must be someone who put this into an orderly system, and that orderly solar system-maker is God.

Mine hand also hath laid the foundation of the earth, and my right hand hath spanned the heavens: when I call unto them, they stand up together. ~ Isaiah 48:13

Biology

July 7

Students are taught about light and dark-colored peppered moths in almost all biology textbooks. Here's the story: prior to the Industrial Revolution, light-colored peppered moths were prevalent in England. During the Industrial Revolution, soot covered the trees, and the dark-colored peppered moths were better camouflaged. Therefore, they had an advantage and survived better than the light-colored moths. This is often called an example of "evolution in action."

Today, England's trees are not soot covered, and light-colored moths are as prevalent as before the Industrial Revolution. This shift in colors is not evolution in action; remember, both varieties of moths were present from the start. As the environment changed, the dark-colored moths had greater opportunity to pass on their genes for darkness than the light-colored ones. With the environment changing again, we now see the lighter ones flourishing. This is natural selection in action, not evolution. Evolution needs proof that one creature changes into another completely different kind of creature. No such proof has ever been seen.

Furthermore, these light and dark-colored peppered moths did NOT spend time on exposed tree trunks and rocks as the famous textbook pictures show. Those promoting this idea in textbooks have now admitted that **they glued the moths on the tree trunks; the photographs were fakes**. In reality, peppered moths are nocturnal and rest in tree tops during the day. Don't believe everything you read in your textbooks! But do believe everything in the Bible. God, not evolution, created peppered moths from the beginning.

In the beginning God created the heaven and the earth.
~ Genesis 1:1

July 8

Microbiology

Not so long ago, scientists discovered that eating undercooked pork could cause an infection from a parasite called trichinosis. This parasitic worm can infest pigs and be passed on to us when we eat insufficiently cooked pork. When someone eats pork with this parasite, digestive juices dissolve the cyst, releasing the parasite larvae into the body. These larvae penetrate the small intestine walls where they grow, mate, and produce more parasites. Yuck! The adult female can produce thousands of larvae that enter the bloodstream and then burrow into the muscles and other tissues.

The best way to protect against this parasite is to kill it off before you eat pork. This can be done either by freezing the meat below 5°F for 21 days prior to eating pork or making sure the internal temperature is at least 145°F when cooking. Also, today's hog farms are meticulous, preventing the trichinosis parasite altogether. Did the Israelites know about this prevention? God knew the problems with eating undercooked pork, so He prohibited His people from eating pork in order to keep them safe. In fact, it has been found that those who followed the Israelite's dietary rules were far healthier than other cultures that did not. **God always has our best interests at heart** even though we may not understand the specific reasons.

And the swine,..... it is unclean unto you : ye shall not eat of their flesh
~ Deuteronomy 14:8

Design

July 9

Have you considered the snowflake? It has been said that no two snowflakes are alike. Is this true? The average snowflake contains 10^{18} or 1,000,000,000,000,000,000 water molecules. How many ways can these molecules be arranged? Let's compare this to arranging 15 books on a shelf. There are 15 choices for arranging the first book, 14 for the second book, 13 choices for the third book and so on. When we multiply this out there are over a trillion ways to arrange only 15 books. If we took one hundred books and figured all the possible ways of arranging them, the number is 10^{158} or a 1 with 158 zeros. **This number is greater than the atoms in the universe!** Remember, a snowflake contains 10^{18} water molecules, which can be arranged. The number of possible ways is far greater than arranging 100 books.

From simple water vapor condensing on dust and changing into ice, we find endless amounts of six-sided, complex, symmetrical patterns. Who is the creative genius who came up with such endless variety and design? God is the master designer. Just as He asked Job, *"Have you entered the treasury of the snow?"* May we take the time to see these treasures of beauty that God created for our enjoyment.

Hast thou entered into the treasures of the snow?
Job 38:22

July 10

Geology

One of the most significant confirmations of the Earth's recent creation has been the measurement of carbon-14 (^{14}C) within diamonds.[1] Why is this so significant? **There should not be a single atom of ^{14}C left within diamonds!**

Almost all sources of carbon contain a small amount of an unstable ^{14}C. ^{14}C has a half-life of 5730 years. This means one-half of any remaining ^{14}C disappears every 5730 years. Modern measurement equipment is so accurate that you'd have to divide the starting amount of ^{14}C in half 18 times before it could no longer detect the presence of **any** remaining ^{14}C.

Diamonds are made of carbon and also contain minute amounts of ^{14}C that had to have been present at their very formation. Since diamonds are the hardest natural substance known to mankind, it is impossible that any modern carbon contamination could have worked its way inside of a diamond. There is also no known way that ^{14}C could magically be generated deep inside an already formed diamond. Thus, any ^{14}C within diamonds essentially proves that diamonds are far younger than 100,000 years. Evidence indicates that diamonds formed deep within the Earth. Therefore, because the Earth is believed to be billions of years old, it is routinely taught that diamonds are also billions of years old. Yet, if this were true, there would not be a single atom of ^{14}C left within their structure. It is a fact of science that diamonds contain levels of ^{14}C more than a hundred times greater than the equipment detection limit.[2] Thus, **both diamonds, and the rock layers deep within the Earth are thousands, not billions, of years old.**

The next time you see someone wearing a glittering bit of carbon (a diamond), remember, **this is one of the strongest evidences that God recently created this Earth** for our amazement and enjoyment.

...upholding all things by the word of his power...
~ Hebrews 1:3b

Biology

July 11

Have you considered the vegan spider? We normally think of spiders as "meat eaters" because they spend their lives trapping and eating insects. Yet, in Mexico, living in Acacia trees, are special spiders (*Bagheera kilingi*) that jump from leaf to leaf, eating the tips and drinking nectar from petioles (the leaf stalks). Biologists documented the life of over 140 of these spiders, and only on four occasions did these spiders display any carnivorous behavior. Occasionally, when the opportunity presented itself, they would snatch an ant larva from a passing ant nursemaid. Analysis of spider tissues also confirms that they eat plants and are not carnivores. **One scientist was shocked after hearing of a vegetarian spider**. To Bible-believing scientists, this should not be at all shocking; a vegetarian spider would be reminiscent of life before Adam sinned.

to every thing that creepeth upon the earth, wherein there is life, <u>I have given every green herb for meat:</u> and it was so. ~ Genesis 1:30

July 12
Biblical Accuracy

Why do I believe the Bible to be true? One of the reasons is the large number of fulfilled prophecies. **No other book can claim that although many have tried**. For instance, the Koran has one specific prophecy (that Mohammad would return to Mecca), but it is a self-fulfilling prophecy, which the writer was capable of making come true - he did return to Mecca. This is quite different from the prophecy concerning Jesus, who said that HE would return from the grave. Jesus was dead for three days and then came back from the dead. Mohammed's prophecy was easily fulfilled while Jesus' prophecy was not humanly possible!

In the same way, other fulfilled prophecies in the Bible prove the Bible true. Consider the prophecies about Sidon and Tyre. The prophecy regarding the city of Sidon was that the people would be decimated, but the city would continue (Ezekiel 28:21-23). The city of Sidon was attacked, and 40,000 were killed, but the city still stands today. What about Tyre? At its height, the prophet declared that the coastal city of Tyre would be destroyed; the walls would be broken down so that, *"I will scrape her dust from her and make her like the top of a rock. It shall be a place for the spreading of nets.....They shall lay thy stones and thy timber and thy dust in the midst of the water...I will make thee like the top of a rock....never to be rebuilt and never again to be inhabited?* (Ezekiel 26:4-5,12,14 emp. added). At its height, the city of Tyre was besieged by the powerful King Nebuchadnezzar. For 13 years, Tyre held off the attack; finally, the walls were breached, and many were killed. Thousands, however, had fled to an island ½ mile out in the Mediterranean Sea to rebuild their city. Two hundred fifty years later, Alexander the Great came to Tyre and commanded the city to surrender. The people, feeling secure on their island fortress, laughed. **So Alexander came up with a bold and daring plan**. He would build a causeway across one-half mile of sea to Tyre. Alexander used every timber, stone, and piece of rubble from old Tyre and scraped the site of the city clean – right down to the bedrock. Today Tyre is like the top of a rock, good only for the spreading of nets. *"For I have spoken it, saith the Lord GOD...."* (Ezekiel 26:5).

For verily I say unto you, Till heaven and earth pass, one jot or one tittle shall in no wise pass from the law, till all be fulfilled.
~ Matthew 5:18

History

July 13

Did dinosaurs recently live in the Amazon? Vance Nelson, researcher/explorer, travels the world finding the untold secrets of planet Earth. On his latest expedition, he traveled to the Amazon River. In 1940, an American explorer traveled through this same region, and he reported that the indigenous people saw a strange creature that lived in the nearby river; the description fitting a sauropod dinosaur. Nelson hired a local, secular archeologist to guide him to the locations of rock art in the jungle.

One cave's wall depicts a hunting scene with a large animal in the center surrounded by nine hunters with one of the hunters holding a raised spear. Obviously, these hunters were hunting a living creature; this creature had a long neck, small head, big body, and large tail. This is not a picture of a llama but of an animal very much like a long-necked, sauropod dinosaur. This indicates that **the indigenous people saw and hunted dinosaurs** very recently in the Amazon River Basin. This is one of the many untold secrets of planet Earth. It is not such a secret, after all, that dinosaurs and man lived together in the relatively recent past.

Behold now behemoth, which I made with thee; he eateth grass as an ox. Lo now, his strength is in his loins, and his force is in the navel of his belly. He moveth his tail like a cedar: the sinews of his stones are wrapped together. His bones are as strong pieces of brass; his bones are like bars of iron. He is the chief of the ways of God:
~ Job 40:15-19a

July 14

Biology

Have you considered the chambered nautilus? This South Pacific Ocean creature has a unique shell that is divided into separate gas-filled chambers. The nautilus can sink to the ocean bottom or rise to the surface by changing the gas pressure within the sealed chambers; for example, the nautilus will flood some of the chambers with water to descend. **This is exactly how submarines work**. Submarines have tanks that can be filled with water or air. When the tanks are filled with air, the submarine rises, if the tanks are filled with water, it sinks.

Evolutionists believe that the nautilus evolved from mollusks that grew extra sections of their shell as floatation devices. Fossil nautiluses, however, look just like today's nautiluses, showing no intermediate evolutionary change. No one would believe that a submarine happened by accident and chance, so why would anyone believe that "nature's submarine," the nautilus, happened by accident and chance? The nautilus simply gives glory to God's ingenuity.

Thou rulest the raging of the sea....
~ Psalm 89:9

History

July 15

What happened to the dinosaurs? The biblical explanation is that the majority were killed during the Flood of Noah. This is the reason why we find their fossilized bones buried in the rock layers that formed during the Flood. Yet, Noah was told to take land-dwelling, air-breathing creatures upon the Ark, and this would have included young, small dinosaurs. These creatures must have gone extinct after the Flood. But why? Let's look at two modern examples; the demise of the Asian elephant and the tiger.

Today, across Asia, wild elephants are killing hundreds of people every year. Here are some accounts from just the last few years:

- In Thailand, an elephant stomped three rubber plantation workers to death.
- In Nepal, 11 people were killed by elephants in one week while gathering firewood.
- In Vietnam, a herd of elephants killed at least 10 people.

In response, villagers are fighting back, and the elephant population is shrinking with each passing year.

Back in 1819, Singapore was primarily swampland and teeming with tigers. By 1840, tigers were killing 200-300 people a year. As the city grew, 600-800 people a year were reported being killed by tigers, and a certain area was even called *"Tiger Resort."* Desperate authorities offered bounties, and by 1930, the last wild tiger was shot in Singapore. **It took less than 100 years for the most fearsome predator of mankind to go from killing almost 1000 people per year to complete extinction in an entire region of the world!**

The parallel between the extinction of dinosaurs and the localized "extinction" of elephants and tigers is obvious. As the human population grew, dangerous dinosaurs had to be eradicated. What happened to the dinosaurs? They were quite likely hunted into extinction.

(Into the Ark went) every beast after his kind, and all the cattle after their kind, and every creeping thing that creepeth upon the earth after his kind, and every fowl after his kind, every bird of every sort. And they went in unto Noah into the ark, two and two of all flesh, wherein is the breath of life. ~ Genesis 7:14-15

July 16 — Biology

What animal looks like it sweats blood? The 7,000-pound hippopotamus. The five-inch-thick hippo skin has sweat glands that ooze a red slime, which later turns brown. This oozing slime protects the hippo in three ways. First, it gives the hippo its own sunblock protection. This is great because hippos spend a lot of time in the sun. In addition, the red slime is an insect repellant. Also, the red slime has antibiotic qualities. Hippos live in less than pure water and have very aggressive daily territorial fights with each other, often resulting in terrible cuts and wounds. To have built-in antibiotics would stop deadly bacteria in their tracks. Where did these glands come from? **How many millions of years did it take to get the glands just right?** God knew what the hippo would need and provided for his protection from sun, insects and deadly bacteria.

Make a joyful noise unto the Lord, all ye lands. ~ Psalm 100:1

Biology

July 17

Did you know that blind cave fish were designed to go blind! Scientists once thought it was by accident. Cave fish are a generic term for freshwater fish found in - you guessed it, caves. Geneticists have found that blind fish living in caves are almost identical to those in the river outside the cave. The only difference seems to be that the cave fish have smaller eyes, or no eyes, or eyes lighter in color. Actually, for fish living in a dark cave, this is an advantage. A highly developed visual system uses up to 15% more energy and soft eye tissue is easily damaged if bumped into the walls of a cave. Instead, cave fish depend on their sense of smell and sensitivity to water pressure changes. Also, being in a dark cave, eye coloring has no purpose and it takes extra energy to maintain eye color. So if cave fish have eyes, they are lighter in color. Are these changes a mutational degeneration? Actually, cave fish are not regressing, but well designed to live in caves.

Conrad Waddington, a biologist, proposed the idea that many animals have a mechanism allowing enviromental changes to switch on genes, when the change would benefit the animal. Such a mechanism is found in blind cave fish - involving a protein called HSP90. When a cave fish embryo experiences subtle factors such as lower electrical conductivity in the water (it is believed that cave water has lower conductivity because the water has less salt), the growing embryo senses these outside conditions and turns off the HSP90 protein. This causes a reduction in fish's eye size. These eyes have shallow sockets and can even be scaled over. **When these same blind cave fish were introduced into water outside the cave, their offspring were born with fully functioning eyes within two generations!**

Scientists are discovering that we have "flexible genetics." This is no surprise to Bible-believing Christians; God has simply pre-programmed creatures with the ability to adapt to different environments.

And his brightness was as the light; he had horns coming out of his hand: and there was the hiding of his power.
~ Habakkuk 3:4

July 18

Biblical Accuracy

Did you realize that North American alligator almost went extinct in the 1960s? In response to this situation, alligators were put on the endangered species list in 1967. But this alone did not help in saving them as their numbers continued to decrease. Then an interesting plan was set in place – alligator farms! Alligator farmers started going out into the wild to collect alligator eggs. They raised these gators in captivity for two years and promised to return 20% of the adults back into the wild. The remaining 80% were sold for hides and meat. The result, alligator meat and hides became less expensive - making poaching unprofitable.

The alligator population has increased to such an extent, today that today they are off the endangered species list. **God has called us to manage and care for His Earth,** and He created mankind in His image – with the creativity to do just that. Who would have thought of saving alligators through farming?

And God blessed them, and God said unto them, be fruitful, and multiply, and replenish the earth, and subdue it: and have dominion over the fish of the sea, and over the fowl of the air, and over every living thing that moveth upon the earth. ~ Genesis 1:28

Anatomy

July 19

Teeth are surprisingly tough; we can bite and chew food for decades without cracking. A tooth's dentine is covered with tooth enamel. How can enamel, which by itself is brittle like glass, survive our chewing and biting process without cracking? Researchers have found that the design of the tooth enamel prevents cracks in three ways:

1. Tufts are crack-like flaws deep within the tooth where the enamel and dentine meet. Under the stress of biting or chewing, these tufts distribute the stress - suppressing the growth of cracks.
2. Enamel is made up of rods that criss-cross each other like basket weave. This hinders cracks from spreading.
3. If a crack expands, the tooth fills in the space with material extended from the tufts - which glues the cracked walls and stops further expansion.

Our teeth are extremely tough structures built from brittle materials - yet, they are able to withstand a lifetime of biting and chewing because of their design. When we see a design, we know there must be a designer. The tooth's designer is Jesus.

Thy teeth are as a flock of sheep ....
~ Song of Solomon 6:6

July 20

Botany

Water does not flow uphill. So, how does water get to the leaves high up in a tree? Coast redwood (*Sequoia sempervirens*) trees tower some 35 stories or 379 feet above the ground.[1] Some of these redwoods move as much as 160 gallons of water a day up out of the ground. As you stand near the base of these trees, **listen closely for the sound of their mechanical machinery pumping the water** to the top. You won't hear a sound. So, how do they move all that water?

God has set up a wonderful design in trees – osmosis, capillary action and transpiration. Even though wood seems to be solid, it has thousands of microscopic interior tubes stretching from the roots to the top of the tree. Water enters the roots because of osmosis; higher pressure moves water molecules into the lower pressure area in the roots. Then, capillary action takes place, moving the water upwards. Dip a corner of a paper towel in water and notice the water creeping up the fibers. Working with osmosis and capillary action is transpiration. As sunlight strikes the leaves, the water molecules evaporate, transforming liquid water to a gas. This vapor "flies" into the air while the next water molecule in line starts heating up. The long chain of water molecules is pulled to the very top of the tree as each one at the top evaporates. **On a hot summer day, water molecules can travel up the tree at 25 mph**. All this goes on silently, year after year. There are no mechanical parts, and when something breaks down, the tree has mechanisms to repair itself. We cannot say the same when we pipe water to the top of a tall building. When we see such an advanced plumbing system, we know there must be a plumbing engineer!

As poet Joyce Kilmer famously stated, "… only God can make a tree."

...stand still, and consider the wondrous works of God.
~ Job 37:14b

Biology

July 21

Corals mainly live in shallow tropical waters that are well lighted. The coral polyp is an animal that builds a limestone cup and hides in it during the day. When we pick up a piece of coral, we are picking up the multiple, connected limestone cups. Each cup is where the coral polyp lives. The coral polyp is a tiny soft-bodied creature that comes out at night and waves its tentacles to catch the passing microscopic plankton.

Corals experience three environmental threats: hot sunshine, powerful waves, and coatings of sand. How do corals protect themselves?

1. Coral reefs are found in tropical, sun-drenched oceans and during low tides, the corals can become too hot. To solve that p,roblem, the **corals secrete mucus that acts as a sunscreen**.
2. Corals live along the shores that experience pounding, powerful waves (especially during stormy seasons) that could easily break up the coral. To solve that problem, corals **build strong foundations** to withstand pounding waves.
3. Corals live near sandy beaches so they can easily become coated and even covered with sand. To solve that problem, the coral polyps use their tentacles to **clean the sand off of their limestone housing**.

Who was the original problem solver for these corals? God Himself - He is the One that cares for His creation.

And when they heard that, they lifted up their voice to God with one accord, and said, Lord, thou art God, which hast made heaven, and earth, and the sea, and all that in them is: ~**Acts 4:24**

July 22

Biology

Coral polyps have built in poisonous "harpoons." The coral polyp's tentacles are covered with stinging cells (nematocysts) that shoot and kill the plankton. When zooplankton swim by and accidentally touch one of the stinging cells, the "harpoon" is triggered. In thousandths of a second, the lid on the stinging cell flies open, and the harpoon is released. The barbs on the "harpoon" tear a hole in the prey, and the filament trailing the harpoon enters the hole to inject the poison. The zooplankton dies, and the polyp can then pull the meal into its mouth and digest it in its stomach. Each harpoon can only be used one time. A new harpoon (nematocyst) soon grows in its place. This method of hunting zooplankton requires perfect synchronization of sensory cells, nerve cells and muscle cells of the coral animal. Synchronization takes planning and design. That great planner and designer is God! Coral is not just another pretty ornament – it is a colony of deadly hunters!

God thundereth marvellously with his voice; great things doeth he, which we cannot comprehend. ~ Job 37:5

Geology

July 23

Imagine the world-covering flood event with fast-moving churning waters….

1. As the fountains of the great deep were broken up, many plate tectonic movements generated numerous earthquakes, resulting in an immense number of tsunamis.
2. As the ocean floor plates pushed apart, molten rock emerged, creating a new ocean floor. The new ocean floor was less dense and rose, pushing up the sea level and caused a surge of ocean water onto the continents.
3. Super-storms were generated in the atmosphere as a result of the supersonic steam jets at the crustal fracture zones, catapulting ocean waters aloft before they fell back to Earth as torrential rainfall (Genesis 7:11). It has been estimated that such super-storms and their winds drove water currents at speeds of 100 mph or more.
4. Twice-daily tides. The earth being covered with water, these tidal surges would have experienced no shorelines; thus the tidal surges would have moved across the submerged continents, causing much churning of water and redistribution of pulverized sediments.

Powerful, fast-moving currents and surges ripped up rocks and laid them down, producing the sedimentary layers that we see today on all the continents of the world. The Flood of Noah's day was truly catastrophic!

that calleth for the waters of the sea, and poureth them out upon the face of the earth: The LORD is his name:
~ Amos 9:6b

July 24

Design

Ships traversing the ocean have to be regularly cleaned of barnacles, or they lose significant streamlining and efficiency. **Even many whales can be seen with barnacles clinging to their skin for a free ride.** As a matter of fact, the vast majority of whale species have barnacles clinging to their skin, and each of these whales are home to their own specific species of barnacle. Yet, the pilot whale is barnacle-free. Why don't barnacles cling to pilot whales?

It's all in the skin; tiny nanostructures on a Pilot whale's skin inhibit barnacle larvae from attaching. These "nano-ridges" are microscopic pores that ooze a parasite-resistant gel to keep the barnacles from attaching. Marine researchers are trying to copy the whale's skin so that it can be painted onto ship hulls. Here is yet another invention derived by "thinking God's thoughts" and copying the Master Designer's handiwork!

Many, O LORD my God, *are* thy wonderful works *which* thou hast done....
~ Psalm 40:5

Biology

July 25

Is there life atop a frozen, cinder-covered volcanic peak? Yes, a small insect named Puʻu Wekiu, which means "topmost hill" in the Hawaiian language. It is a tiny, flightless bug whose habitat is the 13,796 foot summit of the tallest volcano in Hawaii, Mauna Kea. The summit of Mauna Kea represents one of the most extreme environments in the Hawaiian Islands with almost no plant life. Daily temperature fluctuations can be between 25ºF and 116ºF with a winter snow pack covering the peak, creating below-freezing temperatures for much of the year.[1] So, how does the insect survive?

Unlike most other lygaeids that eat seeds, the Wekiu feeds on insects that are blown to the top of the mountain and die. This is actually a large resource; snow packs at the summit are often covered with thousands of dead insects. When the snow melts, wekiu bugs can be found at the edge feeding on insects that drop out of the melting snow. Wekiu also have "antifreeze" in their blood that allows them to survive at below-freezing temperatures.[2]

Any other insect would not be able to survive such conditions! From the beginning, God knew what the wekiu needed in order to survive and programmed into the insect the characteristics that were needed. Here we have a small insect, in a harsh environment, testifying to the Creator's care and foreknowledge.

**Sing unto him, sing psalms unto him: talk ye of all his wondrous works.
~ Psalm 105:2**

July 26

History

It is widely and routinely taught in Bible colleges that the Exodus from Egypt never happened. This is one of the most longstanding criticisms of the accuracy of the Old Testament – based on the fact that no Egyptian documents mention the Hebrew slaves and their exodus from Egypt. In addition, the books of Moses (Genesis, Exodus, Leviticus, Numbers, and Deuteronomy) make no mention of specific pharaohs of Egypt. Thus, **Bible skeptics assume there was no exodus from Egypt** and that the Bible cannot be trusted to mean what it says.

To understand this omission from Egyptian documents, we need to understand the Egyptian culture.

1. The Egyptians were infatuated with the afterlife, and their religious dogma convinced them that if they were forgotten by the living, they lost their immortality in the afterlife. This is why they spent enormous effort to record their names and images on monuments throughout Egypt.
2. Egyptians despised their enemies. To not even mention the names of their enemies was the ultimate in contempt and disrespect.
3. Egyptian hieroglyphics alter and ignore historical events to favor Egyptians. Revisionist history (to fit the viewpoint of the historian) is indeed a very old practice.
4. For Moses to not name the pharaohs would be his way of rejecting their authority over him – a practice he may have adopted having been raised in Egypt.

Thus, when the entire nation of Egypt was decimated by a series of plagues; followed by the lowest members of society walking away with much of the wealth of the nation; followed by Egypt's powerful military being drowned in the Red Sea – **it is little wonder that all records of the people responsible for these events (the Israelites) would be purged from Egyptian records and monuments.**

The justification used by theologians and skeptics to ignore God's Word are excuses, not facts. God's word speaks the truth; there was an Exodus.

And the waters returned, and covered the chariots and the horsemen, and all the host of Pharaoh that came into the sea after them; there remained not so much as one of them. ~ Exodus 14:28

Cosmology

July 27

A recent paper published in *The Astronomical Journal* looked at the characteristics of 2,000 "exoplanets" orbiting other stars in our galaxy. Then they extended these results mathematically to other stars in other galaxies throughout the universe. They looked at the habitability characteristics of exoplanet/star systems and ranked the planets in terms of their potential habitability. Then they extended their findings to the estimated 700 quintillion or so exoplanets that may exist in our enormous universe to estimate the odds of finding another life-suitable, potentially inhabitable planet (such as Earth). So what was the conclusion of their statistical analysis? **The Earth is totally unique and statistically the only planet in the entire universe capable of supporting life!**

This conclusion was unexpected and totally destroyed evolutionary assumptions. The authors hedged their finding with all sorts of "apologies" for their conclusions. The paper noted that they may be in error because, *"With these kinds of massive and highly hypothetical calculations, what might refine the predictions could be further discoveries about the composition and position of more exoplanets."* The researchers admit that their findings, *"may need to be taken with a grain of salt."*

But here are the facts.
1. Based on what we now know and observe, in the entire universe, the Earth is the only planet uniquely designed for, and capable of, supporting life.
2. After SETI (the Search for ExtraTerrestrial Intelliegence) spent almost 50 years of searching through every wavelength of the electromagnetic spectrum coming to Earth from every direction in the universe, there is absolutely no evidence for the existence of any intelligent life outside of Earth.

With every scientific observation, God is making the truth about His existence increasingly apparent.

I have made the earth, and created man upon it: I, even my hands, have stretched out the heavens, and all their host have I commanded.
~ Isaiah 45:12

July 28

Design

What are scientists up to now? They are making a "robosnail," a snail-like robot. Why would a scientist be copying a slimy snail? If you want to build something that moves over all terrains, what better creature to copy? **A snail creeps forward on a layer of gooey slime; thicker goo allows it to move faster, while thinner slime offers more resistance**. The ten-inch "robosnail" is a mass of gears, wiring and pieces of plastic that creates a series of slow, undulating waves along its rubbery membrane "foot", which allows it to creep forward slowly. "Robosnail" is only able to move on flat surfaces.

Today, surprisingly, scientists are finding that liquids on a smaller scale behave in a different way. The smaller the scale, the more "sticky" a liquid seems to be. For example, when maple syrup is on a plate and you move your finger back-and-forth, the area covered by the thinnest layer of syrup is the hardest to move through. Scientists still have much to learn. You could say we trail the snail in technology. God knew what He was doing when he designed such a "slick" way of moving.

Give unto the Lord the glory due unto his name;
~ Psalm 29:2a

Geology

July 29

The Heart Mountain slide is a famous rock layer known to every geology student. Yet, **how this happened is a total mystery to secular geologists!**

Near the end of Noah's Flood, an enormous area of sediment broke away from the east side of a volcano near Yellowstone National Park. This one-third mile thick layer of sediment, over 1300 square miles in area, slid across an almost flat surface at an estimated speed of 100 miles per hour! It broke into dozens of huge chunks and settled on top of overlying rock layers (which are assumed to be much "younger"). Thus an extremely "old" layer of rock ended up on top of "younger" rocks. In reality, these layers are all essentially the same age - just laid down and pushed around in different ways and at different times during the flood of Noah's day.

This massive rock slide is not a mystery when we put on our biblical glasses. During the Flood of Noah, rapidly deposited sedimentary layers were filled with water, and the weight of these sediments squeezed water out between the layers. Water resistant minerals, such as gypsum, prevented this liquid from rapidly escaping, thus forming a lubricated surface between layers of rock – similar to water trapped between two sheets of Plexiglas™. Eventually, the pressure became so great that a slight jiggle from an earthquake caused the entire side of the mountain to slide across the landscape, relocating itself over 30 miles away without disturbing the sequence of layers laid down by the Flood. In addition, the friction caused by the slide generated a super-critical layer of carbon dioxide, a condition where gas gets so hot it acts like a fluid to literally "float" massive blocks of stone, resulting in the rock layers sliding even further.

Events such as this are a logical consequence of water-filled sediment that was laid down rapidly during the Flood of Noah's time. The Heart Mountain landslide is a mystery to secular geologists who believe in evolution, but not to those who believe the truth of the Bible. The Heart Mountain slide is clearly a result of the Flood.

> **(God) removeth the mountains, and they know not: which overturneth them in his anger.** ~ Job 9:5

July 30

Paleontology

Snakes alive! **A snake that was longer than a school bus (48 feet long) and weighing more than a ton was found in Columbia!** It's twice as long as the largest living Anaconda, but don't worry, it's long dead. This fossilized snake was dug out of a coal pit mine along with other giant fossils - turtles with shells twice the size of manhole covers, crocodiles more than 12 feet long, seven-foot long lungfish (2-3 times longer than today), exotic leaves and plants. The fossilized snake, named *Titanoboa cerrejonensis* is the largest snake ever found. They even dug up the snake's fragile skull!

Snakes are cold-blooded - meaning their body temperature changes with the outside temperature. Scientists believe such a large snake had to have lived in a rainforest climate to grow so large. The fossil record reveals that before the Flood of Noah's day creatures could grow quite large and the enviroment was very different. grew much larger. Paleontogists have great fun digging up this lost world.

There were giants in the earth in those days....
~ Genesis 6:4

July 31

Christian Truth

America is exactly paralleling the downward moral slide explained in Romans 1:18-32.

This passage expresses God's displeasure at any who "*suppress the truth*" (Romans 1:18 NKJV) about His existence and character. It states that it is creation that testifies to these things in an absolutely obvious way. In other words, creation can never be explained without our Creator. Yet, **mankind accelerated down the path of trying to explain the origin of the universe and life without God about 200 years ago**. In order to maintain this fantasy, only Darwin's evolutionary view of origins is shown to students while the evidence for creation is suppressed.

The second stage of downward deterioration began after the Scopes "Monkey Trial" in 1925 as evolution moved toward becoming the only explanation for life being taught in our schools. Over several generations, this idea became the only framework through which teachers filtered their thinking about all of reality. The foolishness of believing that everything could make itself (without God) became accepted by the majority, "*their foolish hearts were darkened...and professing to be wise they became fools*" (Romans 1:21, 22 NKJV). God has defined foolishness in Psalm 14:1, "T*he fool hath said in his heart, there is no God....*" Our education system is literally filled with people professing to be wise, yet they seem incapable of seeing the obvious - that life has a designer.

The third stage of deterioration occurred in the 1960s. Humans were created to worship, and once they reject the worship of their Creator, the creation itself becomes the center of their adoration. The radical environmental movement, starting in the 1960s, has at its core a spirit of "creation worship." Symptoms abound inside and outside the Christian community: valuing eagle eggs and African lions far above aborted human babies and unfounded hysteria over global climate change. "*[People] exchanged the truth about God for a lie, and worshiped and served created things rather than the Creator.*" (Romans 1:25 NIV)

The fourth stage is actually a judgment of God upon our willful rebellion as he withdraws restraint upon our sinful nature. Whether a human is male or female is locked into every single one of the billions of cells that make up our bodies, and no amount of cross-dressing, hormone treatment, or surgery can change that reality. **The ultimate fist-waving in the face of God is to believe that He will determine nothing about our lives, even our sexuality.** Yet, *"abandoned natural relations… [men and women] were inflamed with lust for one another…."* (Romans 1:26, 27 NIV). Over the last several decades, many countries in the western world have placed homosexual "marriage" on equal footing with Biblical marriage.

During the final stage of rebellion, God gives the culture over to a *"depraved mind"* and *"every kind of wickedness"* as people *"not only continue to do these very things but also approve of those who practice them"* (Romans 1:28-29, 32 NIV). As we look at the list in Romans 1:29-31 - envy, murder, deceit, malice, gossip, arrogance, and so on – **all are on the rise in America today**. Just as in Sodom and Gomorrah, anyone standing against such evil will be persecuted, and ultimately, such a society will be destroyed – either from within or from without.

Notice that the downward slide started with the denial of a Creator. What is the solution? Perhaps part of the answer is sharing with others the evidence for a Creator to whom we are accountable.

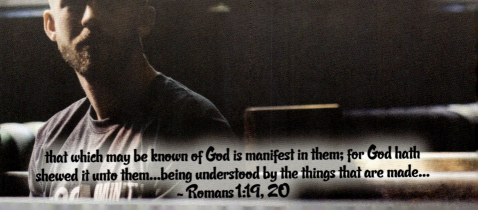

that which may be known of God is manifest in them; for God hath shewed it unto them…being understood by the things that are made…
~ Romans 1:19, 20

If you love me, keep my commandments.
– John 14:15

"If no set of moral ideas were truer or better than any other, there would be no sense in preferring civilized morality to savage morality or Christian morality to Nazi morality."
– C.S. Lewis, chair of Medieval and Renaissance Literature at Cambridge University

August

Geology

August 1

Chalk is a sedimentary rock made up of a collection of the skeletons of phytoplankton. The White Cliffs of Dover, in southern England, is a picture of this massive graveyard. The cliffs are 350 feet high at the English Channel, while across much of England the beds are 1300 feet thick.

Evolutionists believe that such thick chalk deposits require millions of years to accumulate. Under catastrophic conditions caused by the biblical Flood, about 4400 years ago, **explosive blooms of tiny organisms produced chalk beds, however, in a short period of time**. The oceans during the Flood were warmer with massive nutrient loading from the dead plant and animal life. This caused plankton to multiply enormously. The warm, turbulent seawaters caused these tiny skeletons to amass, die, and settle rapidly to the bottom as pure chalk. This cycle continued until the floodwaters were drained from the continents. The unimaginable scale of these blooms was driven by the availability of nutrients and carbon dioxide from dead creatures, and volcanic activity associated with Noah's Flood.

The purity of chalk deposits is one point of evidence supporting their catastrophic origin. If they formed over millions of years, we should find a wide variety of other marine creatures and sedimentary debris within the deposits. Yet, we do not. A second point of supporting evidence is the occasional discovery of large animal fossils found within these deposits. Both dinosaurs and 6-foot long clams have been found fossilized within the chalk. If large animals were not buried very quickly, they would have rotted away. Chalk beds cover 25% of the Earth's surface, and it is the purity of these beds, along with the large fossils found within them, that shout "catastrophe deposits"! This is exactly what would be expected from Noah's Flood.

Shew me thy ways, O Lord; teach me thy paths. Lead me in thy truth, and teach me: for thou art the God of my salvation; on thee do I wait all the day. ~ Psalm 25:4,5

August 2 — History

The ancient Chinese possessed an unusual knowledge of Bible history thats they incorporated into their written pictograph language. The most ancient of Chinese writings are called oracle bones in which the pictographs are inscribed on bones and tortoise shells. The inventor of the original Chinese characters obviously had knowledge of the Genesis account. For example, the word for *desire or covet* is made up of two characters, trees and woman:

Woman + Trees = Desire, Covet

There were two trees in the Garden of Eden, the tree of the knowledge of good and evil (the forbidden tree) and the tree of life. In the Genesis account, Eve saw the fruit of a forbidden tree and desired it.

The word *difficulty, trouble* is made up of tree and garden

Trees + (Garden) Enclosure = Difficulty, Trouble

When Adam and Eve ate of that forbidden fruit in the garden, difficulty resulted. Now there would be thorns and thistles and difficulty during childbirth.

Not only was the Earth cursed, but now death would enter in. The character meaning, *to die, perish* is:

Hands + Trees = Mulberry Tree + Mouths = To Die, Perish

Note how the two mouths (Adam and Eve) indicating eating fruit from the forbidden tree produced death.

These are just a few examples of how the knowledge of the first eleven chapters of Genesis is imbedded in the Chinese pictograph language. When witnessing to the Chinese, you can show them that Christianity is not just a Western religion but that their ancient fathers knew and believed in the One true God of the Bible. The Chinese language is a silent witness to the knowledge of Genesis 1-11.

"The tree of life (was) also in the midst of the garden, and the tree of knowledge of good and evil...And when the woman saw that the tree was good for food, and that it was pleasant to the eyes, and a tree to be desired (covetable)... she took of the fruit thereof, and did eat, and gave also unto her husband with her; and he did eat." ~ Genesis 2:9, 3:6

Biology

August 3

Honeybees are cold-blooded, but by moving their flight muscles in a way reminiscent of our shivering, they can generate heat. This ability does more than keep the hive warm on a cold winter day; it protects the hive from predators. Sometimes the hive is threatened with chalkboard fungus. When this happened, researchers have noticed that bees raise the temperature of the hive to kill the fungus. Researchers also found that when the hive is attacked by a giant hornet, the bees swarm the hornet, surround it, and then begin to "shiver," raising the hive's temperature to 116°F. The honeybees are unable to sting through the hornet's tough armor, so they kill it by heat! Amazingly, if they would increase the temperature just one more degree, to 117°F, the bees themselves would die from the heat. How do the bees know this? How do they know what the temperature is in the hive? Remember, they are all working independently to generate this heat. God has given his creatures the ability to stay healthy and protect themselves.

They compassed me about like bees....
~ Psalm 118:12a

August 4 — Biology

How does a honeybee, a cold-blooded insect, survive the winter? Bees like to keep their hive at 95°F. But how do they do this? As the temperature becomes cooler, the honeybees form a cluster. Those inside the ball of bees are kept warm, and they rotate with the bees on the outside of the ball so that all have a chance to remain warm. As the temperature continues to cool, the bees will move their flight muscles without flying; you could say the bees are "shivering." This generates heat, warming the bee cluster further.

What if the hive gets too hot in the summer? Some of the bees act as cooling fans, standing at the entrance of the hive and beating their wings creating a breeze. If this does not reduce the hive's temperature, other bees leave the hive and bring back water that they spread out on the walls of the hive. Now the fanning of the bees causes the water to evaporate and cool the hive.

Bees appear to be smart engineers, but they are just programmed to do this. The really smart engineer is the One who programmed this within them, and that is God.

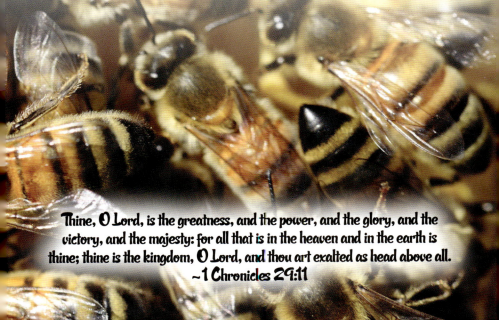

Thine, O Lord, is the greatness, and the power, and the glory, and the victory, and the majesty: for all that is in the heaven and in the earth is thine; thine is the kingdom, O Lord, and thou art exalted as head above all.
~1 Chronicles 29:11

Biology

August 5

Tree frogs live in trees, sticking firmly to branches and leaves -- even walking upside down on these surfaces. How do they keep from falling off? It's all in the feet. Close inspection of a tree frog's foot reveals pads with cracks and crevices from which mucus oozes. This mucus first cleans the dust and dirt off the surface to which the frog wants to cling. Then more mucus oozes out - creating a thin layer of "adhesive" to grip the surface. **These tree frogs have feet that both clean and stick.** Did these sticky feet happen by accident and chance? How many tree frogs fell to their death before they got it right? Who created sticky feet for the tree frogs? God only had to speak, and it came into existence.

Praise ye the Lord: for it is good to sing praises unto our God....
~ Psalm 147:1

August 6

Cosmology

Step outside on a clear, dark night when there is no moon and see a sweeping band of white across the night sky; it's the Milky Way galaxy. It looks like someone spilled a bottle of milk as the hazy white area glows, but in reality, it is the light from a vast number of stars.

The night sky is filled with hundreds of billions of galaxies, each with millions to trillions of stars with each star varying in color, size, temperature and brightness; we also find neutron stars, pulsars, and novas (star explosions) along with nebulae in all their splendor. **The more we study the universe, the more we are amazed by its immensity, complexity, and beauty**.

In the same way, the more we study the Creator God, the more amazing He becomes to us. His power and divine nature are displayed through the things He has made (Romans 1:20). And the things we can observe are but the outer fringe of his works; how faint the whisper we hear of him! (Job 26:14).

We should not be surprised at all the incredible things we find in the universe!

By his spirit he hath garnished the heavens....
~ Job 26:13a

Biology

August 7

Have you ever heard of a bird that sews its nest? This bird, which lives in Southeast Asia, is aptly named the "tailor bird." The tailor bird starts with large, green tree leaves and pokes holes with its sharp beak along the edges of the leaves. Then, it uses spider webs or grasses to sew the leaves into a cylinder shape. Now the bird builds its nest inside of this cylinder. When the chicks hatch, they are hidden away behind a green curtain of leaves.

How does the tailor bird know how to sew? **Did the young, female birds go to sewing classes at bird school?** No, these birds are born with this ability programmed in their brains. Scientists call this programming "instinct," but have never really been able to explain from where these instincts come from. It is as if a program was written in the hard drive of their brain. When we see a program, we know there must be a programmer, and this programmer is God.

Touching the Almighty, we cannot find him out: he is excellent in power....
~ Job 37:23

August 8

Microbiology

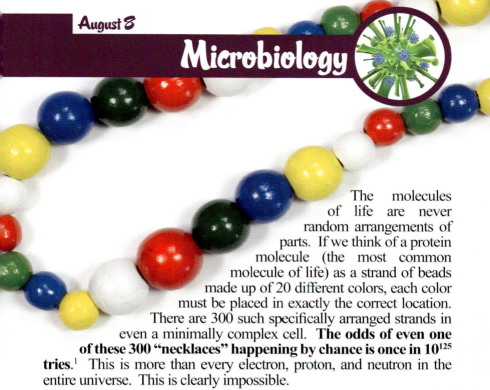

The molecules of life are never random arrangements of parts. If we think of a protein molecule (the most common molecule of life) as a strand of beads made up of 20 different colors, each color must be placed in exactly the correct location. There are 300 such specifically arranged strands in even a minimally complex cell. **The odds of even one of these 300 "necklaces" happening by chance is once in 10^{125} tries**.[1] This is more than every electron, proton, and neutron in the entire universe. This is clearly impossible.

Michael Denton, an Australian scientist, has written that even the simplest cell would require at least 100 functional protein "necklaces" to appear simultaneously and start interacting with each other in perfect coordination.[2] Since just one protein is as unlikely as $1/10^{125}$, the odds of 100 such proteins is $1/10^{2000}$. That is a one followed by 2000 zeros! **It is abundantly clear that life has a designer** of unimaginable intelligence and ability!

Oh, give thanks to the Lord of lords! For His mercy endures forever: To Him who alone does great wonders.
~ Psalm 136:3,4

Biology

August 9

A scientist pondered what she was seeing on the oleander shrub. She had been looking at a shrub and noticed a fly moving around, but upon closer examination, it looked like ants hitching a ride on the fly's wings. But the ants looked too symmetrical, so she got out her microscope. **She was astounded to discover one ant "painted" on each wing of the fruit fly** (*Goniurellia tridens*).

Not only was there a perfect representation of an ant on each wing, but it was so well done that each "painting" displayed an ant's head, thorax, and abdomen (the three parts of an insect), six legs and two antennae. When frightened, the fruit fly fluttered its wings, causing the two ant-like images to move back and forth, confusing a predator and allowing the fruit fly to dart away. How do evolutionists explain how these images got "painted" on the wings? They don't – they simply state that "evolution did it." Did the fruit fly have the mental ability to "paint" these images with its DNA code? When we see perfectly designed images with precise detail, we know there must be a designer, and that designer is God.

Unto thee lift I up mine eyes, O thou that dwellest in the heavens.
~ Psalm 123:1

August 10 — Biology

Who cleans up the seal and penguin colonies? The snowy sheathbill bird. This white bird looks like a cross between a pigeon and domesticated hen and is widespread across the Antarctica region. It hangs out in the seal and penguin colonies during breeding season. **What we think is disgusting, they think is delicious**.

Sheathbills eat dead seals, penguins and their droppings. These birds are the clean-up crew, making the colony a healthier place. By removing dead animals, these birds limit the spread of diseases. God's attention to every detail of life is apparent in His creative details for making healthy seal and penguin colonies at the far ends of the Earth.

The birds round about are against her; come ye, assemble all the beasts of the field, come to devour.
~ Jeremiah 12:9

August 11

Biblical Accuracy

Dr. Duane Gish, author of *Dinosaurs by Design*, documents a few of more than 270 stories from various cultures around the world that talk about a devastating worldwide flood.[1] Here are just a few examples:

- **Hawaii** – Long after the death of the first man, Kuniuhonna, the world became a wicked, terrible place to live. There was one good man left; his name was Nu-u. He made a great canoe with a house on it and filled it with animals. The waters came up over all the Earth and killed all the people. Only Nu-u and his family were saved.
- **China** – Fuhi is considered the "father of their civilization," Fuhi, his wife, three sons, and three daughters escaped a great flood. He and his family were the only people left alive on Earth. After the great flood, they repopulated the Earth.
- **Babylonia** – Ancient documents list 10 great kings that lived before a great flood came to destroy the Earth. One man survived this flood, and all people on Earth descended from this one man.
- **Toltec** – The Toltec Indians of Mexico tell of a "first world" that lasted for 1716 years before a great flood covered even the highest mountains. A few men escaped this flood in a "closed chest." Following the flood, the men built a great tower to provide safety. Their languages, however, were confused and they wandered to other parts of the world.
- **Genesis** – God sent a worldwide Flood to judge the sinfulness of man. One righteous family of eight was saved by building a boat and bringing animals on board. At the end of the Flood, the boat rested on top of a high mountain. They came down from the mountain and repopulated the world.

All of the 270 cultural stories have similarities to the Genesis Flood account described in the Bible because they all came from the same original source – people's knowledge of this real event. The stories just became distorted over time.

And Noah went forth, and his sons, and his wife, and his sons' wives with him: Every beast, every creeping thing, and every fowl, and whatsoever creepeth upon the earth, after their kinds, went forth out of the ark. ~ Genesis 8:18-19

August 12  **History**

What do Australian Aborigines and people of India have in common? Apparently, they are related. Recent genetic testing found strong DNA similarities between them. The large number of similar genetic markers across the genome gives a clear signal that **the people of India and Australia intermarried 4,000 - 5,000 years ago**. This would also help explain the many linguistic similarities between the peoples of southern India and many of the Aboriginal tribes. How is this viewed from a biblical perspective? After the Flood of Noah's time, the people built a tower of Babel and then were dispersed (Genesis 10, 11). The dispersion of the people from the tower of Babel may have happened several hundred years after the Flood (over 4,000 years ago). As a result, some groups of people would have settled in India, and others traveled further on to Australia. Modern DNA testing confirms this migration and the corresponding dates. Science finally catches up with the Bible.

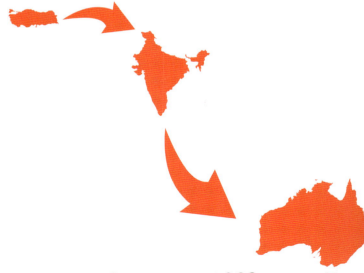

Therefore is the name of it called Babel; because the LORD did there confound the language of all the earth: and from thence did the LORD scatter them abroad upon the face of all the earth. ~ Genesis 11:9

Biology

August 13

Did you know that the lampsillis mussel has its own fishing lure? These mussels live in streams and lakes. When it is time to send out its larvae, it pushes part of its soft body out of its shell. **This fleshy mantle mimics a little minnow – it even has "eyes."** The lure movement is also astonishingly like a live minnow, even gulping with its mouth.

When a "host fish." a largemouth bass, comes close to the mussel and "takes the bait." the mussel shoots a cloud of larvae into the fish's mouth where they clamp onto its gills. Here the larvae stay for weeks sucking the blood from the host fish; finally, they drop off when they are large enough to survive as adult mussels.

How can a mussel evolve the right lure for the host fish? How can a mussel that has no eyes know what the lure needs to look like or when a bass will come to its lure? If the mussel did not shoot its larvae into the host fish, then it would go extinct. Throwing the word like "evolution" at this amazing process does not explain how it could have developed. It had to be designed to work the way it did from the beginning, or it would not work at all.

And blessed be his glorious name for ever: and let the whole earth be filled with his glory; Amen, and Amen.
~ Psalm 72:19

August 14

Biology

Freshwater mussels have a very unusual and complex life cycle. One part of their life cycle requires the use of a fish as a host. But how does the mussel get its larvae into the fish? One mussel found in the waters of North America, the "snuff box mussel," uses an amazing method. **This mussel does what many sport fishermen do; it catches a fish, and then releases it**.

When the mussel is ready to release its larvae for the next stage in its reproductive life cycle, it catches a host fish by closing its shell on its head or snout and holds onto the fish until the larvae are released and attach themselves to the fish's gills. Then the mussel releases the fish. Weeks later, the larvae have grown and dropped off the fish to continue the mussel's life cycle. How does evolution explain this? How does a mussel that has no eyes grab a logperch fish? The best explanation is that God designed this specific life cycle to reveal His cleverness to us.

For great is the Lord, and greatly to be praised....
~1 Chronicles 16:25

Paleontology

August 15

Noah took two of every kind of land animal on board the Ark, including dinosaurs. After getting off the Ark, these dinosaurs spread around the world. The ancient histories of many cultures document dinosaur encounters.

Britain's history contains hundreds of stories about large reptiles called dragons.

- According to one account, a large reptile killed and ate King Morvidus in 336 B.C.
- Just over 100 years ago, elderly Welsh folk told of a colony of winged serpents (pterosaurs?) that lived in the woods around Penllin Castle in Glamorgan. These *"winged serpents were the terror of old and young alike…they were described as very beautiful,… looked as if they were covered with jewels of all sorts…when angry, they flew over people's heads… they were as bad for poultry as foxes…they were terrors in farmyards."*
- In 1405, after an unsuccessful attempt by local archers to kill the dragon with its impenetrable hide, the villagers near Sudbury drove into a swamp a *"dragon vast in body with a crested head, teeth like a saw, and a tail extending to an enormous length. Having slaughtered the shepherd of a flock, it devoured many sheep."*

After the Flood, people also spread across the Earth, but who would want these terrifying creatures living near their village? Many dinosaurs likely went extinct due to human expansion. When we put on our biblical glasses, it is no surprise to find these types of widespread "dragon" reports. Dinosaurs definitely did not go extinct 65 million years ago!

Every beast, every creeping thing, and every fowl, and whatsoever creepeth upon the earth, after their kinds, went forth out of the ark.
~ Genesis 8:19

August 16

Biology

A hermit crab cannot make its own shell to live in but has to find an empty shell to occupy. Once found, he backs into the shell; his twisted body is ideally designed to fit into a spiral shell. The crab uses his two back legs to grip the inside of the shell, keeping him firmly in place. The two front legs are used for walking, with the right one being much larger than the left. This right claw can be used as a "door" when he wants to blockade himself inside the shell. When the hermit crab gets too large for his shell, he leaves it and finds another larger shell to live in.

Often, a hermit crab carries a sea anemone on his shell. Sea anemones are covered with stinging cells, which release poison and kill the crab's enemies when touched. When a hermit crab has to move to a new home, he will "plant" the anemone on his new shell. How did the hermit crab get his spirally curved body that fits perfectly in a shell? How did he get his extra-large right claw that acts as a door to his home? And how did he discover that it was good to have a sea anemone living on his shell? **How does evolution explain these features?** It is much easier to explain them if we accept that God created the hermit crab with these special features.

The foxes have holes, and the birds of the air have nests...
~ Matthew 8:20a

Christian Truth

August 17

What is the greatest commandment? Love the Lord your God with all your heart, soul, strength and MIND (Luke 10:27). Christians are not to park their brains at the church door but are called to be thinking Christians. Here are some questions that can help you when discussing issues such as evolution.

1. What do you mean by __(*Evolution or other terms*)____?
2. How do you know what you are saying is true?
3. What difference does that make in your life? Or, So What?
4. What if you're wrong?
5. What would you accept as evidence that you may be wrong?

Use these questions wisely. You can use them in two ways - as a hammer or pry bar. We want the pry bar. In 2 Corinthians 10:5, we are called to destroy speculations, not people!

We, as Christians, need to be soft-hearted toward people and hard-headed in our thinking.

Casting down imaginations, and every high thing that exalteth itself against the knowledge of God, and bringing into captivity every thought to the obedience of Christ; ~ **2 Corinthians 10:5**

August 18 — Anatomy

The evolutionary idea of vestigial (or useless) organs, as leftovers from our evolutionary past, has produced tragic consequences. For many years, the thyroid gland (which has no duct to release secretions) mystified doctors. **So when people had an enlarged thyroid (goiter), it was simply removed**. In the 1870s, Dr. Theodore Kocker noticed some of his patients were going insane a few years after their operation. Through examining his surgical notes, he found that if he had left any thyroid behind, the patients did not go mad. However, the operations continued, and it was another 30 years before the function of thyroxine (the secretion from this gland) was discovered.

Today, we know that the thyroid gland is vitally important for making and storing hormones that help regulate such things as heart rate, blood pressure, body temperature, and growth rate. If we do not have enough of this hormone, we can feel overly tired, cold, or otherwise low in energy. If we have too much of this hormone, it is like a car idling too fast - we are likely to become overly nervous/irritated, have trouble concentrating, have trouble sleeping, and so on. **The thyroid gland is hardly a useless, leftover organ!** The more scientists study the body, the more they become convinced that the body did not happen by accident and chance but was designed by someone of great intelligence; that someone is God.

But now, O LORD, thou art our father; we are the clay, and thou our potter; and we all are the work of thy hand.
~ Isaiah 64:8

Botany

August 19

Have you considered how seeds get moved around the Earth? Land plants are stuck in one spot by their roots. They can't move, so God designed their seeds to be moved around. God's creativity and imagination in this area is astounding. Seeds are dispersed by wind, water, ingestion, hitchhiking, and exploding into the air. They are designed with parachutes, barbs, airfoils, draglines, airbags, wings, hooks, and rocket shapes. If wind is being used to disperse the seed, how would that seed be designed? Lightweight and maybe with a wing or parachute to give it more lift to float it afar. If water is being used to disperse a seed, the seed is designed waterproof and floatable. If animals are used to disperse seeds, they need to eat the fruit first.

The seeds within the fruit must remain undigested as they pass through digestive systems before being deposited in another place. If hitchhiking, then the seed needs hooks and barbs to attach itself to the animals' skin, feathers, or fur. If the seed is thrown from the plant, it would involve lots of physics. For instance, once the seeds are ripe, **a squirting cucumber literally shoots its seeds as much as 40 feet away!**

When you go for a walk in the meadows or woods, look to see God's creativity in how He designed a stationary plant to move around the world.

Then the earth shall yield her increase.
~ Psalm 67:6

August 20

Biology

There is no need for a bug zapper when a chameleon is around. With stealth and patience, the chameleon moves along a branch. His feet are ideally made to grasp branches with little effort. His tail is ever ready to catch the branch should he fall. His eyes are unique, like turrets on a tank, swiveling independently to see in every direction – a full 360 degrees. **Each eye is also like a telephoto lens**, adjusting and calculating distances with precise accuracy.

When prey is located, both eyes focus on the bug, and Zap! The chameleon's catapulting tongue shoots out five times faster than the speed of a jet fighter plane being catapulted from the deck of an aircraft carrier – 16 times the acceleration of gravity (16 g). The tongue itself is about twice as long as his body as it is propelled forward. This long tongue is stored on a bone – similar to how a long, sleeved sweater can be pushed up one's arm. When the chameleon sees the bug, he takes aim, cocks, and fires his tongue forward with a catapult motion. A fraction of a second before contact, a sticky tongue pad forms into a suction cup at the tip of the tongue – complete with finger-like extensions at the tip (like an elephant's trunk) to wrap around the bug. The bug is caught and brought in for lunch. **All this happens faster than the blink of an eye!** How many years did the chameleon stumble along trying to develop his feet, eyes, and specialized tongue in order to catch lunch? What we see is marvelous design that should bring us to our knees in worship of the Designer, God.

And all men shall fear, and shall declare the work of God;
for they shall wisely consider of his doing.
- Psalm 64:9

Geology

August 21

If there was a worldwide flood, would not sediments have been transported vast distances? As the Flood waters swept over the continents, they would have deposited sedimentary layers. Let's look at just one example.

The Grand Canyon has a bright white layer of sandstone near the top lip commonly called "the bathtub ring." This Coconino sandstone layer consists of pure quartz sand averaging 315 feet thick and covering some 200,000 square miles, containing at least 10,000 cubic miles of sand. Where did all this sand come from? Within the Coconino sandstone are sloping sand "waves" pointing southward, indicating that the water flowed from the north. It has been postulated that the source of this sand was northern Utah or Wyoming.

Higher in the strata sequence above the rim of the Grand Canyon is the Navaho Sandstone. It can be seen in Zion National Park, just north of the Grand Canyon. This sandstone also consists of very pure quartz sand, giving it its brilliant white color, and it also has sand "waves" indicating that the sand came from the northeast. Within this sandstone is the mineral zircon, which is easily traced to its source material. It has been postulated that these sand grains in the Navajo Sandstone could have come from the Appalachians of Pennsylvania and New York and farther north into Canada. These sand grains were transported about 1,250 miles across North America. If there was a world-wide flood, sediments would have been transported vast distances, and that is what we are now discovering. This speaks of a global Flood some 4400 years ago.

Whereby the world that then was, being overflowed with water, perished. ~ 2 Peter 3:6b

August 22

Design

One of the most beautiful moths in the world is the Atlas moth (*Attacus atlas*) from the forests of Southeast Asia. Most people are impressed with this rare moth's incredible 12-inch wingspan, making it one of the largest living insects of today. The patterns on the moth's wings are gorgeous. But take a closer look at the moth's wing tips. **They resemble a cobra's head**, complete with staring eyes and a grimacing mouth. What better way to scare off predators than to have a poisonous snake "painted" on your wings!

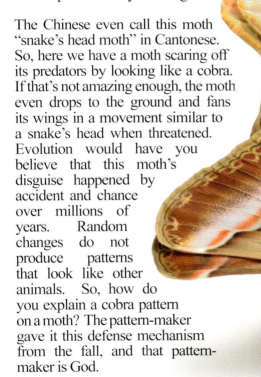

The Chinese even call this moth "snake's head moth" in Cantonese. So, here we have a moth scaring off its predators by looking like a cobra. If that's not amazing enough, the moth even drops to the ground and fans its wings in a movement similar to a snake's head when threatened. Evolution would have you believe that this moth's disguise happened by accident and chance over millions of years. Random changes do not produce patterns that look like other animals. So, how do you explain a cobra pattern on a moth? The pattern-maker gave it this defense mechanism from the fall, and that pattern-maker is God.

All things were made by him; and without him was not anything made that was made. ~ John 1:3

History

August 23

Of all the fish in the world, the 'o'opu 'alamo'o (opu) - native only to the island of Hawaii, is one of the most amazing. This fish only lays its eggs far inland from the ocean in the upper reaches of the Kolekole stream. Once the eggs hatch, the larvae are swept downstream by the swift current of the river and flushed into the warm, clear waters of the Pacific Ocean, where they mature into colorful 5-inch-long fish. To produce the next generation of fish, the female must swim back upstream to lay her eggs in the fresh water of the mountain stream. Here is where the miraculous occurs! Between where the mother lays her eggs and her ocean habitat is the Akaka Waterfall - which plummets 440 feet from a narrow opening on a sheer cliff wall. How can a fish swim up a 440 foot waterfall?

Unique to all the fish in the world, this particular species has a special set of fins fused together to form a suction cup directly between its front pectoral fins. The Opu laboriously attaches its suction cup fins to the water-slickened surface of the falls, and drags itself upward against the force of the flowing water, and reattaches itself again. Moving a fraction of an inch at a time, over many days, she literally free-climbs the 440 foot falls against the flow of the water to the top of the stream where she lays her eggs.

The following question arises; how did this fish learn to do this? Without the suction-cup shaped fins, the climb would be impossible! The opu had to have the ability to climb with suction cups from the beginning or no more opu fish. God created the opu fish to delight us in His creative ability. Only God could create a waterfall-climbing fish!

For by him were all things created, that are in heaven, and that are in earth, visible and invisible, whether they be thrones, or dominions, or principalities, or powers: all things were created by him, and for him:
- Colossians 1:16

August 24
History

Often, we think man is more intelligent now than in the past. Have you considered when man **began to write?**

- One of the great wonders of the ancient world was the library of Alexandria built in 300 B.C. and located in Alexandria, Egypt. This **vast library** contained over a million scrolls.
- In 900 B.C., King Solomon writes in Ecclesiastes, "my son, be admonished: of making **many books** there is no end…." (Ecclesiastes 12:12).
- In 2000 B.C., Job wrote, "Oh that my words were now written! Oh that they were **printed in a book!**" (Job 19:23). Here we see Job, writing some 500 years before Moses (1500 B.C.), contemplating printing a book!
- Going back further, we find in Babylon, on one of King Ashurbanipal's tablets, a comment that he "**loved to read the writing of the age before the Flood**." His library had over 100,000 volumes![1] Arguments that writing did not exist in the time of Moses are not true. Here a king records that he was reading writing prior to the Flood of Noah's day (2348 B.C.).
- Another **Babylonian tablet lists the *ten* kings of Babylon who lived before the Flood**, in the Bible; Noah was the *tenth* generation from Adam.

Man was created intelligent from the beginning! The evolutionary idea that man started as a caveman who was an unintelligent, knuckle-dragging idiot is not true. Man was created intelligent from the beginning. Man was made in the image of God to communicate, using both speech and writing, from the very beginning.

Oh that my words were now written! Oh that they were printed in a book! That they were graven with an iron pen and lead in the rock forever!
~ Job 19:23, 24

Design

August 25

Scientists have recently unlocked the secret of beautifully color, tropical Indonesian Peacock or Swallowtail (*Papilio blumei*) butterflies. On their wings are brilliant iridescent bands of bright green. These colors are not produced by pigments but by light bouncing off what looks like the inside of an egg carton (only on the microscopic level). The intensity of colors is produced because there are multiple "egg-carton-shaped" layers alternate with layers of air on a nanostructure level. Scientists have copied the butterfly's nanostructure design - resulting in the same intense colors being produced.

Now scientists want to bring this butterfly scale technology to market. These artificial structures could be used in paper money or passports to prevent forgery. Scientists have copied what was already present; they recognized a good design when they saw it. The next time you look at your passport, take a look and see if there is a butterfly scale shimmering back at you and think of the **ONE** who is the real Creator of this technology.

He hath made every thing beautiful in his time:
~ Ecclesiastes 3:11a

August 26 — Geology

A brand new island was "born" off the coast of Iceland in 1963. This new island, named Surtsey, was created by an erupting undersea volcano. Within a few months of its formation, this sterile, volcanic rock island was already being transformed into a "mature" island. Wide sandy beaches, gravel banks, impressive cliffs, gullies, channels, and boulders were all being worn by the relentlessly pounding surf. **Had no-one been around to see the island form recently, one might say it looks millions of years old**.

Iceland's chief geologist Sigurdur Thorarinsson, was amazed at how old the island looked only months after its formation. Biologists, too, were surprised; the island was colonized by plants quickly. Birds started having chicks there in 1970 (7 years later) - bringing in seeds with their excrement. Growing plants supported insects, that attracted birds, that in turn brought in more plants, and the cycle continued. There is now a fully functioning ecosystem on Surtsey. What happened on Surtsey provides insight into what happened after the Flood of Noah's day – the rapid redistribution of plants and animals around the world. Surtsey continues to teach us more, for it is also rapidly eroding - about 2.5 acres a year. Within a few centuries, Surtsey could be gone!

Surtsey, sixteen days after the onset of the eruption

Surtsey has been full of surprises - teaching us that mature landscapes can form rapidly, biological diversity can develop quickly, and erosion can transform landscapes swiftly.

The waters wear the stones:
~ Job 14:19a

Biology

August 27

Does this sound like the plot from a poor horror movie? A parrot attacks and kills a sheep - even burrowing into the sheep's body to devour its kidneys while the sheep is still alive! That is what was happening in New Zealand's high country during the late 1800s. Naturalists were stunned as they discovered that local birds (called keas) were killing and eating thousands of sheep. These parrots normally ate seeds and fruit. Why was this taking place? As sheep were introduced into New Zealand's highland country, the habitat changed drastically, and the parrot's old food source was greatly diminished. How they learned to eat meat is not known. The New Zealand kea became so hated that in the hundred year period between 1870 -1970, an estimated 150,000 were killed. Today's keas are not showing this type of behavior.

In 2002, a British researcher reported that he saw a sheep eating a bird; the sheep had snatched and eaten a grouse in the scrublands. This was not normal behavior for a sheep, for they are herbivores, not carnivores. But that was not the only such report, CNN in 1999 reported that Hussein al-Marqouqi's sheep ate nine chickens. Also, out of China's Sichuan province comes a report of a panda killing and eating 26 goats. **These types of accounts of plant-eating animals devouring meat are not as uncommon as one might think**. After the Fall, certain animals started eating meat; prior to the Fall, all were plant eaters. These reports can give us insights into how animals became carnivores.

And to every beast of the earth, and to every fowl of the air, and to every thing that creepeth upon the earth, wherein there is life, I have given every green herb for meat: and it was so.
~ Genesis 1:30

August 28
Christian Truth

Where in the Bible does it say the Earth is 6,000 years old? There is no place in the Bible that gives the exact date of creation. By studying the genealogies of Genesis, however, we can figure out an approximate timeline from Creation to the time of Abraham.

VERSE IN GENESIS	FATHER	SON	FATHER'S AGE AT SON'S BIRTH
1:1-31	Creation		0
5:03	Adam	Seth	130
5:06	Seth	Enosh	105
5:09	Enosh	Kenan	90
5:12	Kenan	Mahalalel	70
5:15	Mahalalel	Jared	65
5:18	Jared	Enosh	162
5:21	Enosh	Methuselah	65
5:25	Methuselah	Lamech	187
5:28	Lamech	Noah	182
7:01	Age of Noah at the Flood		600
	CREATION TO FLOOD		1656
11:10	Shem	Arphashad	2yrs after flood
11:12	Arphashad	Shelah	35
11:14	Shelah	Eber	30
11:16	Eber	Peleg	34
11:18	Peleg	Reu	30
11:20	Reu	Serug	32
11:22	Serug	Nahor	30
11:24	Nahor	Terah	29
11:26, 32; 12:4, Acts 7:4	Terah	Abram	130
	Age of Earth at time of Abram's Birth		2008

From creation week to Abram's birth was 2008 years. If we round the number to 2000 years from creation to Abraham, and 2000 years from Abraham to Jesus, and 2000 years from Jesus to now, that's about 6000 years since creation. If we trust the Bible to mean what it says, the Earth/universe is about 6,000 years old, **NOT** hundreds of thousands of years, **NOT** millions of years, **NOT** billions of years.

Note- The Jewish calendar states the Hebrew year is 5779, (2018 A.D).

In the beginning God created the heaven and the earth.
~ Genesis 1:1

August 29

Biology

The archer fish, named for its expertise in archery, has a distinctive way of getting its supper. **This fish shoots its prey with water bullets!** The aquatic sharpshooter shoots these "bullets" up to nine feet away with deadly accuracy to knock its prey off overhanging leaves and branches. To accomplish this requires the fish to have a unique design.

This small fish has a mouth that is angled upward with the roof of its mouth having a groove to hold the tongue. When the gills 'pop' or slam shut, water is shot through the mouth as the tongue presses into the groove. The tip of the tongue directs the water bullets - adjusting for velocity and volume in order to precisely hit the insect. The cricket, grasshopper, or butterfly falls into the water to be quickly eaten.

But the archer fish's design is brilliant in many other ways. In order to conceal its position when hunting for insects above the water, its dorsal fins (the fins on its back) are farther back than almost all other fish. In this way, the hunter remains underwater and does not reveal its location. The archer fish's eyes are also unique. They have a special portion of the retina that swivels into place allowing it to look at the air above the water. Try this when you are swimming, with your mask on underwater, try looking up into the air above the water. It is almost impossible to see anything clearly above the surface of the water in this way - but not for the archer fish!

The archer fish is uniquely made - from its angled mouth to the groove in the roof of its mouth; from the dorsal fin placed farther back to the swiveling retina allowing it to clearly see up out of the water and into the air. How does evolution explain this? Remember that the only option evolution has for explaining life is non-directed, non-purposeful mutations over millions of years. Other fish get their food in the water; **no fish ever hunted its food in the air!** So where did the archer fish get this idea? He didn't. The archer fish testifies to the genius of its Maker.

The Lord sitteth upon the flood; yea, the Lord sitteth King for ever.
~ Psalm 29:10

August 30

Paleontology

What a fossil find! It was a blood-filled female mosquito locked in oil shale. Jurassic Park, here we come! Near Glacier National Park in Montana, fossil collectors have dug up more than 16,000 tiny insect fossils in oil shale. One of the most unique finds was a female mosquito whose abdomen was filled with blood. She was buried and fossilized so rapidly that her last blood meal never had time to be digested. **That itself is testimony to the catastrophic nature of the worldwide Flood that created these oil shales**.

"The abdomen of a blood-engorged mosquito is like a balloon ready to burst. It is very fragile," said the lead paleontologist. The odds against this mosquito becoming fossilized by slow evolutionary processes are simply astronomical. From an evolutionary view, our blood-filled mosquito had to have been blown to the water's surface, sunk quickly to the bottom, and covered with oxygen-free sediment to prevent rapid degradation - all without disrupting the engorged abdomen that was, "ready to burst." A better explanation is a sudden catastrophic burial of this mosquito along with countless other creatures beneath tons of water-borne sediment from the global Flood.

Much of the fossil record is a record of the order of burial, not the evolving of one creature into another. In fact, this supposed 46 million year old mosquito looks exactly like today's mosquitoes from North America. **Not a hint of evolutionary transformation!** This fossilized, blood-filled mosquito is a testimony to the recent global Flood of Noah's time.

And the waters prevailed upon the earth an hundred and fifty days.
~ Genesis 7:24

History

August 31

Ancient people were great movers of stone - as evidenced by Egypt's pyramids, Easter Island's megalithic head statues and England's Stonehenge. Yet, the largest cut stone has been found near Baalbek, Lebanon, in the ruins of an ancient city known as Heliopolis. Amidst these ruins is found the Temple of Jupiter with 70-foot columns that date back to the peak of the Roman Empire (~2000 years ago). They had quarried these columns in Egypt, barged them to Lebanon, and hauled them across the mountains in order to erect them. Quite a feat!

But the base upon which the columns stand is the real marvel. At the base of this Temple are three hewn stones called the "trilithon." It is believed that these stones were in place before the Romans arrived, and they simply engineered their building on this foundation. Each of these foundation stones weigh over a million pounds. The individual limestone blocks measure 10 feet by 13 feet by 60 feet long. These stones were quarried three-quarters of a mile away and raised 26 feet into the air. We don't even know how the builders transported these massive objects to their final location. Surprisingly, an even larger stone was found at the quarry measuring 14 feet high, 13 feet wide and 70 feet long - **weighing an estimated 1.7 million pounds!**

Compare the ingenuity of early man with NASA's movement of a similar weight object in 1965 – the giant Saturn V rocket. This rocket weighted approximately 400,000 pounds. It was moved from its construction building to the launch pad on a giant tracked vehicle called the Crawler-transporter. **This object weighted only half what these ancient stones weighted yet required a specially design vehicle to move it.** People 3000 - 4000 years ago moved stones weighing twice as much WITHOUT modern crawler-transporters! Students are routinely given the impression that ignorant, Stone Age "hunter-gatherers" from this period were little more than bumbling cavemen. Hardly! Ancients were quite intelligent; just look at the stone structures they left behind. Man was created intelligent from the beginning.

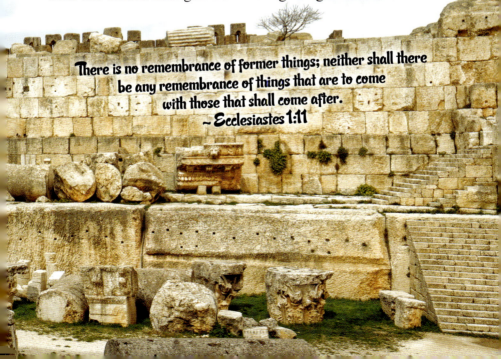

There is no remembrance of former things; neither shall there be any remembrance of things that are to come with those that shall come after.
~ Ecclesiastes 1:11

Professing to be wise, they became fools.
– Romans 1:22

"(An evolutionary origin of the human brain) is difficult to understand, because, unlike a computer, it was not built with specific purposes or principles...(no designer) only natural selection, the engine of evolution, is responsible."
- Gerald Fischbach, Scientific American, Vol.267, No.3, p.24.

september

September 1
Christian Truth

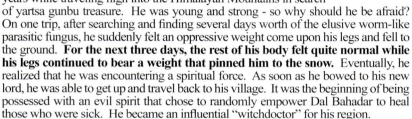

Not everything we observe in our world has scientific explanations. The following is the testimony of a Nepal Christian as recorded by missionary Paul Michaels:

A teenager named Dal Bahadar had been cheating death for several years while traveling high into the Himalayan Mountains in search of yartsa gunbu treasure. He was young and strong - so why should he be afraid? On one trip, after searching and finding several days worth of the elusive worm-like parasitic fungus, he suddenly felt an oppressive weight come upon his legs and fell to the ground. **For the next three days, the rest of his body felt quite normal while his legs continued to bear a weight that pinned him to the snow.** Eventually, he realized that he was encountering a spiritual force. As soon as he bowed to his new lord, he was able to get up and travel back to his village. It was the beginning of being possessed with an evil spirit that chose to randomly empower Dal Bahadar to heal those who were sick. He became an influential "witchdoctor" for his region.

Why he was chosen was as much a mystery as the powers that would unpredictably overcome him for the next seven years. Once these powers were newly manifested, his father-in-law sent him to a cave-dwelling Shaman to hone his powers. Some may think that possessing such power is a high calling, but Dal Bahadar found it to be a life of constant torment. He was continually sick and was trapped to serve his ruthless spiritual ruler. Possessing healing powers led others to revere him, but the physical and spiritual oppression drove his wife to find another man, and her abandonment only added to his torment.

Then one day a man from his village, Bhem, who had also been tormented with years of sickness, was made well by another healer. Everyone in the village was curious. How did this happen? Bhem told them, "A more powerful Ruler had healed him." He had been told of the Redeemer-King, Jesus, and he believed in him. When Dal Bahadar heard this news, he begged Bhem to take him to this church in a village several hours away. He too wanted to be set free. As he attended the church each week, he heard the good news of God's forgiveness comes through faith in His Son, Jesus Christ. On his fourth visit, he believed in Jesus Christ, and the church prayed for him. **A peace he had never known before began to flood his soul.**

Dal Bahadar has now been a believer for four years, leads a small fellowship of Christians in the village of Sayakhola, and is one of the students being trained for church planting in Mugu. Now his life's goal is to bring the freedom that Jesus offers to every village in the province of Mugu over the next five years. His treasure hunt for a healing fungus high in the Himalayan Mountains ultimately led Dal Bahadar to a far greater treasure.

As for me, I will call upon God; and the Lord shall save me. Evening, and morning, and at noon, will I pray, and cry aloud: and he shall hear my voice. ~ Psalm 55:16-17

September 2

Biology

A United States entomologist has estimated that one pair of Colorado potato beetles, if allowed to reproduce unchecked, would increase to over 60 million in one season. One female fly, beginning reproduction in May, would produce 143,875 bushels of flies by August. Aphids reproduce quickly, and in one season they can produce over 13 generations. If not held in check, the world's aphid population would be ten sextillion aphids in one year. Imagine living in a world where insects were not controlled. But what controls insect reproduction rates?

Fortunately, birds have a large appetite for insects. It has been found that a scarlet tanager can eat over 600 gypsy moth caterpillars in 18 minutes. It has been estimated that chickadees alone eat over 8 billion insects per year. Birds keep the insect population in balance. Now consider what evolutionists say about the origin of birds – they did not evolve until many millions of years *after* insects appeared on our planet!

Without birds, insects would have decimated the world's vegetation. The world would have been a bleak place with little life. What we see is actually what God has said, that He created both birds and insects during the first week of creation at the very beginning of time.

*As soon then as they were come to land,
they saw a fire of coals there, and fish laid thereon, and bread.
~ John 21:9*

Biology

September 3

There are over 245 different species of poison dart frogs that live in the rainforests of the Americas. They display a dizzying array of bright colors ranging from deep blue to strawberry red and metallic green to polka-dotted yellow! **The golden poison dart frog is one of the deadliest**; if a person has the equivalent of two grains of table salt of the toxin in his bloodstream, he is dead within minutes! This toxin is so powerful that if an animal even touches the spot where a golden poison dart frog has recently sat, it dies!

When indigenous Colombian natives go hunting, they will catch these golden poison dart frogs and rub their darts on the frog's back. They then use blow guns with their poisonous darts to kill monkeys, birds, or even jaguars. One golden poison dart frog has enough poison to kill 10-12 people. Yet, the same frogs in captivity are not poisonous. Why?

Poison dart frogs obtain their poison from the foods they eat - such as ants and beetles. In captivity, they are not fed their usual rainforest food. How does a poisonous dart frog fit into the biblical account of a perfect, death-free world as described in the Garden of Eden? In the beginning, everything was good; dart frogs did not have an active poison. **Adam and Eve could have held these dart frogs, examined their dazzlingly beautiful colors of red, blue, and yellow - and not been harmed**. When Adam sinned, nature became cursed. Animals started to eat one another, and inactive defensive mechanisms became activated. Thus, the dart frogs became poisonous only after eating other creatures. God gave these tiny frogs protection from predators in a fallen world.

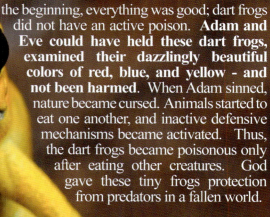

Our help is in the name of the Lord, who made heaven and earth.
~ Psalm 124:8

September 4

Design

If you listen closely, you will realize that birds are extremely skillful musicians. When birds sing, you can hear melody, harmony, and rhythm. Many birds sing in "absolute pitch", that is, if they sing a song in G major today, the same song will be sung in EXACTLY the G major pitch all other days. There is also evidence that birds can transpose songs from one key to another. Male blackbirds have been observed to sing in matched counter-singing, i.e. each blackbird takes turns singing a tune back to other birds. Some birds even sing a variation on a theme. When human musicians attempt a matching counter-singing, it requires planning, talent, practice, and design.

Some birds sing duets; the African robin performs its duet antiphonally (where 2 birds sing alternate notes in a song). To execute this type of duet requires split second timing! When you hear a bird singing, notice that the songs contain consonsant intervals, which produce a pleasant sound, rather than dissonant intervals. Hermit thrushes have been found to sing the pentatonic scales. Other birds can sing two notes at the same time because of the position of their voice boxes.

Both Mozart and Beethoven recognized birds' musical abilities and borrowed bird songs as inspiration for their music. Bird songs show evidence of structure and beauty. If evolution was true and songs evolved by accident or chance, then at least half the songs should be grating, irritating, and nonsensical. We do not hear that! The worldwide morning song of birds is known as the "Dawn Chorus" - welcoming in a new day. When we hear beautiful music, we know it has been composed and that there must be a composer. Bird songs are beautiful – take time to listen to what Jesus, the Greatest Composer of all, has composed for our pleasure.

Let everything that hath breath praise the LORD.
~ Psalm 150:6

September 5

Paleontology

When Europeans first settled in Australia, they recorded Aboriginal stories of a creature called the bunyip. This huge creature lived in swamps and had a "blood-chilling cry." In the 1800s, in Victoria, Australia, the bones of a bunyip were found. It was reported in the July 1845 edition of the *Goolong Advertiser* newspaper that an Aboriginal had identified this as a bunyip bone. He then drew a picture of the bunyip. This picture was taken to other Aborigines, who had no chance to communicate with the first one, and each identified the bone and picture as a bunyip. The newspaper reported a number of sightings of the bunyip; it looked like an alligator standing 12 feet tall. Its hind legs were thick and strong, with forelegs longer. It had long claws. It could swim. It walked on land with its hind legs and head erect. It was covered with multicolored scales and laid pale blue eggs double the size of an emu's egg. Its snout was like a duck's bill.

The description and newspaper sketch bear a strong resemblance to the duck-billed dinosaurs - **13 years before the first fossil duck-billed dinosaur bone was described**. Dinosaurs and man did live together. Today, many dinosaurs have gone extinct. When we put on our biblical glasses, we would expect these types of widespread reports after the Flood as the dinosaurs left the ark and spread out and filled the Earth.

Every beast, every creeping thing, and every fowl, and whatsoever creepeth upon the earth, after their kinds, went forth out of the ark.
~ Genesis 8:19

September 6

Biology

One of Australia's more bizarre creatures is the thorny devil. It looks like a walking cactus with sharp spikes all over its body. In the desert, there is not much water, but during the cool nights, dew collects on the lizard's spikes. Tiny grooves or channels between the spikes direct the condensed water to the thorny devil's mouth - allowing him to quench his thirst. **The water is not moved by a pump or gravity, but by capillary action**. You can see capillary action by placing a straw into a glass of water. Notice that the water rises up into the straw above the level of water in the glass. The smaller the channel, the further up the water will flow. Once water is in the grooves, all the lizard needs to do is swallow - this action sucks the water to his mouth, which in turn causes more water to move along the grooves.

Not only can the thorny lizard capture moisture at night from dew, it can also remove moisture from the vegetation it moves through by rubbing his belly on wet rocks or kicking damp sand on his back. What a design! The system effectively and efficiently sucks water from all over his body. He uses this superpower to the hilt, like a walking sponge; the thorny devil gathers all the water he needs. It is hard to believe that this system of grooves came about by accident and chance through millions of years. This system of spikes and grooves needed to be present from the beginning in order for the lizard to survive in a desert environment. What an ingenious water-collecting system!

The beast of the field shall honour me, the dragons and the owls: because I give waters in the wilderness.... ~ Isaiah 43:20

Cosmology

September 7

Why would God make galaxies? We live in the Milky Way galaxy, which contains over 100 billion stars. Our galaxy is disk-shaped with a bulge in the middle. The Earth is located on one of the arms of this spiral galaxy. About 30 of our closest galaxies are grouped into a cluster called "The Local Group." Another cluster is called the "Virgo cluster," which has about 2,000 galaxies. Between these clusters of galaxies are voids. It is estimated that there are 100 billion galaxies. But why aren't stars just randomly dispersed across the universe?

Galaxies have a special purpose. **Galaxies are visible from greater distances than a single star could ever be.** It is much easier to see a group of stars in a galaxy than one lone star! Take a piece of paper, and draw one star on it. Take another paper, and draw many stars on it. Now walk to the other side of the room. Which is easier to see, one star or a large group of stars? Galaxies allow us to understand the enormous size of the universe and the power of God in a way that single stars evenly dispersed around the universe could not. The heavens do declare the glory of God, but we could never know the vastness and the quantity of the stars in the universe if they were not grouped into galaxies.

Lift up your eyes on high, and behold who hath created these things, that bringeth out their host by number: he calleth them all by names by the greatness of his might, for that he is strong in power; not one faileth. ~ Isaiah 40:26

September 8

Biology

Have you considered the tiger swallowtail butterfly? In order not to be eaten, it has three disguises it uses through its various stages to adulthood.

1. The newly hatched larva looks like bird droppings. What bird would want to eat bird poop?! Three molts later, the caterpillar has turned green to match the leaves upon which it feeds.
2. In addition, the head of the caterpillar's green plump body has two large spots that resemble snake eyes. Birds that eat caterpillars hate snakes!
3. Finally, in its pupa stage, the tiger swallowtail looks like a broken twig on a tree.

These three disguises reflect a great deal of knowledge about the behavior of the creature that wants to eat this butterfly.

1. How did the larva grow itself to look like bird droppings? Did he look at droppings, know that birds don't eat droppings, and decide to transform his body to look like that?
2. At its third molt, how did it know to put the eyes of a snake on its green body? How did it know that birds are afraid of snakes? Had the caterpillar seen a snake?
3. During its pupa stage, how did it figure out how to color itself with the color and shape of a broken twig?

Evolutionists believe that because these things give the tiger swallowtail a survival advantage, they all just happened over huge time periods by accident and chance. Does this really make sense? The tiger swallowtail is a master of disguises, but he was provided that by our loving Creator.

The LORD will preserve him and keep him alive...
~ Psalm 41:2a

September 9
Microbiology

There are billion-dollar hotels in Las Vegas because the owners know that they are going to make money from the majority of people coming through their doors. Statistics is science and assures us that certain things are either going to happen or not.

Statistics can also be used to prove that life could never have made itself. There are an estimated 10^{80} atoms in the entire universe. Even if our universe were 15 billion years old (10^{18} seconds) and each of these atoms are interacting with each other every trillionth of a second, this would *only* allow 10^{112} possible chemical interactions since the beginning of time. Let's compare that number (10^{112}) to the odds of the correct proteins and enzymes, needed for life, coming into existance by chance processes.

It is believed that the very simplest form of life would require at least 20 proteins and 387 enzymes – all with very specific sequences of amino acids.[1] If the average sequence of these chemicals is 10 amino acids, the odds of these amino acid arrangements forming by random chance would be 20 raised to the 10th power raised to the 387th power . In other words, once in 10^{5035} tries. This is absurdly less likely than the 10^{112} possible interactions of every atom in the history of the universe. Once in a trillion odds would be like flipping a coin and randomly getting heads 40 times in a row. No-one would ever believe this could happen. Once in 10^{5035} is an inconceivable impossibility.

God has made it absolutely obvious; the molecules of life were designed by intelligence, not chance.

(I will do mighty wonders) that they may see, and know, and consider, and understand together, that the hand of the Lord hath done this, that the Holy One of Israel hath created it. ~ Isaiah 41:20

September 10 — Design

A common illustration used in biology textbooks shows the forelimb of a bat, bird, dolphin, and human. These forearm bones have a similar design even though the specific parts are completely different in size, shape, and function. This comparison is known as "homologous structures." It is taught that similar features of different organisms prove that they had a common ancestor. Advanced biology books state that the source of similar structures is the "common gene coding areas" in each embryo's DNA coding. Yet, this was disproven over 30 years ago. We know that similar structures in different creatures come from completely different genes[1] – meaning there is no scientific reason to believe that homologous structures are the result of common origin.

Even more dishonest is the selective use of "similar structures" to support the belief in evolution. The eye of a cephalopod (octopus) is FAR more similar to the human eyeball than the arm of a human is similar to the arm of a bat, bird, or dolphin. Yet nobody thinks there is any close ancestral relationship between an octopus and a human. Thus, quite **dissimilar features** (like the flipper of a dolphin and the arm of a human) **ARE** considered proof of evolution while almost **exact similarities** (like the eye of an octopus and that of a human) **ARE NOT** considered ancestral relationships. This smacks of a double standard.

The picking and choosing of which features to accept and which features to ignore is evidence that evolution is actually story-telling and not science. Similarity in features, which appear throughout the animal kingdom, is evidence of a common designer. God designed the best from the beginning and just continued using the same design when needed.

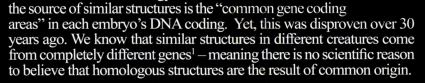

For my thoughts are not your thoughts, neither are your ways my ways, saith the Lord. ~ Isaiah 55:8

Biology

September 11

Even the poop from baby song-birds reveal the design of God.

Baby song birds are always hungry, and the parent is continually feeding them, but what goes in one end…must come out the other! The nest could easily become a real mess. Imagine the bird nests filling up with bird excrement as the baby birds are pushed closer and closer to the rim by the rising sewage.

The presence of this fecal matter would not only be unhealthy but enable predators to easily detect their location. How does nature solve this problem? Disposable diapers. Each chick's fecal matter has a mucous membrane that surrounds it. The chick generally defecates within seconds of being fed. The parent then removes this fecal sac and deposits it away from the nest as it flies off to find additional food for the chicks. Shortly before the chicks fledge (fly away from the nest), they stop producing fecal sacs.

When you see tiny baby birds in their nests, think of how God has provided for their cleanliness and safety using the world's FIRST biodegradable, disposable diapers!

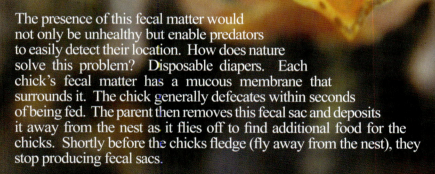

*I know all the fowls of the mountains:
and the wild beasts of the field are mine.
~ Psalm 50:11*

September 12
Biblical Accuracy

Under a thick ice sheet in Greenland, scientists discovered a new "Grand Canyon." Using airborne radar to see through the two mile thick ice sheets, scientists discovered a huge canyon, similar to the Grand Canyon, that is located in Arizona. This hidden Greenland canyon is about half as deep (2,600 feet deep) but twice as long (almost 600 miles) as the Grand Canyon.

Greenland's canyon begins in the middle of the country and continues northward to the sea; it is the world's longest canyon. Scientists were surprised to find the canyon with "the distinctive V-shaped walls" because this means it must be a river valley and not a U-shaped glacier-carved valley. The valley must have been carved prior to Greenland being covered with ice. **If we put on our biblical glasses, we will understand exactly how this valley was formed**. During the closing stages of the global Flood, the fast-moving, sediment-filled, high-energy runoff waters carved canyons at many locations around the world. This happened as the year-long Flood waters drained off the continents, about 4400 years ago, carving out canyons in the newly-formed land masses. Later, tiny rivers flowed at the bottom of these huge canyons, or in the case of Greenland, a huge canyon to be later covered by miles of ice.

**Whereby the world that then was, being overflowed with water, perished:
~ 2 Peter 3:6**

Paleontology

September 13

Trilobites once lived on the ocean floor. We have identified many different species of trilobites; most had two compound eyes, some had no eyes, and others had eyes on stalks like snails. But all trilobite eyes have been found to be unique and complex. Their eyes were not made of living cells, but of a see-through-crystal substance like tiny "rock crystals". That is why the eyes of these creatures were easily fossilized and we can know so much about them. Each compound eye is made up of many single lenses. The optics of these "rock crystals" allowed the trilobite to see things equally well whether they were far away or close up - at the same time! How trilobites were able to do this is very complicated. Each "rock crystal" was made up of two materials. These two lenses were affixed to each other and so designed that they solved the problem of blurriness or spherical aberration. We did not solve these optics problems until Rene Descartes (1637), Christian Huygen (1690), and others addressed the problem. These scientists had to employ difficult mathematical formulas that allow us to enjoy the optics we use today. Yet, the trilobites' eyes used these laws of optics for their complex lenses.

Trilobites are mostly found in Cambrian rock. The Cambrian layer is near the bottom of the geological column that evolutionists claim contain **the fossilized remains of the simplest creatures**. Do trilobite eyes sound simple? Dr. Riccardo Levi-Setti, an expert on trilobites, said that the eyes of a trilobite could qualify for a patent. The design of the trilobite eye makes use of Fermat's principle, the Abbe sine law, Snell's laws of refraction, and the optics of birefringent crystals. Of course, the God of the universe, who made the trilobite eye, does not need to patent his invention. He owns everything anyway.

One generation shall praise thy works to another, and shall declare thy mighty acts. ~ Psalm 145:4

September 14

Biology

Have you ever noticed that you cannot see moths' eyes reflecting back? Moths see well at night, but their eyes have a special built-in anti-glare feature so that light is not reflected to alert predators of their location. Scientists were intrigued by this special anti-glare feature and wanted to copy the moth's eye so that our TVs, cell phones and other products could have glare-free displays. What they found was an orderly array of tiny bumps on the surface of the moth's eye. These tiny bumps are so small that the wavelengths of visible light are

deflected and absorbed instead of being reflected back. This is very similar to how a sound-proof room is made, except, on a larger scale; ridge-shaped foam lines the room, so the incoming sound waves are deflected into the walls and absorbed. When the moth-eye nanostructure technology was applied to solar cells, the glare was reduced from 35-40 % to only 2%.

When we have a glaring problem, like the reflection of light on solar cells, look to see how God has solved the problem. These scientists simply copied what had already been made, that is, **they recognized a good design when they saw it**. In the future, your anti-glare cell phone may have moth eyes!

O Lord, thou art my God; I will exalt thee, I will praise thy name; for thou hast done wonderful things; thy counsels of old are faithfulness and truth.
~ Isaiah 25:1

History

September 15

If there was an Ice Age ending only about 3500 years ago, shouldn't the ancient cultures have a remembrance of it? We find just that in the ancient people groups' legends. They speak of "the Great Cold" or "evil winters." The Mayans of Central America record in the *Popol Vuh* that their ancient ancestors had sailed to their land from the east during a time of black rain and constant twilight. This would be consistent with rampant volcanic upheavals during the Ice Age bringing ash in the rain and constant twilight (dense cloud-cover). The ancient Avesta writing coming out of western Russia describe the early Ice Age as "*Ten months of winter are there now, two months of summer, and these are cold as to the water, cold as to the earth, cold as to the trees… There all around falls deep snow, that is the direst of plagues.*" These are not the only people groups that described this event. Here are some others: Toba Indians in South America, the Incas, the Tarahumara of northern Mexico, the Araucanians of Chile, the Mataco Indians of Argentina and many more. Many of these cultures associate the Flood with the subsequent period of cold, earthquakes, volcanoes, periods of darkness, and continual cloud cover. The Mayan *Popol Vuh* records that after the Flood there was "much hail, black rain and mist, and indescribable cold." Another Mayan source says "sunlight did not return till the twenty-sixth year after the flood. These people knew about the Ice Age and wrote of their experiences. All this fits perfectly within the biblical worldview!

Out of the south cometh the whirlwind: and cold out of the north.
~ Job 37:9

September 16

Biology

Some of the most interesting examples of design are found in animals that help each other survive (symbiosis). An example found in most tropical seas is between the blind shrimp and goby fish. The blind shrimp digs a hole and uses its front claws like a bulldozer to keep the entrance clear of debris. The blind shrimp, however, is blind. That's where the goby fish comes in - it guards the entrance to the shrimp's home. The blind shrimp always keeps a feeler (antenna) touching the fish. **When danger approaches, the fish signals the shrimp with a flick of its tail and both dive into the hole**.

Whenever you see a blind shrimp, there will always be goby fish nearby! The blind shrimp is protected from trouble while the goby fish is given a spot to hide. How does evolution explain this partnership? They say, "Since the partnership is useful it must have evolved." **This explains nothing about how these instincts could have evolved slowly over time**. This type of partnership had to have been programmed into them from the beginning - by their Creator God.

I will praise the name of God with a song, and will magnify him with thanksgiving. ~ Psalm 69:30

Christian Truth

September 17

It is often AFTER the children leave home that parents wonder why their children have ditched the faith. One blogging mother, Natasha Crain, propsed a discerning question to determine whether your child is headed for the exit door or not.

Is your child <u>asking you questions</u> about Christianity? If they are not, they are headed for trouble!

- Just because they are not asking questions doesn't mean they have answers to faith questions.
- They may have never been shown why Chistianity is so radically different (and more logical) than other religious beliefs - including humanism and atheism.
- They may have already made the shift away from Christianity because of science indoctrination. Youngsters of Christian families experience real inner turmoil when experts sources contradict the Bible. Christian students believe and trust their teachers, as they should; however, we need to help them understand why the teacher has to teach from a non-biblical perspective.

If they are not asking questions about their faith, then when they leave home, they have a good chance of ditching the faith. **Statistics find that around 2/3 of children who grew up in Christian homes are leaving the church**.

Parents must be the first, at a young age, to challenge them on why they believe what they believe--why they did not evolve from green slime-- then you will know where they stand in their faith walk. Many parents are lulled into a false belief that their children are toeing the line until they leave home. **Are your children asking questions about Christianity?** If not, challenge them.

I have no greater joy than to hear that my children walk in truth.
~ 3 John 4

September 18 — Anatomy

Our teeth not only show amazing design but reveal His signature at a microscopic level.

Enamel is the bright white exposed part of the tooth. It is the hardest living tissue in the human body. This is why long after the bones of buried animals have disintegrated the teeth often remain. This hard enamel shell protects the tooth's life support system – the blood vessels and nerves. It is the design of enamel that allows us to bite, tear, and chew our food.

But, perhaps, the most stunning thing about our teeth is buried within the enamel. The enamel is designed using fish-shaped rods on a microscopic level. This shape interlocks the enamel crystals giving them incredible strength – like nuts threaded onto a bolt. It's very curious that the cross-sections of these structures are fish-shaped. From the earliest historical times, the symbol that Christians used to identify themselves with Jesus Christ was the symbol of a fish. **Jesus Christ called us to be "fishers of men" and our very teeth are made from "rods" that look like "fish!"** Could this be coincidence, or was it God's design? I'll let you be the judge!

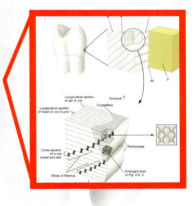

And he saith unto them, "Follow me, and I will make you fishers of men."
~ Matthew 4:19

Botany

September 19

When we think of plants, we think of photosynthesis and sunlight. But what if they receive too much UV-B light? UV-B is ultraviolet light that burns biological tissues. It is the reason we put on sunscreen to protect our skin from the Sun's damaging wavelengths.

When UV-B reaches damaging levels the leaves, plants make their own sunscreen chemicals! Plants have special photoreceptors that detect high levels of UV-B light. These switch on genes to make the plant's sunscreen. These chemicals are then deposited in the leaf tissues, ready to absorb the high levels of UV-B. This protects the cells below. At the same time, if any of the cells are found to be damaged, enzymes go into action repairing the damaged DNA. This keeps the photosynthetic machinery humming along.

How did this incredible system of detection, protection and repair come about? By accident and chance? How could plants exist before sunscreen? We have man-made sunscreen to protect ourselves while plants have God-made sunscreen.

*For the sun is no sooner risen with a burning heat,
but it withereth the grass, and the flower thereof falleth,
and the grace of the fashion of it perisheth:
~ James 1:11*

September 20

Biology

The Crucian carp is an amazing fish that can survive for extended periods without oxygen. "Look Ma, no air!" As the deep snow piles up on the frozen Scandinavian lakes, no light is able to penetrate into the lake water deep below the ice. This results in a lack of oxygen in the lake water. In most creatures, including most fish, the lack of oxygen results in the build-up of lactic acid – ultimately resulting in death. The Crucian carp, however, is able to survive. How?

God has designed this fish to slow its heartbeat as the oxygen levels decrease. As oxygen levels continue to drop, an amazing change occurs. The carp changes its metabolic chemistry, so it does not need oxygen. Meanwhile, **it starts transforming the deadly lactic acids into sugars to create energy without needing oxygen**. How do evolutionists explain this? Did carp get together with their chemistry sets and decide they needed to create a new way of surviving without oxygen? How would they know what to do? The carp needed this built-in ability from the beginning in order to survive harsh Scandinavian winters. The creativity of Jesus is revealed in the design of these carp!

I will meditate also of all thy work, and talk of thy doings. Thy way, O God, is in the sanctuary: who is so great a God as our God? ~ Psalm 77:12-13

September 21

Geology

When traveling in the western states, you may come across cross-bedding. Cross-bedding is found in sedimentary rock; it is a series of visible layers within the rock that suddenly change direction. Most layers are horizontal; however, cross-bedding has layers that are at a distinct angle to the horizon. Cross-bedding is found most often in sandstone. **Cross-beds exist because of Noah's Flood**.

Desert sand dunes have steep faces with sand beds at an angle greater than 25 degrees. If the sand bed angle is less than 25 degrees, most likely it was water-deposited. By measuring the angle of the sand layers in these cross beds, we can determine if the sandstone came from an ancient desert or a flood. You can do an experiment to establish whether

a cross-bedded sand dune was created by wind or water. First, establish the horizon, lay a protractor on that, and determine the angle of the cross-bed. If the angle of the sand bed is greater than 25 degrees, it formed in a dry environment. If the angle of the sand bed is less than 25 degrees, the sand was most likely laid down in a flood environment. If you do not have a protractor with you, take a picture and do the measurements at home. It is the wide extent of cross-bedding throughout sandstone layers of the western United States that testify to the worldwide nature of the Flood that laid these rock layers down. So, the next time you visit national parks in the West, take along your protractor, and do the protractor test. Sedimentary rock layers with cross-bedding are a testimony to Noah's Flood!

How precious also are thy thoughts unto me, O God! how great is the sum of them! If I should count them, they are more in number than the sand: when I awake, I am still with thee.   ~ Psalm 139:17-18

September 22

Design

Moles are made for life underground. They are one of the most efficient excavating mammals on the planet - spending their entire lives digging underground tunnels. Tunnels near the surface are used for searching for earthworms, grubs and insects while deeper tunnels (10 feet deep) are used for living areas. Moles have voracious appetites and eat an equivalent of their body weight each day.

These animals are perfectly designed for digging with the following characteristics:

- Compact bodies
- Large front paws with broad, sharp, hard claws that face backwards, so they can dig with breast-stroke style motion
- Short, stubby tail that can be used as a lever
- Cone-shaped muzzle for probing insects in the dirt
- An ultra-sensitive nose to help find insects
- Velvety, thick fur that stands straight up, allowing the fur to move in any direction without rubbing the wrong way and trapping dirt within the velvety coat
- Small eyes that can be covered with thin skin while digging
- External ears are ridges in the skin covered with fur, preventing dirt from entering the ears
- Nostrils that open sideways, not forward, so dirt doesn't plug them

God created the mole with all these features so that it could be a successful tunnel digger.

And the earth was full of His praise.
~ Habakkuk 3:3b

September 23

Biology

Have you considered the shark? You may have been aware of the shark's ability to smell. But, did you know, they are able to detect the smell of blood from miles away? Are you aware, however, of their ability to sense electricity in the water? On a shark's snout are located nerve receptors called the ampullae of Lorenzini. These tiny receptor holes allow the shark to pick up the electricity given off by a beating heart. These tiny sensory receptors work with the shark's brain to give an exact location of a possible meal.

Theoretically, it has been determined that a shark could locate the position of a 9-volt battery over 1,000 miles away! Man has not even come close to copying such a wonder!

O give thanks unto the Lord; for he is good:
because his mercy endureth for ever.
~ Psalm 118:1

September 24

History

As difficult as it is to imagine, during the Ice Age, people were measuring and mapping the globe. The Piri Reis map, dating from 1513, has an accurate rendering of Antarctica and its coastline. It was not until 1949 that sonar mapping discovered where the coastline is located - underneath 5000 feet of solid ice. Yet, this map and another drawn by Oronteus Finaeus in 1531 showed Antarctica with mountain ranges, rivers, and bays prior to becoming covered by thousands of feet of snow and ice.

These two maps were a compilation of information that was moved from the Library of Alexandria in Egypt to Turkey before that great ancient depository of knowledge was destroyed by fire. The Turkish cartographers wrote on these maps that their source maps were made by the ancient seafarers, Phoenicians. Antarctica was officially "discovered" by the Russians in 1818 AD, or should I say, rediscovered! **During the Ice Age, the very warm ocean floodwaters (from the fountains of the deep, volcanism, and plate tectonics) would have kept the coastline of Antarctica free from ice for centuries**. Eventually, as the oceans continued to cool, great ice sheets covered it, as we find it today.

The one and only Ice Age took place just after the Flood (2348 BC) and is believed to have lasted about 700 years - 500 years to build up and 200 years to melt down. This would have provided ample time for the ancient explorers to sail the seas and map the globe before Antarctica was permanently covered by ice. **These maps provide EXTREMELY convincing evidence that the biblical understanding of Earth's history is correct**.

They that go down to the sea in ships, that do business in great waters;
~ Psalm 107:23

September 25
Microbiology

From the time of the ancient Greeks, up through the middle of the 19th century, it was widely taught that life formed all by itself via the "spontaneous generation of life." Scientists throughout this period insisted that observation confirmed this "fact of science" as they watched mold appearing on food and maggots crawling out of raw dead meat. Louis Pasteur (1822-1895), the father of microbiology, proved spontaneous generation was wrong- dead things do not make living things.

Pasteur showed that it was invisible microorganisms that explained things like the formation of alcohol within beer, the spoilage of milk, and the spread of disease. As a result, he developed pasteurization of milk, vaccinations for the prevention of diseases, and sterilization procedures. Literally millions of lives have been saved because of his work. Louis Pasteur performed experiments that proved that microorganisms can never create themselves. From his experiments with boiled broth in flasks, he discovered the Law of Biogenesis, that life comes from life. Nothing developed in sterilized, sealed flasks while open flasks developed microorganisms. Dead, sterile broth is dead; it can not make a living microorganism. You can still see one of his sealed flasks of broth on display at the Pasteur Foundation in Paris; nothing has grown in it since the 1860s.

But what was the inspiration behind his developments? **Pasteur realized that life could not have made itself but only exists as a result of the creation by God**. It is ironic that Pasteur proved the spontaneous generation of life wrong in the same year that Charles Darwin published *Origin of the Species*, 1859, that said spontaneous generation was right. Darwin spent the last decades of his life campaigning to convince others that life developed and advanced all by itself without God. Pasteur used reproducible experimentation to develop a law of science, the Law of Biogenesis - that life comes from life, just as God said in Scripture. Darwin used unobserved speculation to convince a world, anxious to get rid of accountability to their Creator, that life made itself and bacteria turned into people while Pasteur used the scientific method. Be very careful which side of this controversy you find yourself supporting.

(Solomon) spoke of trees, from the cedar tree that is in Lebanon even unto the hyssop that springeth out of the wall: he spoke also of beasts, and of fowl, and of creeping things, and of fishes. And there came of all people to hear the wisdom of Solomon, from all kings of the earth, which had heard of his wisdom. ~ I Kings 4:33, 34

September 26 — Geology

One of the great mysteries in geology is the inselberg, like Ayers Rock in central Australia. The German word inselberg means a hill jutting up from a plain, like an island in a placid sea or "island mountain." From a distance, that is exactly how an inselberg looks, like an island rising from a flat sea. They are found on all continents. Some famous inselbergs are Sugarloaf towering 1,300 feet high out of the Rio de Janeiro harbor in Brazil or Stone Mountain in Georgia standing 825 feet above the land.

Inselbergs are said to be millions of years old, but **if that were true they should have eroded down to nothing, yet they are still steep-sided**. From a biblical perspective, the retreating waters of the Flood of Noah's day explain inselbergs. The retreating floodwaters would have scoured soft sediment away, planing the surrounding land off flat. As the waters decreased, they become channelized in places, cutting away the land but leaving isolated remnants with steep sides, that is, the tall inselberg structures. The Genesis Flood explains this and many other "mysterious" landforms that are found worldwide.

Fifteen cubits upward did the waters prevail; and the mountains were covered.
~ Genesis 7:20

Paleontology

September 27

One of the greatest mysteries of evolution is not how things change but why things don't change for the better. Mutations are real, and random changes deteriorate the DNA coding as each new generation makes copies of itself. It is inevitable that any organism will change over time as these copying mistakes destroy useful information within an organism. Thus, the result is downward deterioration, not upward advancement. But even more startling is the idea that any creature could remain unchanged for hundreds of millions of generations. Yet, this unchanging nature of creatures in the fossil record (called stasis) is quite common. Small changes over time have been made but not enough for a current species to be unrecognizable from its fossilized form.

It is widely taught that birds exist because of small changes in dinosaurs over time. In other words, over millions of years, dinosaurs turned into birds. Yet, dinosaur bones have been found buried with a host of other creatures - such as crocodiles, dragonflies, redwood trees, grass, clams, and birds. They look essentially identical to modern living examples, so we call them "living fossils." Dinosaurs evolved into birds while other creatures remained unchanged?! God's word is clear; He created birds on Day 5 and dinosaurs on Day 6 of creation week. Dinosaurs did not evolve into birds!

And God said, Let the earth bring forth the living creature after his kind, cattle, and creeping thing, and beast of the earth after his kind: and it was so. ~ Genesis 1:24

September 28 — Geology

One of the many evidences supporting a worldwide Flood is the frequent finding of oval-shaped petrified trees. Why is this significant?

Almost every museum display on the formation of fossils shows the slow accumulation of sediment around organisms to form the fossils. It seems likely that petrified trees formed in this way would have turned to solid rock long before they were buried under millions of pounds of sediment (dirt). **So, if evolutionary processes produced petrified trees - they would almost all be circular in cross section**.

On the other hand, if petrified trees exist because enormous mats of vegetation were deeply buried during the worldwide Flood of Noah, millions of pounds of sediment would have pushed down on the trees before they became fossilized. Thus, many would have been flattened by the weight of rapidly accumulating sediment before they became petrified. In other words, because fossilization is a process that has been shown to occur quite rapidly (within decades, not millions of years), the trees could have been flattened into an oval shape before they were fossilized. This is exactly what we find in many locations.

Observational evidence supports the reality of a recent worldwide Flood upon our planet.

Then the earth shook and trembled; the foundations also of the hills moved and were shaken.... ~ Psalm 18:7

Biology

September 29

What bird makes the longest non-stop migration? The Bar-tailed Godwit flies non-stop for five or more days from Alaska to New Zealand/Australia - approximately 7,000 miles. During the day, they analyze polarized light to get the Sun's position even when it is cloudy. By night, they follow the stars, which means they know how the constellations move in both the northern and southern hemisphere! But as amazing as their navigational ability is, their endurance is even more awe-inspiring.

Just before they migrate from Alaska, they gorge themselves on clams and other creatures in the coastal mudflats. Fat builds up in thick rolls under their skin, increasing their total weight by 55%. Yet, even the type of fat these birds produce is unique. This fat is low in water content and very concentrated. As soon as they stop eating, a very unusual change takes place. The birds' internal organs -- the intestines, kidney and liver – all shrivel up. Now the fat fills in the empty space and the birds' bodies are once again streamlined for flight. How would the first Godwit that migrated from Alaska to Australia know that it needed to shrivel its organs in order to pack on the fat? **Can you shrivel your organs and survive?** This is truly a uniquely God-designed creature.

Hast thou not known? Hast thou not heard, that the everlasting God, the Lord, the Creator of the ends of the earth, fainteth not, neither is weary? There is no searching of his understanding. – Isaiah 40:28

September 30
Biblical Accuracy

There are more than 100 specific prophecies concerning Babylon. Three thousand years ago, ancient Babylon had magnificent hanging gardens with outer walls **rising 200 feet tall and 187 feet thick, with regularly spaced towers 300 feet high defending the city!** These walls enclosed an area of 196 square miles. By comparison, the Great Wall of China is much longer, but it is not nearly as tall or strong. The ancient historian Herodotus wrote that the fields around Babylon were so fertile he hesitated to write about them lest people think him insane. In Jeremiah 51:58, 62, God made a specific prediction concerning this massive fortress of the ancient world, *"The broad walls of Babylon shall be utterly broken...It shall be desolate forever."*

Today, Babylon is a trackless wasteland containing huge mounds of rubble. Nothing grows there. Not even a blade of grass survives in this barren desert. Babylon lies in total ruin. The area can best be described as "totally desolate." Over 2300 years ago, the mighty Alexander the Great decided he would rebuild Babylon. He determined that this would be a great spot for the capital of his mighty empire. He issued supplies to his soldiers to rebuild Babylon, but immediately after declaring his decision to rebuild Babylon, Alexander the Great was struck dead. A coincidence? God stated that Babylon would never be rebuilt, and what God declares, happens!

...thy word is truth. ~ John 17:17b

For by him were all things created, that are in heaven, and that are in earth, visible and invisible, whether they be thrones, or dominions, or principalities, or powers: all things were created by him, and for him: And he is before all things, and by him all things consist.
– Colossians 1:16-17

"(Evolution) is not only deceptive, but it threatens to be mischievous in a high degree...In all its bearing upon scriptural truth, the evolutionary theory is in direct opposition to it. If God's Word is true, evolution is a lie. I will not mince the matter, this is not the time for soft speaking."
- Charles Spurgeon, 19th Century evangelist and pastor, from his sermon, 'Hideous Discovery', July 25, 1886.

Biology

October 1

Have you considered the Arctic ground squirrel? It lives in the land of frigid temperatures--the northern tundra. This squirrel is unable to dig deep into the ground because the ground is permanently frozen, hard as rock, year-round. So, it has to hibernate close to the surface of the ground where temperatures can get as low as 5°F. Even though the ground squirrel is warm-blooded, it has the ability to drop its body temperature to 27°F; that's 5 degrees below freezing! This arctic squirrel does not turn into a "squirrelsicle" - instead its blood super-cools without freezing. **Meanwhile, the squirrel's heartbeat drops from 350 beats per minute to about 3 beats per minute**. Its breathing rate is reduced to once every several minutes with only a trickle of blood entering the brain -- causing brain wave activity to register zero. If this were seen in a human, he would be declared brain-dead! But not with the Arctic ground squirrel. He's only hibernating!

The squirrel hibernates up to ten months every year, rousing itself about 12 times during this period. Remember, hibernation affects every cell; it is not just simply going to sleep. **Vast, complex, internal changes take place**. If these changes (slowing of the heartbeat and breathing, dropping the internal temperature, etc...) were due to slow gradual evolutionary processes, there would be no Arctic ground squirrels! All would have died in the process of trying to find the correct internal changes for successful hibernation. When we study the Arctic ground squirrel and all the processes involved in hibernation, it becomes obvious that it could not have happened by accident and chance! There was One who created the Arctic ground squirrel with the ability to hibernate. And who is that hibernator maker? God, Himself! He cares for His creation!

Then the beasts go into dens, and remain in their places.
~ Job 37:8

October 2

Geology

Have you considered how little sediment exists on the seafloor? Every year, wind and water erode dirt off the continents, and it runs off into the oceans. Most of this dirt (sediment) stays near the continents. Scientists know how much dirt comes off the continents each year – about 20 billion tons. What is the average thickness of sediment all over the sea floor? Not even 1,300 feet. When we do the math, the amount of dirt (sediment) that has piled up at the bottom of the world's oceans can be accounted for in less than 12 million years. Evolutionists say the Earth's oceans are billions of years old. **There should be 250 times more sediment at the bottom of the oceans if this were true**. So, then, where's the dirt? The lack of seafloor sediment shows us that the Earth is not old, but young.

One final thought - "12 million years-worth" of sediment in the oceans does not prove the oceans are 12 million years old. That calculation is based on today's accumulation rate. During Noah's Flood, only about 4400 years ago, sediment would have been flowing into the oceans millions of times faster than anything we see happening today.

They that go down to the sea in ships, that do business in great waters; These see the works of the Lord, and his wonders in the deep.
~ Psalm 107:23-24

October 3

Microbiology

Off the coast of Hawaii lives a little squid about two inches long. During the day, the bobtail squid sleeps, huddled down in the sand. At night, it hunts. It swims near the surface, revealing a silhouette as viewed from below. To avoid detection, he wears an "invisibility cloak" made of glowing bacteria on his underbelly that mimics moonlight. This bioluminescent bacteria (*Vibro Fischeri*) is harbored in a special organ in the squid's mantle, where the squid provides food for them. The bobtail squid then uses filters to adjust how much of the bacteria's brightness shows so that it matches the moonlight. **If it's a full moon; it mimics the light of a full moon**, with a crescent moon, it mimics the lower light level of a crescent, and if a cloud suddenly covers the Moon, no problem!

Each morning as the squid buries itself in the sand, it releases most of the glowing bacteria. During the day, the remaining bacteria multiply so they are ready to go by nightfall. How does the squid know which bacteria to "capture"? How did it know that it needed an "invisibility cloak" to hide its silhouette? How did it know that it needed a filter to dim or brighten the bioluminescent bacteria? All these features shout design! When we see a design, we know there must be a Designer, and that Designer is God!

Thou art my hiding place and my shield...
~ Psalm 119:114a

October 4
Paleontology

Every summer, paleontologist Philip Bell searches the riverbeds of a certain area in Alberta, Canada, looking for newly exposed fossils from the spring run-off. June of 2012 proved to provide a jackpot! On the riverbed cliff a hadrosaur (duck-billed dinosaur) with actual skin was exposed! Philip found **not just an impression of skin, but actual dinosaur skin!** The skin was glossy black but still contained pigment. Scientists are studying the skin's melanosomes to determine the actual color.

Was this type of dinosaur grey, green or orange? The bigger question is, "How could dinosaur skin have lasted for some 65 million years?" Shouldn't it have been totally decomposed? Since when does skin last 65 million years!? If we put on our biblical glasses, we can see how such dinosaur skin can still exist. Dinosaurs were caught and buried quickly in the Flood of Noah only about 4400 years ago. Real dinosaur skin shouts the Genesis Flood!

Behold now behemoth...his strength is in his loins, and his force is in the navel of his belly. He moveth his tail like a cedar: the sinews of his stones are wrapped together. His bones are as strong pieces of brass; his bones are like bars of iron. ~ Job 40:15a, 16-18

Biology

October 5

Whales have enormous bones. If the oceans were billions of years old and these bones did not disappear, the ocean floor would be littered with whale bones. Fortunately, the oceans are not billions of years old, and God planned ahead with an amazing trash recycling system. Deep within the ocean, there exists an amazing creature commonly known as

the "Zombie Worm." It is apparently called this because its job is to eat dead bones. Its scientific name is *Osedax mucofloris*, whose literal translation is "bone-eating snot flower." This "bone-eating snot flower" attaches itself to the bones of dead whales and burrows into them, creating a root system. The remainder of its body is exposed outside the bone, covered with mucus, and looks like a flower. The Zombie worm oozes out an acid which transforms the bone material into edible proteins and collagen molecules. Then, parasites living within the Zombie worm's body eat this food. The parasites provide a by-product, that feeds the worm. The Zombie worm needs the parasites, and the parasites need the Zombie worm!

Aside from the astonishing fact that an acid-producing, bone-dissolving, snot-covered worm exists to dispose of whale bones, one has to ask, how did it survive before it found the parasite (or the parasite found it)? Why did it start producing acid to dissolve bones? Unless everything was in place from the beginning, neither the parasite nor the Zombie worm could have survived. Everything needed for survival of these two separate and distinct creatures had to be in place from the very moment of their creation. God, in his wisdom and creativity, produced such wonders for our amazement and appreciation!

The eyes of all wait upon thee; and thou givest them their meat in due season.
~ Psalm 145:15

October 6

Design

Imagine a vase for flowers. Where did it come from? Of course, you would say that someone made it, but how do you know? Did you see someone making it? How do you know the vase had a maker? Even though you did not see someone making the vase, you can see skill and design. Even though a vase is a simple structure, it still reveals design that could not have come about by accidental change or chance over time. Someone must have made the vase. Why did she make it? Perhaps it was so she could enjoy the flowers she just received.

Now, let's consider the flowers in the vase. A plant that grows flowers is unbelievably complex! A plant cell is far greater in complexity than any machine mankind has ever made. Photosynthesis alone is astonishingly complex; we are still not capable of unlocking the secrets of how it really works. **How is it logical to say that a vase was made by someone but not the flowers?** Flowers show so much design that they must have come from the mind of a super-intelligent creator. That Creator is God!

Consider the lilies how they grow: they toil not, they spin not; and yet I say unto you, that Solomon in all his glory was not arrayed like one of these. ~ Luke 12:27

October 7

History

The Ice Age had different effects around the world. In the northern latitudes, there were ice and cold with countless blizzards. In the middle latitudes, there were heavy rains. During the Ice Age, the Sahara Desert region was a well-watered place with a patchwork of rivers and lakes supporting subtropical flora and fauna. The Sahara Ice Age art has literally thousands of figures etched into rocks; depictions of tropical and aquatic animals, gazelles, cattle, crocodiles and men fishing along these ancient lakes. Geologists were surprised to find bones of elephants, buffalo, antelope, rhinos, giraffes, and other animals in this area. Also found were many bones of aquatic animals such as hippos, amphibians, crocodiles, fish, and clams, showing that this desert was once well-watered. Satellite ground-penetrating radar revealed an old drainage network in the Sahara; several of the channels were the size of the Nile River Valley. During the Ice Age, many places in the middle latitudes received much rain, and therefore, had a wonderfully lush environment. For example -

- The Great Basin in the area of Nevada, USA, was also once well-watered and lush. During the Ice Age, the Great Basin area had 120 lakes. The Great Salt Lake remains from what is now called Lake Bonneville; it was six times larger and 800 feet deeper than present day Great Salt Lake. The ancient shorelines can be seen on the surrounding hills and mountainsides. Lake Bonneville was the size of Lake Michigan.
- Eastern Pakistan and northwest India were once a beautiful grassy and forested land, as compared to the now-dried-up Sarasvati River. In fact, in Vedic literature, the Sarasvati is memorialized as a large river.
- Eastern Turkey was quite different in the past. Sargon of Agade of Mesopotamia, the world's first great military leader, had to put down some strife in the then-Hittite territory in Turkey. He and his army had to hack through jungles full of wild game and exotic birds. Today, no jungles are found within thousands of miles of this area; it is an arid region.
- In South America, Lake Titicaca in the Andes Mountains had a port city of huge megalithic blocks, Tiahuanaco. It is now a desolate wasteland without vegetation located five miles from the receded shoreline. During the Ice Age, it was rainy with lush vegetation.

During the one and only Ice Age, caused by Noah's Flood, the middle latitudes were well-watered. After the Ice Age, these places experienced a great drying out. **This was the REAL climate change!**

Also by watering he wearieth the thick cloud: he scattereth his bright cloud: And it is turned round about by his counsels: that they may do whatsoever he commandeth them upon the face of the world in the earth. ~ Job 37:11-12

October 8

Biology

Chameleons are famous for their color-changing ability. Chameleons have highly structured skin. The outer layer of skin is transparent. Beneath the top layer are two layers of skin with red and yellow pigments. Below these are two more layers, one reflecting blue light and the other reflecting white light. Deeper still is a layer of dark brown pigment. The color change happens when the pigment cells at any particular layer expand or contract. For example, when a chameleon is calm, and the skin is not excited, the yellow pigments are partly contracted - letting the reflected blue light through (blue and yellow make the chameleon appear green). When a chameleon is angry, he may turn yellow because the yellow pigments expand (blocking the blue light from reflecting through).

Chameleons can show a dazzling display of reds, pinks, yellow, blues, greens, and browns. Their basic color pattern is camouflage green; however, they will change color due to heat, light, and mood. The brain sends a signal to the pigments to contract or expand causing the chameleon to change color in about 20 seconds. This system of changing colors is extraordinarily complex! The more we study creation, the more we find amazing complexities that point to a Master Designer!

Thine, O Lord is the greatness, and the power, and the glory, and the victory, and the majesty: for all that is in the heaven and in the earth is thine; thine is the kingdom, O Lord, and thou art exalted as head above all.
~1 Chronicles 29:11

October 9
Botany

Have you noticed that the gooey inside of a fig bar is also crunchy? That cruch is the little seeds of the fruit. Inside the bulb of a fig are hundreds of flowers that develop into tiny fruits. In 1882, the Smyrna female fig tree was brought from Turkey to California. But many years after the fig trees were planted, no one understood why no fruit was growing on the trees until botanist George Roeding discovered that the trees were all female and needed to be pollinated by wild fig wasps.

So back to Turkey the California farmers went to find the wild fig trees and the wild fig wasps. **The wild fig wasp is so tiny it can fit through the eye of a sewing needle**. Success! Each summer, the Smyrna fig orchards of California are covered with large paper bags. Inside are the wild fig wasps dusted with pollen from the male wild fig trees. Only the wild fig wasp can pollinate the female Smryna fig tree. All these three are needed for success; the female Smryna fig tree, the male wild fig tree and the fig wasp. The fig trees need the wasp, and the wasp needs the fig trees. Any missing pieces would cause the demise of all.

Here's the problem for those who leave God out of the process. The fig wasp appears in the evolutionary timeline tens of millions of years **before** figs. If this were true, we would not have Smyrna figs. The biblical view tells us that God created figs on day 3 and fig wasps on day 5. So as you munch on that crunchy fig bar, thank God for the fig wasp.

For the Lord thy God bringeth thee into a good land, a land of brooks of water, of fountains and depths that spring out of valleys and hills; A land of wheat, and barley, and vines, and <u>fig trees</u>, and pomegranates; a land of oil olive, and honey;...
~ Deuteronomy 8:7-8 (emphasis added)

October 10

Biology

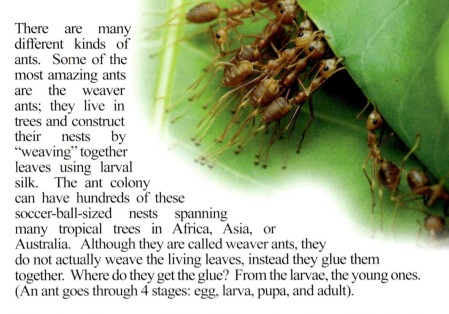

There are many different kinds of ants. Some of the most amazing ants are the weaver ants; they live in trees and construct their nests by "weaving" together leaves using larval silk. The ant colony can have hundreds of these soccer-ball-sized nests spanning many tropical trees in Africa, Asia, or Australia. Although they are called weaver ants, they do not actually weave the living leaves, instead they glue them together. Where do they get the glue? From the larvae, the young ones. (An ant goes through 4 stages: egg, larva, pupa, and adult).

When the worker ants are building their nest, they grab one leaf and hold the edge of another leaf. During this time, another worker ant brings in a larva which is about to enter into the pupa stage of metamorphosis. Instead of the larva spinning a cocoon, the worker ant squeezes the larva just as we might squeeze a tube of toothpaste, causing sticky silk to come out. The larva is then passed from ant to ant, glueing the leaves together, and thus constructing a secure nest. Evolutionary theory says that slowly over millions of years, the weaver ants evolved this method of sticking leaves together. Question - didn't ant nests need to be secure right from the beginning? If it did not work the first time, or millionth time, why build a nest in a tree? Weaver ants, just like all ants, work by instinct; they just know how to build a nest. When we see an instinct, we know there must be an instinct maker, and that is God.

There be four things which are little upon the earth, but they are exceeding wise: The ants are a people not strong, yet they prepare their meat in the summer;
~ Proverbs 30:24-25

Christian Truth

October 11

A recent study of beliefs in Iceland revealed that there was not a single individual under the age of 25 who believed in creation! In America, two-thirds of all church-going young people leave the church once they leave for college. Our young people are being taken captive by the "empty philosophies of this world." How do we stop this loss of the next generation? **A study on the brushing of teeth may give us some insight.**

In a controlled study, one group of young people was told why brushing their teeth was good for them. A second group was given the same information but also warned that false reports would try to convince them that teeth-brushing was harmful to their teeth and told how to refute such lies. Then both groups were exposed to the misinformation. **The results were stunning**. Those that were told ONLY the benefit of brushing were far less likely to consistently brush than those who were both warned that they would be lied to about the dangers of brushing and told how to refute this misinformation.

Christians need to understand the implications of this simple study. For our young people to hold onto their faith and not be taken captive, they need to hear both the why the Bible is true AND to be warned about the lies the enemy will say about it. Young people need to understand the Christian worldview as well as the lies from other worldviews that attack Christian truth - such as Evolutionism, Secular Humanism, Postmodernism, Communism, and Islam. All are widespread and rapidly increasing "empty philosophies" that are prevalent in our culture today.

Beware lest any man spoil you through philosophy and vain deceit, after the tradition of men,
~ Colossians 2:8a

October 12

Biology

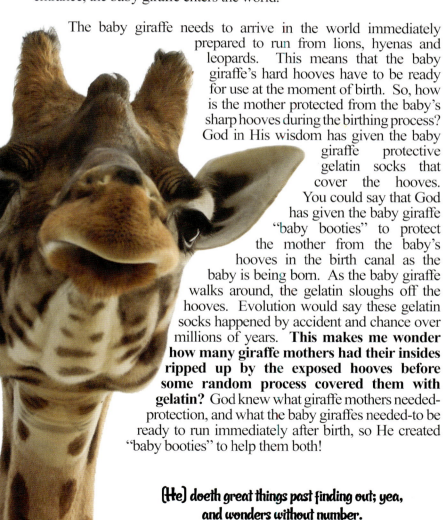

Did you realize that baby giraffes wear "baby booties" during birth? A mother giraffe is pregnant with the baby for 15 months. When she is ready to give birth, she does not lie down, but remains standing, **and the newborn baby drops six feet to the ground!** With such an abrupt entrance, the baby giraffe enters the world.

The baby giraffe needs to arrive in the world immediately prepared to run from lions, hyenas and leopards. This means that the baby giraffe's hard hooves have to be ready for use at the moment of birth. So, how is the mother protected from the baby's sharp hooves during the birthing process? God in His wisdom has given the baby giraffe protective gelatin socks that cover the hooves. You could say that God has given the baby giraffe "baby booties" to protect the mother from the baby's hooves in the birth canal as the baby is being born. As the baby giraffe walks around, the gelatin sloughs off the hooves. Evolution would say these gelatin socks happened by accident and chance over millions of years. **This makes me wonder how many giraffe mothers had their insides ripped up by the exposed hooves before some random process covered them with gelatin?** God knew what giraffe mothers needed- protection, and what the baby giraffes needed-to be ready to run immediately after birth, so He created "baby booties" to help them both!

(He) doeth great things past finding out; yea, and wonders without number.
~ Job 9:10

History

October 13

Evidence of a worldwide flood can be found in the historical records around the world. In Mexico, the Toltec Indians have an account of "the first world" lasting 1,716 years before being destroyed by a great flood. This great flood covered even the highest mountains. Only a few people escaped this world-wide flood in a "toptlipetlocali," which means a closed chest. After the flood, these few people began to multiply and built a very high "zacuali" or tower. During the time they were building the high tower, the languages were confused. Does any of this sound familiar to the same history we find in Genesis?

The Toltecs began with seven friends and their wives who spoke the same language, crossed great waters, lived in caves, and wandered 104 years until they came to "Hue Hue Tlapalan" or southern Mexico. This all took place 520 years after the great Flood. **Of course, the most reliable Flood account is found in the Bible**. When the biblical genealogies are counted, we find that the pre-Flood world lasted 1656 years, and the languages were confused at the tower of Babel about 100 years after the Flood. The Toltecs historical account is amazingly similar to the biblical account!

So the Lord scattered them abroad from thence upon the face of all the earth: and they left off to build the city. Therefore is the name of it called Babel; because the Lord did there confound the language of all the earth: and from thence did the Lord scatter them abroad upon the face of all the earth. ~ Genesis 11: 8-9

October 14

Biology

One of the most bizarre looking creatures in the world today is the star-nosed mole of North America. It got its name from 22 "tentacles" hanging off its nose. This star-shaped structure is more sensitive to touch than an elephant's trunk. The star structure contains more than 25,000 projections that send messages via more than 100,000 nerve fibers to the brain. Since the mole lives in total darkness, **the star tentacles function very much like our eyes - but use touch instead!**

The bottom pair of tentacles has the highest density of nerve endings, acting like our central vision. The other tentacles act like our peripheral vision, allowing the mole to pick up the big picture. The mole uses these 22 tentacles to "scan" the environment with a rapid series of touches, too fast for our eyes even to see. In one laboratory test, a star-nosed mole was able to find five pieces of earthworm in a single second!

Evolutionists believe that these tentacles evolved over time by accident and chance. If the star-nosed mole did not have his tentacles from the beginning, how would he have found his food? If he found his food without his tentacles, why would he have needed to evolve these tentacles? He was already eating! God designed the star-nosed mole from the beginning with its unique "seeing system."

O Lord, revive thy work in the midst of the years, in the midst of the years make known; ~ Habakkuk 3:2

Biblical Accuracy

October 15

Babylon was both an empire and one of the greatest cities of the ancient world. The Bible proclaims more than 100 prophecies concerning this city. One prophecy states that she will never be rebuilt. Today, Babylon is still in ruins, a mound of rubble haunted by jackals, vipers and scorpions. But let's consider two specific prophecies about Babylon that are seemingly contradictory. Jeremiah 51:42 states, "The sea is come up upon Babylon: she is covered with the multitude of the waves thereof" while Jeremiah 51:43 states that Babylon will become, "a desolation, a dry land, and a wilderness." **How could Babylon be both covered with water and be a dry desolate desert?**

In 1811, an archeologist named Claudius James Rich wrote a book titled ***Narrative of a Journey to the Site of Babylon***, in which he made the following observation, *"For the space of two months throughout the year the ruins of Babylon are inundated by the annual overflowing of the Euphrates so as to render many parts inaccessible by converting the valleys into morasses."* After the water subsides, the site becomes a dry, parched desert. Both prophecies are true! Babylon is both covered with waves and a dry desolate ruin that has never been rebuilt. God gave us more than 2,000 prophecies in order that we may believe His promises. His one great future promise is "that whosoever believeth in him should not perish, but have everlasting life" (John 3:16b), and "he that believeth not the Son shall not see life; but the wrath of God abideth on him" (John 3:36b). God's word is true, and it will come to pass.

Thy word is true from the beginning:
~ Psalm 119:160

October 16

Biology

Sharks are cold-blooded animals. These type of creatures take on the surrounding temperature. So So how do great whites, common threshers or shortfin mako sharks keep their internal core temperature some 13-48 °F ABOVE the waters in which they swim? These sharks have their own build in heat-exchangers!

The heat created by their muscle activity is moved to vessels that flow by the gills; water can be very cold as it flows by the gills, which extract oxygen. These very small blood vessels make a mesh (rete mirabile) of capillaries causing the heated blood to flow next to the cold (oxygenated) blood. As this happens, heat is exchanged to the incoming cold blood, keeping the shark warm. Now with heated and oxygenated blood, the shark is able to swim in cold waters at high speeds. **These sharks have their own built-in countercurrent heat exchangers!**

We use heat exchangers in much of our technology - such as refrigeration and air conditioning. Would we say this technology happened accidentally over millions of years? Then why would we say it happened by accident in a shark? God knew sharks would have to swim fast even though some would live in cold waters. To solve the problem, He designed them with heat exchangers.

Sing unto him, sing psalms unto him: talk ye of all his wondrous works.
~ Psalm 105:2

October 17

Biology

What is one of the most ravenous carnivores in the ocean? Children immediately respond – "A Shark!" But they are wrong. It turns out to be a starfish! A single sea star (or starfish) can devour 12 clams a day.

As the starfish creeps over the ocean floor, it finds its primary food source - bivalves such as oysters and clams. It then crawls on top of the clam, wrapping its arms around each half and pulls. At first, the clam's muscles keep its shell tightly shut. The starfish's numerous tube feet, which act like suction cups, keep the pressure on. Slowly, the clam tires and it opens up - just a bit. At that exact instant, the starfish thrusts its stomach (which looks like a parachute) out of its mouth and slips it inside the clam.

The starfish stomach begins to digest a tasty clam meal while inside the clam's own shell! After eating, the stomach returns with its contents to the starfish. Aren't you glad that we do not eat our food this way! Imagine eating dinner - you thrust your stomach out of your mouth, onto the table, and digest the food right there! When finished, you would pull your stomach back in. I hope you can stomach one of the most remarkable methods of eating in the world. God loves to show us His creativity!

Great things doeth He, which we cannot comprehend.
~ Job 37:5b

October 18

Design

When we look at any object, how do we know whether it is designed by intelligence or the product of natural forces? How can we KNOW whether or not a living organism is the result of natural forces or intelligent design?

For that matter, how can we scientifically prove whether any complex object, such as an airplane, is the product of intelligent design or chance occurrences? Very few people have ever seen an airplane constructed, so how can we know it did not make itself? This may seem like a silly question, but there is actually a very simple way to know the truth. A passenger jet is capable of flight yet is made from thousands of complex parts that -

- Do not occur naturally
- Have individual components incapable of flight
- All have to be present and arranged in specific positions to allow flight to take place

Thus, an airplane could not have made itself. It is absolutely obvious that an airplane was designed, constructed, and assembled by an intelligent source for the purpose of flight. In the same way, a living cell is made up of millions of non-living parts that -

- Do not occur naturally outside of a cell
- Are not themselves alive
- All have to be present in specific locations in order for the cell to be alive

The simplest living cell far exceeds the complexity of a jet airplane because a cell can reproduce an exact copy of itself – no man-made machine is capable of this feat. Both the airplane and cell were designed by intelligence. The airplane by man's intelligence, the cell by God's intelligence!

The glory of the Lord shall endure forever: the Lord shall rejoice in his works. ~ Psalm 104:31

Microbiology

October 19

In the salty marshes off the East Coast of the USA, "farmer" snails live. They cut long gashes down the blades of the cord-grass. As they slice, they leave their droppings along the cut, and the gash soon has fungus growing on it. This fungus is then eaten by the snails – allowing them to thrive on the special nutrition supplied by the fungus. In experiments by biologists, **without eating this fungus, the snails hardly grew, and twice as many of their young died**. These snails need the fungus in order to flourish. How does evolution explain these snails' farming technique? How did snails know they needed this fungus for better health? How did snails exist prior to farming it? If those snails did exist without the fungus, why grow it? The Creator knew what these snails needed in order to flourish and provided them with the knowledge to farm in such a manner.

Praise ye the Lord: for it is good to sing praises unto our God;
~ Psalm 147:1a

October 20

Cosmology

Our Sun is remarkably unique. We do not have a run-of-the-mill star that lights our planet, but an exceptionally distinct star. The Sun is in the top 10% by mass as compared to other stars in the neighborhood of the Milky Way galaxy. **This makes it perfect for sustaining life on Earth.** If it were the size of super-giant Betelgeuse (in the constellation of Orion), it would engulf the inner planets (Mercury, Venus, Earth, and Mars). If it were as bright as Rigel (25,000 times brighter than the sun), it would emit too much radiation. If it were smaller, it would not support life on our Earth. If our sun were in a multi-star system (small group of stars gravitationally bound to each other), it would cause the Earth to experience extreme temperature variations. Most observable stars are part of multi-star systems.

The Sun's position in the Milky Way galaxy is also perfect. Our Sun is located on the outer edge of one of the spiral arms - far away from common inner galaxy star explosions (supernovae). Our Sun is an exceptionally stable star whereas other single stars of the same size, brightness, and composition have violent ejections called coronal mass ejections about once every 100 years. In 1989, the Sun experienced just one of these superflares - causing a huge disruption of the power grids in northern Quebec. Yet, this was a small superflare as compared to other stars; they produce superflares 100 million times more powerful than the ones that blacked out Quebec. If the Sun ejected such a superflare, the Earth's ozone layer would be destroyed, and all life on Earth would be wiped out. Our Sun is remarkably unique! Praise the Lord! Because it is so stable, so ideally located, so ideally sized - it is the perfect sun, ideally made by God for us - the crown of His creation.

From the rising of the sun unto the going down of the same the Lord's name is to be praised. ~ Psalm 113:3

Biology

October 21

Have you considered how reindeer (caribou) survive in extremely cold climates? Sure, they are the only deer with fur on their noses, but they also eat moss! That's right, moss. Most animals do not eat moss because it contains little nutritional value, and it is hard to digest. But moss contains a special chemical that keeps fluids (such as reindeer blood) from freezing inside the reindeer. You could say that **eating moss is like adding antifreeze to the reindeer's radiator** - keeping these animals from freezing on the coldest of days. Do we say man-made antifreeze happened by accident and chance? Then, why would we say reindeer antifreeze happened by accident and chance?

Make known his deeds among the people. Sing unto him, sing psalms unto him: talk ye of all his wondrous works.
~ Psalm 105:1b~2

October 22
Christian Truth

Did you realize the Chinese have known about a single Creator God for more than 4000 years? From the beginning of their history, the ancient Chinese worshipped a being they called "ShangDi" and acknowledged Him as the Creator of the universe and all life. ShangDi means "God above" or "Most High God."

For more than 4000 years ago, the Chinese emperors also sacrificed an unblemished bull to ShangDi. Once a year, the emperor would sacrifice an unblemished bull in a ceremony accompanied by prayers and hymns of praise. This was called the border sacrifice. **This sacrifice was originally done on the eastern border on top of Mount Tai** in Shan-Dong. In the 15th century it was moved to Beijing, and the Temple of Heaven Complex was built for this purpose. (Today, the Altar of Heaven complex is a prime tourist attraction, and few people concern themselves with its origin and meaning.) Do you see the parallel with the practices of the ancient Israelites? Where did Adam make an offering to God and teach his sons to do the same? It was likely at the border of the Garden of Eden that they were forbidden to enter. Why sacrifice a perfect (unblemished) bull? This pointed to the sacrificial death of Jesus. The emperors continued doing this for thousands of years without realizing the significance of their actions. They had not been told that the sacrifice of the sinless Son of God (Jesus) had already taken place as a once-and-for-all payment for their sins. It was not until 1911 when the last emperor was deposed that the annual border sacrifices were stopped.

How did the Chinese know about a righteous, just, Creator God who required payment for their sinfulness? After the Flood of Noah's day, people began to multiply on the Earth. After the Flood, the people built a tower, the Tower of Babel. God confused their languages and scattered them abroad. As the ancestors of the Chinese left the Tower of Babel, they settled in China, but they brought with them the same knowledge of God that the Hebrews had learned from their common ancestor – Noah. The ancient Chinese worshipped the God of the Bible; it was the faith of their fathers.

When the whole nation is guilty...
the bullock shall be killed before the Lord.
~ Leviticus 4:13,15

Geology

October 23

"Don't stand that close to the cliff edge!"
"Why? I'll be careful!"
"That cliff could give way at any moment."
Perhaps Mom had more wisdom than we realized!

We are programmed with the concept that rocks are "rock solid" - millions of years old and never changing. But around the world, there are recent examples of "unexpected collapses" of famous geological features. In Australia, for example, the famous *London Bridge* formation collapsed on January 15, 1990, and one of the *Twelve Apostles* (*sea stacks*) collapsed dramatically as a tourist watched in 2005. The *Cliffs of Moher* in Ireland and the *North Cliffs* in Cornwall were recently caught dramatically falling away as tourists recorded the events on their hand-held video devices.

At the Arches National Park in Utah, the famous *Wall Arch* – (spanning 71 feet wide and 33 feet high) collapsed in a single night on August 4, 2008. **Just since 1970, forty-three arches have collapsed at Arches National Park while not a single new arch has formed**. What we are seeing is massive rapid-scale erosion, not slow erosion expected by an evolutionary timescale. What we observe are cliffs collapsing at any moment. The evolutionary idea that cliffs erode slowly over time could cause you great harm on your next vacation if you are standing on a cliff that catastrophically collapses.

Your understanding of history really does affect where you stand!

...Go forth, and stand upon the mount before the Lord. And, behold, the Lord passed by, and *a great and strong wind rent the mountains, and brake in pieces the rocks* before the Lord; but the Lord was not in the wind: and after the wind an earthquake; but the Lord was not in the earthquake: And after the earthquake a fire; but the Lord was not in the fire: and after the fire *a still small voice.*
~1 Kings 19:11-12 (emphasis added)

October 24
Biblical Accuracy

Was the Flood mentioned in Scripture local or worldwide? Let's take a look:

1. The most common Hebrew word for the description of the Flood is the Hebrew word for "all or every". Here are a few examples (emphasis added):

   - "**ALL** flesh had become corrupted upon the earth" (Gen. 6:12)
   - "the end of **ALL** flesh is before me" (Gen. 6:13)
   - " I will bring a flood upon the earth to destroy **ALL** flesh (that has the breath of life under heaven) …**EVERYTHING** that is upon the earth shall die" (Gen. 6:17)
   - "**EVERY** living thing of **ALL** flesh (shall come two by two onto the ark)…" (Gen. 6:19)
   - "**EVERY** living substance I have made I will destroy off of the **FACE OF THE EARTH**" (Gen. 7:4)
   - "**ALL** the fountains of the great deep broke open" (Gen. 7:11)
   - "**EVERY** beast…**ALL** the cattle…**EVERY** creeping thing…**EVERY** bird of **EVERY** kind (wherein is the breath of life)…two by two went onto the ark" (Gen. 7:14,15)
   - "the waters prevailed exceedingly and **ALL** the high hills, **UNDER THE WHOLE HEAVEN**, were covered" (Gen. 7:19)
   - "15 cubits (about 24 feet) **ABOVE THE HIGH MOUNTAINS** the water prevailed" (Gen. 7:20)
   - **ALL** flesh dies…**ALL** whose nostrils were the breath of life…**ALL** that was in the dry land…" (Gen. 7:21,22)

2. The ark was large enough to hold two (in some cases seven) of every known kind of land animal that had the breath of life in its nostrils. Without getting into all the math, the 16,000-plus animals would have **occupied much less than half the space** in the Ark.

3. Noah stayed on the ark for almost 5 months AFTER it had landed. This allowed the land to dry and plants to root so that the released animals had the best chance of survival in order to repopulate the Earth.

4. God promised that, "*all flesh would never again be cut off by the waters of a flood; neither shall there be any more a flood to destroy the earth*" (Genesis 9:11). Yet, there have been thousands of floods destroying large areas of the Earth. Either God is a liar, or the Flood of Noah was global.

The primary reason for misinterpreting Genesis 6-9 as "a local flood" is an attempt to gain credibility with modern geological thought (which needs huge time periods within the Earth's rock layers to explain life without God). It is long overdue that Christian colleges, theologians, and pastors see the damage done by the distortion and disregard of God's Word in this area. God's words are **always** true.

Thou coveredst (the Earth) with the deep as with a garment: the waters stood above the mountains. Thou hast set a bound that they may not pass over; that they turn not again to cover the earth.
~ Psalm 104:6, 9

Biology

October 25

Horses are uniquely made to work alongside of us. One of their unique features are the millions of sweat glands all over their bodies. Most mammals are not like the horse. Most have their sweat glands in their foot pads. Few mammals have sweat glands that cool their entire body. Have you ever seen a sweaty dog? **The only animal you will probably ever see dripping with sweat is the horse.** Horse sweat is not like human sweat which is clear and watery; horse sweat is white and lathery. Horse sweat contains latherin, a detergent, that enables the sweat to spread rapidly over the horse's skin and hair. Sweating is like having a built-in air conditioner. As the sweat evaporates, it cools the body. The horse's ability to sweat allows it to work all day in the heat along with us. Our Creator gave us a unique animal to serve us, and, indeed, horses have worked with mankind throughout the centuries.

In the sweat of thy face shalt thou eat bread, till thou return unto the ground;
~ Genesis 3:19

October 26

Biology

Most animals have a heart to body size that follows a generally linear relationship, that is, the larger the animal, the larger is its heart in proportion. An exception is the horse's heart that is smaller than expected for such a large animal. Thus, the horse's small heart has difficulty pumping the required amount of blood throughout the horse's large body. So, God gave the horse four more pumps to help move the blood around its body. These "pumps" are located in the horse's hooves.

On the underside of the horse's hoof is a "v" shaped structure called a "frog." The frog pumps blood throughout the leg. When a horse steps down, it compresses the frog that pushes up against the blood vessels, squeezing the blood up the leg. When a horse lifts its leg, the blood moves down the leg. Horses have five pumps circulating blood, the heart and four frogs. This makes the horse extremely well designed for traveling long distances with speed, strength, and endurance. When running, the horse needs more blood circulating throughout its muscles, so the four frog pumps provide that. Why didn't God build a larger heart? Then, it would be operating all the time. **God didn't need to put a huge heart into the horse's design because he had a better idea**. A smaller heart assisted by four, turbo-charged, auxiliary pumps located in the hooves of the horse provided the answer! God is a great designer.

Some trust in chariots, and some in horses: but we will remember the name of the Lord our God. ~ Psalm 20:7

Biology

October 27

Imagine developing an artificial sweetener so potent that a single drop could make a lime taste as sweet as candy and transform fiery tabasco sauce to the sweetness of honey. The chemist who discoveres such a miracle sweetener will find both fame and fortune. Such a sweetener has already been invented by God, but He seldom receives either appreciation or credit for His brilliance.

Europeans visiting West Africa in the 1700s noticed the locals chewing on the fruit of a local shrub (later named *Synsepalum dulcificum*) and discovered that the fleshy pulp around the seed completely transformed the taste of bitter, sour, or spicy foods to sweetness. After years of study, it was discovered that a chemical called miraculin (apparently in honor of its miraculous taste transforming properties) binds to the tongue's taste buds, and under acidic conditions, it magnifies a person's sweetness receptors a thousand-fold. Since even spicy, sour, or bitter foods have some sugar, the enhanced sweetness is all that is tasted!

What a God we serve who can take even the bitter and make it sweet. If He can do this with something as complex as the chemistry of taste, He can do the same with the sorrow and bitter circumstances of our life.

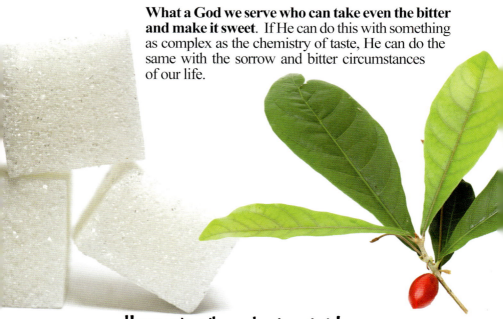

How sweet are thy words unto my taste! yea, sweeter than honey to my mouth! ~ Psalm 119:103

October 28

Biology

Brittle stars, a relative of the star fish or sea star, have 5 arms around a disc. They received their name because they seem to be brittle. If a brittle star is picked up, one of the arms may fall off to help it escape, but later it will regenerate the missing arm. Scientists were surprised to find that even though brittle stars do not seem to have any eyes, they can flee from predators, catch prey, and change color from dark brown during the daytime to grey at night. How are they able to do these things without eyes?

Biologists found an array of spherical structures made of calcite covering this organism's body. These spherical structures act as a micro-lens to focus light onto a tiny area the size of a dust speck. The resulting image is then focused onto nerve fibers that feed into nerve bundles; in other words, **the entire body of a Brittle Star functions as one huge compound eye!** What seemed to be an eyeless creature turned out to be all eye! Researchers have even commented that this visual system is far superior to anything man has made.[1] When you are visiting an ocean, take a look under rocks - you may find a Brittle Star staring back at you with its big compound eye.

The hearing ear, and the seeing eye, the Lord hath made even both of them.
~ Proverbs 20:12

Biology

October 29

On a cold winter day, you may notice a duck walking on ice and another walking in snow. How is it possible that their feet don't freeze and fall off - given their bare legs and feet? Like many birds, ducks have a unique warming system called a "countercurrent" heat exchanger inside their legs and feet.

Engineers have long understood that when two pipes are touching each other with the fluid flowing in the <u>same</u> direction, half the heat is transferred to the other pipe's fluid. If, however, the two fluids move in <u>opposite</u> directions, nearly 100% of the heat can move from the warmer pipe to the colder pipe. That is what happens in ducks! The pipe (artery) carrying warm blood runs down to the feet and passes next to the pipe (vein) with the cold blood coming from the feet. When the exchange takes place the heated blood transfers about 95% of its heat before it reaches the feet. In engineering design, this is called a countercurrent heat exchanger. Combine this with the legs and feet made mostly of bones/hard parts, and you get feet that neither freeze nor waste heat energy. **God in His wisdom created the countercurrent heat exchanger long before engineers discovered the principle**.

The next time you see a duck or bird standing in snow, tell your friend why birds do not have to wear winter boots. God built into these creatures a countercurrent heat exchanger!

If any of you lack wisdom, let him ask of God, that giveth to all men liberally, and upbraideth not; and it shall be given him. ~ James 1:5

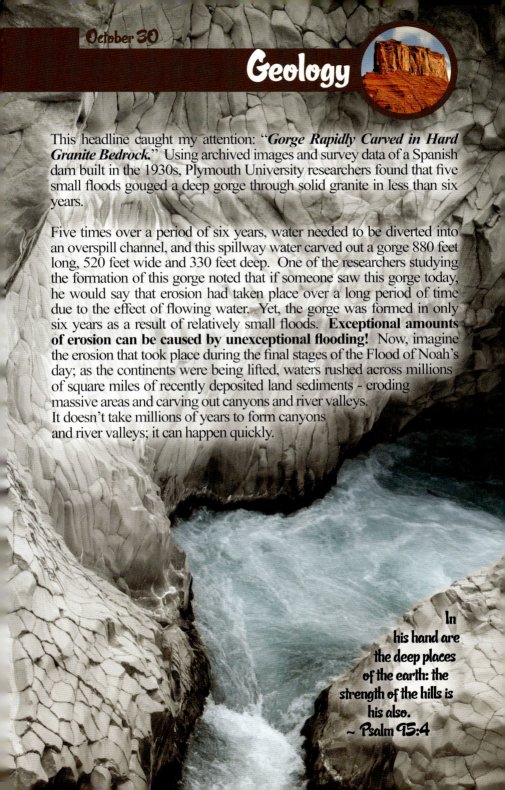

October 30

Geology

This headline caught my attention: "**Gorge Rapidly Carved in Hard Granite Bedrock.**" Using archived images and survey data of a Spanish dam built in the 1930s, Plymouth University researchers found that five small floods gouged a deep gorge through solid granite in less than six years.

Five times over a period of six years, water needed to be diverted into an overspill channel, and this spillway water carved out a gorge 880 feet long, 520 feet wide and 330 feet deep. One of the researchers studying the formation of this gorge noted that if someone saw this gorge today, he would say that erosion had taken place over a long period of time due to the effect of flowing water. Yet, the gorge was formed in only six years as a result of relatively small floods. **Exceptional amounts of erosion can be caused by unexceptional flooding!** Now, imagine the erosion that took place during the final stages of the Flood of Noah's day; as the continents were being lifted, waters rushed across millions of square miles of recently deposited land sediments - eroding massive areas and carving out canyons and river valleys. It doesn't take millions of years to form canyons and river valleys; it can happen quickly.

In his hand are the deep places of the earth: the strength of the hills is his also.
~ Psalm 95:4

October 31
Biblical Accuracy

According to biblical chronology, Joseph was sold into slavery and taken to Egypt about 3700 years ago (Genesis 39:1, 2). Joseph was eventually elevated to rule the country under Pharaoh (Gen. 41). Nine years later, Jacob and his family came to Egypt, (Gen. 47:9), and some of his members were appointed to prominent positions in the government (Gen. 47:6). The Israelites were located in the Land of Goshen, and they "*grew and multiplied exceedingly*" (Gen. 47:27). Some time after Joseph's death (Gen. 50:26), the Israelites continued to multiply, "*and the land was filled with them*" (Exodus 1:7). This alarmed the then reigning pharaoh who conscripted them into slavery. "*They set taskmasters over them to afflict them with their burdens. And they built for Pharaoh supply cities, Pithom and Ramses*" (Ex. 1:11). About 3550 years ago, Moses was born and adopted by the daughter of Pharaoh. Forty years later Moses showed his allegiance to his own people by murdering an Egyptian who was mistreating an Israelite and was obliged to flee (Ex. 2). After forty years in exile, he returned to lead the Israelites out of bondage to the

Promised Land. There followed the ten plagues, the destruction of the Egyptian army, (Ex. 14:26), and the death of Pharaoh (Psalm 136:15). This happened about 3450 years ago (1 Kings 6:1).

These events cannot be satisfactorily synchronized with the traditionally held dates of Egyptian history. The 18th dynasty (1550 - 1298 BC) is supposed to have occurred from about 3300 - 3600 years ago. This was the most powerful, most affluent dynasty that ever ruled the land of Egypt. **During this dynasty there is no record of mass slavery, no trace of Israelite occupation, and no indication of disasters of the magnitude of the ten recorded plagues/the loss of the powerful Egyptian army/loss of the pharaoh**. The 18th dynasty is also the best recorded dynasty that ever ruled in Egypt. Every king is known and both monuments and papyri provide a clear picture of the history of this dynasty. **If there was an Exodus during this dynasty there should be some indication of it, but there isn't**. Either the biblical record is wrong, or there is something wrong with the standard Egyptian timeline. The latter turns out to be the case, but it is so ingrained in Egyptology that it will take decades for that truth to be acknowledged.

Here is Egyptian archeologists have found. During the 12th Dynasty (assumed to be 3960 - 3991 years ago), the Old Egyptian Kingdom shows evidence that the land of Goshen was filled with large numbers of people from the land of Canaan (i.e. Israelites). One of the pharaohs (Sesostris I) is known to have had a vizier (first in command after him) whose powers were similar to those granted to Joseph. Moses would have been born under another ruler (Amenemhet III) whose daughter had no children and would have adopted Moses. Moses confronted yet another pharaoh (Neferhotep I) 80 years later. This ruler's body was never found and the land of Egypt descended into utter desolation as the Old Kingdom ended. It was not until the rise of the 18th Dynasty that the New Kingdom began, many generations after the time of Moses and the Exodus. If the dates for the 18th Dynasty are merely shifted 300 years forward, the Biblical and Egyptian Chronologies line up perfectly.

Shortly after the Rosetta stone was translated in the late 1800s, several thousand years were lopped off the "standard Egyptian chronology". The same is likely to happen again as approximately 300 years are lopped off the current "standard Egyptian chronology" and experts eventually realize the Bible's timeline and history for the nation of Egypt is absolutely accurate.

Then Joseph came and told Pharaoh, and said, My father and my brethren, and their flocks, and their herds, and all that they have, are come out of the land of Canaan; and, behold, they are in the land of Goshen.
- Genesis 47:1

And be not conformed to this world: but be transformed by the renewing of your mind, that you may know what is that good, and acceptable, and perfect, will of God.
- Romans 12:2

"It is the duty of all nations to acknowledge the providence of All Mighty God, to obey his will, and to be grateful for His benefits."
– George Washington (1732-1799), 1st President of the United States

November 1
Christian Truth

Romans 1:19-26 describes the progressive slide into moral degeneration that any culture experiences once they reject God as creator. Once a creator is denied, people start worshipping (making the object of their adoration) the creation instead of the creator. Romans chapter 1 states that the next step along this path is the distortion of sexuality from its obvious design to a distortion of sexuality in all possible forms. As we look at our degenerating society, the rampant spread of pornography, sexual promiscuity, and homosexuality is everywhere apparent. In the Western world today, this rejection of God has reached such a fantasy level that people have come to believe that they can even change their own sex from male to female (or vice versa) – even though every cell in their body testifies to their actual sex.

Pornography drives this sexual distortion and immorality. Forty million Americans between the ages of 12–60 visit porn sites on a regular basis.[2] Not only is pornography widespread (with an estimated $12 billion dollars in 2017 sales), but it is celebrated and promoted as normal by the entertainment media. Yet, there is a deep internal shame experienced by those addicted to pornography. Those caught in the progressively degenerating trap of porn find themselves increasingly obsessed with the habit to the exclusion of healthy relationships and other productive activities. **It is no wonder so few have time to ponder the reality of creation and God's existence.**

In one way, porn addiction is like the worst illness of the Old Testament - leprosy. Leprosy was a source of shame and hidden from others as long as possible. Once identified, lepers were cut off from healthy relationships and banished from society. Whether leprosy or porn, the victim struggles with shame. So what is the solution to porn addiction? The starting place is the return to acknowledging that all forms of sexual perversion are sinful - whether premarital sex, adultery, homosexuality, or pornography. Then, return God to the object of your adoration, find a way to hold yourself accountable, and allow God to transform your mind.[1] An excellent resource to help with this is a small book called *Seven Times* by Keith Grabill.

> **And be not conformed to this world: but be ye transformed by the renewing of your mind, that ye may prove what is that good, and acceptable, and perfect, will of God. ~ Romans 12:2**

November 2

Biology

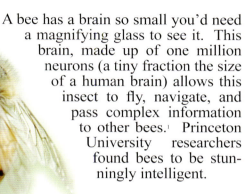

A bee has a brain so small you'd need a magnifying glass to see it. This brain, made up of one million neurons (a tiny fraction the size of a human brain) allows this insect to fly, navigate, and pass complex information to other bees.[1] Princeton University researchers found bees to be stunningly intelligent.

These researchers wanted to see if bees could find their food source if the food was moved increasingly farther away from the hive. First, the researchers moved their prime food source 150 feet away from the hive. The bees found the food in less than one minute. Next, they moved the food source another 150 feet away in the same direction. Again, the bees took less than a minute to find the food source. They did this two more times, moving it precisely 150 feet each time until it was 600 feet away. Each time, the bees rapidly located the food. But then the astounding happened. **While researchers were studying the bees, the bees were studying the researchers!**

When the researchers moved the food a fifth time to a location 750 feet away from the hive, they found the bees already at the new location waiting for them! The bees saw the pattern, calculated the next move, anticipated the actions of the researchers, and beat them to the new location![2] Evolutionists believe intelligence evolved by accident and chance over millions of years. The ability of bees to learn quickly, actually shows the hand of the Creator, not accident and chance.

Forasmuch as there is none like unto thee, O Lord; thou art great, and thy name is great in might.
~ Jeremiah 10:6

November 3
Geology

How do Bible-affirming geologists and evolutionary geologists differ as they interpret the rock layers of the Earth?

	Biblical Geologist (global flood)	**Geologist** (NO global flood)
Time to form geological column	Sedimentary rocks formed mostly during and subsequent to the year-long Flood	Over 500 million years
Oldest fossils	Made by the Flood (~2400 BC)	Millions of years old
What are "first" and "last" fossils	First = Buried earliest or before Flood Last = buried late in /or after the Flood	First = early in evolution history Last = final survivor
Dinosaurs	Alive at same time as people	Died 65 million years ago before people evolved from monkey-people

Flood geology and evolution have **two VERY different ways of looking** at the geological column and the fossils. Originally, the geological column explained the Flood of Noah's time; later, evolutionists changed the meaning.

Scientists routinely find fossilized pollen, spores, and wood from land plants in the Cambrian rock layer (which is at the base of the geological column). Evolutionary geologists are surprised because land plants were not supposed to have evolved until much later in time. Flood geologists are not surprised at finding pollen and spores in the Cambrian layer because the geological column represents the order in which creatures and plants were buried by Noah's Flood. **Spores and pollen can blow from one place to another, but not from one time to another!** The Bible's description of a worldwide flood fits the fossil evidence much better than the evolutionary explanation.

Then the waters had overwhelmed us, the stream had gone over our soul: Then the proud waters had gone over our soul.
~ Psalm 124:4-5

November 4

Geology

Have you considered the origin of caves? Most caves are found in nearly pure limestone layers hundreds of feet thick. To explain the origin of caves, one must first explain where the limestone layers came from, then how the caves came into existence with its magnificent cave wonders.

Here are the three stages:
- First, the deposition of limestone in thick layers
- Second, the carving out of the cavity within the limestone layer
- Third, the "decorating" of the caves (stalactites, stalagmites, etc…)

First, the Flood of Noah's day laid down these nearly pure layers of precipitated limestone as the "fountains of the deep" (Genesis 7:11) spewed forth enormous quantities of hot, mineral-laden water. Second, at the end of the Flood, enormous tectonic activity took place as, "the mountains rose; the valleys sank down" (Psalm 104:8 NAS). These tectonic activities caused many cracks in the limestone which allowed waters to drain through. In unique, localized areas, these waters were rich in acids from volcanic activity, decaying dead animals, and vegetation from the Flood, and **this quickly ate away limestone** – rapidly forming the enormous cave tunnels.

Cave decorating occurred during stage three. Cave mineral formations, such as stalagmites, developed from calcium-loaded water draining through the cavities. Just after the Flood, the ground was much wetter, due to the Flood waters and the post-Flood Ice Age. **Mineral-rich waters dripped from the cave ceilings and evaporated, leaving behind a variety of cave decorations.** Since that time, the water supplies have decreased, and the growth of cave decorations has slowed. When we put on our Biblical glasses, we can see where cave formation and decorations fit; limestone cave formations began with the Flood of Noah's day some 4400 years ago.

The waters stood above the mountains. At thy rebuke they fled; at the voice of thy thunder they hasted away. They go up by the mountains; they go down by the valleys unto the place which thou hast founded for them. ~ Psalm 104:6-8

History

November 5

Have you considered that ancient man was intelligent? Archaeologists recently examined some stone tools that were made by Neanderthal man. They found that the **Neanderthals had made superglue**! The wooden handles were glued to flint knives by birch pitch superglue. This adhesive was made by a dry distillation method that is difficult to reproduce even using modern manufacturing methods.

Smoldering birch bark must be heated to between 644 - 752°F and oxygen must be excluded to keep the resin from bursting into flames. If the temperature were lower than 644°F, the birch resin would not form the glue. If the temperature were above 752°F, it would blacken, form carbon, or burn. Making superglue from birch bark took some know-how! **Were the Neanderthals bumbling, primitive cavemen** as evolutionists have taught for years? Hardly! God made man intelligent from the beginning.

NEANDERTHAL SUPERGLUE

Tubalcain, an instructer of every artificer in brass and iron:....
~ Genesis 4:22

November 6

Biology

Humpback whales, the gentle giants of the deep, are warm-blooded animals. These mammals must maintain a certain body temperature to survive, yet they live continuously in water that can often be ice-cold. These warm-blooded whales must also move between warm, shallow waters and cool, deep waters, which cause them to experience huge temperature differences rapidly. To prevent these mammals from experiencing hypothermia in the cool waters, God gave whales a layer of blubber, which acts like the best winter coat ever designed.

This blubber can be 1½ to 2 feet thick, giving the humpback whale a total of nearly 40,000 pounds of insulating blubber. Think about wearing a huge winter coat outside on a 100°F summer day! You would immediately overheat. So why doesn't a whale overheat when swimming in warm water? God has solved this problem by building the whale's fins to act like huge air conditioners. Just like the African elephant with its large ears filled with blood vessels, the whale's fins contain millions of tiny capillaries that can rapidly either warm or cool the blood. Do we say air conditioners happened by accident and chance, or do we say they were designed? God designed the humpback to survive in both cool and warm ocean waters.

O Lord, how manifold are Your works! In wisdom You have made them all. The earth is full of Your possessions— This great and wide sea, In which are innumerable teeming things, Living things both small and great.
~ Psalm 104:24-25

Cosmology

November 7

Water on the Moon? Scientists were amazed when they analayzed the Apollo Moon rocks from 1969 -1972 and found water within the rocks. They found a significant amount of water chemically bound up inside these Moon rocks. **This puzzles evolutionists** because all of their models for the origin of the Moon begin 4.5 billion years ago with molten or unconsolidated material. This material would have boiled off any water, which would have evaporated into space, leaving the Moon "bone dry."

Yet, we have now documented that deep within the Moon there are significant concentrations of water held within tiny volcanic glass beads. The discovery that the Moon is not waterless, but full of water bound up in the volcanic rock, is a mystery to scientists because it does not fit with their idea of the Moon's origin. **The Bible describes the Moon being created on Day 4, about 6000 years ago.** So, finding water within Moon rocks is no surprise to those who believe Scripture.

Then God made two great lights: the greater light to rule the day, and the lesser light to rule the night...the fourth day.
~ Genesis 1:16, 19

November 8

Biology

Every year on hot summer days, the treetops ring with the high-pitched sound of an insect called the annual cicada. Its call can be heard more than 400 yards away. The sound you hear is the male calling to the female. They mate and live for only a few weeks. After the eggs hatch, the nymphs drop to the ground, burrow into the soil, and feed on the sap of plant roots until the following year. Then, on hot summer days, they emerge, molt, climb high into a tree, find a mate, and the cycle repeats.

Another type of cicada is called the periodic cicada. The periodic cicadas' lifecycle is a bit more unusual; they stay underground as nymphs for 17 years (13 years for another species). The 17-year cicadas live in Northeast USA, while the 13-year cicadas live in the Midwest and Southeastern parts of the USA. All of these cicadas emerge from the ground on the same day, either 17 or 13 years after the eggs were laid. Imagine millions of cicadas emerging all at the same time and singing incredibly loudly from the tree tops. **Imagine all these insects emerging within a few hours** of one another, all timed 17 or 13 years after the eggs were first laid! What a strange and wonderful "alarm clock" built within them that tells millions of nymphs it is time to come out of the ground and mate. How did they get this built-in alarm clock? Clocks do not happen by accident and chance. There had to be a clockmaker, and the cicadas' clockmaker is God!

To every thing there is a season, and a time to every purpose under the heaven: ~ Ecclesiastes 3:1

Microbiology

November 9

Scientists have been able to transcribe the human DNA code and lay it out like the letters in a book. With every passing year, they are decoding more of the language in order to gain a better understanding of how our bodies work. Yet, the DNA code is so complex that we may never completely understand the intricacies of its meanings and functions. We have even discovered that the sequence of information can be read forwards and backwards, overlapped to have different functions and meanings, and letters can be turned "on & off" depending on conditions within a cell.[1] **This is analogous to a book that can be simultaneously read in English, French, German, and Spanish - and be understandable when read forwards or backwards!** Yet, in each different language, the same sequence of letters will have a different understandable meaning. The author of such a book would be celebrated as an incomprehensible, brilliant genius. This is exactly what our limited understanding of the DNA code reveals.

Could this code come about by accident and chance? To believe this code wrote itself by random, one-small-change-at-a-time mutations is to believe in the impossible. We really have no excuse for not believing in and worshipping the Author of Life – Jesus Christ. The very DNA language that God invented is written within every one of our estimated 10 to 35 trillion cells. This DNA language testifies to His existence, genius, and majesty.

> Looking unto Jesus the author and finisher of our faith; who for the joy that was set before him endured the cross, despising the shame, and is set down at the right hand of the throne of God. ~ Hebrews 12:2

November 10 — Design

One summer, I was hiking in a forest out West and came into a clearing. I was surprised to find a log cabin with a stone fireplace there. The forest ranger had told me this area was uninhabited. "What is this?" I thought. I went inside to investigate. The walls were made of large logs without bark. "Oh," I see, "a huge bolt of lightning hit the trees and stripped them of their bark." I'd seen pictures of trees hit by lightning and bark strewn everywhere. Once the trees were debarked, a strong wind must have come down the mountain pass and blown the trees over causing them to come to rest on top of each other - forming the log cabin.

Next, I examined the stone fireplace. No mortar was needed as each stone fit nicely together. Thinking about this, I walked outside and noticed that the nearby river bed had the same rocks. "Oh," I reasoned, "a big flood must have swept down the river and picked up the rocks." And because moving water can sort stones, I figured that was how they fit together so nicely to form the stone fireplace. Satisfied with how the log cabin got there, I continued my hike.

What do you think of my story? **Is it true that the log cabin made itself?** We know that complex structures do not just come about by themselves. It takes an intelligent source. When we see a building, we know there must be a builder; a painting requires a painter; a design requires a designer. Life is too complex to come about by accident and chance. **The more we study science, the more we see design** - which means there must be a designer, and that Designer is God!

O ye sons of men, how long will ye turn my glory into shame? how long will ye love vanity, and seek after leasing? - Psalm 4:2

Geology

November 11

One of the ways to determine whether a canyon or cliff has been recently formed--or is very old--is to look at the pile of rubble at the base of the cliff or canyon. This rubble is the result of wind, rain, and temperature changes wearing away at the cliff face – resulting in material falling away from the vertical face and accumulating as a pile at the bottom of the cliff. This rubble at the base of a steep slope is called "talus." **The older the canyon or cliff, the more talus there should be at the bottom.** Eventually, the vertical wall should completely disappear and be replaced by a sloped pile of accumulated talus.

The fact is many, if not most, cliffs and canyons in the Western United States, and many other places around the world, still have vertically-walled valleys and have relatively small piles of talus at the base of cliffs. This is strong evidence for young geological features. If these vertical canyons and cliff walls were millions of years old, they would have eroded away long ago. Vertical canyons and cliff walls with little talus testify to a young Earth. So the next time you see a canyon or cliff, examine how much talus exists at its base.

And surely the mountains falling cometh to nought...
~ Job 14:18

November 12
Geology

A 2013 study estimated that 345 billion barrels of oil are recoverable from oil-containing-shale rock layers. This is typically done by a common oil-drilling process known as fracking. Shale is a clay-rich sedimentary rock that *seals* in the oil and gas – preventing movement of the fluids.

Where did all this oil come from? It is possible that some oil was created along with all the other resources of the earth, but most seem to be derived from organic matter. Oil has its own "fingerprint," and most oils match up with marine algae deposits (type 1 oil) and marine planktonic deposits (type 2 oil). To create oil, these deposits of organic debris needed to be heated; this is done by the Earth's thermal gradient. In other words, these deposits were buried at a certain depth, 8,000 to 15,000 feet, in order to "cook" at a temperature of 180°- 250°F. This is called the "oil window." Of course, there are variations; if there is a nearby active volcano, the area does not need to be buried as deeply to produce oil. If, the organic debris passes through the "oil window" and cooks at higher temperatures, the result will be a natural gas deposit.

Do we see oil forming naturally today? NO. Nearly all organic debris is eaten by microorganisms and scavengers prior to becoming trapped in sediment. So, what event in history led to the creation of oil and gas? Noah's Flood buried huge amounts of marine algae and plankton, trapping them faster than they could naturally decay and covering it with lots of sediment. **The Earth's oil reserves are young, not millions of years old.** If the oils were old, they would have been destroyed by bacterial action by now. Even the 2010 Deepwater Horizon oil spill in the Gulf of Mexico saw surface oil quickly eaten by bacterial action. We also know that bacteria live virtually everywhere, even deep within the Earth. So, we can assume that old oil would not exist after millions of years. The Flood of Noah's day has provided us with this much needed blessing for our modern world.

Every good gift and every perfect gift is from above, and cometh down from the Father of lights, with whom is no variableness, neither shadow of turning. ~ James 1:17

November 13
Biblical Accuracy

Have you considered our genetic code? Genetic scientists can now track genetic mistakes on the human genome. They are finding that each generation is adding genetic mistakes, not getting better. **The genetic code is rapidly deteriorating**; there is an increasing incident of birth defects. With such rapid deterioration of the human genome, evolutionists can hardly believe that humans exist! That's because they assume that humans have been around for some 100,000 years (some say millions). Yet, humans do exist and are not extinct. This can only mean that humans have not been around as long as evolutionists assume.

The biblical view that humans have been around for about 6,000 years, with only 200 or so generations since Adam and Eve. This agrees with what we see in science and observations of the rapidly deteriorating the human genome. Human DNA currently contains over 5000 mistakes leading to various genetic deseases. Adam and Eve were created perfect. Their children married brothers and sisters. **It was not until the time of Moses that God prohibited the marriage between close relatives.** God saw that this was necessary to minimize offspring becoming deformed. Our genetic code is deteriorating - not improving. How old is the Earth and its creatures? When we examine the genetic code, it says we live in a young Earth, just as God tells us in the Bible.

For we know that the whole creation groaneth and travaileth in pain together until now.
~ Romans 8:22

November 14
Paleontology

Ask people when the dinosaurs died out, and they will usually answer 65 million years ago. Then why are scientists now finding soft tissues in some dinosaur bones? Dr. Mary Schweitzer was analyzing the fossilized thigh bone of a T-rex found in the Hell Creek formation of Montana and found, to her amazement, blood vessels, cells with nuclei, tissue elasticity and intact protein fragments. Can these survive 65 million years? No! Could they have survived since the Flood of Noah's day (~ 4400 years ago)? Yes!

Many studies of Egyptian mummies and other humans of old age show the same sort of details as Schweitzer reported in her T. rex. Since Schweitzer's discovery, more paleontologists are cracking open dinosaur bones and finding, to their amazement, the same thing: blood vessels, cell nuclei, tissue elasticity and protein fragments. **Dinosaurs' soft tissues reveal they**

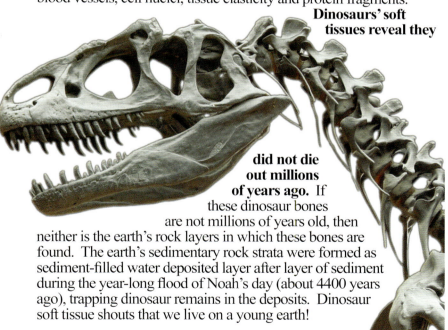

did not die out millions of years ago. If these dinosaur bones are not millions of years old, then neither is the earth's rock layers in which these bones are found. The earth's sedimentary rock strata were formed as sediment-filled water deposited layer after layer of sediment during the year-long flood of Noah's day (about 4400 years ago), trapping dinosaur remains in the deposits. Dinosaur soft tissue shouts that we live on a young earth!

And the waters decreased continually until the tenth month: in the tenth month, on the first day of the month, were the tops of the mountains seen.
- Genesis 8:5

November 15

Biology

In 1998, a new type of octopus was discovered - the mimic octopus (*Thaumoctopus mimicus*). It has the amazing ability to change shape, color, texture and swimming patterns in seconds to impersonate poisonous marine animals. This brown and white striped octopus is 2 feet long with pencil thin tentacles about ten inches long. This octopus lives off the sandy shores of the Indonesian islands. Scientists are astounded at the wide variety of marine animals that this mimic octopus can transform itself into within seconds. It can transform itself to look like the poisonous flat fish or the poisonous lion fish. When damselfish are near, it transforms itself to look like the poisonous sea snake; sea snakes are a known predator of damselfish.

Scientists have documented the mimic octopus doing 15 different imitations in order to escape its predators. **This means that the mimic octopus knows which animals will threaten the predator that is threatening him!** How does evolution explain the mimic octopus's ability to know the predator's predator and then impersonate it? God gave to the mimic octopus the intelligence to discern which dangerous marine creature to mimic--so the predator would be afraid--AND the ability to mimic the predator's predator.

The mimic octopus testifies to God's creativeness and skill!

Blessed be the Lord God, the God of Israel, who only doeth wondrous things. ~ Psalm 72:18

November 16

Microbiology

The third largest land animal today is the rhinoceros – often weighing over 6000 pounds (as much as three compact cars)! Pound per pound, it is also the fastest land animal – capable of running almost 30 mph and knocking over a SUV loaded with gawking tourists! **Yet, this mighty beast is dependent on the smallest of creatures for its survival.**

The rhino is a herbivore designed to eat plants that many animals cannot. Rhinos survive in harsh environments filled with low nutrient (even poisonous) plants that deer and other herbivores cannot digest. What is the rhino's secret to survival? It has an integrated system of bacteria and specialized organs that allow it to thrive.

The microbes that process a rhino's food live in the caecum (a special section of the intestine downstream of the small intestine), and they break down the cellulose materials that the rhino eats – turning them into sugars, vitamin B, and amino acids that the rhino cannot directly obtain from plants. But this symbiotic relationship between the biggest and smallest of organisms is even more amazing. The transformation of nutrients takes place downstream of the rhino's small intestine, but nutrients the rhino needs must be absorbed upstream (in the small intestine). So how does the rhino survive? Powerful muscular contractions in the rhino's digestive tract move things in both directions in the rhino, either driving nutrients upstream for absorption by his body or driving waste downstream for elimination. **The unique design of such a complex system testifies to the genius of its Creator.**

Let my mouth be filled with thy praise and with thy honour all the day.
~ Psalm 71:8

November 17

Biology

Frogs go through metamorphosis from egg to tadpole to frog. They begin life in the water like a fish and later develop legs and lungs to live on land and water. This is an amazing body transformation; **virtually every organ and body system is radically reworked in a specific order so that a tadpole can survive while it is turning into a frog**. A tadpole gets oxygen from the water using gills; it changes to a frog that uses lungs to get oxygen from the air. A tadpole goes from having a tail to a frog with legs and no tail. The tadpole goes from living in the water to a frog living on both land and water.

If evolution were true, how would a tadpole, a fish-like creature, mutate with both the ability and the desire to drop its tail, get legs, rid itself of gills and make lungs? **Could genetic mistakes rework virtually everything in order to go from a tadpole to a frog?** Remember that it is the frog and not the tadpole that makes babies. If evolution says that the tadpoles evolved—well—no babies. Frogs and their metamorphosis cry out design; the frog's life cycle had to work all at once, or it would not have happened. Perhaps God chose this unique and fascinating method for a frog's development so we would know He exists.

Thou art good, and doest good; teach me thy statutes.
~ Psalm 119:68

November 18

Biology

What bird did the Wright brothers copy in order to make an airplane? The turkey vulture. More than 100 years ago, Bible-believers Orville and Wilbur Wright spent years studying and working to produce the first motorized airplane. They began by observing birds in flight through their binoculars. **One of the many things they noticed were birds changing the shape of their wings as they flew into the wind.** The birds would curve the surface of their wings allowing the air to flow over the curved surface - creating lift. The Wright brothers' first powered flight lasted 12 seconds and flew 120 feet. That same day, they flew several more times; the last flight was 59 seconds and covered 852 feet.

Since that cold, wind-swept December day on a beach in North Carolina in 1903, the airplane industry has worked hard to develop well-designed airplanes. Our best design ideas for airplanes have come from observing birds and how they fly. When we see an airplane, we know there must be an airplane designer. When we see a bird, we know there must be a bird designer, and that designer is God.

The way of an eagle in the air... (is) too wonderful for me....
~ Proverbs 30:19, 18

Anatomy

November 19

Try the following three movements:
1. Rotate your wrist in a 360 degree circle.
2. Move your extended arm at the elbow straight up and down like a hinge on a door.
3. Swing your arm in a circle at the shoulder.

Your arm is designed with three completely different types of joints to allow an amazing range of movement - from throwing a baseball to picking up a pebble and placing it overhead into a cup. **Without all three of these very differently designed joints, this range of movements would be impossible.**

Guess what engineers have discovered as they have worked to design robots used for everything from painting cars on an assembly line to the robotic arm on the space shuttle? They need to use exactly the same three types of joints! Every robotic arm has some combination of a rotational joint (similar to our wrist), a hinge joint (similar to our elbow) and a universal joint (similar to our shoulder). Yet, the manmade joints are crude, cumbersome, and wear out far quicker than those designed for our bodies. Isn't it obvious the designer of our bodies was the greatest engineer of all?

Who hath believed our report? and to whom is the arm of the Lord revealed? - Isaiah 53:1

November 20

Botany

High in the Himalayas, there is a mystery. In the permafrost lives a parasitic fungus called the yartsa gunbu. This fungus attacks a live host (such as a worm or ant), invading and replacing tissues in the worm or ant's body. In some species, the parasitic fungus can even force its host, such an ant, to climb a tree and attach itself to a leaf before it dies - such that the spores from the fungus spread under optimal conditions. **How could a "primitive" fungus learn to control its host?** How the worm that hosts the yartsa gunbu fungus is even able to survive high in the Himalayan Mountains and reproduce in such a cold climate is as strange as the medicinal herb the worm's body becomes. Once the worm bores underground, the fungus kills it, and out of its dead body grows a plant-like shoot, that pierces the frosty ground - enabling courageous Nepali explorers to find this strange medicinal herb.

In Eastern medicinal practices, the fungus grown from the dead worm is marketed as a powerful healing herb that sells like gold. The price of this parasite has risen almost 1000% from the 1980s to today (from 1000 Yuan/kg to 100,000 Yuan/kg). Its value has drawn the strongest Nepalese to risk their lives and trek three to four days from their remote villages into the thin, bitterly cold atmosphere. There are many stories of men who never return.[1]

Use of yartsa gunbu has been recorded as far back as the 15th century in a Tibetan text translated *An Ocean of Aphrodisiacal Qualities*. Related species have shown interesting biological and pharmacological properties, such as an immunosuppressive drug helpful in human organ transplants and as a drug used to treat multiple mclerosis. There are many wonders in nature that God has prepared for our benefit!

**I have made the earth, and created man upon it...
~ Isaiah 45:12**

November 21
Biology

Have you considered the camel's ability to go days without water, suffer extreme dehydration, and then drink up to 40 gallons at one time? It's all in their red blood cell design.

Camels have red blood cells that are shaped flat, oval, and much smaller than human red blood cells. Human red blood cells are round. When humans become dehydrated, our blood becomes "sluggish" as the blood cells get stuck; a 5% water loss can result in serious medical problems. **For humans, a 12 % water loss can result in death by dehydration;** but not so for a camel, with its smaller, flatter, oval-shaped red blood cells. Even as the camel's water level drops, its blood just keeps 'a flowin'. **A camel can lose up to 40 % of its water and still survive.**

The camel also has an enormous ability to store water in its body. Some camels have been documented to drink 40 gallons at one time. If we drink too much water at one sitting (~ ½ gallon or 2 ½ liters), our red blood cells start to swell and can actually burst. The camel's red blood cells are able to expand up to 240% without rupturing while most animals' red blood cells are only able to expand up to 150%. How did the camel know it needed to have this type of red blood cell to survive harsh conditions? How would this cell evolve? The red blood cells of a camel were obviously designed by God in order for the camel to survive and thrive in dry desert environments.

The beast of the field shall honour me, the dragons and the owls: because I give waters in the wilderness, and rivers in the desert, to give drink to my people, my chosen.   - Isaiah 43:20

November 22
Geology

You may have watched CSI (Crime Scene Investigation) shows on TV. These detectives use various clues left at the scene of a crime to reconstruct an event, which they were not present to witness. The same can be done at the scene of the greatest catastrophe in Earth history – the worldwide Flood. But the "crime scene" of this event is the entire Earth! How the evidence is interpreted depends on your starting philosophical viewpoint. If you are trained to believe in enormous periods of time in Earth history, evidence that supports the worldwide extent of Noah's Flood is missed or denied. **The Tapeats Sandstone deposit, as found in the Grand Canyon, is a perfect example.**

This sedimentary rock layer was deposited right at the bottom rock record, on top of a scoured and often tilted layer of the Earth's foundational rock layers. Tapeats Sandstone is a bed of sand that has been cemented together. It shows a distinct pattern of waves and cross bedding - which indicates the direction and speed with which the water deposited this sand. A clue used to identify the Tapeats Sandstone is its chemical composition. This rock layer contains a specific amount of the mineral feldspar and more potassium than any other common sandstone layers, such as the overlying Coconino Sandstone. The final clue that can be used to identify this very specific sandstone layer is its fossil content. The Tapeats Sandstone often contains an extinct creature called the trilobite, while sandstone layers further up (which would have formed later in the worldwide Flood) often contain amphibian or reptile fossils (because these creatures would have been more mobile and able to survive into the later stages of the Flood.)

The reason a scientist can reconstruct the "crime scene" of Noah's Flood and know it was worldwide in extent is because of the characteristics of the Tapeats Sandstone- its chemical composition and fossil content. This extensive rock layer extends across entire continents (often given different names at different locations) from the Grand Canyon, AZ (Tapeats Sandstone); Chippewa Falls, WI (Mt. Simon Sandstone); Libya, North Africa (Sauk Sandstone); and Timna, Israel (Amudei Sandstone). All are identical - **indicating that they are all the same deposit, laid down at the same time, by the same event.** Only a world-covering Flood could explain such evidence.

And he answered and said unto them, I tell you that, if these should hold their peace, the stones would immediately cry out.
~ Luke 19:40

November 23

Design

How did the seahorse get its square tail? That's right; a seahorse has a unique tail - it is square, not round. Almost all animal tails have circular or oval cross-sections, but not the seahorse! **This square cross-section tail allows the seahorse to grip better than if it had curved sections.** When examining the tail, notice how it is made up of about 36 square segments that become smaller in size along the tail length.

A 3D printer duplicated the tail, and when the tail was submitted to crushing tests, it was found to provide better crush resistance than a cylindrical tail. Today's scientists are doing more research on the seahorse tail in order to develop new robotic systems. Scientists are just copying the Master Designer, God!

Declare his glory among the heathen, his wonders among all people. For the Lord is great, and greatly to be praised....
~ Psalm 96:3-4

November 24 — Biology

It is often asked how freshwater fish could survive the Flood of Noah's day when the whole Earth was covered with salt water. We do not know for certain what the salt content was of the Genesis floodwaters; they probably were salty but not as salty as today. One way freshwater fish could have survived in salty water was through the formation of a halocline (or density gradient) within the water layers. **Very salty water poured into fresh water can form layers that remain separated indefinitely.** The floodwaters could have formed a density gradient with fresh water on top and salt water in a layer below. For example, in 1993, the Great Mississippi Flood flowed into the Gulf of Mexico producing a layer of freshwater that was traceable all the way from the Mississippi River delta to the Florida Keys and a thousand miles up the East Coast.

Another possibility for survival was revealed in an experiment that was done in the 1970s by biologist Arthur Jones for his doctoral research. He hypothesized that "all, or at least most, fish kinds that survived the Flood must be able to survive both sea water and fresh, and much mixing of the two." In this particular experiment he used a kind of fish called cichlids. His research found that **freshwater cichlids not only survived for over two years in pure sea water, but they also "lived and reproduced normally."** Another fish that can survive in both fresh and salty waters is salmon. God created life with the ability to adapt to different environmental situations.

Let the heaven and earth praise him, the seas, and every thing that moveth therein.
~ Psalm 69:34

November 25

Cosmology

What about the Big Bang Theory? The Big Bang Theory says there was absolutely nothing, and then all the energy and matter in the universe appeared as a single point that suddenly explosively expanded. This created hydrogen gas that was flung out and spread throughout the universe. Then, clouds of hydrogen gas pulled themselves together, forming stars. From the stars, the planets were flung out, and you and I were made. Question - Where did the energy come from? How did it get so compressed to form a single point? What caused the explosion? Do explosions make order and design? (Explosions just make big messes.) And what was before the Big Bang? Evolutionists say there was nothing. **Do I get something from nothing?**

It takes more faith to believe in the Big Bang Theory than to believe there is a God. God clearly told us that He was the One who made the heavens and the Earth – God made them from nothing.

In the beginning God created the heaven and the earth.
~ Genesis 1:1

November 26
Microbiology

DNA found in dinosaur bones! The DNA molecule is one of the most fragile and easily fragmented of all organic structures, yet that is what has been found in dinosaur bones. Since Dr. Mary Schweitzer first reported finding soft tissue in dinosaur bones in 2000[1], so many fossils have been documented to contain soft protein and other undecayed biological material that it has become routine. Recently *undecayed DNA sequences* were found within soft dinosaur tissue![1] This is the "final nail" in the coffin of the belief that these fossils laid in the ground for millions of years.

Studies have been done to see how long DNA would exist if held at certain temperatures. For example, if the DNA were held at 77°F, it could survive for 22,000 years; after that, no measurable genetic sequence would be left. Here are the results of the study:

    77°F – 22,000 years
    59°F – 131,000 years
    41°F – 882,000 years
    23°F – 6.8 million years

Notice for DNA to survive for millions of years, the temperature had to be below freezing. Fossils trapped in rock layers do not experience subfreezing temperatures for millions of years! Also notice, the millions of years mentioned are only 1/10th of the time as compared to the evolutionary idea of dinosaurs dying out 65 million years ago. Dinosaur fossils and the rock layers they are trapped in are not that old. These dinosaurs were caught in the Flood of Noah's day some 4400 years ago. It is no surprise then that small amounts of the DNA structure could occasionally be found in these dinosaur fossils. **DNA in dinosaur bones shouts, "It's a young Earth!"**

Canst thou draw out leviathan with an hook?... Out of his mouth go burning lamps, and sparks of fire leap out. Out of his nostrils goeth smoke, as out of a seething pot or caldron. His breath kindleth coals, and a flame goeth out of his mouth. **- Job 41:1, 19-21**

November 27

Geology

The apostle Peter tells us that at a time, which he calls "The last days," scoffers will laugh at the Genesis Flood account (2Peter 3:3,6). I think we are there! What evidence is there for a worldwide flood? One evidence comes from observing sedimentary rock layers. Sedimentary rock layers cover ¾ of the world's continents. Try this simple experiment to see how rapidly sedimentary layers can form. (I am using food, but two different sizes of sand grains will work just as well.)

Blend together the following recipe for "Russian Tea":
- 2 cups orange-flavored drink mix (e.g. Tang)
- 1½ cup sugar
- 1 cup instant tea powder
- 1 (3 oz.) pack lemonade mix (or 2 packs of lemon Kool-aid)
- 2 tsp. cinnamon
- ½ tsp. ground cloves
- Mix well.

Now, slowly pour the mixture through a funnel into a tall, clear glass. What you should observe is layering as the mixture separates. **Multiple thin layers result as the falling materials sort themselves.** Evolutionists would have us believe that layers form slowly over time, yet in this demonstration (which can also be done with different sized grains of sand), we see that layers actually form rapidly. The same thing can happen over huge regions as water sorts sediment into distinct horizontal layers.

So make yourself a cup of Russian Tea (2 Tbs. or more of the mixture to a cup of water, heated), sit back, look at your layers, and know that God's Word is true. There was a world-wide Genesis Flood that produced the sedimentary rock layers that cover 75% of the world's continents.

Fifteen cubits (22 feet) upward did the waters prevail;
and the mountains were covered.
~ Genesis 7:20

November 28

Biology

When winter comes, some animals hibernate while others migrate, but have you heard of the Arctic springtail's method of surviving the winter? Arctic Springtails are tiny little insects less than 2/10th of an inch long. They spend their spring and summer living in the mossy areas of the Arctic. Once it starts becoming chilly, they start to darken in color and lose massive amounts of water until they shrivel up - looking like a dried, crumpled leaf. **They spend the winter dehydrated and dormant**. This is called cryoprotective dehydration and is also used by the Antarctic nematode and the Antarctic midge larvae. When the spring warmth returns, the Arctic springtail rehydrates itself and crawls away as if nothing happened.

Evolutionists believe that the springtails' ability to dry out and later rehydrate themselves happened over millions of years. Yet, this simply cannot be true because the springtails, nematodes, and midge larvae all had to get it right the first time in order to survive the first brutal Arctic winter. God provided this unique hibernation ability from the very beginning.

O Lord, how great are thy works! ~ Psalm 92:5a

Biology

November 29

You probably know that God created many birds and mammals with incredible parenting skills. But you may be amazed at the effort a tiny amphibian living in the remote forests of Central America takes to ensure its offspring's survival. Many frog species simply lay their eggs in water and leave the scene. **Not so with the strawberry poison dart frog.** She lays her eggs on the damp rainforest floor instead of in a pond like most frogs. The father stays vigilant over the fertilized eggs keeping them moist. When a tadpole hatches, it wriggles onto the mother's back. She hops away, usually looking for the rain-filled part of the bromeliad plant, which holds pools of water. Here she leaves her tadpole in the plant's pool of water and goes back to fetch her other tadpoles, giving each a piggyback ride to a different pool of water. Daily, she will visit 3-9 tadpoles and feeds each one an unfertilized egg. She cares for her tadpoles, in this manner, for six to eight weeks until they become frogs and can hop out.

How does the tadpole know to hop onto the mom's back? How does the mom know to give him a piggyback ride to a pool of water? How does the mom remember each place to visit? How does she know to feed them an unfertilized egg? **Most frogs just lay their eggs and hop away.** If the strawberry poison dart frog had hopped away like other frogs, there would be no more strawberry poison dart frogs; this behavior and all its parts had to happen the first time! God designed this just to show us how creative He could be.

Let everything that hath breath praise the Lord. Praise ye the Lord.
~ Psalm 150:6

November 30
Geology

What is the tallest mountain in the world? This record actually belongs to Mauna Kea in Hawaii that rises 30,610 feet from the bottom of the sea…and a staggering 56,447 feet from its underground mountain roots.[1] Mt. Everest is only 29,029 feet. Whereas Mt. Everest is made primarily of sedimentary rock, Mauna Kea is entirely composed of volcanic lava. Both mountains were formed during or shortly after Noah's Flood.

Skeptics of a biblical timeline point to the enormous size of the Hawaiian Island volcanoes, measure how slowly volcanoes are growing today, and state as a fact that the Earth must be millions of years old for such large volcanic mountain chains to have formed. What they fail to realize is that during the Flood of Noah, "all the fountains of the deep broke up" (Genesis 7:11) causing copious amounts of lava to pour forth. **The rate of volcanic activity today can be compared to a leaky faucet slowly dripping water while during the Flood of Noah, the lava would have been like a torrent of water coming from a fire hose.** During the Flood, lava was pouring forth to form Mauna Kea and could easily have been flowing at 1000 times the rate we see today. Although no one knows when the peak first broke through the surface of the Pacific Ocean, there is no reason to believe it could not have been during or subsequent to the Flood of Noah's day about 4400 years ago.

Keep silence before me, O islands; and let the people renew their strength: let them come near; then let them speak…. ~ Isaiah 41:1

"Trust in the Lord with all thine heart; and lean not unto thine own understanding. In all thy ways acknowledge him, and he shall direct thy paths."
- Proverbs 3:5-6

"Then the Grinch thought of something he hadn't before. What if Christmas, he thought, doesn't come from a store. What if Christmas, perhaps, means a little bit more."
– Dr. Seuss (1904 – 1991), beloved children's book author

December

Microbiology

December 1

During Darwin's time, only the cell wall, cytoplasm, and nucleus could be seen. It was not until the advent of advanced microscopes that we could peer deeply into a cell. What scientists found amazed them! They found a micro-city.

The nucleus is like the city hall, directing the cell's activities. The mitochondria is the cell's power plant, giving the cell its energy to work. Every city needs grocery stores, and that is the job of the Golgi bodies. Golgi bodies store supplies of chemicals that the cell makes. Whenever proteins or fats are needed in another part of the cell, the Golgi body wraps them up and sends them to where they are needed. The endoplasmic reticulum transports things within the cell like a mailman. It also acts like a garbage collector, picking up waste, so the cell does not become polluted. The lysomes are the cell's police force, protecting it by destroying invaders (like bacteria). They also send trash out through the city wall (the cell membrane).

Darwin never knew all the activity that was going on within a microscopic cell. It really is like a miniature city abuzz with activity. Does a city build itself by accident and chance? Just like a city takes planning and organizing, so too, our not-so-simple cells needed a planner and organizer. That planner and organizer was God who ensured that each part was present and working from the beginning.

Now unto him that is able to do exceeding abundantly above all that we ask or think, according to the power that worketh in us.
~ Ephesians 3:20

December 2

Geology

Diamonds are valuable because they are rare. Diamonds are rare because they formed almost 90 miles below the surface of the Earth and were only thrust up to the surface in a few localized areas. But when did this release of these beautiful gemstones occur? One of the clues is the relatively unstable nature of the carbon structure that created the diamonds

Diamonds are made from pure carbon, but they are dazzlingly clear - unlike black carbon that makes up coal, or the grey form of carbon, called graphite (used in pencils). Although diamonds are the hardest known naturally occurring mineral, they are both brittle (easily fractured along their crystalline lines) and unstable. Temperatures and pressures slightly below and above where they form cause diamonds to rapidly degenerate to a softer and more stable form of carbon known as graphite. Thus, **it is believed that diamonds could only have formed about 90 miles below the Earth's surface** where the temperature is between 900°C – 1200°C (~1,650°F - 2,200°F) and the pressure is just right for the diamond crystal structure to form. IF it took years (or even days) for these diamonds to travel to the surface of the Earth, they would have passed through a zone where the temperature and pressure would have forced the diamond structure to revert into a more stable graphite structure. But they did not revert and made it to the Earth's surface as diamonds. Thus, most experts accept that diamonds must have been explosively spewed from 90 miles below to the Earth's surface **within a matter of 7-20 hours**. What event in history would cause this to happen?

During Noah's Flood, the Bible states that "all the fountains of the deep broke up" (Genesis 7:11). **This was a unique one-time event, and nothing like it has happened before or since.** For diamonds to be carried rapidly to the surface, molten blobs of lava rock from the mantle of the Earth needed to burst through the rock layers of the Earth. This molten mantle material called kimberlite would have had to burst from sources starting 125 miles below the surface of the Earth and travel all the way to the Earth's surface through chimney-like pipes. The process carried diamonds with it as the molten rock passed the 90 mile "diamond-making" depth. We do not see this happening today; today's volcanoes spew lava slowly from depths much closer to the surface. It is in these kimberlite crater areas (primarily at specific locations in southern/central Africa, Canada, Siberia, Australia, and Brazil) where modern diamond hunters seek their fortunes.

It was the fracturing of the Earth during Noah's Flood that made it possible for us to enjoy the beauty of the diamond. In fact, every woman wearing a diamond can use it as a witnessing tool. Diamonds were formed at the diamond-making depth and then thrust upward with the magma in the kimberlite pipes in a matter of hours during the violent upheaval of the Flood of Noah's time. How diamonds are made proclaim that the biblical Flood is truth!

In the six hundredth year of Noah's life, in the second month, the seventeenth day of the month, the same day were all the fountains of the great deep broken up,.... ~ Genesis 7:11

December 3

Biology

The North African desert scorpion is continually exposed to sandstorms. These same sandstorms can sandblast paint right off steel. So, how is the scorpion's exoskeleton able to withstand such abuse?

Curious scientists discovered that the scorpion's exoskeleton is not smooth but covered with tiny domes only 10 micron high. Computer simulations reveal that these domes deflect the airflow, reducing the sandblasting force by 50 % when compared to a smooth surface. **Scientists are now applying this bumpy technology to turbine blades and helicopter rotors to increase their life.** These design engineers are just copying what God has already designed.

As one great scientist, Johannes Kepler, once stated, "We are just thinking God's thoughts after Him."

I am the Lord that maketh all things...
~ Isaiah 44:24

December 4
Biblical Accuracy

Tracing the DNA lineage of all humans back to an original source has revealed that all humans originally came from a single woman and single man.[1] This is no surprise to Christians, who were told this thousands of years ago in the first chapters of the Bible. It has just taken modern science 6000 years to catch up with what God has told us in the Bible. But we have also traced the lineage of other creatures. For instance, DNA testing has now revealed that **all living goats, are descended from five original female goats** and all living sheep are descended from three or four original females.[2] Why multiple pairs and not one original goat or sheep pair? Once again, the Bible provides the answer.

Noah was told to take seven pairs of each type of "clean" animal on board the ark. Some of these animals were subsequently used for sacrifice. All the sheep and goats in the world today have descended from the remaining animals. The DNA test results exactly match what would be expected if the Bible and the worldwide Flood are accurate. God's word is always true!

> Of every clean beast thou shalt take to thee by sevens, the male and his female...And Noah builded an altar unto the Lord; and took of every clean beast, and of every clean fowl, and offered burnt offerings on the altar.
> ~ Genesis 7:2a & 8:20

December 5

Biology

Did you know that shrimp have some of the most amazing eyes in the animal kingdom? Mantis shrimp have photoreceptors capable of receiving 16 different wavelengths of light. Humans only have 3 photoreceptors (red, green, and blue), which we combine to see all the visible colors. **One can only imagine the fantastic visual experience possible with 16 photoreceptors!** Besides this, mantis shrimp see UV, heat (infra-red), and polarized light. In fact, they can also detect circular polarized light.

Furthermore, each of its two compound eyes can perceive depth and move independently. These eyes are being studied in hopes of producing better DVD players. Some scientists now specialize in a new field of study called biomimicry. In essence, human designers are simply copying ideas from the Master Designer. God is the one who made the heavens, the Earth, the seas and all that is in them. There is an infinite amount to learn from Him.

Thy mercy, O Lord, is in the heavens; and thy faithfulness reacheth unto the clouds. Thy righteousness is like the great mountains; thy judgments are a great deep: O Lord, thou preservest man and beast. ~ Psalm 36:5,6

December 6

History

Scientists agree that James Clerk Maxwell's (1831-1879) greatest contribution to science was his brilliant 913 page treatise on the mathematical unification of electricity with magnetism. This forever changed the world of physics and is the foundation of radio transmissions, television, computers, space travel, and all modern electronics. Maxwell stands at the forefront of the most brilliant scientists who ever lived, and his legacy is the modern world we all enjoy. Some physicists have shown that even atoms can be explained as the result of the movement of charges and that matter itself is really an electrical simulation – all based on Maxwell's equations.1

Although Maxwell lived a short 48 years, he was also responsible for mathematically explaining Saturn's rings as a massive cloud of particles. He made major contributions to the fields of statistics, astronomy, gas theory, color theory (producing the first color photograph), and thermodynamics.

As a contemporary to Charles Darwin, Maxwell soundly rejected naturalistic explanations for life stating, "No theory of evolution can be formed to account for the singularity of molecules, for evolution necessarily implies continuous change…" A prayer written by Maxwell stated, "Almighty God, who has created man in Thine own image, and made him a living soul that he might seek after Thee and have dominion over Thy creatures, teach us to study the works of Thy hands…"

A deeply sincere follower of Jesus Christ, Maxwell used his faith as the foundation from which he made his great discoveries. Do not be deceived that belief in creation is a detriment to scientific advancement … the very opposite is true. Maxwell had this verse inscribed upon the entrance to his science laboratory at Cambridge University:

The works of the Lord are great, sought out of all them that have pleasure therein.
~ Psalm 111:2

Biology

December 7

Have you considered the giraffe's tongue? This 18-inch-long tongue is so agile that it is able to flick individual ants from an acacia tree leaf. Acacia leaves are the giraffe's main food, but stinging, biting ants that live on the acacia tree try to stop the giraffe from eating the leaves. Giraffes are large animals that can reach 18 feet in height, and it takes lots of food to keep this animal alive. **A giraffe can eat up to 75 pounds of acacia leaves in a single day.** But biting ants aren't the only hazard with which the giraffe has to deal. Acacia trees have thorns or spikes - many longer than one of your fingers! What if one of these spikes happens to get in with the leaves and is swallowed? You can imagine a fish bone stuck in your throat; now imagine a 4-inch-long thorn stuck in the ten-foot-long throat of a giraffe!

The giraffe's Creator has taken care of that by designing thick saliva to cover the spike - allowing it to slide down the throat without getting stuck. The thorns are coated so thickly that they exit the giraffe in the same condition they entered without any harm to the digestive system. This thick saliva had to be present from the beginning, or the first giraffes would have gotten thorns stuck in their throats – driving them to extinction. **Evolution would have us believe that this thick saliva happened by accident and chance over millions of years.** If this is true, would we have any giraffes left? God knew what giraffes would experience and provided the solution. If God cares about a giraffe's saliva, think how much more He cares for you.

With him is wisdom and strength, he hath counsel and understanding. - Job 12:13

December 8

Biology

Giraffes have many unique features. They can tower up to 18 feet above the ground. Have you ever wondered how it keeps its 500 pound neck upright? The giraffe has a very long ligament called the nuchal ligament that runs from the back of the skull all the way down to the base of its tail. This ligament acts like a giant rubber band pulling the head and neck into its upright position.

Another unique feature is the design of the patches. Giraffes can become overheated in the African savannas. How do they regulate their temperature? Those irregular, brown patches help to regulate their temperature. Each patch has a large blood vessel around its border that branches off into smaller blood vessels into the patch. To release heat, a giraffe sends blood to the smaller branches in the middle of the patch - thereby radiating the heat away from its body. If the giraffe is too cold, the blood is not sent into these blood vessels.

Giraffes are uniquely designed animals that possess a myriad of specialized design features. **It is easy to see the power and creativity of God when looking at a giraffe.**

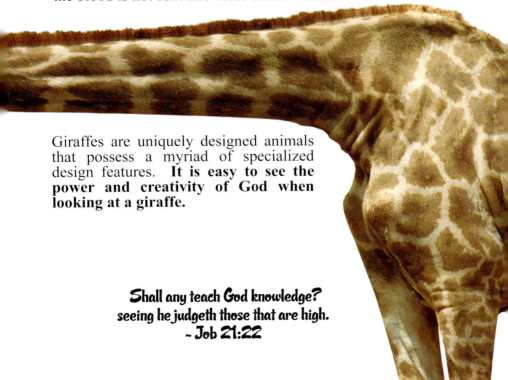

Shall any teach God knowledge? seeing he judgeth those that are high.
~ Job 21:22

Anatomy

December 9

Have you ever heard of the term "brainwaves"? Before the 1900s, nobody had ever considered the possibility that such a thing existed, let alone that these waves could be detected or measured. But in 1933, a scientist named Alfred Loomis attached electrodes to his own and other family members' heads and invented a machine to magnify and record the electrical signals that he detected coming from the brain. This discovery was the basis for the invention of the electroencephalograph (EEG), an instrument still used today to detect abnormalities related to electrical activity of the brain.

Loomis discovered that there were different patterns of electrical activity when we are sleeping, dreaming, awake, or emotionally excited. He also discovered that the mind responds to words and sounds even when deeply asleep. Our brain's pattern of electrical signals repeats in a very periodic, wave-like pattern. This observation solved a mystery that had been noted for centuries. Why could some people look at a clock before going to sleep, decide to wake up at a given time, and then wake up within seconds of that time without an alarm clock?

Since our sleeping brain produces waves in a perfectly repeatable, periodic pattern, **it literally can act as a clock to wake us at the exact moment desired by keeping track of the number of waves that pass from the moment it drops into subconscious sleep!** The human brain is truly a marvelous organ, which we have barely begun to understand - even 80 years after the invention of the EEG.

yea, his heart taketh not rest in the night.
~ Ecclesiastes 2:23

December 10

Botany

It's a lazy summer day in the cornfields of Iowa; **yet, an all-out war is taking place.**

Into the cornfield comes a caterpillar with a voracious appetite for corn leaves. As the caterpillar munches on corn leaf after corn leaf, what's a corn plant to do? The damaged corn plant releases volatile chemical compounds, that send a message warning the other corn plants to activate their own defense genes. A different volatile chemical attracts parasitoid wasps to the corn plant, where the caterpillar is eating. The parasitoid wasp lays its eggs under the caterpillar's skin. The eggs hatch and the larvae eat the caterpillar from the inside out. If the corn leaf is damaged by wind or hail, does the plant still release these signals? No. **The corn plant only cries for help when the caterpillar's saliva is recognized; false alarms do not happen!**

It is the caterpillar's saliva plus the wounding of the plant that starts what scientists call a signal transduction pathway in the corn. This complex process results in the making and releasing of volatile chemicals crying for help. Was this battle in the cornfield taking place before man sinned? Is this what God calls "very good" at the end of Creation week? No. It was not always like this. Like so many predator/prey relationships, it reveals the tragic consequences of man's sin. God the Creator equipped each organism with the necessary ability to adapt to sin's consequences - which affected everything in the universe.

According to Scripture, plants are not "alive" in the same way as people and animals. In the beginning, plants were created as food. Creation scientists speculate that originally wasps may have laid their eggs in protein-rich plants and not in the caterpillars. After the Fall, everything deteriorated. Wasps needed more protein-rich sources (like caterpillars) and alternative defense mechanisms arose. Sin's consequences affects EVERYTHING!

Cursed is the ground for your sake; In toil you shall eat of it all the days of your life. Both thorns and thistles it shall bring forth for you, and you shall eat the herb of the field.
~ Genesis 3:17-18

December 11
Biology

Corals are actually animals, not plants. Each animal builds a castle around itself and lives in the castle. The animal is actually called a "polyp," and the castle it makes is the hard structure we call coral. At night, the coral polyp comes out to feed by waving its tentacles to catch microscopic animals. During the day, the coral polyp processes its food with the help of tiny algae called zooxanthellae. (The algae are caught by the coral and live within the coral polyp's tissue.) This algae uses sunlight in the process of photosynthesis to make sugar. (That is one of the reason's corals are only found in brightly lit water.) This sugar is then transferred to the coral polyp. **The plant (algae) feeds the animal (coral). The coral, in turn, provides the algae with a protective home and carbon dioxide.** Carbon dioxide is what the algae need in order to make food. If the algae is not present within the coral, the corals become fragile and ultimately die. Corals need algae, and the algae need corals. In fact, there is about three times more algal tissue than polyp tissue in a coral colony.

The algae also provide coral with their color. The algae's chlorophyll mixes with the coral polyp creating the color. When corals lose their algae, zooxanthellae, they become white or bleached. Coral and algae help each other out! How did the coral know that it needed this type of algae, Zooxanthellae, to help it survive? How did it survive originally without it? How could they have evolved independently? Scientists call this symbiotic evolution, but throwing a word at something does not explain how it developed. God created these two to work together for each other's benefit and to show His glory.

With trumpets and sound of cornet make a joyful noise before the Lord, the King. Let the sea roar, and the fullness thereof; the world, and they that dwell therein. ~ Psalm 98:6-7

December 12

Geology

Imagine walking through an underground city carved out of salt. Imagine this underground city with chapels, bedrooms, dining rooms with chandeliers and sculptures of biblical scenes, saints, and famous historical figures – all carved from salt. Since the 13th century, over 700 years ago, the Wielickzka salt mine near Krakow, Poland, has been mined, and an underground city has been carved out in the process. This salt mine is over 1,000 feet deep and 180 miles long. But how did all this salt get there?

Seawater contains salt. When seawater evaporates, it leaves behind salt and other minerals. Evolutionists believe that these thick, extensive salt deposits came about from the evaporation of seawater over great ages. These underground salt deposits, however, are ultra-pure sodium chloride, free of contaminants and ready for use on roads and for consumption. **Where are all the sand and sea creatures trapped in this evaporating seawater over millions of years?**

A better explanation is that during the Flood of Noah's day, "all the fountains of the great deep (were) broken up" (Genesis 7:11), spewing out hot liquids into the cooler, deep oceans. Once cooled, these superheated, super-saturated waters lost the ability to hold their load of dissolved minerals, resulting in great layers of precipitated salts. Salt deposits are better explained as precipitates, not evaporites. So if you ever spend the night in a "salt bedroom," or just add salt to your popcorn, think biblically about where that salt originated; salt is a result of Noah's Flood--and then tell others from where it came.

As Jesus said, "You are the salt of the earth...." ~ Matthew 5:13

Design

December 13

Scientists have been studying the shark's skin. When viewed under an electron microscope, the shark's skin has tiny scales called denticles. The size and position of denticles allow water to flow by quickly, enabling the shark to swim fast. Scientists replicated these denticles on swimsuits. During the 2000 Sydney Olympics, athletes that wore Speedo's Fastskin (shark suit) swimsuits were able to swim faster, breaking 13 of the 15 world records. Continued research created the LZR Racer (which was named the 2008 "best invention" by TIME Magazine). Michael Phelps wore this suit at the Beijing Olympics - winning eight record-breaking gold medals. **Copying the design of shark's skin for swimsuits at swim meets gives users such an advantage that these types of sharkskin swimsuits are now banned in competition!**

Naval designers have also applied this sharkskin design to the bottoms of boats. They are finding that cargo ships use less fuel when they add these denticles to the hulls. Also, scientists noticed that on a shark's skin, there is not much parasitic growth. Now researchers are testing the concept of applying this design to hospital surfaces in order to resist bacterial growth. All this technology is from studying the Great Designer's design and copying it!

> O Lord, how manifold are thy works! in wisdom hast thou made them all: the earth is full of thy riches.
> ~ Psalm 104:24

December 14
Geology

Have you noticed that many mountain ranges lie next to deep valleys?

- The Himalaya Mountains lie next to the Ganges Plain. The Ganges Plain is a deep valley filled in with sedimentary rocks.
- The Teton Range of mountains is adjacent to Jackson Hole (which lies in a valley) where there appears to be only 6,000 feet of vertical change from the valley to the top of the mountains. Jackson Hole is built on the top of many layers of sedimentary rock. If we go all the way to the bottom of this sediment, all the way to the basement granite rock layers, **we find this sedimentary rock has dropped down 20,000 feet below sea level**. Now add the Teton Mountains (13,000 feet above sea level) to the 20,000 feet of sedimentary rock at the base of that mountain, and it represents a sediment thickness of 33,000 feet!

As the waters rushed off the rising mountains at the end of the Flood, sediments were carried with it. This filled the basins we see near the mountains. The mountains did rise up, and the valleys did sink just as it says in Psalm 104:8. The earth's landscapes bear witness to an absolutely devastating Genesis Flood.

They go up by the mountains; they go down by the valleys unto the place which thou hast founded for them.
~ Psalm 104:8

History

December 15

We often think that man was primitive in the past. But, then, how do you explain some of the technology of the past? For example, the **ancient Egyptians had a blue-colored pigment that was both beautiful and intense, not even fading with severe sunlight exposure.** This paint colorant was used by the ancient Egyptians and then passed onto the Greeks and Romans. Yet, during the "dark ages," Europeans lost the knowledge of how to manufacture this paint (about 1100 years ago). It was not until the 19th century, when Pompeii was uncovered, that a small pot of this pigment was found and analyzed, allowing us to regain this knowledge. Egyptian Blue is calcium copper tetrasilicate. The paint samples contained silica, calcium oxide, and copper oxide. These compounds were mixed together in precise proportions and heated to 1650°F (900°C) for many hours to produce the brilliant, durable, blue pigment.

The ancient Egyptians used chemistry to create an intense, non-fading, blue colorant. Primitive? Hardly! God created Adam genetically perfect and with the maximum human intellect. In Genesis 4:20-22, mankind is described as having knowledge of livestock, metalworking, and music. After the Flood, the tower of Babel was built, and man was dispersed. Some of Noah's descendants moved to Egypt and brought with them the knowledge and technology of the pre-Flood world. This explains why ancient civilizations seemed to spring up overnight, like in ancient Egypt. This Egyptian blue is a testimony that man was highly skilled right from the beginning - giving proof that the Genesis account is true.

He was the father of those who dwell in tents and have livestock. His brother's name was Jubal. He was the father of all those who play the harp and flute. And as for Zillah, she also bore Tubal-Cain, an instructor of every craftsman in bronze and iron...
~ Genesis 4:20-22

December 16

Cosmology

For decades, planetary scientists have claimed that the Earth's ocean water came from comets colliding with the early Earth. But once they measured the composition of the water on comets, scientists found it did not match the characteristics of ocean water. Thus, this explanation fell upon hard times. What's an evolutionary cosmologist to do?

The latest attempt to rescue the idea that the Earth made itself violates all rules of logic and science. It is now being proposed that water clung to dust particles as they coalesced to form the Earth approximately 5 billion years ago. Here's the elephant-in-the-living-room problem with this idea:

- These dust particles circling the Sun would have been heated to between 150 and 1080 ºC – way above the boiling point of water for millions of years while the planet was coalescing. The water would simply have boiled away!
- It is repeatedly assumed that dust circling the Sun clumped into planetesimals (giving something we don't understand a long name apparently makes it more believable), and then the planetesimals accreted into planets. Yet, it has never been satisfactorily explained how this process could happen because realistic modeling scenarios indicate the particles are driven apart far faster than they "accrete."
- One of the researchers stated, "The new results will force scientists to re-evaluate the process of Earth's formation. **Perhaps** the team's absorption model is correct, or **perhaps** water came to Earth aboard a kind of **asteroid that hasn't yet been found, or no longer exists**..."

Notice the faith of these scientists. Their beliefs are not based on testable, reproducible observations of science but in "perhaps stories" and things that "haven't been found or no longer exist." For Christians, our faith is in what God has told us, "He created the heavens and the earth."

And my right hand hath spanned the heavens: when I call unto them, they stand up together.
~ Isaiah 48:13

December 17

History

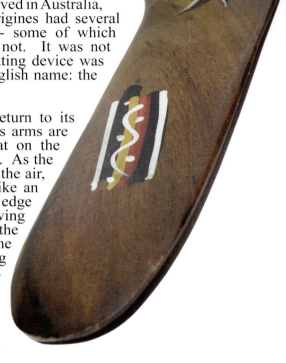

It seems very counterintuitive that if I throw a stick it would return to me, but that is exactly what a boomerang does. When the English arrived in Australia, they noticed that the Aborigines had several types of throwing sticks - some of which returned while others did not. It was not until 1822 that this fascinating device was described and given an English name: the boomerang.

How does a boomerang return to its thrower? The boomerang's arms are curved on the top and flat on the bottom - creating an airfoil. As the boomerang moves through the air, its wings create lift, just like an airplane. As it spins, the edge of the forward spinning wing creates more lift than the opposite arm. This causes the boomerang to tip, resulting in a principle known as gyroscopic precession. This uneven lift causes a constant turning pressure that then causes the boomerang to return to its thrower.

The boomerang is not some primitive object made by some primitive man, but it was made by an intelligent person capable of using sophisticated aerodynamic principles. Boomerangs are a testimony of mankind's brilliance from the moment of creation.

For enquire, I pray thee, of the former age, and prepare thyself to the search of their fathers: (For we are but of yesterday, and know nothing, because our days upon earth are a shadow:) Shall not they teach thee, and tell thee, and utter words out of their heart?

~ Job 8:8-10

December 18

History

A man, a plan, a canal, Panama! A century ago, the world marveled at the engineering of the Panama Canal, but it would not have been built if not for a devout Christian military doctor named William Gorgas. The French had started to build the 50-mile-long Panama Canal through the ridges and mountains that separated the Atlantic and the Pacific Oceans, but many of the workers died of yellow fever, and the French abandoned the project. The leading scientists of the day believed the disease was spread by air from surrounding marshes and filthy slums. The reality was much different; yellow fever came from the bite of a mosquito *Aedes aegypti* - the same mosquito that now carries the Zika virus.

Against the conventional scientific wisdom of their day, William Gorgas and Walter Reed did careful experimentation to find the mode of disease transmission. They even had volunteers sleep in the noxious excretions of yellow fever victims for a week; no one died. Then they studied the habits of the mosquito *A. aegypti*. It never traveled more than 200 yards from its birth place AND laid eggs only in fresh water. Armed with this knowledge, Gorgas was assigned to the Panama Canal project. He immediately ran into roadblocks as the majority of doctors refused to believe or accept his conclusions. **It took President Roosevelt's private doctor encouraging the President to enforce Gorgas' methods.** So began the largest public health project in the history of the world up to that time. A massive effort was begun to kill the mosquitoes by fumigating houses and putting screens on windows, lids on cisterns, and even floating oil on standing water. The war succeeded! Once the mosquito that carried yellow fever was killed off, the focus shifted to engineering the Panama Canal.

Gorgas was a Christian who understood that the truth is often opposed. Gorgas knew he was fighting "settled science." Today, we have greatly benefited from Gorgas' determination to do true science, but we are still fighting a battle for truth as only evolutionary thought is allowed throughout our public school systems. **We, too, need to fight "settled science" and keep the truth in front of people.**

A man's heart deviseth his way: but the Lord directeth his steps.
~ Proverbs 16:9

Geology

December 19

Where did the Great Salt Lake get its salt? Why is it not a fresh water lake? The Dead Sea, Aral Sea, and Caspian Sea are also dried up ocean water lakes. Evolutionists believe that the waters are from oceans that were trapped; creationists agree. Salty waters were caught in basins as the Genesis floodwaters rushed off the land.

After Noah's Flood, the Ice Age began. About a thousand years later, **the Ice Age ended bringing on dramatic, worldwide climate change.** Lakes dried leaving dry basins. Lake Bonneville (Utah) has ancient shorelines that can be seen 1,000 feet above the basin in the surrounding mountains. Salt lakes, dry lake basins, and elevated shorelines testify to one world-covering flood, the Flood of Noah's day.

Doth a fountain send forth at the same place sweet water and bitter?
~ James 3:11

December 20

Biology

Today, anthropologists like to classify people into different groups (races) based on their skin color and hair: Caucasoid (Europeans), Mongoloid (Chinese), Negroid, Australoid and Malayan. Yet, skin color is based simply on how much melanin is produced in each skin cell. If a person has a lot of melanin, he will be dark-skinned. If the person does not have much melanin, he will be light-skinned. When a person with lots of melanin (dark-skinned) lives in a northern country that receives little sunshine, he will not be able to absorb much vitamin D and may develop rickets. If a person with little melanin, light-skinned, lives near the equator with lots of sunshine, he may develop skin cancer. As a result, there would be natural thinning of the genetic pool in response to the environment.

During the Ice Age, people groups left the tower of Babel and spread out. People of higher latitudes began to 'acquire' light skin while those near the equator 'acquired' dark skin. But what about the Eskimo (Inuit) people living in the far north and the people of Central and South America? Why do they have middle-brown skin? Shouldn't the Eskimos be light-skinned and the South Americans living on the equator be dark-skinned? These people groups moved out from the Tower of Babel and simply lacked the gene for lots of melanin (dark skin) that resulted in these American people groups having middle-brown skinned people. **The gene pool is more important than the environment; new information cannot be added.**

Adam, from whom we are all descended, had the best possible gene pool. Noah and his family were probably middle brown, possessing genes for both dark and light skin. Today, most people are middle brown. In fact, we are all one big extended family!

And (God) hath made of one blood all nations of men for to dwell on all the face of the earth .... ~ Acts 17:26

December 21
Microbiology

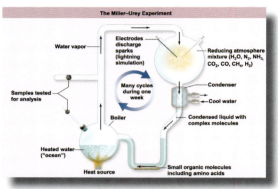

Stanley Miller's famous experiment in 1953 attempted to show that life began when lightning passed through a particular atmosphere and made chemicals called amino acids. Amino acids are the building blocks of proteins, and proteins are required by all living cells. Miller did show that some amino acids could be made in this way, but it's quite another thing to get them to build a living cell! Just as a few concrete blocks in a parking lot will never turn themselves into a complex building, the existence of a few amino acids can never explain the origin of a living cell.

These amino acids supposedly linked together to form proteins (like beads on a necklace). These proteins then somehow would have to form the first DNA that went on to form the first living cell. Generations of schoolchildren have been taught this fairytale as if it were a fact of history. Now even many atheists are bailing out and admitting life could not have possibly formed in this way. Why?

1. Amino acids in water do not concentrate themselves; they disperse.
2. Amino acids need to be in the pure form in order to make proteins. Contaminants in ocean water would have stopped protein formation.
3. Under natural conditions, pure amino acids will not form proteins.
4. Living things use only left-handed amino acids, yet Miller-type experiments always result in a useless 50:50 mixture of right and left-hand amino acids.

What Miller's experiment actually showed was that life could not possibly have formed in this way. The complex organization of life requires an intelligent Creator! It is by observing creation that God makes His awesome power and creativity apparent to everyone.

*Because that which may be known of God is manifest in them;
for God hath shewed it unto them.
~ Romans 1:19*

December 22

Geology

Deep below the ground near a silver and lead mine of Chihuahua, Mexico, at the Naica Mine, two men were blasting a tunnel and discovered a cavern crammed full of colossal crystals as large as mature pine trees - 50 feet long and 4 feet across. These are the largest known crystals in the world!

These crystals were made of a mineral called selenite. The cavern's unbearable heat measured 150 °F with 100% humidity. Geologists believe that under this cavern is a huge chamber of superheated molten rock that forced fluids rich in minerals up through the fault lines to the surface. These fluids dissolved the limestone caverns and filled some with silver, lead, and zinc deposits; others became nurseries for gypsum crystals (selenite is one variety). The selenite crystals would have grown while the fluid completely filled the cavern. Roberto Villasuso, the mine exploration superintendent, stated that **these crystals probably formed within a 30-50 year period.** Why such a short time and not millions of years? Because the minerals grew so evenly. If there had been any movement of water, it would have altered the crystallization patterns. **The crystals' clarity and size testify to rapid formation, not millions of years.** It does not take millions of years, just the right conditions.

And the likeness of the firmament upon the heads of the living creature was as the colour of the terrible crystal, stretched forth over their heads above. ~ Ezekiel 1:22

Geology

December 23

Visitors on cave tours are almost always told that the stalactites and stalagmites have taken thousands, if not millions, of year to form. The claim is frequently made that a stalactite takes a full century to grow only one inch. Always consider, however, **what you are not being told!** For instance:

1. Stalactites in the basement of the Lincoln Memorial are huge. The memorial was built during the 1930s with a basement. **Rainwater seeping through the marble floor has formed stalactites up to five feet in height!**
2. A **concrete** railroad bridge in Wooster, Ohio, had a stalactite growing underneath that was over 12 inches long. **Only twelve years earlier, the bridge had been cleaned of stalactites.**
3. Foot-long stalactites have grown in lime-rich mines of Newcastle, Australia. **These mines are less than 40 years old.**

Stalactites grow where water seeps through limestone rock, dissolving limestone. When water containing the dissolved limestone enters the cave roof, the water evaporates leaving the limestone behind. If there are any remaining water droplets, they fall to the cave floor and evaporate, leaving behind the deposit, in this case, a stalagmite.

During past periods of massive water movement through the ground (such as during the Ice Age), water would percolate through the ground into empty cave formations to form many stalactites and stalagmites very rapidly. After the Ice Age, there was a great drying out of climates worldwide.

To make a stalactite and stalagmite doesn't take millions of years, just the right conditions.

I tell you that, if these should hold their peace, the stones would immediately cry out. ~ Luke 19:40

December 24

History

In 1991, a 3,000 year old frozen corpse was found in the Austrian-Italian Alps. This "ice-man" was named Otzi. Along with his frozen corpse were found a longbow of yew wood, a framed backpack, copper ax, dried fruit, other foods, a first aid kit of birch bracket fungus (which is a powerful pharmaceutical), and a fire-making kit that included flint and ores for making sparks. His last meal was goat meat and bread cooked over a charcoal oven. **Otzi doesn't sound like a stone-age brute, does he?** In actuality, sophisticated, intelligent human beings have always existed.

But the surprises didn't stop there. Scientists also found a strain of ulcer-causing *Helicobacter pylori* within his body that is **essentially identical to what we find today** in Central and South Asia. This *H. pylori* has not changed for thousands of years! Otzi had an ulcer just like modern man, and it was caused by the same bug *Helicobacter pylori*.

Otzi, the ice man, fits the true history of the Bible. Adam and Eve and their descendants were intelligent people. After the Flood, the Tower of Babel was built; God confused their languages, and people were scattered across the face of the Earth. Otzi was one of those descendants.

So the Lord scattered them abroad from thence upon the face of all the earth: and they left off to build the city. Therefore is the name of it called Babel; because the Lord did there confound the language of all the earth: and from thence did the Lord scatter them abroad upon the face of all the earth. ~ Genesis 11:8-9

Biblical Accuracy

December 25

The Old Testament has hundreds of specific prophecies concerning Jesus Christ. These prophecies were spoken of hundreds of years prior to his birth. Here are but a few:

PREDICTION	OLD TESTAMENT	NEW TESTAMENT
Virgin birth	Isaiah 7:14	Matt. 1:23
Birth in Bethlehem	Micah 5:2	Matt. 2:6
Fleeing to Egypt	Hosea 1:1	Matt. 2:15
Crying in Ramah	Jeremiah 31:15	Matt. 2:18
John's voice in the wilderness	Isaiah 40:3	Matt. 3:3
Holy Spirit descending on Jesus	Isaiah 11:2, 61:1	Matt. 3:16
Blind receive sight	Isaiah 35:6	Matt 11:5
Jesus' 3 days & 3 nights buried	Jonah 1:17	Matt. 12:40
Speaking in parables	Psalm 78:2	Matt: 13:35
Jesus' entry on donkey	Zechariah 9:9	Matt. 21:5
Jesus would cleanse the Temple	Malachi 3:1	Matt. 21:12
Jesus betrayed for 30 silver pcs.	Zechariah 11:13	Matt. 27:9-10
Dividing Jesus' garments by lots	Psalm 22:18	Matt. 27:35
Crucified between two robbers	Isaiah 53:12	Matt. 27:38
Jesus buried in rich man's tomb	Isaiah 53:9	Matt. 27:57-60
Not a bone would be broken	Ps. 34:20	John 19:33
Jesus' side would be pierced	Psalm 22:18	John 19:23
Jesus ascends into heaven	Psalm 68:18	Acts 1:9

No ordinary book would have hundreds of prophecies fulfilled. This is God's method of validating that the Bible was inspired for our benefit by the One who made time. Therefore He knows the future. The Bible is truly the inspired word of God!

(Jesus Christ) has been made manifest, and by the prophetic Scriptures has been made known to all nations...
~ Romans 16:26 (NKJV)

December 26

Design

What causes the wind? Wind is air in motion. It moves from regions of higher pressure to those of lower pressure. The pressure variations are a result of the uneven heating of the Earth by the Sun. Along the equator, more solar radiation is absorbed. The warmed air moves north or south. Wind is constantly stirring up the atmosphere. The wind direction depends on many factors - such as the spin of the Earth, cloud cover, barometric pressure, land topography (mountains and valleys), etc… **Without wind, our world would be a hot, stagnant place!**

Farmers often put up a weather vane in order to know the wind direction and be prepared. When reading a wind vane, farmers know the arrow points **into** the wind. A metal image of a rooster is often placed atop a weather vane to allow the wind orientation to be easily seen. Why do many of our wind vanes have a rooster on display? The rooster represents Jesus' prophecy of Peter's betrayal - that Peter would deny him three times before the rooster crowed.

In Scripture, the Holy Spirit is compared to wind. How is wind like the Holy Spirit? The wind has no shape or form. It is invisible and mysterious, yet its presence is known by its effects - the same as the Holy Spirit. The wind is a powerful force; it cannot be stopped or controlled by anyone, the same as the Holy Spirit. The wind shows great variety, from a gentle soft breeze to hurricane force. In the same way, the Holy Spirit may gently bring a person to know Christ or use a dramatic method (such as an earthquake with the jailer in Acts 16). *"The wind blows wherever it pleases. You hear its sound, but you cannot tell where it comes from or where it is going. So it is with everyone born of the Spirit"* -John 3:8.

I tell thee, Peter, the cock shall not crow this day, before that thou shalt thrice deny that thou knowest me.
~ Luke 22:34

Anatomy
December 27

We are still discovering new capabilities and features of the human body. It has long been assumed that humans cannot hear ultrasonic sound because the mechanisms within our ear do not respond to sound wavelengths that small. Yet, Dr. Patrick Flanagan was issued two patents in 1958 for his invention of a device he called the Neurophone,™ which coverts normal sound into ultrasonic signals. He showed that the human brain was able to "hear" and interpret these signals. It has taken almost 50 years to explain this capability.

Dr. Martin Lenhardt of the University of Virginia recently discovered that a tiny organ in our inner ear (that is normally associated with balance) is also responsible for our ability to sense ultrasonic sound. This organ, called the saccule, is capable of responding to ultrasonic sound and sending the signals to the human brain. Lenhardt discovered that nerves from the pea-sized saccule are distributed throughout the brain - some going to the area of the brain that computes sound while others are distributed into areas concerned with long-term memory.

In an age where some would have us believe almost all discoveries of science have already been made, **there is much yet to be learned about the creation** – including the design of our own bodies!

There is none holy as the Lord: for there is none beside thee: neither is there any rock like our God.
~1 Samuel 2:2

December 28
Paleontology

The geological column in our textbooks has been used by evolutionists to represent creatures evolving over millions of years. Did you realize, however, that there are many "inconvenient" fossils? Here are just a few:

- Evolutionists have to explain from where birds came. So, they assume two-legged, upright walking dinosaurs evolved into birds. Yet, a **fossil dinosaur with three fully-formed birds in its stomach** has been found in China.
- Grass has been found in fossilized dinosaur dung (coprolite). Yet, for a century, evolutionists have taught that **grass appeared 10 million years after the dinosaurs** went extinct. How could a dinosaur eat something that did not yet exist?
- The remains of a dinosaur were found alongside a fossil of a dog-like mammal. Mammals of this size were not supposed to have evolved until **long after the dinosaurs** disappeared.
- Fossil pollen, evidence of flowering plants, has been found in the Precambrian layer 550 mya (million years ago), but flower pollen should not appear in the fossil record until 160 mya.
- Also found in the same layers and fossil beds with dinosaur fossils are ducks, squirrels, badger-like creatures, beaver-like creatures, platypuses, bees, pine trees, frogs, and others. According to a standard evolutionary timescale, **these creatures belong in different geological times** and should not be there. Yet they are.

These are just a few of the evolutionists' "inconvenient fossils" found in the fossil layers. The Flood of Noah's day generally buried things in ecological zones where they lived but at times washed creatures in from different zones. This is the best explanation for these "inconvenient fossils." They were buried simultaneously, because they lived simultaneously. The simplest explanation is also the correct explanation - the Flood of Noah's day best explains these "inconvenient fossils."

And all flesh died that moved upon the earth, both of fowl, and of cattle, and of beast, and of every creeping thing that creepeth upon the earth, and every man: All in whose nostrils was the breath of life, of all that was in the dry land, died. And every living substance was destroyed which was upon the face of the ground, both man, and cattle, and the creeping things, and the fowl of the heaven; and they were destroyed from the earth: and Noah only remained alive, and they that were with him in the ark. ~ Genesis 7:21-23

Biology

December 29

Did you know that sea turtles have a built-in compass? Magnetic compasses are important for navigation; they enable people to tell directions by using Earth's magnetic field. Loggerhead turtles (Caretta caretta) must stay within the North Atlantic Gyre, the circular ocean current system that surrounds the Sargasso Sea. Biologists tested these turtles by putting them in water tanks surrounded by electric coils that generated an artificial magnetic field. As they changed the variables, they found that the turtles again and again would swim to where they thought the gyre was.

The conclusion is that these sea turtles use magnetic measurements to stay in the North Atlantic Gyre. Did a compass happen by accident and chance? When you see a compass, you know there must be a compass-maker. God cares for His sea turtles by giving them built-in compasses.

The sea is his, and he made it:.... ~ Psalm 95:5

December 30 — Geology

In October of 2015, a massive crack mysteriously opened up in the foothills of the Bighorn Mountains (Wyoming, USA). This massive gash appeared within two weeks. The "gash" (as the locals like to call it) measured 2250 feet long and 150 feet wide. There were no earthquakes reported in the area. One geologist wrote, *"It's an impressive example of just how quickly very large geological events can occur under the right conditions."* Another wrote of being *"awed to see the Earth change so dramatically, so quickly."*

Evolutionists are trained to interpret almost all geological features in terms of slow, gradual processes; so rapid changes such as this are a surprise to them. Meanwhile, those who have a "Flood geology" framework realize that catastrophes can happen in the present and have happened in the past. **The Earth can change dramatically and quickly.**

And the earth opened her mouth, and swallowed them up together with Korah.... ~ Numbers 26:10

Cosmology

December 31

There is an active and vigorous debate amongst creation researchers as to the order of events as God created the entire universe early in creation week. One of the most common questions asked by Christians concerning the age and size of the universe is **how light could have reached the Earth in six literal days when the universe is so large.** It currently takes light 13 billion years to travel from one side to the other. There are at least four competing models that address this problem, but it is yet to be determined which model most satisfactorily answers all the related observations.

1) According to special relativity, **time itself is variable and depends upon the gravitational pull in the vicinity** where the passage of time is being measured. Thus, a mere six days could have been passing on earth, while God was expanding the universe and billions of years were passing further out in space.[1]

2) **Space itself expanded millions of times faster than the speed of light**, allowing plenty of time for light to reach the Earth in a literal six day period.[2]

3) All of the observations of general and special relativity can be mathematically explained by **allowing the speed of light to be variable.** This would allow light to reach Earth from distant stars in a biblical timeframe.[3,4]

4) The initial material from which God made the universe was a body of neutrons equal to the mass of the entire universe. This material would naturally expand, forming the stars and all the elements of the universe in a matter of days without the heat and timeframe required by traditional Big Bang cosmology.[5]

Although each of these possible cosmological models has its own set of issues, they are miniscule compared with the enormous issues surrounding the Big Bang cosmology. For instance:

1. The Big Bang does not work without the assumption of an initial expansion rate one hundred trillion trillion times faster than the speed of light (commonly call the "inflation period" of the Big Bang).

Nobody has ever observed such an expansion or explained why or how it could happen or what slowed it down. It is just assumed to be true because, without it, the Big Bang does not work.

2. Stars and galaxies cannot form from hydrogen gas and have never been seen to form. Gases expand; they do not coalesce together. So, it is assumed that 95% of all the matter and energy in the universe is a mathematical convenience called "dark matter and dark energy." This invisible construct has never been observed, measured, nor seen – it is just assumed to exist because without it, the Big Bang does not work.

3. A consequence of the Big Bang is that half of all material created at the beginning should be antimatter. Yet, all matter we see and measure is "real matter." Thus, experiments show that the processes that supposedly made everything do not match everything we measure and observe. This problem is simply ignored.

4. The most basic observable and testable law of science continuously confirms that matter and energy can never pop into existence. Nothing produces nothing, yet the Big Bang ignores this and has to assume that everything came from nothing.

5. The constants of the universe are PERFECTLY tuned. To explain the universe as it now exists based on a Big Bang explosive expansion requires a total mass that could not be changed by even the weight of a single grain of sand. This is so incredible to researchers that the most common solution amongst cosmologists is to believe we are just one of an infinite number of unobservable universes, and since the number of universes out there is infinite, every possible variation is guaranteed. This nonsense is accepted as science because without believing in this, the Big Bang is untenable.

By leaving God out of their thinking and seeking to become wise without acknowledging God has been involved in creation, modern scientists have become fools.

(They) forgat his works, and his wonders
that he had shewed them.

~ Psalm 78:11

References

Date	Reference
2-Jan	Hennigan, Tom. July 2015. "Miniature Metropolises". Answers Magazine. Retrieved June 2016 from https://answersingenesis.org/creepy-crawlies/insects/miniature-metropolises/
4-Jan	Bartz, Paul A. 2014. "Are 'Cavemen' primitive?" Letting God Create Your Day, vol. 7, Foley, MN: Creation Moments p.89.http://www.mcclatchydc.com/news/nation-world/world/article24516295.html
5-Jan	Frazen, Jennifer. July 23, 2015.How do sea sapphires become invisible? Scientific American. Retrieved June 2016 from http://blogs.scientificamerican.com/artful-amoeba/how-do-sea-sapphires-become-invisible/DeMarco, Emily. July 17, 2017. Video: solving the mystery of the invisible 'sea sapphire'. Science. Retrieved June 2016 from http://www.sciencemag.org/news/2015/07/video-solving-mystery-invisible-sea-sapphire
6-Jan	Gitt, Werner. 2006. Stars and their Purpose. Green Forest, AR: Master Books p. 20-21.
7-Jan	Smith, Norbert E. 2007. "Buzz pollination", Creation Research Society Quarterly, 43(4) 261-262. Retrieved June 2016 from http://www.creationresearch.org/members-only/crsq/43/43_4/2007v43n4p261.pdf
9-Jan	1. Burgess, Stuart. 2000. Hallmarks of Design, Day One Publications. Ryelands Road, Leominster, UK. p.152-154. 2. http://nutritiondata.self.com/facts/fruits-and-fruit-juices/1846/2
10-Jan	Catchpoole, David, "Bunchberry bang!", Creation, 31 (2):32-34, March 2009.
11-Jan	Bartz, Paul. "The Fish with three lines of defense". Letting God Create Your Day. Foley, MN Creation Moments. Retrieved June 2016 from http://www.creationmoments.com/radio/transcripts/fish-three-lines-defense https://www.svsu.edu/~tkschult/moia/porcupinefish.html
12-Jan	Fullbright, Jeannie K. 2006. Exploring Zoology 2: Swimming Creatures of the Fifth Day. Anderson, IN: Apologia Education Ministries pp.181-182.
14-Jan	Weiland, Carl. September 15, 2009. "Fossil Squid Ink that still writes!" Creation. Retrieved June 2016 from http://creation.com/fossil-squid-ink
15-Jan	Stelzer, Becky, Gary Vaterlaus, (Ed.). 2007. Museum Guide: A Bible-based Handbook to Natural History Museums, Answers in Genesis, Green Forest, AR: Master Books, p.77.
16-Jan	2014. "Neanderthal leatherworking discovery", Creation, 36(1) 9.
17-Jan	Coxworth, Ben. February 2010. "Scientists create sensors for subs based on fish anatomy". Gizmag. Retrieved June 2016 from http://www.gizmag.com/researchers-create-lateral-line-sensors/14141/
18-Jan	Hughes, Erin and Lita Cosner. 2015. "What is Science?" Creation, 37(2) 30-33.
19-Jan	Behe, Michael. 2006. Darwin's Black Box: The Biochemical Challenge to Evolution. New York: Free Press, 74-98.
20-Jan	Sarfati, Jonathan. 2007. Venus Flytrap. Creation, 29(4) 36-37. Fulbright, Jeannie K. 2004. Exploring Creation with Botany, Anderson, IN: Apologia Educational Ministries. 43-44.
21-Jan	Morell,Virginia. July 2015. "Feeding Frenzy: Orcas show their smarts by working together to whip up a meal". National Geographic Magazine, 76-87.
22-Jan	Snelling, Dr. Andrew A. April 1994. "Can flood geology explain thick chalk beds?" Answers Magazine. Retrieved June 2016 from https://answersingenesis.org/geology/sedimentation/can-flood-geology-explain-thick-chalk-beds/
23-Jan	Catchpoole, David. 2014. "'Bug Eye' widens field of view", Creation, 36 (3) 45. Retrieved June 2016 from http://creation.com/bug-eye-broadens-field-of-view
24-Jan	PBS's video. 2012. Inside Nature's Giants: Camel. Retrieved June 2016 from http://video.pbs.org/program/inside-natures-giants/
25-Jan	Johnson, James J.S., J.D. TH. D. 2015. "Sound science about dinosaurs". Acts & Facts, I.C.R. 44(1). Retrieved June 2016 from http://www.icr.org/article/8508 Beechick, Ruth. 1997. Genesis Finding our Roots. Pollock Pines, CA: Arrow Press, 11.
26-Jan	http://www.barringercrater.com/about/history_2.php "The First Proven Meteorite Crater". Answers Magazine. April 2016. 11(2)43.
27-Jan	http://creation.com/focus-182
28-Jan	Allen, David. December 2002. "Warped Earth". Creation, 40-43. Retrieved June 2016 from http://www.answersingenesis.org/articles/cm/v25/n1/warped
29-Jan	AstroBiology http://www.astrobio.net/exclusive/2419/our-earliest-animal-ancestors, 2010.
30-Jan	Thomas, Brian. September 2015. "The Mystery of Missing Talus". Acts & Facts, I.C.R. 44(9). Retrieved June 2016 from http://www.icr.org/article/8943
31-Jan	Fell, Barry. 2010. America B.C. Muskogee, OK: Artisan Publishers. 15-17.
1-Feb	Newcomer, Jim. April 2016. "A Word is Worth a Thousand Pictures". Answers Magazine, 11(2) 91-92.
2-Feb	"Gold Veins produced 'in an instant'". Creation, 35 (3)7.
3-Feb	Wahl, John. April-June 2015. "'Butterflies' Unsung Rivals". Answers Magazine, 10(2) 41-43.

Date	Reference
4-Feb	Horton, Jennifer. April 3, 2008. "Where do butterflies get their striking colors?" Retrieved June 2016 from animals.howstuffworks.com/insects/butterfly-colors2.htm Chiang, Mona. 1999. "You Asked…" Science World.
5-Feb	Gurney, Robert. 2013. "The Serpent". Creation, 35(3)34-37. Retrieved June 2016 from xa.yimg.com/kq/groups/21372679/957541644/name/Apologetics'
6-Feb	Catchpoole, David. July 2011. "Turtles as loggerhead with evolution". Creation, 33(3)28-31. Retrieved June 2016 from http://creation.com/turtles-at-loggerheads-with-evolution
7-Feb	www.CreationAstronomy.com Creation Astronomy News, April 2013, Spike Psarris Lisle, Jason. 2006. Taking Back Astronomy. Green Forest, AR: Master Books. 63-64. Lisle, Dr. Jason. 2005. What does the Bible say about Astronomy? Petersburg, Kentucky: Answers in Genesis. 11-12.
8-Feb	Johnson, Lanny and Marilyn. May-June 2007. "Bee wings". Alpha Omega Newsletter. Retrieved June 2016 from http://www.insectman.us/articles/bees-wasps/bee-wings.htm http://www.dave-cushman.net/bee/legwing.html
9-Feb	Powell, Corey. February 2015. Popular Science. p.32. Brahic, Catherine. July 16, 2014. "Meet the electric life forms that live on pure energy". New Scientist. Retrieved June 2016 from https://www.newscientist.com/article/dn25894-meet-the-electric-life-forms-that-live-on-pure-energy/
10-Feb	Burgess, Stuart. 2012. He Made the Stars Also What the Bible says about the Stars. Ryelands Road, Leominster, UK: Day One Publications. 62-66.
11-Feb	Bartz, Paul A. "Little Dipper". Letting God Create your Day. Foley, MN: Creation Moments. Retrieved June 2016 from http://www.creationmoments.com/radio/transcripts/little-dipper
13-Feb	Bell, Phillip. September 2003. "Bishop Bell's brass behemoths". Creation. 25(4) 40-44. Retrieved June 2016 from www.creation.com/bishop-bells-brass-behemoths Catchpoole, David. July 23, 2013. "Hadrosaur skin found". Retrieved June 2016 from http://creation.com/hadrosaur-skin Weiland, Carl. January 22, 2013. "Radiocarbon in dino bones". Retrieved June 2016 from http://creation.com/c14-dinos Sarfati, Dr. Johanthan D. December 11, 2012. "DNA and bone cells found in dinosaur bones". Retrieved June 2016 from http://creation.com/dino-dna-bone-cells
14-Feb	Batten, Don. March 1996. "Dogs breeding dogs". Creation, 18(2)20-23. Retrieved June 2016 from http://creation.com/dogs-breeding-dogs
15-Feb	Ham, Ken (Ed.). 2013. The New Answers Book 4. Green Forest, AR: Master Books. p. 139. Nienhuis, James I. 2006. Ice Age Civilizations. Houston, Texas: Genesis Veracity. p. 6.
16-Feb	Snelling, Dr. Andrew. 1990. The Revised Quote Book. Petersburg, Kentucky: Answers in Genesis. p.11.
17-Feb	"Unicorn deer found in Italy". Answers Magazine. June 14, 2008. Retrieved June 2016 from https://answersingenesis.org/mammals/unicorn-deer-found-in-italy/
18-Feb	O'Brien, Jonathan. (2016). All one people. Creation, 38(2) 15. Retrieve from http://www.cnn.com/2015/03/03/living/feat-black-white-twins/
19-Feb	Sarfati, Jonathan. January 2015. "Pitcher plants and animal sanitation". Creation, 37(1)29. Retrieved June 2016 from http://creation.com/pitcher-plants-and-animal-sanitation Adams, Cat. April 20, 2015. "The Giant plants that eat meat". BBC. Retrieved June 2016 from http://www.bbc.com/earth/story/20150420-the-giant-plants-that-eat-meat http://www.thefreelibrary.com/Red-flashing+fish+have+chlorophyll+eyes.-a020909589
20-Feb	Bartz, Paul A. "The Red-eyed sniper fish". Letting God Create your Day. Foley, MN: Creation Moments. Retrieved June 2016 from http://www.creationmoments.com/node/2287
21-Feb	Adapted from presentation of Dr. Randy Guliuzza (DATE, Place)
22-Feb	Snelling, Andrew and John Woodmorappe. December 1998. "Rapid Rocks". Creation, 21(1) 42-44. Retrieved June 2016 from http://creation.com/rapid-rocks
23-Feb	Walker, Tas. August 2003. "Granite grain size: not a problem for rapid cooling of Plutons". Journal of Creation, 17(2) 49-55.
24-Feb	Mulfinger, George & Orozco, Mulfinger Julia, *Christian Men of Science: Eleven Men Who Channged the World*, 2001, pp.71-97.
25-Feb	Kennedy, D. James. 2005. Why I Believe. Thomas Nelson, p. 22-23. McDowell, Josh. 1993. A Ready Defense. Thomas Nelson, p. 71-72. http://biblehub.com/topical/e/edom.htm
26-Feb	Faulkner, Dr. Danny. October 2015. "Pluto's Surface is Young". Answers Magazine, 10(4) 11.
27-Feb	Sherwin, Frank. 2007. "The Amazing Jewel Beetle". Acts & Facts, 36(5). Retrieved June 2016 from https://www.icr.org/article/3268/, Marshall, Michael. May 24, 2012. "Zoologger: infrared-sensing beetles born in fire". New Scientist. https://www.newscientist.com/article/dn21842-zoologger-infrared-sensing-beetles-born-in-fire/
28-Feb	Oard, Michael. 2014. The Genesis Flood and Floating Log Mats. Creation Book Publishers.

Date	Reference
2-Mar	Bartz, Paul A. "Those Astonishing Bee Engineers". Letting God Create your Day, vol. 2, Foley, MN: Creation Moments p.240.
3-Mar	Doolan, Robert, September 1995. "Dancing Bees". Creation 17(4):46–48. Retrieved June 2016 from http://creation.com/dancing-bees
	Christian, Melinda, April 1, 2011. "Honeybees- Always on the Move". Answers Magazine. Retrieved June 2016 from https://answersingenesis.org/creepy-crawlies/insects/honeybees/
4-Mar	http://www.sciencedaily.com/terms/yellowstone_caldera.htm
5-Mar	Bell, Philip. 2013. "Sunstones and Viking Magic". Creation, 35(4) 50-51.
6-Mar	"Weird and Wonderful The Marvellous Moloch". Creation, 18(3):29–32.
7-Mar	Burgess, Stuart. 2012. He Made the Stars Also What the Bible says about the stars. Day One Publications. Ryelands Road, Leominster, UK. pp.50-57.
8-Mar	Carpenter, Tom. July-August 2011. "Night Music". MN Conservation Volunteer. MN D.N.R. pp. 59-61.
9-Mar	Sherwin, Frank, M.A., 2003. "Reheating the Prebiotic Soup", Acts and Facts by ICR, 32(9).
10-Mar	http://www.wisegeek.org/how-many-species-of-bacteria-are-there.htm
11-Mar	Personal correspondence with Edward Sandoval
12-Mar	O'Brien, Jonathan. 2014. "Diamonds Are they really all that old?". Creation 36(2) 22-23.
13-Mar	Snelling, Dr. Andrew A. December 27, 2006. "The Origin of Oil". Answers Magazine. Retrieved June 2016 from https://answersingenesis.org/geology/the-origin-of-oil/
14-Mar	"'Primitive' electric eel not so primitive after all". Retrieved June 2016 from http://www.creationmoments.com/radio/transcripts/primitive-electric-eel-not-so-primitive-after-all http://askanaturalist.com/how-do-electric-eels-generate-electricity/
15-Mar	www.setterfield.org
16-Mar	Oard, Michael. September 2004. "Dead Whales: telling tales?". Creation 26(4):10–14. Retrieved June 2016 from http://creation.com/dead-whales-telling-tales
17-Mar	"Painted ladies migrate thousands of miles, radars discover, they are just too high for you to see them". 2012. The Telegraph. Retrieved June 2016 from http://www.telegraph.co.uk/news/earth/earthnews/9617298/Painted-ladies-migrate-thousands-of-miles-radars-discover-they-are-just-too-high-for-you-to-see-them.html
18-Mar	Lyons, Eric, and Kyle Butt. "Darwin, Evolution, and Racism", Apologetics Press, 2009. Retrieved June 2016 from https://www.apologeticspress.org/apcontent.aspx?category=7&article=2654
19-Mar	Catchpoole, David. 2015. "Why the Elephant is Losing its Tusks (And it's Not Evolution!)", Creation,37 (1) 21.
20-Mar	Woetzel, Dave. 2013. Chronicles of Dinosauria. Green Forest, AR: Master Books, p. 41.
	Catchpoole, David. December 2008. "Unique two-head reptile fossil". Creation 31(1)51. Retrieved June 2016 from http://creation.com/2-head-reptile
	Weiland, Sean. December 2006. "To close for comfort". Creation 29(1)56. Retrieved June 2016 from http://creation.com/too-close-for-comfort
21-Mar	Sarfati, Dr. Jonathan. June 2007. "Performing surgery upon evolutionary thinking". Creation. 29(3)46-48. Retrieved June 2016 from http://creation.com/performing-surgery-upon-evolutionary-thinking-interview-with-ross-pettigrew
	Bergman, Jerry. 1990. "Vestigial Organs" are Fully Functional. Creation Research Society. p.47-49.
22-Mar	Hennigan, Tom. July 2015. "Miniature metropolises". Answers Magazine. Retrieved June 2016 from https://answersingenesis.org/creepy-crawlies/insects/miniature-metropolises/
	Moffett, Mark W. 2010. Adventures among Ants: A global Safari with a Cast of Trillions. University of California press. p.142.
23-Mar	Sarfati, Dr. Jonathan. 2008. By Design: Evidence for Nature's Intelligent Designer-The God of the Bible. Creation Book Publishers. p. 47-48.
24-Mar	"Where are all the human fossils?". Retrieved June 16 from http://creation.com/images/pdfs/cabook/chapter15.pdf
24-Mar	Brown, Walt. In the Beginning. updated August 15, 2016. Retrieved June 2016 from http://www.creationscience.com/onlinebook/Liquefaction7.html
25-Mar	Catchpoole, David. July 2012. "Woodpecker head-banging wonder". Creation. 34(3)43. Retrieved June 2016 from http://creation.com/woodpecker-head-banging-wonder
	Soniak, David. "Why don't woodpeckers get brain damage". Retrieved June 2016 from http://mentalfloss.com/article/30731/why-dont-woodpeckers-get-brain-damage
	Palmer, Jason. "How woodpeckers avoid head injury". BBC News. Retrieved June 2016 from http://www.bbc.co.uk/news/mobile/science-environment-15458633
26-Mar	Pennisi, Elizabeth. May 23, 2012. "Whoopee-cushion sized organ helps whales feed". Science. Retrieved June 2016 from http://www.sciencemag.org/news/2012/05/whoopee-cushion-sized-organ-helps-whales-feed
	Pyenson, Nicholas. Jan. 2012. Science. p.
27-Mar	Ham, Ken (Ed). 2013. The New Answers Book 4. Master Books, p.27-28, 40-43.
28-Mar	Catchpoole, David. June 26, 2007. "Amazing discovery: Bird wing has "leading edge" technology". Creation. Retrieved June 2016 from http://creation.com/amazing-discovery-bird-wing-has-leading-edge-technology
29-Mar	Walker, Tas. March 2007. "Vanishing Coastlines". Creation 29(2) 19-21. Retrieved June 2016 from http://creation.com/vanishing-coastlines

Date	Reference
30-Mar	Oard, Michael, Tara Wolfe and Chris Turbuck. 2012. Exploring Geology with Mr. Hibb. Creation Book Publishers, Powder Springs, Georgia. p.21-24
31-Mar	1. M. Schweitzer et al., "A role for iron and oxygen chemistry in preserving soft tissues, cells and molecules from deep time," Proceedings of the Royal Society B, (online 27 November 2013) 281:20132741 2. Mark Armitage, personal correspondence with Creation Summit dated October 2, 2014.
2-Apr	1. Waters, Hannah. April 25, 2013. 14 Fun Facts about Penguins. Retrieved June 2016 from http://www.smithsonianmag.com/science-nature/14-fun-facts-about-penguins-41774295/?no-ist 2. Kallok, Michael. "MN Wild Anglers". MN Conservation Volunteer. Retrieved June 2016 from http://files.dnr.state.mn.us/mcvmagazine/young_naturalists/young-naturalists-article/wild_anglers/wild_anglers.pdf 3. Cornell Lab of Ornithology All about Birds Retrieved June 2016 from https://www.allaboutbirds.org/guide/common_loon/lifehistory
3-Apr	"Where are all the human fossils?". pp. 191-198. Retrieved June 2016 from http://creation.com/images/pdfs/cabook/chapter15.pdf
4-Apr	"Mutualism". Retrieved June 2016 from http://www.cas.miamioh.edu/mbi-ws/BiodiversitySymbiosis/mutualism.htm
5-Apr	http://www.richard-seaman.com/Birds/NewZealand/Gannets/TheColonies/
6-Apr	Martin, Jobe and Dan Breeding. 2009. Creation Proclaims: Climbers and Creepers, DVD, vol. 1, Biblical Discipleship Ministries: Rockwall, Texas.
7-Apr	Burgess, Stuart. 2012. He Made the Stars Also What the Bible says about the stars. Day One Publications: Ryelands Road, Leominster, UK. pp.67-68.
8-Apr	"Coywolves: Hybrid reveal clues about dog kind", 2016. Creation 38(2)10.
9-Apr	1. Bacteriologist Dr. Alan Linton, Quoted from The Myth of Junk DNA, Jonathan Wells, Discovery Institute Press, 2011, p. 12. 2. Ibid., p. 68. 3. www.bbc.co.uk/news/science-environment-14933298
10-Apr	DeYoung, Donald and Derrik Hobbs. 2009. Discovery Design. Master Books: Green Forest, AR. p. 150. Suddath, Claire. June 15, 2010. "A Brief History of: Velcro" Retrieved June 2016 from http://content.time.com/time/nation/article/0,8599,1996883,00.html
11-Apr	Milius, Susan. "Hot bother: ground squirrels taunt with infrared". Science news online. Retrieved June 2016 from http://www.phschool.com/ science/science_news/articles/hot_bother.html "Dancing infrared ground squirrels". Creation Moments Retrieved June 2016 from http://www.creationmoments.com/radio/transcripts/dancing-infrared-ground-squirrels
12-Apr	Noebel, David & Chuck Edwards. 1999. Thinking like a Christian, student journal. Summit Press: Manitou Springs, CO. p.42.
13-Apr	"Owl Mystery unraveled: Scientists explain how bird can rotate its head without cutting off blood supply to brain" July 31, 2013. John Hopkins Medicine. Retrieved June 2016 from http://www.hopkinsmedicine.org/news/media/releases/owl_mystery_unraveled_scientists_explain_how_bird_can_rotate_its_head_without_cutting_off_blood_supply_to_brain
15-Apr	Catchpole, David. 2015. "Squid do…fly!". Creation. 37(4) 12-13.
16-Apr	Klingaman, William and Nicholas Klingaman. 2013. The Year without Summer: 1816 and the Volcano that darkened the World and Changed History. St. Martins Griffin: New York.
17-Apr	"Guinea Ebola outbreak: Bat-eating banned to curb outbreak". March 25, 2014. BBC news. Retrieved June 2016 from http://www.bbc.com/news/world-africa-26735118
19-Apr	"Scientists build world's first artificial stomach". November 10, 2006. NBC news. Retrieved June 2016 from www.nbcnews.com/id/15655255/ns/health-health_care/t/scientists-build-worlds-first-artificial-stomach/#.VoL2T3nnbrc
20-Apr	"Evolution can't digest this fly". Creation Moments. Retrieved June 2016 from http://www.creationmoments.com/radio/transcripts/evolution-cant-digest-fly
21-Apr	Walker, Tas. "A Monstrous mound of… minerals!" September 2005. Creation 27(4)56. Retrieved June 2016 from http://creation.com/a-monstrous-mound-of-minerals
22-Apr	Sherwin, Frank. 2013. Guide to Animals. Institute of Creation Research: Dallas, Texas. p.50-51.
24-Apr	DeYoung, Donald B. 1992. Weather and the Bible. Baker Book House: Grand Rapids, Michigan. p.31-32.
25-Apr	1. Science, Sept. 2013. more info needed 2. Answers Magazine, Vol. 9 No. 1, Jan. 2014, p.13.
26-Apr	Bierle, Dr. Don. 1992. Surprised by Faith. Emerald Books: Lynnwood,WA. p.32-34.
27-Apr	Snelling, Dr. Andrew A. November 1, 2012. "#5 Rapidly Decaying Magnetic Field: Ten Best Evidences from Science that Confirm a Young Earth". Answers Magazine. Retrieved June 2016 from https://answersingenesis.org/evidence-for-creation/5-rapidly-decaying-magnetic-field
28-Apr	Seaburn, Paul. July 19, 2014. "Barnacle superglue finally comes unglued". Retrieved June 2016 from http://mysteriousuniverse.org/2014/07/barnacle-superglue-finally-comes-unglued/ "Nature's Strongest Glue comes Unstuck". Newcastle University, UK. Retrieved June 2016 from http://www.ncl.ac.uk/press/news/legacy/2014/07/naturesstrongestgluecomesunstuck.html
29-Apr	Oard, Mike. 2008. Flood by Design. Master Books: Green Forest, AR. p. 95-108.
30-Apr	1. Thomas, Brian. 2016. "Rats, bats and pitcher plants". Creation 38(1): 18-19. 2. Millner, Jack. July 14, 2015. "The Carnivorous Plant that uses sonar to coax bats to roost inside…so it can eat their poo". Daily Mail. Retrieved June 2016 from http://www.dailymail.co.uk/sciencetech/article-3160700/The-carnivorous-plant-uses-SONAR-coax-bats-roost-inside-eat-POO.html

Date	Reference
1-May	"The 10 Best Evidences from science that confirms a Young Earth". Oct-Dec. 2012. Answers Magazine. Retrieved June 2016 from https://answersingenesis.org/evidence-for-creation/the-10-best-evidences-from-science-that-confirm-a-young-earth/
2-May	Sarfati, Dr. Jonathan. July 17, 2012. "Mantis shrimp "fist" could inspire new body armor". Creation 36(4)40-41. Retrieved June 2016 from http://creation.com/mantis-shrimp-fist-body-armour
3-May	Austin, Steve and John Morris. Footprints in the Ash, Master Books: Green Forest, AR, p. 102-103. Hergenrather, John & Tom Vail & Mike Oard & Dennnis Bokovoy. 2012. The True North Series: Your Guide to Yellowstone and Grand Teton National Parks. Master Books: Green Forest, AR. p.160-161.
4-May	Kennedy, D. James & Jerry Newcombe. 1994. What if Jesus Had Never Been Born? Thomas Nelson Publishers: Nashville, Tennessee. p.91-106.
5-May	"The Wombat's backward pouch". Creation Moments. Retrieved June 2016 from http://www.creationmoments.com/radio/transcripts/wombats-backward-pouch
5-May	"Greenhouse thermostat discovered". Creation Moments. Retrieved June 2016 from http://www.creationmoments.com/radio/transcripts/greenhouse-thermostat-discovered
6-May	The Privileged Planet, Illustra Media, DVD
8-May	"Did Life begin in the water?" Retrieved June 2016 from http://www.earthage.org/did_life_begin_in_water.htm
9-May	Parker, Gregory & Keith Graham & Delores Shimmin & George Thompson. 1997. Biology God's Living Creation. A Beka Book: Pensacola, Florida. p.187-189.
10-May	Parker, Gregory & Keith Graham & Delores Shimmin & George Thompson. 1997. Biology God's Living Creation. A Beka Book: Pensacola, Florida. p. 563-564. Zollinger, Sue anne. April 28, 2009. "Terminator sponges". Moment of science. Retrieved June 2016 from http://indianapublicmedia.org/amomentofscience/terminator-sponges/ Picture reference: http://www.uic.edu/classes/bios/bios100/labs/spongeflow.jpg do we add?
11-May	Sherwin, Frank. 2013. Guide to Animals. Institute of Creation Research: Dallas, Texas. p.73. "Fiery Flying Serpent". Genesis Park. Retrieve June 2016 from http://www.genesispark.com/exhibits/evidence/scriptural/the-fiery-flying-serpent/
12-May	DeYoung, Dr. Don. 2005. Thousands... not Billions: Challenging an Icon of Evolution-Questioning the Age of the Earth. New Leaf Publishing Group.
13-May	Bell, Philip. December 2005. "The Super-senses of oilbirds". Creation 28(1)38-41. Retrieved June 2016 from http://creation.com/the-super-senses-of-oilbirds
	Wrong date bacteria compass 14-May Helder, Margaret. March 1998. "The World's Smallest Compass". Creation 20(2) 52-53. Retrieved June 2016 from http://creation.com/the-worlds-smallest-compasses
	Correct date 14-May Kennedy, D. James & Jerry Newcombe. 2005. Lord of All Developing a Christian World-and-Life View. Crossway Books. p. 27-28.
15-May	Gitt, Dr. Werner. 2005. If Animals could Talk. Master Books: Green Forest, AR. p.90 "Wonderful Worms". March 1998. Creation. 20(2)56. Retrieved June 2016 from http://creation.com/wonderful-worms
17-May	Martin, Jobe. May 12, 2008. "Melipona Bee Defies Evolution". Exploration films.com. Retrieved June 2016 from https://www.youtube.com/watch?v=7DV7TS3XB94
18-May	http://news.nationalgeographic.com/news/2008/08/080608-cuttlefish-camouflage-missions_2.html PBS Nova's King of Camouflage the Cuttlefish. 2007. Retrieved June 2016 from https://www.youtube.com/watch?v=s7Mbh4L_HsE
21-May	1. Catchpoole, David. 2015. "Cats: Big and Small". Creation, 37(4)34-37. 2. Hendry, Andrew et. al. March 23, 2007. "The Speed of Ecological Speciation". Functional Ecology.pages
22-May	McKeever, Stacie. November 10, 2008. "Seeds of Dissent". Answers Magazine. Retrieved June 2016 from https://answersingenesis.org/jesus-christ/jesus-is-god/seeds-of-dissent/
25-May	Snelling, Dr. Andrew A. March 5, 2015. New Answers Book 3. Retrieved June 2016 from https://answersingenesis.org/the-flood/what-are-some-of-the-best-flood-evidences/
26-May	Parker, Gary and Mary. 2005. The Fossil Book. Master Books: Green Forest, AR. p.18-22.
27-May	Dreves, Dennis. March 1993. "Beavers – aquatic architects". Creation 15(2)38-41. Retrieved June 2016 from http://creation.com/beavers
28-May	Parker, Gregory & Keith Graham & Delores Shimmin & George Thompson. 1997. Biology God's Living Creation. A Beka Book: Pensacola, Florida. p. 452.
29-May	"Umbrella Bird". Creation Moments. Retrieved June 2016 from http://www.creationmoments.com/radio/transcripts/umbrella-bird
30-May	"Dinosaurs in Ancient Cambodian Temple". Retrieved June 2016 from http://www.bible.ca/tracks/tracks-cambodia.htm Catchpoole, David. September 2007. "Angkor saw a Stegosaur?" Creation: 29(4)56. Retrieved June 2016 from http://creation.com/angkor-saw-a-stegosaur
31-May	1. Humphreys, D.R., 1994. Starlight and Time: Solving the Puzzle of Distant Starlight in a Young Universe. Master Books: Green Forest, AR. p.66-68. 2. Samec, Ronald. 2014. "Explaining nearby objects that are old in time dilation cosmologies". Journal of Creation 28(3)9. 3. Humphreys, D.R. 2014. "New view of gravity explains cosmic microwave background radiation". Journal of Creation. 28(3)106-114.
1-Jun	DeYoung, Donald, "One Leg up on Architects", *Creation Magazine*, Sept. 2009.

Date	Reference
2-Jun	"Asymmetric burrow openings create passive ventilation: prairie dog". Ask Nature. Retrieved June 2016 from http://www.asknature.org/strategy/e27b89ebcdec8c9b5b2cd9ac84b8f8a0
3-Jun	1. Schamndt, B. et.al., 2014. "Dehydration melting at the top of the lower mantle". Science 344 (6189):1265-1268. 2. Mitchell, Elizabeth. October 15, 2011. "Comets had a Role in Forming Earth's Oceans: Study Shows". Answers magazine. Retrieved June 2016 from https://answersingenesis.org/astronomy/comets/comets-role-forming-earth-oceans/
4-Jun	Sarfati, Jonathan. December 1998. "Salty seas evidence for a young earth". Creation 21(1)16-17. Retrieved June 2016 from http://creation.com/salty-seas-evidence-for-a-young-earth#20120328
5-Jun	DeYoung, Dr. Don. July 2010. "Water Striders-Walking on water". Answers Magazine. Retrieved June 2016 from https://answersingenesis.org/creepy-crawlies/insects/water-striders-walking-on-water/
6-Jun	Burgess, Stuart. 2001. He Made the Stars Also What the Bible says about the Stars. Day One Publications: Rylands Road, Leominster, U.K. p. 176.
7-Jun	"No Heartbeat? Don't Worry". Creation Moments. Retrieved June 2016 from http://www.creationmoments.com/content/no-heartbeat-dont-worry
8-Jun	https://en.wikipedia.org/wiki/Engine_efficiency Sarfati, Jonathan. July 15, 2015. CMI conference lecture. Myrtle Beach, N.C.
9-Jun	Noebel, Dr. David. 1991. Understanding the Times. Harvest House Publishers. p.96.
10-Jun	DeYoung, Dr. Don. April 2014. "Bird-saving spider webs". Answers. Retrieved June 2016 from https://answersingenesis.org/technology/bird-saving-spider-webs/
11-Jun	Sarfati, Jonathan. April 2011. "Spiderweb stickiness secret". Creation 33(2)34-35. Retrieved June 2016 from http://creation.com/spiderweb-stickiness
12-Jun	McDowell, Josh. 1998.A Ready Defense. Thomas Nelson Publishing. p.72-3.
13-Jun	White, Monty, "The Amazing Stone Bears of Yorkshire", *Creation Magazine,* June-Aug. 2002, pp. 48-49. Weiland, Carl, :The Earth: How Old Does it Look?", *Creation Magazine,* June-Aug. 2000, pp. 8-13.
14-Jun	Kever, Jeannie. August 18, 2014. "Researchers Draw Inspiration for Camouflage System From Marine Life". University of Houston News. Retrieved August 19, 2014 from http://www.uh.edu/news-events/stories/2014/August/0818Cephalopods Yu, C. et al. "Adaptive optoelectronic camouflage systems with designs inspired by cephalopod skins". Proceedings of the National Academy of Sciences. Published online before print. "Awesome New Camouflage Sheet Was Inspired By Octopus Skin". Newsy. Posted on sciencedaily.com August 19, 2014, accessed August 19, 2014. Meyer, Fox. "How Octopuses and squids change color". Retrieved June 2016 from http://ocean.si.edu/ocean-news/how-octopuses-and-squids-change-color Thomas, Brian. August 27, 2014. "Octopus skin inspires high-tech camouflage fabric". Retrieved June 2016 from http://www.icr.org/article/octopus-skin-inspires-high-tech-camouflage/
15-Jun	Nelson, Vance. 2012. Dire Dragons. Untold Secrets of Planet Earth Publishing Co: Red Deer, Alberta.
16-Jun	Breeding, Dan & Jobe Martin. August 26, 2014. Retrieved June 2016 from www.answersingenesis.org/kids/videos/horned-toad-lizard/
18-Jun	Morris, J. 2005. "Does the Gallbladder Have a Necessary Function?" Acts & Facts. 34 (2)
19-Jun	DeYoung, Dr. Don. Jan-Mar 20016. "Why not a square tree?" Answers Magazine. p.38-39.
20-Jun	Fulbright, Jeannie K. 2006. Exploring Creation with Zoology 2: Swimming Creatures of the Fifth Day. Apologia Educational Ministries Inc.: Anderson, IN. p.194.
21-Jun	1. Crowner, Robert. "The Decent of Evolution". World Magazine, Posted Feb. 6, 2016. 2. Darwin, Charles. 1958. The Origin of the Species. Penguin: New York, NY, p. 280. 3. Wells, Jonathan. 2000. Icons of Evolution. Regnery Publishing: Washington, D.C. p.38 4. Ibid., p.37 5. Ibid., p. 221
22-Jun	Catchpoole, David. July 2010. "Speedy sharks and golf balls." Creation 32(3) 44. Retrieved June 2016 from http://creation.com/speedy-sharks-and-golf-balls
24-Jun	Robinson, Philip. August 2014. "Cactus spines, sharper than you think!" Creation 28(2)9-11. Retrieved June 2016 from http://creation.com/cactus-spines-sharper-than-you-think
26-Jun	Graham, Gary. September 2009. "Fast Octopus Fossils reveal no evolution". Creation 31(4)40-41. Retrieved June 2016 from http://creation.com/fast-octopus-fossils
27-Jun	Catchpoole, David. April 2013. "Amazing Preservation: Three birds in a dinosaur". Creation 35(2)32-33. Retrieved June 2016 from http://creation.com/3-birds-in-a-dinosaur
28-Jun	"Bucky Beaver Lives Here". February 1, 1997. Creation Science Association of Alberta. Retrieved June 2016 from http://www.create.ab.ca/bucky-beaver-lives-here/ "Beavers build more than dams". Creation Moments. Retrieved June 2016 from http://www.creationmoments.com/radio/transcripts/beavers-build-more-dams
29-Jun	"Dinosaur feather evolution trapped in Canadian amber". September 15, 2011. BBC News. Retrieved June 2016 from www.bbc.co.uk/news/science-environment-14933298 Catchpoole, David. March 2009. "Amber needed water (and lots of it)". Creation:31(2)20-22. Retrieved June 2016 from http://creation.com/amber-needed-water
30-Jun	Spencer, Wayne. January 2011. "Planets around other stars". Creation: 33(1)45-47. Retrieved June 2016 from http://creation.com/extrasolar-planets-problems-for-evolution
1-Jul	The Foundations, DVD set 2011. Answers in Genesis, participant guide, p. 43-44.
2-Jul	"Cyanide for Breakfast?" Creation Moments. Retrieved June 2016 from http://www.creationmoments.com/radio/transcripts/cyanide-breakfast

Date	Reference
	https://en.wikipedia.org/wiki/Sara_Longwing
3-Jul	Oard, Michael J. & Tara Wolfe, Chris Turbuck. 2012. Exploring Geology with Mr. Hibb. Creation Book Publishers: Powder Springs, Georgia. p.55-58.
	"How long does it take coal to form?". August 26, 2011. Creation Revolution. Retrieved June 2016 from http://creationrevolution.com/how-long-does-it-take-coal-to-form/
4-Jul	Malone, Bruce. 2014. Brilliant. Search for the Truth Ministries: Midland, Michigan. p.76-77
5-Jul	Sarfati, Jonathan. Refuting Evolution-chapter 2. Retrieved June 2016 from http://creation.com/refuting-evolution-chapter-2-variation-and-natural-selection-versus-evolution
	Sherwin, Frank. 2013. Guide to Animals. Institute of Creation Research: Dallas, Texas. p.18-19.
6-Jul	"Solar System structure Confounds Scientists". Creation Moments. Retrieved June 2016 from http://www.creationmoments.com/node/2515
7-Jul	Morris, Dr. John D. 1999. "What about the peppered moths?" Acts & Facts 28(4). Retrieved June 2016 From http://www.icr.org/article/1195
8-Jul	Fulbright, Jeannie K. 2008. Exploring Creation with Zoology 3: Land Animals of the Sixth Day. Apologia Educational Ministries Inc. Anderson, IN. p.166.
9-Jul	Libbrecht, Kenneth. Retrieved June 2016 from www.snowcrystals.com and http://www.its.caltech.edu/~atomic/snowcrystals/alike/alike.htm
10-Jul	1. Snelling, Dr. Andrew. April-June, 2015. "Dazzling Diamonds by Special Delivery," Answers Magazine. 10(2)52-55. 2. Taylor, R.E. and J.R. Southon. 2007. "Use of Natural Diamonds to Monitor 14C AMS Instrument Backgrounds". Nuclear Instruments and Methods in Physics Research, B259 Is this correct?. pp. 282-287.
11-Jul	Catchpoole, David. September 2009. "Vegetarian Spider". Creation 31(4)46. Retrieved June 2016 from http://creation.com/vegetarian-spider
12-Jul	Kennedy, D. James. 2005. Why I Believe. Thomas Nelson Inc.: Nashville, Tennessee. p.16-21.
13-Jul	Nelson, Vance. Untold Secrets of Planet Earth: Amazon Expedition. Online video retrieved June 2016 from https://answersingenesis.org/store/specials/untold-secrets/?utm_source=discountsdeals&utm_medium=email&utm_con tent=feature1&utm_campaign=20160309&mc_cid=5a670e7048&mc_eid=4fa8f78a68
14-Jul	Chapman, Geoff. 2000. Weird and Wonderful. Creation Resources Trust: U.K. p.22.
15-Jul	Catchpoole, David. 2015 "Enraged elephants, terrifying tigers, and dangerous dinosaurs". Creation 37(1)34-37.
16-Jul	Dykes, Jeffery. September 2007. "Hippo Habits". Creation 29(4)50-53. Retrieved June 2016 from http://creation.com/hippo-habits "Hippo slim cool and healthy". Retrieved June 2016 from http://creation.com/focus-271
17-Jul	Littleton, Jeanette. 2016, July-Sept. "Designed to go blind", Answers Magazine, vol. 11, #3, 38-39.
18-Jul	Fulbright, Jeannie K. 2008. Exploring Creation with Zoology 3: Land Animals of the Sixth Day. Apologia Educational Ministries Inc.: Anderson, IN. p.202-3.
19-Jul	Sarfati, Jonathan. May 14, 2009. "Tooth enamel: sophisticated materials science." Creation 32(3)53. Retrieved 2016 from http://creation.com/tooth-enamel-sophisticated-materials-science
20-Jul	Johnson, Lanny and Marilyn. July-August 2008. "The Thirsty Tree". Alpha Omega Institute. www.wikipedia, Hyperion (tree), accessed 5/14/2016. is this correct in layout?
21-Jul	Weston, Paula. December 1, 2002. "Coral: Animal, vegetable and mineral." Answers. Retrieved June 2016 from https://answersingenesis.org/aquatic-animals/coral-animal-vegetable-and-mineral/
22-Jul	Weston, Paula. December 1, 2002. "Coral: Animal, vegetable and mineral." Answers. Retrieved June 2016 from https://answersingenesis.org/aquatic-animals/coral-animal-vegetable-and-mineral/
23-Jul	Ham, Ken et al. 2013. The New Answers Book 4. Master Books: Green Forest, AR. p.179-181.
24-Jul	"Whale of an idea". Retrieved June 2016 from http://creation.com/focus-243
25-Jul	1. http://www.ifa.hawaii.edu/info/vis/natural-history/fauna/wekiu-bug.html 2. http://en.wikipedia.org/wiki/W%C4%93kiu_bug I will let you do these, thanks.
26-Jul	Mahoney, Timothy P. & Steve Law. 2015. Patterns of Evidence: The Exodus. Thinking Man Media: St. Louis Park, MN. Is this the correct author, you had a different man listed?
27-Jul	Dockrill, Peter. February 24, 2016. "Earth could be unique among 700 quintillion planets in the Universe: Study finds". Science Alert. Retrieved June 2016 from http://www.sciencealert.com/earth-could-be-unique-among-700-quintillion-planets-in-the-universe-study-finds,
28-Jul	Catchpoole, David. March 2004. "Snail Trail". Creation 26(2)45. Retrieved June 2016 from http://creation.com/snail-trail
29-Jul	Clarey, Tim. April 2016. "Supersized Landslides", Answers Magazine. 11(2)33.
30-Jul	1. http://www.instanthawaii.com/cgi-bin/hi?PlantsCreatures 2. http://en.wikipedia.org/wiki/Petiole_(botany) 3. http://www.instanthawaii.com/cgi-bin/hi?!00butirOTMfX1m0ndooCK93cr2nhn1eXImCau6eC83Cvf5E6afe0nlCSege Hv1bOT9 ntnjaam0nnro7BKA3vtlAaTffzIonUrgvkv22la4g8NOiIn0nSe5vC852ZRvg0
1-Aug	1. Gallop, Roger G. 2011. Evolution- The Greatest Deception in Modern History. Red Butte Press Inc. Jacksonville, Florida. pp.118-119. 2. Oard, Michael J & Tara Wolfe & Chris Turbuck. 2012. Exploring Geology with Mr. Hibb, Creation Book Publishers. Powder Springs, Georgia. p.36-37.
2-Aug	Nelson, Ethel R., Richard E. Broadberry, Ginger Tong Chock. 1997. God's Promise to the Chinese, Read Books Publisher. Dunlap, TN p.36, 47, 48, 52.
3-Aug	"Bees have a Hot Line of Defense". Creation Moments. Retrieved June 2016 from http://www.creationmoments.com/content/bees-have-hot-line-defense
4-Aug	"Bees Environmental Engineers". Creation Moments. Retrieved June 2016 from http://www.creationmoments.com/radio/transcripts/bee-environmental-engineers
5-Aug	DeYoung, Dr. Don. January 1, 2012. "A Sticky Solution God Invented it first". Answers. Retrieved June 2016 from "https://answersingenesis.org/amphibians/a-sticky-solution/

Date	Reference
6-Aug	Lisle, Dr. Jason. 2007. Taking Back Astronomy. Master Books: Green Forest, AR. p.22-23.
7-Aug	http://what-when-how.com/birds/common-tailorbird-birds/
8-Aug	1. who is the author of which book? Meyer, Stephen C. 2004. The Case for a Creator by Lee Stobel". Zondervan: Grand Rapids, MI, p. 229. 2. Denton, Michael. 1986. Evolution: A Theory in Crisis. Adler & Adler, Bethesda, MD, p. 323.
9-Aug	Zacharias, Anna. July 28, 2012. "Fruit fly with wings of beauty". The National UAE news. Retrieved June 2016 from http://www.thenational.ae/news/uae-news/science/fruit-fly-with-the-wings-of-beauty
10-Aug	"Snowy sheathbill". Arkive. Retrieved 2016 from http://www.arkive.org/snowy-sheathbill/chionis-albus/
11-Aug	1. Gish, Duane. 1992. Dinosaurs by Design. Master Books: Green Forest, AR. p. 74. 2. Chart adapted from B.C. Nelson. 1931. The Deluge Story in Stone. Appendix 11, Flood Traditions, Figure 38, Augsburg Publishing, Minneapolis, MN.
12-Aug	"Aboriginal Australians' DNA link to India".2013. Creation 35(3)9. Retrieved June 2016 from http://creation.com/focus-353
13-Aug	Martin, Jobe. Incredible Creatures that Defy Evolution. vol. 3. DVD. Exploration Films.
14-Aug	"Snuffbox (freshwater mussel)". U.S. Fish and Wildlife Services. Retrieved June 2016 from http://www.fws.gov/Midwest/endangered/clams/snuffbox/SnuffboxFactSheet.html
15-Aug	Cooper, Bill. 1995. After the Flood. New Wine Press: U.K. p.131-133.
16-Aug	Chapman, Geoff. 2000. Weird and Wonderful. Creation Resources Trust: U.K. p.18.
17-Aug	Jack, Bill. 2004. Simple Tools for Brain Surgery. DVD.
18-Aug	Sarfati, Jonathan. June 2007. 'Performing Surgery upon Evolutionary Thinking". Creation 29(3)46-48. Retrieved June 2016 from http://creation.com/performing-surgery-upon-evolutionary-thinking-interview-with-ross-pettigrew
19-Aug	Fulbright, Jeannie K. 2004. Exploring Creation with Botany. Apologia Educational Ministries: Anderson, IN. p. 73-78.
20-Aug	McDorman, Perry and Stephanie. April 27, 2014. "Chameleons: Bug's Worst Nightmare" Answers. Retrieved June 2016 from https://answersingenesis.org/reptiles/chameleons/
21-Aug	Snelling, Dr. Andrew. March 5, 2015. "What are some of the Best Flood Evidences?" New Answers Book 3. Answers. Retrieved June 2016 from https://answersingenesis.org/the-flood/what-are-some-of-the-best-flood-evidences/
22-Aug	"Atlas Moth". June 30, 2008. Creation. Retrieved June 2016 from http://creation.com/laminin-atlas-moths-and-gay-brains Woollaston, Victoria. September 24, 2014. "This moth is such a 'snake' in the grass: Atlas insect scares off Predators by looking and acting like a cobra". Daily Mail, UK. Retrieved June 2016 from http://www.dailymail.co.uk/sciencetech/article-2767831/This-moth-snake-grass-Atlas-insect-scares-predators-looking-acting-like-cobra.html#ixzz3wlZeXbnZ
24-Aug	"Who said it?" December 1, 1986. Creation 9(1)12. Retrieved June 2016 from www.answersingenesis.org/creation/v9/i1/whosaiditanswer.asp Kennedy, D. James. 2005. Why I Believe. Thomas Nelson Inc.: Nashville, TN. p.37. Petersen, Dennis R. 2002. Unlocking the Mysteries of Creation. Master Books: Green Forest, AR. p.194, 203. Halley, Henry H. Halley's Bible Handbook. Zondervan Publishing House, Grand Rapids, Michigan. p.44.
25-Aug	Retrieved June 2016 http://www.tufts.edu/as/tampl/projects/micro_rs/theory.html "From Butterflies' wings to Bank Notes-- how nature's colors can cut bank fraud". May 30, 2010. Retrieved June 2016 from http://phys.org/news/2010-05-butterflies-wings-bank-nature.html
26-Aug	Catchpoole, David. December 2007. "Surtsey still surprises". Creation 30(1) 32-34. Retrieved June 2016 from http://creation.com/surtsey-still-surprises
27-Aug tack	Weston, Paula, December 2004. "Air Attack". Creation 27(1)28-32. Retrieved June 2016 from http://creation.com/Air-at-
	"Bird killing sheep". June 2002. Creation 24(3)7. Retrieved June 2016 from http://creation.com/focus-243 "Wild and Woolly". September 1999. Creation 21(4)7-9. Retrieved June 2016 from http://creation.com/focus-214
29-Aug	Martin, Jobe. Creation Proclaims – Archer Fish (DVD). Retrieved June 2016 from https://www.youtube.com/watch?v=omOM8yXBlZM
30-Aug	Mitchell, Dr. Elizabeth. October 19, 2013. "First Fossil Mosquito Found with Blood". Answers. Retrieved June 2016 from https://answersingenesis.org/fossils/how-are-fossils-formed/first-fossil-mosquito-found-filled-with-blood/ Yong, Ed. October 14, 2013. "Blood-filled Mosquito is a fossil first". Nature. Retrieved June 2016 from http://www.nature.com/news/blood-filled-mosquito-is-a-fossil-first-1.13946
31-Aug	A new article? TBA. This is old references: Nelson, Vance. 2012. Dire Dragons. Untold Secrets of Planet Earth Publishing: Alberta, Canada. p. 14-17. Hubbard, Samuel. Discoveries Relating to Prehistoric Man. Oakland: Oakland Museum, 1924:9.
1-Sep	personal correspondence with Nepali missionary Paul Michaels, March 7, 2016.
3-Sep	Creation Museum 15 minute video on poison dart frog exhibit by experts Dorman, Perry and Stephanie. October 1, 2012. "Poison Dart Frogs-Drop Dead Gorgeous". Answers. Retrieved 2016 from https://answersingenesis.org/amphibians/poison-dart-frogs-gorgeous/
4-Sep	Burgess, Stuart, *Hallmarks of Design,* pp.98-118.
5-Sep	"Bunyips and dinosaurs". March 1993. Creation 15(2) 51. Retrieved June 2016 from http://creation.com/bunyips-and-dinosaurs "Settlers feared the bunyip". March 2006. Creation 28(2)7-11. Retrieved June 2016 from http://creation.com/focus-news-of-interest-about-creation-and-evolution
6-Sep	"Marvelous Moloch". June 1996. Creation 18(3)29-32. Retrieved June 2016 from http://creation.com/our-world-afk-solar-system-moloch-lizard
7-Sep	Henry, Dr. Jonathan. 1999. The Astronomy Book. Master Books: Green Forest, AR. p.54.
8-Sep	Bartz, Paul A. 2005. "Master of Disguise" Letting God Create Your Day, vol.2. Creation Moments. p.61.

Date	Reference
9-Sep	Sarfati, Jonathan. CMI conference lecture, Myrtle Beach, NC, July 15, 2015.
10-Sep	Denton, Michael. 1985. Evolution a Theory in Crisis. Adler & Adler: Bethesda, MD. p.149,
12-Sep	"Colossal Canyon Discovery". 2014. Creation 36(1)8. Retrieved June 2016 from http://creation.com/focus-361
13-Sep	Fulbright, Jeannie K. 2006. Exploring Creation with Zoology 2: Swimming Creatures of the Fifth Day. Apologia Education Ministries, Inc: Anderson, IN. p.136-137.
	Wise, Dr. Kurt. February 16, 1998. "My Favorite Evidence for Creation!" Answers. Retrieved June 2016 fromhttps://answersingenesis.org/evidence-for-creation/my-favourite-evidence-for-creation/
	Stammers, Charles. December 1998. "Trilobite technology". Creation 21(1)23. Retrieved June 2016 from http://creation.com/trilobite-technology
14-Sep	Hadhazy, Adam. March 25, 2010. "Moths' Eyes inspire Reflection-Free Displays". Live Science. Retrieved June 2016 from http://www.livescience.com/6526-moths-eyes-inspire-reflection-free-displays.html
	"Moth eye inspire anti-reflective surface- but difficult to copy". October 2010. Creation 32(4)7-11. Retrieved June 16 from http://creation.com/focus-creation-324
15-Sep	Nienhuis, James I. 2006. Ice Age Civilizations. Genesis Veracity: Houston, Texas. p.51, 54, 57
	Landis, Don ed. 2012. The Genius of Ancient Man. Master Books: Green Forest, AR. p.77
17- Sep	Doolan, Robert. June 1995. "Helpful Animals". Creation 17(3)10-14. Retrieved June 2016 from http://creation.com/helpful-animals
	Bates, Gary. August 18, 2016. "A no brainer" test for measuring the faith of our young ones." Creation. Retrieved August 2016 from http://creation.com/no-brainer-test
	Cosner, Lita. May 10, 2016. "They want to convert your children!" Creation. Retrieved August 2016 from http://creation.com/convert-children
18-Sep	Personal correspondence with Edward Sandoval
19-Sep	"How plants 'Know' when to make sunscreen", 2012 Creation 34(1)11.
20-Sep	"Oxygen Optional Carp". Creation Moments. Retrieved June 2016 from http://www.creationmoments.com/radio/transcripts/oxygen-optional-carp
21-Sep	Thomas, Brian. September 2014. "Do Sand-Dune Sandstone Disprove Noah's Flood?" Acts & Facts. I.C.R.: Houston, Texas. p. 18-19.
22-Sep	Weston, Paula & Carl Weiland. March 2003. "The Mole". Creation 25(2) 46-50. Retrieved June 2016 from http://creation.com/the-mole http://www.backyardnature.net/moles.htm
23-Sep	Fields, Douglas. August 2007. "The Shark's Electric Sense" Scientific American 297(2) 76.
24-Sep	Malone, Bruce. 2014. Brilliant. Search for the Truth Ministries: Midland, Michigan. p.44-45.
	Nienhuis, James I. 2006. Ice Age Civilizations. Genesis Veracity: Houston, Texas. p. 19-24.
25-Sep	http://www.sciencemuseum.org.uk/online_science/explore_our_collections/objects/index/smxg-117718
26-Sep	Michael Oard. 2008. Flood By Design. Master Books: Green Forest, AR. p.72-75.
29-Sep	Catchpoole, David. September 2001. "Wings on the wind". Creation 23(4)16-23. Retrieved June 2016 from http://creation.com/wings-on-the-wind
30-Sep	Kennedy, D. James. 2005. Why I Believe. Thomas Nelson, Inc., Nashville, TN. p.23-27.
1-Oct	"Hibernation: not simply sleep". Creation moments. Retrieved June 2016 from www.creationmoments.com/content/hibernation-not-simply-sleep "Deep Frozen Squirrel". Creation Moments. Retrieved June 2016 from www.creationmoments.com/radio/transcripts/deep-frozen-squirrel Hennigan, Tom. March 2008. "Squirrels". Creation 30(2) 28-31. Retrieved June 2016 from www.creation.com/squirrels
2-Oct	Snelling, Dr. Andrew A. October 1, 2012. "#1 Very little sediment on seafloor". Answers. Retrieved June 2016 from https://answersingenesis.org/geology/sedimentation/1-very-little-sediment-on-the-seafloor/
3-Oct	Heimbuch, Jayme. August 8, 2013. "Nature Blows my Mind! The bobtail squid and its amazing invisibility cloak". Retrieved June 2016 from www.treehugger.com/natural-sciences/nature-blows-mind-bobtail-squid-amazing-invisibility-cloak.html
4-Oct	Catchpoole, David. July 23, 2013. "Hadrosaur skin found, Creation. Retrieved June 2016 from http://creation.com/hadrosaur-skin
5-Oct	Short, Aaron. January 9, 2014. "10 most ridiculously weird facts about whales". Retrieved June 2016 from Listverse.com/2014/01/09/10-more-ridiculously-weird-facts-about-whales/
	"Zombie worms crave bone". Ocean Portal, Smithsonian. Retrieved June 2016 from http://ocean.si.edu/ocean-news/zombie-worms-crave-bone
6-Oct	Batten, Don. September 2009. "A Vase of Flowers-by special arrangement". Creation 31(4)56.
7-Oct	Oard, Michael. 2004. Frozen in Time. Master Books: Green Forest, AR. p. 42-44.
	Nienhuis, James I. 2006. Ice Age Civilizations. Genesis Veracity. Houston, TX. p. 35-44, 56, 58-60.
8-Oct	Sarfati, Jonathan. September 2004. "A coat of many colours captivating chameleons". Creation 26(4)28-33. Retrieved June 2016 from http://creation.com/a-coat-of-many-colours-captivating-chameleons
9-Oct	Lamb, Robert. "Are figs really full of baby wasps?" How stuff works. Retrieved June 2016 from http://animals.howstuffworks.com/insects/fig-wasp1.htm
	Souza Dorothy. 2002. Freaky Flowers. Children's Press. p. 20-22.
	2014, "Evolutionary timeline doesn't fig-ure", Creation 36(2)10. Retrieved June 2016 from http://creation.com/focus-362
10-Oct	Chapman, Geoff. 2000. Weird and Wonderful. Creation Resources Trust, U.K p.12.
11-Oct	Burgess, Stuart, *The Origin of Man: The Image of God or the Image of Ape?*, p.124-133, 2004.
12-Oct	PBS Nature "Tall Blondes" Part II. Retrieved June 2016 from https://www.youtube.com/watch?v=JyD-BRMsnIk
13-Oct	Gish, Duane. 1992. Dinosaurs by Design. Master Books. Green Forest, AR. p.75.
14-Oct	Weston, Paula and Carl Weiland. March 2003. "The Mole". Creation 25(2)46-50. Retrieved June 2016 from

Date	Reference
15-Oct	http://creation.com/the-mole Kennedy, D. James. 2005. Why I Believe. Thomas Nelson, Inc.: Nashville, TN. p. 25-27.
16-Oct	Asfour, David. April 1, 2011. "Hot-blooded Sharks". Answers. Retrieved June 2016 from https://answersingenesis.org/aquatic-animals/fish/hot-blooded-sharks/
17-Oct	
18-Oct	Parker, Gregory, Keith Graham, Delores Shimmin, George Thompson. 1997. Biology God's Living Creation, A Beka Book: Pensacola, FL. p.558.
19-Oct	"Old MacDonald has a shell". Creation Moments. Retrieved June 2016 from http://www.creationmoments.com/radio/transcripts/old-macdonald-has-shell
20-Oct	Sarfati, Jonathan. December 1999. "The sun: our special star". Creation 22(1)27-31. Retrieved June 2016 from http://creation.com/the-sun-our-special-star
21-Oct	Fulbright, Jeannie K. 2004. Exploring Creation with Botany. Apologia Educational Ministries: Anderson, IN. p.152. Stelzer, Becky and Gary Vaterlaus, ed. 2006. Zoo Guide – A Bible-based Handbook to the Zoo. Answers in Genesis. p. 81.
22-Oct	Nelson, Ethel R., Richard E. Broadberry, Ginger Tong Chock. 1997. God's Promise to the Chinese. Read Books Publisher, Dunlap, TN.
23-Oct	Catchpoole, David. 2015. "A Dangerous View". Creation 37(2)12-15.
24-Oct	Menton, Dr. David. July 2015. "Climate-Controlled Coworkers". Answers 10(3)56.
25-Oct	Martin, Jobe. Incredible Creatures that Defy Evolution, vol. 3. DVD. Exploration Films.
27-Oct	Catchpoole, David. "Miracle Fruit". Creation 37(2)56.
28-Oct	Sarfati, Jonathan & David Catchpoole. August 22, 2007. " Brilliant brittlestars: Entire skeleton forms one big compound eye". Creation 30(3) 54-55. Retrieved June 2016 from http://creation.com/brilliant-brittlestars
29-Oct	DeYoung, Dr. Don. October 1, 2015. "Cold Feet Design in Nature". Answers. Retrieved June 2016 from https://answersingenesis.org/birds/cold-feet/
30-Oct	2016. "Gorge Rapidly Carved in Hard Rock". Creation 38(2)11.
1-Nov	Grabill, Keith. 2013. Seven Times. Search for the Truth Publications: Midland, MI.
2-Nov	"Bees outsmart scientists" Creation Moments. Retrieved June 2016 from http://www.creationmoments.com/radio/transcripts/bees-outsmart-scientists
3-Nov	Parker, Gary and Mary. 2005. The Fossil Book. Master Books: Green Forest, AR. p.24-25.
4-Nov	Oard, Michael J., Tara Wolfe & Chris Turbuck. 2012. Exploring Geology with Mr. Hibb. Creation Book Publishers: Powder Springs, Georgia. p.61-63
5-Nov	"Neandertal superglue". June 2002. Creation 24(3)7. Retrieved June 2016 from http://creation.com/focus-243
6-Nov	Martin, Jobe. Incredible Creatures that Defy Evolution, Vol. 2, DVD. Exploration Films.
7-Nov	O'Brian, Jonathan. January 2014. "Water in the Moon!" Creation 36(1)52-53. Retrieved June 2016 from http://creation.com/water-in-moon
8-Nov	Fulbright, Jeannie K. 2005. Exploring Creation with Zoology: Flying Creatures of the Fifth Day. Apologia Educational Ministries, Inc.: Anderson, IN. p. 209-210.
10-Nov	Noebel, Dr. David & Chuck Edwards. 1999. Thinking Like a Christian (Leaders Guide). Summit Press. p. 52-53.
12-Nov	1993. Science Order and Reality. A Beka Book Publications: Pensacola, FL. p. 441.
12-Nov	Clarey, Dr. Tim. October 2013. "Oil, Fracking, and a Recent Global Flood". Acts & Facts. Institute Creation Research. p. 14-15.
13-Nov	Catchpoole, David. July 2012. "Time No Friend of Evolution". Creation 34 (3)30-31.
14-Nov	Menton, David. October 2012. "Soft Tissue in Fossil". Answers Magazine. Retrieved June 2016 from https://answersingenesis.org/fossils/3-soft-tissue-in-fossils/
15-Nov	"Mimic octopuses". Marinebio. Retrieved June 2016 from http://marinebio.org/species.asp?id=260 "Most Intelligent mimic octopus in the world". November 4, 2010. Retrieved June 2016 from https://www.youtube.com/watch?v=t-LTWFnGmeg
16-Nov	Hennigan, Tom. October 2015. " Low-Octane Tanks of the African Plains". Answers 10(4) 24-26.
18-Nov	http://creation.com/aig-cmi-article-adds-insult-to-injury-for-creationists
19-Nov	October 2015. "Joint Effort", Answers 10(4) 27. Retrieved June 2016 from https://answersingenesis.org/human-body/joint-effort/
20-Nov	1. personal correspondence with Nepali missionary Paul Michaels. March 7, 2016. 2. https://en.wikipedia.org/wiki/Cordyceps
21-Nov	Clayton, John N. "Dromedary Camel". Dandy Design. Retrieved June 2016 from http://www.dandydesign.org/id36.html "Blood Cells protect from Dehydration: Dromedary Camel". Ask Nature. Retrieved June 2016 from http://www.asknature.org/strategy/b69c5de2019f07f6069a3fd7fb224ea1
22-Nov	Snelling, Dr. Andrew. October 2015. "Sifting Through Layers of Meaning". Answers 10(4) 30-36.
23-Nov	"How the Seahorse got its Square Tail". Creation Moments. Retrieved June 2016 from http://www.creationmoments.com/radio/transcripts/how-seahorse-got-its-square-tail
24-Nov	Sherwin, Frank. 2004, The Ocean Book. Master Books: Green Forest, AR. p. 67-68.
25-Nov	Grigg, Russell. 2006. "Sun, Shine! Moon, Glow! Stars Twinkle! – Day 4". Creation 28(3)24-27. Retrieved June 2016 from http://creation.com/sun-shine-moon-glow-stars-twinkle-day-4
26-Nov	Sarfati, Jonathan. July 15, 2015. CMI conference lecture, Myrtle Beach, N.C.
28-Nov	"Springtail dries out for winter: study shows genetic details of arthropod's extreme survival". The Free Library. Retrieved June 2016 from

	http://www.thefreelibrary.com/Springtail+dries+out+for+the+winter%3A+study+shows+genetic+details+of...-a0206173877
29-Nov	McDorman, Perry. July 1, 2013. "Piggybacking Pollywogs". Answers. Retrieved June 2016 from https://answersingenesis.org/amphibians/piggybacking-pollywogs/
30-Nov	http://en.wikipedia.org/wiki/Mauna_Kea
1-Dec	Fullbright, Jeannie, Exploring *Creation with Human Anatomy and Physiology*, pp.26-31, 2010.
2-Dec	Snelling, Dr. Andrew. April 2015. "Dazzling Diamonds by Special Delivery." Answers. p.52-55.
3-Dec	Sarfati, Jonathan. April 2013. "Learning from bumpy scorpion armour". Creation 35(2)56. Retrieved June 2016 from http://creation.com/scorpion-armour-bumps-biomimetics
4-Dec	Do you need to add more? 1. Proceedings of the National Academy of Sciences, October 2006. 2. Science News, B. Bower, Oct 14, 2006.
5-Dec	Sarfati, Jonathan. April 2012. "DVD Makers copy mantis shrimp eye design". Creation 34(2)56. Retrieved June 2016 from http://creation.com/mantis-shrimp-eye Franklin, Amanda M. September 4, 2013. "Mantis shrimp have the world's best eyes-but why?" Retrieved June 2016 from http://phys.org/news/2013-09-mantis-shrimp-world-eyesbut.html
6-Dec	Mulfinger, George & Orozco, Mulfinger Julia, *Christian Men of Science: Eleven Men Who Channged the World*, 2001, pp.183-210.
7-Dec	Kovalchik, Kara. "Tongue length and other things you should know about giraffes". Mental Floss. Retrieved 2016 from http://mentalfloss.com/article/27517/tongue-length-and-other-things-you-should-know-about-giraffes
8-Dec	Pitman, David. October 2011. "Giraffes Walking Tall … by Design". Creation 33(4)28-31.
10-Dec	Sherwin, Frank. 2005. "All out War in the Corn Field". Acts & Facts 34(8). Institute of Creation Research. Retrieved June 2016 from http://www.icr.org/article/2461/294
11-Dec	Weston, Paula. December 2002. "Coral: Animal, Vegetable and Mineral". Answers 25(1)28-32. Retrieved June 2016 from https://answersingenesis.org/aquatic-animals/coral-animal-vegetable-and-mineral/ "Corals Zooxanthellae … What's That?" NOAA. Retrieved June 2016 from http://oceanservice.noaa.gov/education/kits/corals/coral02_zooxanthellae.html
12-Dec	Morris, Dr. John D. October 2012. The Global Flood Unlocking Earth's Geologic History. Institute of Creation Research: Dallas, Texas. p.127. https://en.wikipedia.org/wiki/Wieliczka_Salt_Mine
13-Dec	Asfour, David. April 1, 2011. "Hot-blooded sharks". Answers. Retrieved June 2016 from https://answersingenesis.org/aquatic-animals/fish/hot-blooded-sharks/ Gunther, Shea. February 8, 2010. "7 amazing examples of biomimicry". Mother Nature Network. Retrieved June 2016 from http://www.mnn.com/earth-matters/wilderness-resources/photos/7-amazing-examples-of-biomimicry/sharkskin-swimsuit#ixzz36v4GgbDf Speedo USA. http://explore.speedousa.com/heritage.html
14-Dec	Oard, Mike. 2008. Flood by Design. Master Books: Green Forest, AR. p. 39-41.
15-Dec	Clarke, Patrick. 2012. "Egyptian Blue" Creation 34 (1)18-19.
16-Dec	November 2015. "New Earth Ocean Theory is All Wet". Creation Matters 20(6)10. Rosen, J. November 12, 2015. "Earth may have kept its own water rather than getting it from asteroids". Science Magazine.vol.…..need more
18-Dec	Olasky, Marvin. May 28, 2016. "A Man, A Plan, A Canal, Panama". World Magazine. P.45-49.
20-Dec	Gallop, Roger. G, Ph.D. 2011. Evolution the Greatest Deception in Modern History. Red Butte Press Inc.: Jacksonville, FL. p. 101.
21-Dec	Heinze, Thomas, "Did God Create Life, Asl a Protein?", *Creation Magazine*, June 2006, pp.50-52.
22-Dec	Walker, Tas. September 2006. "Colossal Crystals". Creation 28(4)18-19. Retrieved June 2016 from http://creation.com/colossal-crystals
23-Dec	Bartz, Paul. 2004. "Is the Lincoln Memorial Thousands of Years old?" Letting God Create your Day vol. 4. Creation Moments: Foley, MN. p.145. Bartz, Paul 2005. "Cave Mysteries". Letting God Create your Day vol. 1.Creation Moments: Foley, MN. p.183. Bartz, Paul. 2004. "Fast Rocks". Letting God Create your Day vol. 4. Creation Moments: Foley, MN. p.117.
24-Dec	December 2003. "Hi-tech Otzi". Creation 26(1)7-9. Retrieved June 2016 from http://creation.com/focus-261 2016. "Otzi Bugged by Still-Common Stomach Bug". Creation 38(3)……need page number
25-Dec	Gothard, Bill, *Character Sketches*, Vol III, Institue in Basic Youth Conflicts, 1985, p.147.
26-Dec	DeYoung, Donald B. 1992. Weather and the Bible. Baker Book House: Grand Rapids, MI. p. 63-65. https://en.wikipedia.org/wiki/Weather_vane
27-Dec	"Brain Waves". Retrieved June 2016 from http://phisciences.co/brain-waves Science, Vol. 253, 5, 1991, 82. do we need this?
28-Dec	Bates, Gary & Lita Cosner. April 17, 2014. "Are there out-of-sequence fossils that are problematic for Evolutionists?" Creation Ministries. Retrieved June 2016 from http://creation.com/fossils-out-of-order
29-Dec	Sarfati, Jonathan. "Turtles can read magnetic maps". Creation 21(2)30. Retrieve June 2016 from http://creation.com/turtles-can-read-magnetic-maps
30-Dec	2016. "A Sudden Gash in the Hills". Creation 38(3)10.

Index by Subject Reference

Subject:	Date:
abiogenesis	8-Jan
aborigines	12-Aug
absolute truth	12-Feb
adaptation	21-Feb
airbags	5-Apr
airplane, design	18-Nov
airplane, design	18-Oct
Akaka Falls	23-Aug
alligators	18-Jul
amino acids	9-Sep
amino acids	8-May
amino acids	9-Mar
anaconda	20-Jul
Angkor temple	30-May
ant, pine needle nests	2-Jan
ant, weaver	10-Oct
anti-cling coating	24-Jul
ants, dairy	12-Nov
ants, flooded homes	22-Mar
apologetics	1-Apr
apologetics	1-Mar
apologetics	1-Jul
arm	19-Nov
artic springtails	28-Nov
ATP, motors	8-Jun
Ayers Rock	26-Sep
Babylon, prophecy	15-Oct
Babylon, prophecy	30-Sep
bacteria	14-May
bacteria	12-Feb
bacteria, DNA transfer	10-Mar
bacteria, electric generating	9-Feb
banana	9-Jan
barameter	24-Apr
barnacles	24-Jul
barnacles	28-Apr
bats, ebola virus	17-Apr
bats, guano	30-Apr
beaver, dams	28-Jun
beaver, design	27-May
bee, bunblebee	7-Jan
bee, dance	3-Mar
bee, honeycomb	2-Mar
bee, intelligence	2-Nov
bee, protection	3-Aug
bee, temperature control	4-Aug
bee, wings	8-Feb
beetle, black fire	22-Feb
beetle, jewel	22-Feb
Bible, inspired	12-Apr
Bible, manuscripts	26-Apr
Big Bang theory	25-Nov
Big Bang theory	31-Dec
bioluminescence	3-Oct
bird, Bristle-Thighed Curlew	23-May
bird, diving ability	5-Apr
bird, dodo	27-Mar
bird, feet design	29-Oct
bird, flight	18-Nov
bird, Godwit	29-Sep
bird, migration	29-Sep
bird, neck design	13-Apr
bird, oilbird	13-May
bird, owl	13-Apr
bird, perching	28-May
bird, perfect pitch	4-Sep
bird, poop	11-Sep
bird, sheep killing	27-Aug
bird, snowy sheathbill	10-Aug
bird, tailor bird nest	7-Aug
bird, tiger swallowtail	8-Sep
bird, umbrella	29-May
bird, water ouzel	11-Feb
bird, whip-poor-will	8-Mar
bird, wings	28-Mar
bird, woodpecker	25-Mar
bird,migration	23-May
black heron	29-May
blind shrimp	16-Sep
Blind cave fish	17-Jul
blood clotting	19-Jan
Borneo	30-Apr
box analogy	9-May
brain concussion	25-Mar
brainwaves	9-Dec
breeding	14-Feb
Bristle-Thighed Curlew	23-May
brittle stars	28-Oct
buffalo	23-Jun
bunchberry dogwood	10-Jan
butterfly, beauty	3-Feb
butterfly, Heliconius sara	2-Jul

Index by Subject Reference Continued

Subject:	Date:		
butterfly, iridescence	25-Aug	conifers	20-Apr
butterfly, iridescence	4-Feb	consensation reaction	8-May
butterfly, migration	17-Mar	coral, nematocysts	22-Jul
butterfly, Painted Lady	17-Mar	coral, photosynthesis	11-Dec
cactus	24-Jun	coral, threats	21-Jul
caldera	4-Mar	corn	10-Dec
cambrian explosion	26-May	coywolf	8-Apr
cambrian explosion	21-Jun	crab, boxer	20-Jun
camel, blood	21-Nov	cratons	2-Dec
camel, hunp	24-Jan	cross bedding	21-Sep
cameleon, color change	8-Oct	current sensing ability	23-Sep
cameleon, hunting	20-Aug	cuttlefish, camouflage	18-May
carbon-14	10-Jul	cyanide	2-Jul
carbon-14	12-Mar	dark energy	25-Jun
carbon-14, dating	12-May	dark matter	25-Jun
cats	21-May	days of creation	6-Dec
caulk	22-Jan	dehydration	21-Nov
cavemen	4-Jan	design, criteria	18-Oct
caves	4-Nov	diamonds	10-Jul
caves, crystals	22-Dec	diamonds	2-Dec
caves, stalactites	23-Dec	diamonds	12-Mar
caves, blind fish	17-Jul	diatomite deposit	16-Mar
cell, complexity	1-Dec	dinoasuar, sauropod	13-Jul
chalk	1-Aug	dinosaur, dragon	15-Jun
Charles Darwin	18-Mar	dinosaur, duck-billed	5-Sep
Chinese, knowledge of Bible		dinosaur, extinction	15-Jul
	22-Oct	dinosaur, fossils	27-Sep
Chinese, written language		dinosaur, recent creation	13-Feb
	2-Aug	dinosaur, skin	4-Oct
chlorophyll	20-Feb	dinosaur, soft tissue	14-Nov
chromophores	18-May	dinosaur, soft tissue	26-Nov
cicada	8-Nov	dinosaur, sounds	25-Jan
cliff erosion	10-Jan	dinosaur, stegosaur	30-May
Cliffs of Dover	1-Aug	dinosaur, stegosaur	17-Jul
Cliffs of Dover	22-Jan	dinosaurs, bird transition	27-Jun
climate change	15-Apr		
climate change	7-Oct	dinosaurs, dragons	31-Aug
cloning	17-Jun	dinosaurs, dragons	27-Mar
clouds	13-Jan	dinosaurs, England	15-Aug
clouds	5-May	dinosaurs, soft tissue	31-Mar
coal, fomation	3-Jul	dinosaurs, transition to birds	
coastlines, shrinking	29-Mar		29-Jun
Coconino sandstone	21-Aug	dinosaur, prints	28-Feb
Colorado Potato beetle	2-Sep	DNA, book analogy	9-Nov
Columbus	31-Jan	DNA, degeneration rate	26-Nov
compass	14-May	DNA, junk	9-Apr
compound eye	28-Oct	DNA, opening	8-Jun
conifer sawfly	20-Apr	dog, breeds	22-Apr

Index by Subject Reference Continued

Subject:	Date:
dogs, panting	23-Apr
dolphins, echolocation	23-Mar
dragons	15-Jun
dragons	31-Aug
Earth design	10-Feb
Earth, age	1-May
Earth, age	28-Aug
Earth, brightness	7-Apr
earth, formation	3-Jun
Earth, four corners	15-Mar
Earth, magnetic field	27-Apr
Earth, old age origin	31-Jan
Earth, rapid geological change	30-Dec
Earth, tilt	25-Dec
Earth, uniqueness	27-Jul
Earth, weather patterns	26-Dec
earthquakes	30-Mar
Edom, prophecy	26-Feb
EEG	9-Dec
eel, electric	14-Mar
Eiffel tower	1-Jun
Egypt, exodus	31-Oct
Egypt, history	26-Jul
Egyptian paint	15-Dec
elephant, tusk	19-Mar
erosion	29-Apr
erosion, canyon	30-Oct
erosion, cliff	23-Oct
erosion, Devil's Tower	4-Sep
erosion, Surtsey, Iceland	26-Aug
erosion, talus formation	11-Nov
eternal life	18-Apr
evolution, rapid acceptance	14-May
exodus	26-Jul
exoplanet	30-Jun
extraterrestrial life	30-Jun
eye, compound	23-Jan
Faraday, Michael	24-Feb
feathers	29-Jun
fish, archer	29-Aug
fish, carp	20-Sep
fish, dragon	20-Feb
fish, fins	16-Feb
fish, goby	16-Sep
fish, lateral line	17-Jan
fish, 'o'opu 'alamo'o	23-Aug
fish, porcupine	11-Jan
flies	23-Jan
Flood, legends	11-Aug
Flood, legends	13-Oct
Flood, local	24-Oct
Flood, global	24-Oct
flowers, design	11-Mar
folded sediment	25-May
formic acid	9-Mar
fossil formation	16-Mar
fossil record	21-Jun
fossil, dating	12-May
fossil, teddy bear	13-Jun
fossils, living	14-Apr
fossils, out of place	28-Dec
frog, feet	5-Aug
frog, metamorphosis	17-Nov
frog, poison dart	3-Sep
frog, smoothie	8-Jan
frog, strawberry poison dart	29-Nov
frog, tree frog	5-Aug
fruit fly	9-Aug
galaxies, purpose	7-Sep
gallbladder	18-Jun
gears	25-Apr
gecko, feet	25-Feb
general revelation	9-Jun
general revelation	1-Feb
Genesis tree	5-Feb
genetic mistakes	13-Nov
geological column	26-May
geological column	3-Nov
geological column	3-Jan
giraffe, baby feet covering	12-Oct
giraffe, ligament	8-Dec
giraffe, patches	8-Dec
giraffe, tongue	7-Dec
Godwit	29-Sep
gold, veins	2-Feb
golf balls	22-Jun
grass, cord	19-Oct
Great Meteor Crater	26-Jan
Great Salt Lake	19-Dec
Greenland, canyons	12-Sep
halocline	24-Nov

Index by Subject Reference Continued

Subject:	Date:
Heart Mountain landslide	29-Jul
hermit crab	16-Aug
herring ball	21-Jan
hibernation	28-Nov
hippo, sweat	16-Jul
homologous features	10-Sep
hormones	29-Feb
homosexuality	1-Nov
homosexuality	31-Jul
horned toad	16-Jun
horse, heart	26-Oct
horse, sweat	25-Oct
house design	10-Nov
human, brain	27-Dec
human, egg	29-Feb
human, brain	29-Feb
human, eyes	29-Feb
Ice Age, civilizations	15-Feb
ice age, frozen man	24-Dec
Ice Age, landlocked lakes	19-Dec
Ice Age, legends	15-Sep
Ice Age, mapping	24-Sep
Ice Age, worldwide rainfall	7-Oct
iguana, heartbeat	7-Jun
indoctrination	21-Dec
Indorctination, effect	11-Oct
Inflation	31-Dec
inselbergs	26-Sep
instincts	28-Jun
instincts	23-May
iridescence	25-Aug
iron preservation	31-Mar
jellyfish, fossils	29-Jan
Jewish people, prophecy	12-Jun
Keas	27-Aug
kimberlite	2-Dec
kimberlite	12-Mar
KodaChrome Basin State Park	24-Mar
krill	26-Mar
lactic acid	20-Sep
leafhopper	25-Apr
limestone	4-Nov
lizard, thorny devil	6-Sep
logic	1-Apr
logic	1-Mar
Louis Pastuer	25-Sep
magnetic field	29-Dec
mangrove swamps	22-Mar
Mauna Kea	25-Jul
Mauna Kea	30-Nov
Maxwell, James	6-Dec
Mercury, magnetic field	7-Feb
migration	23-May
migration	29-Sep
Milky Way	6-Aug
Miller's experiment	9-Mar
Miller's experiment	21-Dec
mimicry	22-Aug
mimicry, biological	19-Nov
mineral water formation	21-Apr
miracle fruit	27-Oct
Miraculin	27-Oct
missions	1-Sep
mole, design	22-Sep
mole, star-nosed	14-Oct
moon, water content	7-Nov
mosquito, fossil	30-Aug
moth, atlas	22-Aug
moth, eyes	14-Sep
moths	3-Feb
mound builders	4-Jul
mountain/valley formation	14-Dec
Mt. Everest	30-Nov
Mussel, fishing lure	13-Aug
Mussel, reproduction method	14-Aug
Mussel, snuff box	14-Aug
mustard seed	22-May
mutations	13-Nov
Native Americans	4-Jul
natural selection	21-Feb
nautilus	14-Jul
Navaho sandstone	21-Aug
Neaderthal, abilities	16-Jan
Neaderthal, superglue	5-Nov
Noah's Ark	21-May
ocean, age	4-Jun
ocean, salt level	4-Jun
octopus, eye design	10-Sep
octopus, fossil	26-Jun

Index by Subject Reference Continued

Subject:	Date:
octopus, mimic	15-Nov
octopus, skin	14-Jun
oil spills	24-Jun
oil, formation	13-Mar
Oil, origin	12-Nov
orcas	21-Jan
pain	16-May
Panama canal	18-Dec
parasitic fungus	20-Nov
pasteurization	25-Sep
penguin, Spiny mouth	2-Apr
peppered moths	7-Jul
petrified trees	3-May
petrified trees, swashed	28-Sep
photosynthesis	11-Dec
photosynthesis	19-Sep
pitcher plant	30-Apr
pitcher plant, giant	19-Feb
planets, formation	16-Dec
plate analogy	3-Jan
platypus	15-Jan
Pluto	27-Feb
polyp	11-Dec
polyp	21-Jul
pornography	1-Nov
Prairie dogs	2-Jun
protein, formation	9-Sep
protein, formation	8-May
protein, formation	9-Mar
Protein, odds of formation	8-Aug
prophecy	19-Dec
pterosaur, cross	11-May
puffer fish, Japanese	23-Jun
question for children	7-Sep
race, skin color	20-Dec
races	18-Feb
racism	18-Mar
rattlesnake	11-Apr
rebellion	31-Jul
reindeer, antifreeze	21-Oct
reptiles, multi-headed	20-Mar
rhino, bacteria	16-Nov
river canyon formation	11-Nov
robots	19-Nov
rock layers	3-Apr
Russell Humphreys	31-May
salt, deposits	12-Dec
sandstone instrusions	24-Mar
Science, historical/operational	18-Jan
scientific method	4-May
scorpion, exoskelton	3-Dec
sea anemones	20-Jun
sea cucumber	12-Jan
Sea sapphire	5-Jan
sea star	17-Oct
sea turtles	29-Dec
seafloor sediment	2-Oct
seahorse, tail	23-Nov
seasons	25-Dec
sediment, folded	28-Jan
sedimentary rock, formation	19-May
sedimentary rock, experiment	27-Nov
seeds, dispersion	19-Aug
Setterfield, Barry	15-Mar
SETI	27-Jul
sexual perversion	1-Nov
shark, heat exchanger	16-Oct
shark, skin	22-Jun
shark, swimsuit design	13-Dec
sharks	23-Sep
sheep, origin	4-Dec
shimp, mantis	5-Dec
shrimp, Peacock mantis	2-May
Sir Richard Owens	31-Aug
snail, slime	28-Jul
snails	19-Oct
snakes, fangs	27-Jan
snowflakes, uniqueness	9-Jul
soil	15-May
solar cells	14-Sep
solar system, order	6-Jul
sorrow	16-May
special revelation	9-Jun
speciation	21-May
Specimen Ridge	3-May
spider, vegetarian	11-Jul
spider, web	10-Jun
spider, web	11-Jun
spirtual decay	12-Feb
sponges	10-May
spontaneous generation	25-Sep
squid, bobtail	3-Oct
squid, flying	15-Apr

Index by Subject Reference Continued

Subject:	Date:
squid, ink	14-Jan
squirrel, California ground	11-Apr
squirrel, artic ground	1-Oct
stalactites	4-Nov
starfish	28-Oct
starfish, sea star	17-Oct
stars, distance	6-Jun
stars, number	6-Jan
stasis	27-Sep
stomach	19-Apr
suffering	16-May
sun	20-Oct
sun, uniqueness	6-May
sunscreen	19-Sep
superglue	28-Apr
symbiotic relationship	20-Jun
talus deposits	30-Jan
tapeats sandstone	22-Nov
taste buds	27-Oct
teeth, enamel	18-Sep
teeth, enamel	19-Jul
termites, symbiosis	4-Apr
Thermopolis	21-Apr
thorny devil	6-Mar
thymus gland	21-Mar
thyroid gland	18-Aug
tidal surges	23-Jul
time dilation	31-May
Tower of Babel	12-Aug
tree of life	5-Jul
trees, round	19-Jun
trees, watering system	20-Jul
trebuchet	10-Jan
trichinosis	8-Jul
trilobyte, eye	13-Sep
turtle, loggerhead	6-Feb
Tyre, prophecy	12-Jul
ultrasonic sound	27-Dec
unicorns	17-Feb
universe, design	7-Mar
universities	1-Jan
vanilla	17-May
vase analogy	6-Oct
velco	10-Apr
Venus fly trap	20-Jan
vestigal organs	18-Jun
Viking spar	5-Mar
volatiles	10-Dec
volcanos	15-Apr
wasp	10-Dec
wasp, fig tree	9-Oct
water gaps	29-Apr
water strider	5-Jun
water, in Earth crust	3-Jun
weather patterns	15-Apr
wekiu bug	25-Jul
weta	6-Apr
whale, decay	5-Oct
whale, fins	6-Nov
whale, killer	21-Jan
whale, pilot	24-Jul
whales, blue	26-Mar
William Gorgas	18-Dec
wind	26-Dec
window, UV reflecting	10-Jun
witnessing	17-Aug
wombat	5-May
worms	15-May
Wright brothers	18-Nov
writing	24-Aug
yartsa gunbu	20-Nov
Yellowstone, volcanos	4-Mar
zombie worms	5-Oct
zooxanthellae	11-Dec

Index by Topic Reference

Anatomy:			Botany:				Paleontology:
4-Jan	20-Feb	4-Aug	10-Jan	6-Jul	12-Mar	27-Mar	30-Jul
19-Jan	25-Feb	5-Aug	20-Jan	27-Jul	13-Mar	16-Apr	5-Sep
18-Feb	2-Mar	7-Aug	19-Feb	6-Aug	24-Mar	4-May	14-Jan
19-Apr	3-Mar	9-Aug	22-Mar	7-Sep	29-Mar	14-May	29-Jan
1-Jun	6-Mar	10-Aug	20-Apr	20-Oct	30-Mar	4-Jun	13-Feb
18-Jun	8-Mar	13-Aug	30-Apr	7-Nov	3-Apr	15-Jun	28-Feb
19-Jul	14-Mar	14-Aug	17-May	25-Nov	21-Apr	4-Jul	16-Mar
18-Aug	17-Mar	16-Aug	19-Jun	16-Dec	29-Apr	13-Jul	31-Mar
18-Sep	19-Mar	20-Aug	24-Jun	25-Dec	30-Nov	15-Jul	14-Apr
19-Nov	23-Mar	23-Aug	20-Jul	31-Dec	3-May	26-Jul	12-May
9-Dec	26-Mar	27-Aug	19-Aug		19-May	2-Aug	26-May
27-Dec	2-Apr	29-Aug	19-Sep	Design:	25-May	12-Aug	30-May
	4-Apr	2-Sep	9-Oct	9-Jan	3-Jun	24-Aug	13-Jun
Biblical	5-Apr	3-Sep	20-Nov	23-Jan	3-Jul	31-Aug	21-Jun
Accuracy:	6-Apr	6-Sep	10-Dec	27-Jan	10-Jul	15-Sep	26-Jun
13-Jan	8-Apr	8-Sep		10-Feb	23-Jul	24-Sep	27-Jun
25-Jan	11-Apr	11-Sep	Christian	21-Feb	29-Jul	13-Oct	29-Jun
17-Feb	13-Apr	14-Sep	Truth:	22-Feb	1-Aug	17-Dec	15-Aug
26-Feb	15-Apr	16-Sep	1-Jan	11-Mar	21-Aug	5-Nov	30-Aug
15-Mar	17-Apr	20-Sep	18-Jan	25-Mar	26-Aug	6-Dec	13-Sep
12-Apr	22-Apr	23-Sep	1-Feb	28-Mar	4-Sep	15-Dec	27-Sep
26-Apr	23-Apr	29-Sep	7-Feb	7-Apr	21-Sep	18-Dec	4-Oct
11-May	2-May	1-Oct	12-Feb	10-Apr	26-Sep	24-Dec	14-Nov
22-May	5-May	5-Oct	1-Mar	24-Apr	28-Sep		28-Dec
12-Jun	7-May	8-Oct	1-Apr	25-Apr	2-Oct		
12-Jul	10-May	10-Oct	18-Apr	5-May	23-Oct	Micro-	
18-Jul	13-May	12-Oct	1-May	9-May	30-Oct	biology:	
11-Aug	15-May	14-Oct	16-May	9-Jun	3-Nov	3-Oct	
12-Sep	18-May	16-Oct	17-Jun	22-Jun	4-Nov	19-Oct	
30-Sep	21-May	17-Oct	1-Jul	9-Jul	11-Nov	8-Jan	
15-Oct	27-May	21-Oct	31-Jul	24-Jul	12-Nov	9-Feb	
13-Nov	28-May	25-Oct	17-Sep	28-Jul	22-Nov	9-Mar	
4-Dec	29-May	28-Oct	17-Aug	22-Aug	27-Nov	10-Mar	
24-Oct	2-Jun	29-Oct	28-Aug	25-Aug	2-Dec	9-Apr	
31-Oct	5-Jun	2-Nov	1-Sep	10-Sep	12-Dec	28-Apr	
	7-Jun	6-Nov	11-Oct	22-Sep	14-Dec	8-May	
Biology:	10-Jun	8-Nov	22-Oct	6-Oct	19-Dec	14-May	
2-Jan	11-Jun	15-Nov	1-Nov	18-Oct	22-Dec	24-May	
5-Jan	14-Jun	17-Nov		10-Nov	23-Dec	8-Jun	
7-Jan	16-Jun	18-Nov		23-Nov	30-Dec	8-Jul	
11-Jan	20-Jun	21-Nov	Cosmo-	13-Dec		8-Aug	
12-Jan	23-Jun	28-Nov	logy:	26-Dec	History:	9-Sep	
15-Jan	28-Jun	29-Nov	7-Sep		7-Oct	25-Sep	
17-Jan	2-Jul	3-Dec	6-Jan	Geology:	16-Jan	9-Nov	
21-Jan	5-Jul	5-Dec	26-Jan	12-Nov	31-Jan	16-Nov	
24-Jan	7-Jul	7-Dec	27-Feb	5-Feb	5-Feb	26-Nov	
3-Feb	11-Jul	8-Dec	7-Mar	3-Jan	15-Feb	1-Dec	
4-Feb	14-Jul	11-Dec	27-Apr	10-Jan	23-Feb	21-Dec	
6-Feb	16-Jul	20-Dec	6-May	22-Jan	24-Feb		
8-Feb	17-Jul	29-Dec	31-May	28-Jan	5-Mar		
11-Feb	21-Jul	27-Oct	6-Jun	30-Jan	18-Mar		
14-Feb	22-Jul	26-Oct	25-Jun	2-Feb	20-Mar		
16-Feb	25-Jul	24-Nov	30-Jun	4-Mar	21-Mar		
	3-Aug						

Index by Scripture Reference

Verse	Date
1 Chr. 17:20	22-Feb
1 Chr. 29:11	8-Oct
1 Chr. 16:8	28-Jun
1 Chr. 16:24	7-Jun
1 Chr. 16:25	14-Aug
1 Chr. 16:31,32	14-Jun
1 Chr. 29:11	4-Aug
1 John 1:5a	20-Feb
1 Kings 4:33,34	25-Sep
1 Kings 19:9	4-Jan
1 Kings 19:11,12	23-Oct
1 Samuel 2:2	27-Dec
2 Pet 3:5-6	3-Jun
2 Peter 2:5,9	30-Mar
2 Peter 3:5	24-Mar
2 Peter 3:6	28-Feb 12-Sep
2 Timothy 3:16a	12-Apr
3 John 4	17-Sep
Acts 17:22-24	1-Jul
Acts 17:26	18-Feb 18-Mar 20-Dec
Acts 4:24	12-Jan
Amos 9:6b	23-Jul
Col. 1:16	23-Aug
Col. 2:8	21-Jun 11-Oct
Col. 3:23	24-Feb
Cor. 10:5	17-Aug
Deu. 3:24	26-Mar
Deu. 8:7-8	9-Oct
Deu. 14:8	8-Jul
Ecc. 1:11	31-Aug
Ecc. 12:1	27-May
Ecc. 2:23	9-Dec
Ecc. 3:1	8-Nov
Ecc. 3:11	3-Feb 11-Mar 25-Aug
Ecc. 7:12,13	30-Apr
Ecc. 8:17	22-Jan
Ecc. 11:7	7-Apr
Eph. 3:20	1-Dec
Exo. 14:28	26-Jul
Exo. 20:11	26-May
Ezk. 1:22	22-Dec
Ezk 1:26	5-Jan
Ezk 35:3,4,9	26-Feb
Gen. 1:1	7-Jul 28-Aug 25-Nov
Gen. 1:16,19	7-Nov
Gen. 1:21	29-Jun
Gen. 1:22	2-Sep
Gen. 1:24	14-Feb 22-Apr 27-Sep
Gen. 1:25	5-Jul
Gen. 1:26,27	17-Jun
Gen. 1:28	18-Jan 4-May 18-Jul
Gen. 1:30	11-Jul 27-Aug
Gen. 1:29	8-May
Gen. 1:26	5-Mar
Gen. 2:21	27-Jun
Gen. 2:7	9-Mar
Gen. 2:9, 3:6	2-Aug
Gen. 3:14b	5-Feb
Gen. 3:17,18	10-Dec
Gen. 3:19	25-Oct
Gen. 4:20-22	15-Dec
Gen. 4:22	5-Nov
Gen. 6:4	30-Jul
Gen. 6:13	14-Jan
Gen. 6:17	29-Jan 13-Mar 14-Nov
Gen. 6:7a	26-Jun
Gen. 7:2a, 8:20	4-Dec
Gen. 7:8	21-May
Gen. 7:11,12	4-Mar 3-May 2-Dec
Gen. 7:12,24; 8:5	3-Apr
Gen. 7:14-15	15-Jul
Gen. 7:20	26-Sep 27-Nov
Gen. 7:21-23	28-Dec
Gen. 7:24	30-Aug
Gen. 8:2	21-Apr
Gen. 8:3	29-Apr
Gen. 8:5	14-Nov
Gen. 8:17	15-Jan
Gen. 8:18	11-Aug
Gen. 8:19	15-Aug 5-Sep
Gen. 9:11	28-Jan
Gen. 11:8,9	13-Oct 24-Dec 12-Aug
Gen. 12:2a	12-Jun
Gen. 47:1	31-Oct
Hab. 2:14	2-May
Hab. 3:2	14-Oct
Hab. 3:3b	22-Sep
Hab. 3:4	17-Jul
Heb. 1:3	10-Jul
Heb. 1:10-11	12-May
Heb. 4:12	14-May
Heb. 4:15	1-Feb
Heb. 12:2	9-Nov
Isaiah 12:5	5-May 17-May
Isaiah 25:1	14-Sep
Isaiah 27:1	17-Jul
Isaiah 29:16	9-Apr
Isaiah 40:8	26-Apr
Isaiah 40:22	31-May
Isaiah 40:26	7-Sep
Isaiah 40:28	29-Sep
Isaiah 40:31	28-Mar
Isaiah 41:1	30-Nov
Isaiah 41:20	9-Sep
Isaiah 43:20	21-Nov
Isaiah 43:20	6-Sep
Isaiah 44:24	3-Dec
Isaiah 45:12	27-Jul 20-Nov
Isaiah 45:18	10-Feb 30-Jun
Isaiah 48:13	26-Mar 16-Dec
Isaiah 51:5b	29-Mar
Isaiah 53:1	19-Nov
Isaiah 55:8	10-Sep
Isaiah 64:8	18-Aug
Isaiah 66:2	23-Jun
James 1:11	19-Sep
James 1:17	12-Nov
James 1:5	29-Oct
Jer. 8:7	17-Mar

Index by Scripture Reference continued

Verse	Date
Jer. 10:6	2-Nov
Jer. 12:9	10-Aug
Job 8:8-10	23-Feb. 17-Dec
Job 9:4	20-Jun
Job 9:5	29-Jul
Job 9:10	21-Jan 12-Oct
Job 12:13	7-Dec
Job 12:8,9	17-Jan
Job 14:18	11-Nov
Job 14:19	30-Jan 26-Aug
Job 19:23,24	24-Aug
Job 20:16	27-Jan
Job 21:22	8-Dec
Job 26:11	26-Jan
Job 26:13a	6-Aug
Job 28:25	24-Apr
Job 28:9,12	12-Mar
Job 36:20	21-Jul
Job 37:11,12	20-May 7-Oct
Job 37:14	20-Jul
Job 37:23	7-Aug
Job 37:4	15-Feb
Job 37:5	22-Jul 17-Oct
Job 37:8	1-Oct
Job 37:9	15-Sep
Job 38:22	9-Jul
Job 38:36	1-Apr
Job 38:37	13-Jan
Job 40:15	31-Mar 30-May 13-Jul
Job 40:15a, 16-18	4-Oct
Job 41:1,19-21	13-Feb 26-Nov
Job 43:13	18-Apr
John 1:3	22-Aug
John 1:5a	20-Feb
John 3:14	11-May
John 16:33	16-May
John 17:17b	30-Sep
John 21:3	7-Jan
Judges 5:3	11-Feb
Judges 2:10	4-Jul
Judges 20:16	25-Jan
Lev. 4:22-24	22-Oct
Lev. 11:13-19	17-Apr
Luke 10:8	1-Jun
Luke 12:27	6-Oct
Luke 13:8	19-Feb
Luke 17:27	3-Jul
Luke 19:40	19-May 22-Nov 23-Dec
Luke 22:34	26-Dec
Matt. 4:19	18-Sep
Matt. 5:13	12-Dec
Matt. 5:18	12-Jul
Matt. 6:23	25-Jun
Matt. 6:32	2-Jan
Matt. 8:20a	16-Aug
Matt. 7:15	12-Feb
Matt. 13:31-32	28-May
Matt. 15:16,17	19-Apr
Matt 17:20	22-May
Micah 4:2	23-Apr
Num. 14:21	19-Jun
Num. 23:22	17-Feb
Numbers 26:10	30-Dec
Proverbs 1:7	3-Jan
Proverbs 1:33	10-Mar
Proverbs 2:3-5	21-Feb
Proverbs 6:6-8	22-Mar
Proverbs 14:12	10-Jan, 21-Mar
Proverbs 20:12	28-Oct 9-May
Proverbs 24:3a	6-Mar
Proverbs 24:13	2-Mar
Proverbs 30:18,19	18-Nov
Proverbs 30:24,25	10-Oct
Proverbs 30:28	25-Feb
Psalm 4:2	10-Nov
Psalm 8:1	16-Feb
Psalm 16:9	18-Dec
Psalm 19:1	7-Feb 7-Mar 28-Sep
Psalm 19:10	2-Feb
Psalm 19:1-3	6-Jan 25-Apr
Psalm 20:72	6-Oct
Psalm 25:4,5	1-Aug
Psalm 28:7	28-Apr
Psalm 29:2	28-Jul
Psalm 29:10	21-Aug
Psalm 33:6-9	10-Jun
Psalm 33:9	2-Jul
Psalm 34:8	9-Jan
Psalm 36:5-6	5-Dec
Psalm 40:5	24-Jul
Psalm 41:2a	8-Sep
Psalm 47: 1,2	3-Mar
Psalm 47:7	15-Apr
Psalm 48:1	10-Jan 12-Nov 7-May
Psalm 50:11	11-Sep
Psalm 53:2	27-Feb
Psalm 55:16,17	1-Sep
Psalm 55:22	24-Jan
Psalm 59:1	20-Apr
Psalm 59:14,15	8-Apr
Psalm 60:2	31-Jan
Psalm 64:9	20-Aug
Psalm 67:6	19-Aug
Psalm 69:30	16-Sep
Psalm 69:34	24-Nov
Psalm 71:8	16-Nov
Psalm 71:17	24-June
Psalm 72:18	23-Jan 15-Nov
Psalm 72:19	29-May 13-Aug
Psalm 77: 13b-14	13-Apr
Psalm 77:12	2-Apr
Psalm 77:12-13	20-Sep
Psalm 78:11	31-Dec
Psalm 86:10	25-Mar
Psalm 89:6	5-Apr
Psalm 89:9	14-Jul
Psalm 89:12	24-May
Psalm 90:2	16-Jan
Psalm 90:16	19-Jan

Index by Scripture Reference continued

Verse	Date
Psalm 92:5	28-Nov
Psalm 95:4	30-Oct
Psalm 95:5	4-Jun 29-Dec
Psalm 96:3,4	23-Nov
Psalm 96:4	16-Jun
Psalm 97:1	18-May
Psalm 98:1	29-Aug
Psalm 98:6,7	11-Dec
Psalm 104:2	15-Mar
Psalm 104:6,9	13-Jun 24-Oct
Psalm 104:24,25	11-Apr 6-Nov 13-Dec
Psalm 104:25	22-Jun
Psalm 104:30a	8-Jan
Psalm 104:31	18-Oct
Psalm 104:32	16-Apr
Psalm 104:33	4-Apr
Psalm 104:8	4-Nov 14-Dec
Psalm 105:1,2	9-Feb 25-May 11-Jun
Psalm 105:2	25-Jul 16-Oct 21-Oct
Psalm 105:5	10-May
Psalm 107:23-24	23-Mar 24-Sep 2-Oct
Psalm 111:2	13-May 6-Dec
Psalm 113:3	6-May 20-Oct
Psalm 118:1	15-May 23-Sep
Psalm 118:12a	3-Aug
Psalm 119:68	17-Nov
Psalm 119:114a	3-Oct
Psalm 119:160	15-Oct
Psalm 123:1	9-Aug
Psalm 124:4,5	3-Nov
Psalm 124:8	3-Sep
Psalm 135:6	1-May
Psalm 136:1,25	20-Jan
Psalm 136:3,4	8-Aug
Psalm 136:5,6	27-Apr
Psalm 139:13,14	29-Feb
Psalm 139:17,18	21-Sep
Psalm 145:10	6-Feb
Psalm 145:15	5-Oct
Psalm 145:16	14-Apr
Psalm 145:21	8-Jun
Psalm 145:3	11-Jan
Psalm 145:4	13-Sep
Psalm 145:5	14-Mar
Psalm 145:9	23-May
Psalm 147:1	19-Oct 5-Aug
Psalm 148:13	4-Feb
Psalm 150:6	4-Sep 29-Nov
Rev. 12:3	27-Mar
Rom. 1:19,20	31-Jul
Rom. 1:20	9-Jun
Rom. 1:22	1-Jan 9-Jun
Rom. 6:26	25-Dec
Rom. 8:20-21	19-Mar
Rom. 8:22	13-Nov
Rom. 10:15b	1- Mar
Rom. 11:33a	10-Apr
Rom. 12:2	1-Nov
Song of Sol 2:12	8-Mar

DEDICATION

Here within you will find a veritable encyclopedia of examples supporting the reality of creation which have been published in the creation field. It is our prayer that those reading this devotional will have their faith strengthened. We hope you will come to new insights of ways that God has revealed Himself as "the maker of heaven and earth". This is how powerful our God is: **He made it all**. Meanwhile, the enemy of our souls is both subtly and overtly attempting to convince us that God did not make the heavens and the earth. This book will help you understand and defend the fact that He did create it all! We worship an unbelievably powerful and patiently forgiving God! Therefore, we dedicate this book to S.D.G.

Soli Deo Gloria: "Solely to the glory of God"

ACKNOWLEDGEMENTS

We are amazed at the vast breadth and depth of research which has been done in the last few decades which support the reality that there is a grand designer behind both life and the entire universe. Our thanks go out to all those tireless researchers who have devoted their lives to studying God's creation. This book is our humble attempt at summarizing and categorizing the work of others.

Our thanks to Jamie Walton for bringing the book alive with her graphic design and illustrations. Thanks to Steve Miller for his stunning cover design. A special thanks to Dr. Carl Baugh for bringing Baptist missions to Fiji over 40 years ago and for supporting and enabling the distribution of this book to students throughout the South Pacific. The text has been greatly improved by input from Bill and Carol McFarland, Don and Jeri Slinger, Christine Stark, and Eddie Barnes-Rosa. Thank you for all the time it has taken to read and correct our early drafts of this book. Thanks to Richard and Tina Kleiss for inspiring this book with *A Closer Look at the Evidence* - the original prequel to this volume. Finally, thanks to all of the **Search for the Truth** supporters who have prayed for this ministry, financially supported this work, and given our devotions to tens of thousands of friends, family members, and co-workers. May these saints meet many in heaven whom the Lord used this book to bring to a saving knowledge of His love.

Finally, a special thanks to Jack Van Impe Ministries who supplied significant funding for the first printing of this devotional to bless students throughout the South Pacific.

ABOUT THE AUTHORS

Julie & Vince Von Vett

Julie Von Vett has been teaching creation science and worldviews since 2003 to homeschoolers and doing seminars at churches and community events. She literally has 500 students all over the state of Minnesota! Prior to this, Julie home educated her children, Annette and Caleb, through high school. After attending worldview classes at Summit Ministries in 1992, she began teaching year-long worldview classes to high school students and parents. She realized that the foundation of a biblical worldview begins with creation, Genesis 1-11. Julie has received her B.A. from St. Olaf College. She lives with husband Vince in Minnesota. In their free time they love to travel out West and explore the geology from a creationist perspective and dig dinosaurs. This is her second book with co-author Bruce Malone.

Bruce Malone has spent almost 30 years bringing the scientific evidence for creation to churches and colleges at seminars throughout the United States and many foreign countries. He has authored six books on the evidence for creation with over 500,000 copies in print; served as adjunct speaker for the Institute for Creation Research;

Bruce & Robin Malone

is an associate speaker for Logos Research Associates Inc.; and is a commissioned worldview speaker under Chuck Colson's Centurion program - bringing a recent biblical creation understanding to worldview issues. Bruce has 27 years of research experience with the Dow Chemical Corporation and had 17 issued patents with the company. He left in 2008 to serve as Executive Director of *Search for the Truth Ministries* with the vision of "Awakening Hearts and Minds to Biblical Truth." This organization widely distributes Bible-affirming creation materials to students and prisoners. Bruce has a B.S. degree in Chemical Engineering from the University of Cincinnati and holds 17 patents for new products with the Dow Chemical Corp. Bruce and his wife Robin have been married since 1983 and have 4 grown children and 4 grandchildren. They reside in Midland, Michigan.

For more creation information see our other resources at
www.searchforthetruth.net

Our Rocks Cry Out 18-part Video Creation curriculum:

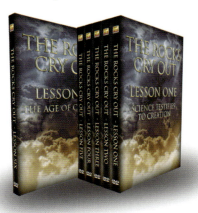

Our other creation devotionals and books:

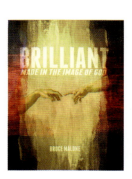

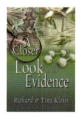
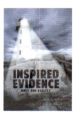

Visit our facebook page for weekly creation blogs and videos:
www.facebook.com/searchforthetruthministries